UKRAINIAN NATIONALISM

UKRAINIAN NATIONALISM

JOHN A. ARMSTRONG

THIRD EDITION

Ukrainian Academic Press

A Division of Libraries Unlimited, Inc.
Englewood, Colorado, U.S.A.

1990

Copyright © 1990 John A. Armstrong
Copyright © 1963, 1955 Columbia University Press
First Edition 1955 published under title
Ukrainian Nationalism, 1939-1945
All Rights Reserved
Printed in the United States of America

No part of this publication may be reproduced, stored in a retrieval system, or transmitted, in any form or by any means, electronic, mechanical, photocopying, recording, or otherwise, without the prior written permission of the publisher.

Ukrainian Academic Press
A Division of Libraries Unlimited, Inc.
P.O. Box 3988
Englewood, Colorado 80155-3988
U.S.A.

Library of Congress Cataloging-in-Publication Data

Armstrong, John Alexander, 1922-
    Ukrainian nationalism / John A. Armstrong. -- 3rd ed.
    xviii, 271 p. 17x25 cm.
    Includes bibliographical references.
    ISBN 0-87287-755-8
    1. Nationalism--Ukraine--History--20th century. 2. World War, 1939-1945--Ukraine. 3. Ukraine--Politics and government--1917- 4. Ukraine--History--Autonomy and independence movements.
I. Title.
DK508.A78   1989
947'.710842--dc20   89-20364
                                                      CIP

For Annette and Janet

Contents

Maps ix
Note on Transliteration xi
Preface to the Third Edition xiii
Preface to the First Edition xvii

    I.   THE EMERGENCE OF NATIONALISM 1

   II.   THE UKRAINIANS AND THE POLISH CATASTROPHE 17

  III.   RETRENCHMENT AND REVOLT 31

  IV.   THE OPENING OF THE UKRAINE 51

   V.   REPRESSION AND REICHSKOMMISSARIAT 73

  VI.   FROM UNDERGROUND TO RESISTANCE 94

 VII.   SALVAGE EFFORTS 124

VIII.   NATIONALISM AND THE CHURCH 145

  IX.   CHANNELS OF NATIONALIST ACTIVITY 162

   X.   NATIONALISM AND THE EAST UKRAINIAN SOCIAL STRUCTURE 181

  XI.   GEOGRAPHICAL VARIATIONS OF NATIONALISM 194

 XII.   PERSPECTIVES OF WARTIME NATIONALISM 211

XIII.   AFTER THE WAR 219

Appendix: Populations of Ukrainian Cities........................241

Note on Sources..245
    Oral Sources..246
    Contemporary Documents....................................249
    Contemporary Newspaper and Periodical Files...............252

Selected Bibliography..255

Index..261

Maps

Penetration of Nationalist Groups into the East
   Ukraine, Summer and Autumn, 1941............................55

Partisan Activity in the Northern Ukraine...........................97
   July, 1941-June, 1942..98
   July-December, 1942...99
   January-May, 1943..100
   June-December, 1943..101

Places Having Ukrainian Newspapers, 1941-43........................176

Regions of the East Ukraine..198

Note on Transliteration

The system used in this study for the transliteration of Ukrainian and Russian words is that employed by the Library of Congress, except that the diacritical marks used there to indicate the substitution of two English letters to represent one Ukrainian or Russian letter have been omitted. For ease in reading, Russian and Ukrainian words appearing in the text have been given English plurals (i.e., they end in "s"). Consequently, an exception to the usual scheme of transliteration has been made in the case of the word *oblast* (a major territorial administrative unit in the Soviet Union). The apostrophe which would ordinarily be used to indicate the "soft sign" following the "t" in Russian, has been omitted altogether, because the "s" in the plural preceded by an apostrophe could easily be confused with the English genitive.

When common English equivalents of Ukrainian and Russian first names exist, these equivalents have been used in the text. The monastic names of members of the Ukrainian ecclesiastical hierarchies have been given in the Latin or Greek forms familiar to Western readers, except in the case of names derived from Slavic saints. In the case of both lay and ecclesiastical authors, the Russian and Ukrainian forms of the first, or monastic, names have been given when referring to their works; but when an author so cited has been mentioned in the text as well, the English equivalent of his name is placed in parentheses after the first citation of each of his works.

Preface to the Third Edition

Two reasons ordinarily suffice for publishing a revised version of any scholarly book: continued demand and lapse of time. Since its first publication in 1955, the demand for *Ukrainian Nationalism*, although modest, has been considerable for a monograph and has not declined. As a result, the work has been in print (in two editions and two printings of the second edition) for most of the thirty-five years since it first appeared. The twenty-six-year period since the second edition was published is obviously long enough for the appearance of enough memoirs, critiques, and secondary treatments to make revision of a book desirable. In the case of *Ukrainian Nationalism*, another factor heightens the need for a new edition: availability of an immense documentation of the wartime Ukraine prepared by German occupation authorities. In the "Note on Sources," the reader will find details on the provenance and present location of this documentation. Here it is sufficient to mention that the German archives were declassified very soon after the second edition appeared, but other duties delayed, from decade to decade, my undertaking the thorough revision called for by the new sources. The recent appearance of critical editions of the German documents pertaining to the Ukraine (notably *Litopys UPA*, 1977-1983) facilitates the work of revision. Conceivably the Soviet archives will provide more relevant materials in the proximate future. This prospect is, however, very uncertain, and it is high time that the third edition be published.

The availability of the German archives means that a major objective of the third edition is complete documentation of the history of wartime Ukrainian nationalism. Because (as explained in the "Note on Sources") I became familiar with many of the documents while they were still classified, substantive changes are fewer than new source citations. For several subjects, the import of the newly available materials is so great, however, that substantial textual revision is in order. The account of the national resistance movement in Chapter VI has been completely reworked. In Chapter VII, discussion of the development of regular Ukrainian military formations, in collaboration with the declining German power, is also thoroughly revised. Secret German communications concerning crucial episodes such as atrocities committed by both the German SS and Soviet secret police in L'vov during the first weeks of the German-Soviet war require concise but detailed analysis in Chapter IV.

Conversely, most chapters require little change except in the footnotes. The book is a monograph, not a history of *all aspects* even of the wartime Ukraine. The historical introduction (Chapter I) could have been completely rewritten from the standpoint of new secondary accounts and conceptual frameworks current in the social sciences. But it appeared preferable to let the text stand as it was first written, except for minor factual modifications, while citing important new historical literature in the notes. Similar considerations affected the limited revision of Chapters II, III, IV, and VIII, where even new historical documentation is sparse. Since Chapters IX, X, and XI constitute a sociological analysis of nationalist penetration of the East Ukraine, one cannot expect a great deal of new information from German reports. Where these are revealing on major local manifestations of nationalism, the documents have been utilized. Finally, as in the second edition, Chapter XII is retained intact, for new evidence has not altered in any major respect my conclusions on wartime nationalism.

During a third of a century, the text of *Ukrainian Nationalism* has acquired, within its limited sphere, a measure of authority—in émigré Ukrainian disputes, as a background interpretation for legal proceedings, and (less frankly) for some Soviet bloc writing. Purely conceptual or stylistic changes in wording might well diminish such established authority. It seems best, therefore, to retain the original wording except where there are clear reasons, derived from facts unattainable thirty-five years ago or interpretations flowing from the newly available factual records, for alteration.

As a social scientist, I believe that monographs should be firmly and explicitly related to appropriate theories. Nevertheless, the compelling practical grounds for retaining the original wording have limited the extent to which I have revised the theoretical frameworks employed in the book. In the historical treatment (primarily Chapters I through VIII) my interpretation of Ukrainian nationalism, derived from Carlton J. H. Hayes' typology of integral nationalism, remains, I believe, appropriate for an early twentieth-century movement (for my comparative perspective, see "Collaborationism in World War II: The Integral Nationalist Variant in Eastern Europe," *Journal of Modern History*, September 1968). Still, if I were undertaking the study anew, I would turn, for a longer chronological perspective, to newer conceptual frameworks emphasizing myth and symbol, such as Kenneth C. Farmer skillfully applied in *Ukrainian Nationalism in the Post-Stalin Era* (The Hague: Martinus Nijhoff, 1980) and I elaborated in my *Nations before Nationalism* (Chapel Hill, N.C.: University of North Carolina Press, 1982).

Chapters VIII-XI examine the *strength* of national sentiment rather than nationalism as an ideology and a movement. Here the appropriate framework must be derived from political sociology. Without explicit elaboration, the first draft (1953) of *Ukrainian Nationalism* combined approaches derived from notions of institutional penetration (churches, voluntary associations, schools, in Chapters VIII and X), communications theory (Chapter IX), and the impact of urbanization (Chapters IX and XI). After that draft had been completed, Karl W. Deutsch's *Nationalism and Social Communication* (Cambridge, Mass.: M.I.T. Press, 1953) presented a sophisticated synthesis of these approaches to modern nationalism in general. The reader can decide how much my relatively crude combination of similar approaches suffices as a framework for assessing wartime East Ukrainian nationalism.

In addition to the middle-level theories just mentioned, for special aspects of the third edition I have drawn on several narrower conceptual frameworks: Franz Borkenau's theory of the escalation of violence among competitive guerrilla movements (Chapter VI), and George M. Kahin's paradigmatic interpretation (Chapter VII) of efforts of national liberation movements to secure the support of the ideologically divided Allies. The comparative dimension provided by these interpretations helps place wartime Ukrainian nationalism in a broader perspective of contemporary events.

My indebtedness to many persons, notably my oral informants, is indicated in the preface to the first edition. Nearly all have since passed away; I can only hope that what I accomplished does some justice to their memory. My mentor throughout my early career, Philip E. Mosely, died seventeen years ago, but his sage advice continues to shape this work. I was inclined to choose a Soviet nationalities topic for my dissertation; but it was Mosely who stressed to me the intrinsic importance of the Ukrainian movement and the richness of available sources. To other members of the Russian Institute (at present Harriman Institute of Russian Studies) staff and to the faculty of Columbia University generally, I am indebted for innumerable suggestions on special aspects of the work.

Columbia University Press, with the support of the Russian Institute, provided invaluable substantive advice on the first two editions, which it published with meticulous care. In 1980 a second printing of the second edition was issued by the Ukrainian Academic Press (a division of Libraries Unlimited, Inc.). Ten years later this press assumed the responsibility of publishing the third edition. To its learned and dynamic publisher, Bohdan S. Wynar; his assistant, Susan R. Penney; in-house editor, Louis Ruybal; and other members of the Libraries Unlimited staff, I am grateful for a complicated task splendidly accomplished. Since I began the Ukrainian project in 1952, my wife, Annette Taylor Armstrong, has borne a major portion of the burden. Without her advice, encouragement, and editorial assistance, there would have been no first edition, much less a third.

St. Augustine, Florida John A. Armstrong

Preface to the First Edition

Because this study is based primarily on widely scattered and little known sources, it would have been impossible for me to have undertaken it without the advice and assistance of many persons and institutions. At the same time, of course, I alone must take full responsibility for all conclusions and opinions expressed.

Foremost among those to whom I am indebted is Philip E. Mosely, Director of the Russian Institute, Columbia University. From the beginning of my study until its completion, Professor Mosely was my constant guide and counselor. Without his encouragement I would scarcely have undertaken this study, and his assistance was indispensable at every stage of its development.

To the other faculty and staff members of the Russian Institute I am also most grateful, not only for specific assistance but for a background of training which in some measure fitted me to cope with my chosen topic. Professors John N. Hazard and Geroid T. Robinson were especially helpful. I am also grateful to Professor Franz L. Neumann of the Department of Public Law and Government, Columbia University; Dr. John S. Reshetar, Department of Politics, Princeton University; and Dr. Fritz T. Epstein of the Slavic Division, Library of Congress, for frequent and invaluable advice.

For the financial assistance which made it possible for me to undertake the travel necessary in connection with my research and to devote an uninterrupted year to the project, I am indebted to the Social Science Research Council, which granted me an Area Research Training Fellowship for 1952-53.

It is impossible within the compass of this preface to mention all those who in some way aided me. Consequently the following listing is an effort to name those persons and institutions which were most helpful in providing advice, written materials, or personal recollections.

The Library of Congress; the National Archives of the United States; the New York Public Library; the Columbia University Libraries; the Yiddish Scientific Institute, New York; the Ukrainian Academy of Arts and Sciences in the United States, New York; the Ukrainian Congress Committee, New York; the United Nations Secretariat; the Committee for the Liberation of the Peoples of Russia, New York; the University of Chicago Library; the Mid-West Interlibrary Center, Chicago.

The School of Slavonic Studies, University of London; the British Museum; the Royal Institute of International Affairs, London; the Centre de Documentation Juive Contemporaine, Paris; the Centre de Documentation Internationale, Paris; the Ost-Europa Institut, Munich; the Institut für Zeitgeschichte, Munich; the Ukrainian Free University, Munich; the Bayerische Staatsbibliothek, Munich; the United States General Consulate, Munich; the Amt für Landeskunde, Remagen.

The Staatsarchiv, Marburg; the Westdeutsche Bibliothek, Marburg; the Herder Institut, Marburg; the Bibliothek des Instituts für Weltwirtschaft, Kiel.

Dmytro Andriievs'kyi, Fritz Arlt, John Bahrianii, Stephen Baran, Theodore Bohatyrchuk, Alexander Boikiv, George Boiko, Simeon Bolan, Taras Borovets', Elie Borschak, Nicholas Chubatii, Martin Cremer, Alexander Dallin, Jane Degras, Ludwig Dehio, Volodymyr Dolenko, Leo Dudin, Alfred Eduard Frauenfeld, Muriel Grinrod, Diomid Gulai, Iaroslav Haivaz, Ludwig von Hammerstein-Equard, Hans von Herwarth, Raul Hilberg, Gustav Hilger, Ihor Hordiievs'kyi, Richard Iarii, Roman Il'nyts'kyi, Arthur Just.

Mykola Kapustians'kyi, Hans Joachim Kausch, Hans Koch, Joseph Korbel, Bohdan Kravtsiv, Volodymyr Kubiiovych, Jean Laloy, Mykola Lebed', Georg Leibbrandt, Borys Levits'kyi, Andrew Livyts'kyi, Katerina Logush, Omelian Logush, Ludwig Lossacker, George Luckyj, Michael Luther, John Maistrenko, Liubomyr Makarushka, Werner Markert, André Mazon, Andrew Mel'nyk, Gerhard von Mende, Vadym Miakovs'kyi, Ivan Mirtschuk, Hanna Nakonechna, Alexander Ohloblyn, Liubomyr Ortyns'kyi, Eugene Ostrovskyi.

Constantine Pankivs'kyi, Zenon Pelens'kyi, Werner Philipp, John Popovych, Myroslav Prokop, Mykola Prykhod'ko, Victor Prykhod'ko, Vasyl' Rivak, Ivan Rudnyts'kyi, Peter Sahaidachnii, Ulas Samchuk, Gertrud Savelsberg, Walther Schenck, Otto Schiller, Paul Seabury, George Semenko, Hans Joachim Seraphim, Paul Shandruk, Constantine Shtepa, Dmytro Shtikalo, Oleh Shtul', Alexander Shul'hyn, Roman Smal-Stots'kyi, Jean-Marie Soutou, Eugene Stakhiv, Volodymyr Stakhiv, Volodymyr Starits'kyi, Iaroslav Stets'ko, George Tarkovych, Eberhardt Taubert.

Arkadii Valiis'kyi, Constantine Varvariv, Michael Vetukhiv, Stephen Vitvits'kyi, John Vlasovs'kyi, Vsevolod Volkonovych, Michael Voskobiinyk, Eric Waldmann, Gerhard L. Weinberg, Sergius Yakobson, Vasyl Zavitnevych.

Archbishop Polykarp Sikors'kyi, the Very Reverend Leo Veselovs'kyi, the Very Reverend Volodymyr Vychnevs'kyi, the Reverend John Hryn'ok.

The maps accompanying this volume were prepared by Anthony J. Sucher, Jr., Arlington, Virginia. His excellent contribution will, I hope, add considerably to the clarity of my presentation.

I am most grateful to the staff of Columbia University Press for its patience and thoroughness in editing the manuscript of this study and in assisting me in numerous aspects of its preparation.

Henry Holt and Company, New York, kindly gave permission for the quotation from Donald Mackenzie Wallace.

In concluding these acknowledgments, I must express my deep gratitude to my wife, who helped me in all phases of my study, and was an unfailing source of encouragement throughout.

Alexandria, Virginia   John A. Armstrong
June, 1954

I
The Emergence of Nationalism

During the summer and autumn of 1941 the German armies rolled across the plains of the Ukraine; by November the entire Ukrainian Soviet Socialist Republic was in their hands. Observers everywhere were aware of the significance of the conquest of this huge area with its forty million inhabitants. The agricultural wealth of the Ukraine, famous as the "granary of the USSR," the gigantic industrial complex of the Donets basin, and the rich mineral deposits were weighed in appraising the loss of the Soviet Union and the gain of Germany. While the political effects of the conquest received less attention at the time, in some ways they were even more important than the economic effects.

While there is a tradition of separate political development in the Ukraine,[1] modern nationalism—the doctrine that persons of a distinctive culture should constitute an independent state—came late to the area. To a close observer, the first stirrings of nationalism among educated groups in the Ukraine would have been apparent early in the nineteenth century, and by the middle of that century Taras Shevchenko, the greatest name in Ukrainian literature, was giving poetic expression to nationalist aspirations. It was considerably later, however, that definitely political organizations were formed to establish the claim of the Ukraine to nationhood.[2] For the student of contemporary politics, it is precisely this late emergence of Ukrainian nationalism which endows it with peculiar interest. Few subjects are of greater importance for the understanding of the political forces shaping contemporary society than the interaction of nationalism, in its numerous manifestations, and socialism, in its divergent branches. Ukrainian nationalism is especially significant in this regard because it took form at the same time that Marxian socialism became influential as an ideology in the Russian Empire. As Ukrainian

---

[1]The term "Ukraine" is used throughout this study (except in cases when another meaning is clearly implied) to refer to the territory comprised in the Ukrainian SSR in 1946. Essentially the same area (with the exception of the Carpatho-Ukraine, which is discussed briefly at several points in this study) was included in the Ukrainian SSR in 1941. This territory corresponds fairly closely— except, as noted in Chapter XI, in the east—to the Ukrainian "ethnographical" territory, the area in which the indigenous population speaks Ukrainian.

[2]John S. Reshetar, *The Ukrainian Revolution, 1917-1920: A Study in Nationalism* (Princeton: Princeton University Press, 1952), p. 12; cf. Jurij Borys, *The Sovietization of Ukraine, 1917-1923: The Communist Doctrine and Practice of National Self-Determination* (Edmonton: Canadian Institute of Ukrainian Studies, 1980).

nationalism acquired definitely political aims and the dominant element of Russian Marxism took on the political form of Soviet Communism, the interrelationship between these two forces became increasingly complex.

This circumstance, together with the intrinsic importance of Ukrainian nationalism as a force directed toward securing the support of one fifth of the population of the Soviet Union, appears to justify a detailed study of Ukrainian nationalism, even though it has never attained its primary aim, the establishment of a truly independent state. Moreover, the importance of the interaction of nationalism and Communism suggests that the study be focused upon that part of Ukrainian ethnographical territory which between 1920 and 1941 was under Soviet control. This region, commonly known as the "East Ukraine," was subjected to the full impact of the Soviet system prior to the period covered in the present study, while the "West Ukraine" was divided among non-Communist Poland, Rumania, and Czechoslovakia during most of the period between the two world wars. While the East Ukraine is emphasized, the West Ukraine is also considered at some length as the region in which nationalism was most vigorous and as that which served as a base for nationalist activities.

The present study is primarily political in theme, being directed to nationalism as a movement aiming at the establishment of an independent state. It is not limited to the political aspect in the narrow sense of the term, however.[3] Since the Ukrainian nationalists did not succeed in organizing a state apparatus, there is little scope for the study of constitutional or legal structures. As will become apparent shortly, the nature of the various nationalist ideologies makes intensive study of Ukrainian political philosophy of limited value. Consequently, an effort has been made to follow the approach sometimes described as the "sociology of politics." The history of the nationalist parties has been traced and, insofar as possible, the diverse social elements of the nationalist movement have been described.

Many efforts have been made to analyze the nature of nationalism and to determine the sources of its vitality. None have been entirely successful, for, like all dynamic movements which spread far beyond their original habitats, nationalism has been colored and transmuted by the varied milieus in which it has become established. It is a problem of peculiar difficulty to determine what has caused the movement to take root at all in many countries; this is especially true of the Ukraine. One of the most frequent stimuli of the nationalist spirit is religion, but the establishment of a separate Ukrainian Orthodox hierarchy was the result of growing nationalist feeling rather than its cause.[4] Another stimulus of nationalism is the existence of distinctive customs and ways of living. In addition to distinctive popular art forms, which will be referred to later, there was a marked difference between the pre-1917 social organization of most Ukrainian peasant communities and their Russian counterparts. The people of the Ukraine, for example, did not usually follow the

---

[3]No effort has been made to consider the primarily cultural aspects of nationalism (such as literary works) during the war period except insofar as they are directly related to nationalism as an organized political movement. In Chapter XIII, however, literary currents which suggest the continuing resonance of nationalist ideas are a major subject.

[4]See Chapter VIII.

predominant Russian system of "repartition," or periodic redistribution of farmlands, with all its implications of subordination of the individual peasant to the community.⁵ In 1905, before this people was generally recognized as a distinct nation, that shrewd observer of the tsar's dominions, Mackenzie Wallace, made these remarks:

> The city [Kiev—Kyïv]⁶ and the surrounding country are, in fact, Little Russian rather than Great Russian, and between these two sections of the population there are profound differences — differences of language, costume, traditions, popular songs, proverbs, folk-lore, domestic arrangements, mode of life, and Communal organization. In these and other respects the Little Russians, South Russians, Ruthenes, or Khokhly, as they are variously designated, differ from the Great Russians of the North, who form the predominant factor in the Empire, and who have given to that wonderful structure its essential characteristics. Indeed, if I did not fear to ruffle unnecessarily the patriotic susceptibilities of my Great Russian friends who have a pet theory on this subject, I should say that we have here two distinct nationalities, further apart from each other than the English and the Scotch. The differences are due, I believe, partly to ethnographical peculiarities and partly to historical conditions.⁷

As Wallace observed, linguistic differences between the Ukrainians and Russians were significant. The factor of language has indeed been used very frequently as the decisive criterion for distinguishing the two ethnic groups.⁸ During the nineteenth century a distinctive, though still evolving, Ukrainian literary language arose based on the speech prevalent among the peasantry. This speech is a member of the East Slavic linguistic group and therefore is closer to Russian than to any other major language, although Russian is not readily understood by most of the peasants. Russian was already established as the literary language of the East Ukraine before literary Ukrainian became prominent, however, and it continued to be familiar to nearly all educated Ukrainians in the Soviet Union.

Fundamentally, though, it is not to the criteria of religion, folkways, or language that the adherents of Ukrainian nationalism have appealed; more

---

⁵Cf. Geroid Tanquary Robinson, *Rural Russia under the Old Regime: A History of the Landlord-Peasant World and a Prologue to the Peasant Revolution of 1917* (New York: The Macmillan Company, 1949), p. 35, on the comparative absence of the practice of repartition.

⁶The second form is the Ukrainian. Usually the place names cited in this study are given in the forms generally used by the power which since 1945 has controlled the area in which they are located. This means that places now in the USSR are designated by the Russian forms, and the few now in Poland by Polish forms. Where the Ukrainian name is different, it is given in parentheses after the first citation. In a few cases (especially rivers) where another form is already familiar to the English reader, this practice has not been followed.

⁷Sir Donald Mackenzie Wallace, *Russia* (New York: Henry Holt and Company, 1905), p. 347.

⁸In this study this general usage of referring to those who speak Ukrainian as their native tongue as "Ukrainians" has been followed, without implying that the speakers are necessarily conscious of national distinctiveness. See especially George Y. Shevelov, "The Language Question in the Ukraine in the Twentieth Century," *Harvard Ukrainian Studies*, XI (June, 1988), pp. 71-171.

basic has been the evocation of a common historical tradition, the claim that the Ukrainian people, once great and independent, had lost their heritage. In the Europe of the turn of the century there were, to the superficial observer, two classes of nations, those which were embodied in independent states and those which were not.[9] Actually, the second group was almost as sharply subdivided into the "historic" nations, which had the memory of having possessed within modern times a stable state form, and those which were not so fortunate. Among the former may be mentioned the Poles, whose republic had vanished only a century previously, and the Czechs, who still preserved a vestige of their ancient state in the Crown of Bohemia. For groups like the Latvians, the Slovenes, and the inhabitants of the Ukraine, however, no such obvious rallying points of statehood existed; hence, the pages of history had to be searched to provide a comparable symbol of unity.

Since it was vital to the emerging nation that its language and its history be embodied in works which could inspire loyalty, it was only natural that the leaders of the nationalist movement should have been writers. The national poet Shevchenko has already been mentioned, and he was but one of many writers, such as Nicholas Kostomarov and John Franko. Historians, headed by Michael Hrushevs'kyi, who perhaps more than any other deserves the title of father of Ukrainian nationalism, were equally important.[10] The early leaders of the movement were almost without exception intellectuals—men more at home with words than deeds—a fact which was to have great significance for the future development of Ukrainian nationalism.

Part of the effort to stimulate the historical sense of the people of the Ukraine centers around an endeavor to demonstrate that their ethnic and spiritual ancestors were the people of Kievan Rus' and to deny that the Russians were descended from the medieval state of Kiev. Much greater energy is devoted, however, to studying the Cossacks of the Zaporozhian Sich (the Stronghold beyond the Rapids—of the Dnieper River) and to attempting to show that their struggles with Poland and Russia were in fact efforts to set up an independent Ukrainian state.[11] This emphasis was understandable, for the memory of free, warlike Cossack ancestors was still alive among the common people. In this connection, the astonishing success against Poland of the seventeenth-century Cossack leader Bohdan Khmel'nyts'kyi, who led his armies to the banks of the Vistula, is given special prominence. The subsequent story of how Khmel'nyts'kyi became a vassal of Moscow in order to maintain his independence of Poland, and of how the tsars then gradually absorbed his successors' realm, furnishes the chief historical basis for the allegation that union with

---

[9]This concept is expressed in Hugh Seton-Watson's *Eastern Europe between the Wars, 1918-1941* (Cambridge: Cambridge University Press, 1946), pp. 268-69.

[10]Cf. Reshetar, *The Ukrainian Revolution*, p. 9.

[11]Compare the proportion of space devoted to the two periods in easily available histories by nationalist Ukrainians, such as Mykhailo (Michael) Hrushevs'kyi, *A History of the Ukraine*, ed. O. J. Frederiksen, Introduction by Professor George Vernadsky (New Haven: Yale University Press, for the Ukrainian National Association, 1941), and Dmytro Doroshenko, *History of the Ukraine*, trans. Hanna Keller (Edmonton: The Institute Press, Ltd., 1939).

Russians was forced upon the Ukrainians, i.e., of the Ukrainian national constitutive myth.[12]

While it could in all probability never have taken root without the existence of distinctive historical traditions, language, and customs, modern Ukrainian nationalism developed in a dual imitative-defensive reaction to foreign nationalisms. The German nationalist movement of the early nineteenth century, with its romantic emphasis on glorification of the national past and the language and customs of the common people, had a strong influence on nascent Ukrainian nationalism. Moreover, within the Austro-Hungarian Empire a culturally advanced segment of the Ukrainian people was in close contact with the intense nationalism of Galician Poles. Poles constituted in effect the ruling class of Galicia, which had once been part of the Polish kingdom. The Ukrainian-speaking half of the population of the province had never lost all awareness of its distinctiveness, since a considerable gap separates the Ukrainian and the Polish languages, and the ethnic division coincided with an ecclesiastical separation. The Poles were Latin Catholics, while the Ukrainians, though also in obedience to the Pope, were nearly all of the Greek (i.e., Byzantine-Slavonic) rite. Consequently, it is not surprising that the ranks of the clergy provided a large proportion of the awakeners of Galician Ukrainian national feeling. Most prominent of such priests was Metropolitan Andrew Sheptyts'kyi. He was the scion of a family which was counted among the Polish nobility, but he felt himself to be Ukrainian; his career embraced almost the entire span of Ukrainian nationalist activity, from the turn of the century to the close of the period covered in this study.[13]

The reasons why a Ukrainian nationalist movement arose within the Russian Empire are not so obvious. By the beginning of the twentieth century, the great bulk of prominent men of Ukrainian ethnic origin appear to have been Russified in culture and feeling, even if they occasionally gave signs of remembering that there were different cultural elements in their family backgrounds.[14] That the Russian Empire could have carried out such a large-scale assimilation is a tribute to the degree to which it was supranational, avoiding the narrower concepts of ethnocentrism. Although a strong current had set in since the sixties, when N. T. Danilevskii's *Rossiia i Evropa* (Russia and

---

[12]See Frank E. Sysyn, *Between Poland and the Ukraine* (Cambridge, Mass.: Harvard Ukrainian Research Institute, 1985); Theodore Mackiw, *Prince Mazepa* (Chicago: Ukrainian Research and Information Institute, Inc., 1967); Orest Subtelny, *The Mazepists* (Boulder: East Ukrainian Monographs, 1981).

[13]See Stepan (Stephen) Baran, *Mytropolyt Andrei Sheptyts'kyi* (Metropolitan Andrew Sheptyts'kyi) (Munich: Vernyhora, Ukraïns'ke Vydavnyche Tovarystvo, 1947), and Il'ko Borschak (Elie Borschak—this author is better known by the French form of his name), *Un Prélat Ukrainien: Le Metropolite Cheptyckyj (1865-1944)* (Paris: Editions Franco-Ukrainiennes, 1946). The fact that the parish priests of the Greek Catholic rite were allowed to marry meant that their nationalist feeling could be passed on from generation to generation, a factor of considerable significance in providing a continuing body of bearers of the "national ideal."

[14]Reshetar, *The Ukrainian Revolution*; Borys, *The Sovietization of Ukraine*; David Saunders, *The Ukrainian Impact on Russian Culture, 1750-1850* (Edmonton: Canadian Institute of Ukrainian Studies, 1985); Izaac Mazepa, *Ukraïna v ohni i buri revoliutsii, 1917-1921* (The Ukraine in the Fire and Storm of Revolution, 1917-21), 3 vols. (Munich: Prometei, 1950-51); and Volodymyr Vynnychenko, *Vidrodzhennia natsii: Istoriia ukraïns'koï revoliutsii, marets', 1917 r.—hruden', 1919 r.* (The Rebirth of a Nation: A History of the Ukrainian Revolution, March, 1917-December, 1919), 3 vols. (Vienna, 1920).

Europe) heralded the advent of Pan-Slavism based on ethnic Russian hegemony, for many, especially for officials in the governing bureaucracy, the rule of the tsars remained an expression of the ecumenical tradition of empire, a "Third Rome," but one which based its authority on symbols of universality rather than national exclusivism.

The claims of the Russian Empire to acceptance, however, were weakened by its failure to solve social questions. However much cultural differences and historical memories may have contributed to the formation of the Ukrainian nationalist movement, it is difficult to conceive how it could have arisen had it not to a large extent corresponded with a basic cleavage in the social structure of the Ukraine. There, to an unusual degree, nationality coincided with economic class. The Ukrainians were, with the exception of a small intelligentsia, almost entirely peasants; the landowners and officials were Poles or Russians, while the commercial bourgeoisie was largely Jewish. Under such circumstances, any nationalist movement was likely to become a class movement as well, a movement whose leaders would stress agrarian reform and liberation of the peasant from "exploiting" groups.

It was in this way, of course, that Ukrainian nationalism became a rival of Communism. Basically, Communism[15] in the Russian Empire in the period before and during the Revolution of 1917 was a movement of townspeople. Both its ideology and its practical possibilities induced it to seek especially the support of the urban industrial workers, led and inspired by a group of dissident intellectuals. The latter were drawn from all the nations of the tsarist realm, but were predominantly Russian and Jewish. The workers were predominantly Russian, and those few Ukrainian laborers who had settled permanently in the cities prior to 1917 had for the most part become Russified in speech and consciousness.[16] But the Communist leadership, with its sharp insight into the real social conditions of the country, realized that no purely urban movement could succeed in a country four-fifths peasant; hence, it sought, especially after the March Revolution in 1917, through the instrumentality of the soviets, to draw the villager into the revolutionary movement. At this point the Communists encountered the opposition of the Ukrainian nationalists. In the confusion and disorganization following the overthrow of the tsar in March, the Ukrainian nationalists had been able to pass from the stage of a quasi-legal group of parties, intent primarily on arousing an attachment to cultural nationalism, to a real, if shaky, political force. From the spring of 1917 to the summer of 1920, this force, though now no longer representing a single "movement," was able to maintain a series of Ukrainian governments on the soil of the Ukraine.

It is no purpose of this study to detail the nature of these governments which have been described elsewhere in comprehensive fashion.[17] For future

---

[15] The Bolshevik faction of the Social Democratic Party in Russia did not adopt the designation "Communist" until 1917, but to avoid confusion I use the latter term throughout to refer to the essentially continuous movement.

[16] Patricia Herlihy, *Odessa: A History, 1794-1914* (Cambridge, Mass.: Harvard Ukrainian Research Institute, 1986); Patricia Herlihy, "Ukrainian Cities in the Nineteenth Century," Ivan L. Rudnytsky (ed.), *Rethinking Ukrainian History* (Edmonton: Canadian Institute of Ukrainian Studies, 1981), pp. 135-55; Steven L. Guthier, "Ukrainian Cities during the Revolution and the Interwar Era," *ibid.*, pp. 156-79.

[17] Reshetar, *The Ukrainian Revolution*.

reference, however, it is necessary at least to list them. The first, formed in April, 1917, was known as the Ukrainian Central Rada (*rada* means council and is the equivalent of the Russian word *soviet*), but during the first months of its activity it was really a semiautonomous administrative organ admitting the supremacy of the Provisional Government in Petrograd. Democratic and strongly socialist in its ideology, the Rada was the creation of the leftist intellectual groups which had predominated in the national movement before the war. It declared Ukrainian independence in January, 1918, but when it collided with the demands of the Germans, who occupied the Ukraine in February, 1918, the Rada was ousted. It was replaced by a quasi-monarchial regime under a member of the landowning aristocracy, Paul Skoropads'kyi, a descendant of a *het'man* or chieftain of the Zaporozhian Cossacks.[18] After the armistice of November, 1918, this government, no longer supported by German troops, fell, and was replaced by a new regime, known as the Ukrainian People's Republic (Ukraïns'ka Narodna Respublika — UNR). This government lasted nearly two years, but was subject to extreme vicissitudes because of the strength of the Communist effort to conquer the Ukraine, attempts of the White anti-Bolshevik armies to reincorporate it in Russia, and the desire of Poland to extend her sphere of influence to the Dnieper. The administration, known as the "Directory," soon came under the control of its most forceful member, Simon Petliura, who, through his military command, acquired such fame in this period that among the less educated elements of the Ukrainian population his name has since been synonymous with the struggle for national independence.

Because they represented a measure of stability, the successive Ukrainian governments attracted the support of many persons who desired a regime independent of Communism. To be sure, many persons in the Ukraine who desired the establishment of a firm authority supported the conservative military commands of Denikin and Wrangel, the White generals. Before the latter became prominent, however, the equally conservative authority of the Het'man attracted the support of a considerable section of the upper classes of the tsarist society, including a number of military officers. Once they had accepted the idea of an independent Ukraine, several of the officers, like Generals Vsevolod Petriv and Michael Omelianovych-Pavlenko, remained adherents of the nationalist Ukrainian regime which succeeded Skoropads'kyi, and were of valuable assistance because of their professional skill.[19] On the other hand, except for Skoropads'kyi's group, the leadership of Ukrainian nationalism

---

[18] Skoropads'kyi was a collateral descendant of Ivan Skoropads'kyi, elected *Het'man* in 1708.

[19] The biographies of these officers are extremely interesting because of the light they throw on the process of Ukrainization of tsarist aristocrats. Thus General Petriv had more Norwegian and Finnish than Ukrainian ancestry, but his family had been settled in the Ukraine for several generations; it is said that "his national consciousness was awakened" by association with ardently nationalist Finnish and Swedish officers from the grand duchy of Finland while on duty in Warsaw in 1904. Actually, the fact that the division of which he was chief of staff when the October Revolution took place was 80 percent Ukrainian may have decided him to throw in his lot with the national movement (cf. *Za Ukraïnu*, January 28, 1945, p. 2, and February 1, 1945, p. 2). Omelianovych-Pavlenko was the son of a Don Cossack general and a Georgian princess, but being stationed in Odessa when the Bolshevik Revolution took place, he joined the Ukrainians. See Myroslav Martynets', "Gen.-Polk. M. Omelianovych-Pavlenko," (Colonel-General M. Omelianovych-Pavlenko), *Visti Bratstva kol. Voiakiv 1. UD UNA*, August-September, 1952, p. 1).

remained predominantly in the hands of intellectuals throughout the revolutionary period, and even many of the Het'man's followers were writers and scholars. The educated youth of the Ukraine was divided between those who desired to join in the Bolshevik movement and those who chose the way of a left-wing nationalism. Victor Prykhod'ko, a nationalist who lived through the period, describes the former as persons who thought on a "planetary" level, desiring to solve all the world's problems at once and regarding the claims of national affinity as "parochial." One, his schoolmate, was Volodymyr Zatons'kyi, who was later to become one of the most implacable of Communist officials in the Ukraine. Even before the war, he, according to the writer, refused to have anything to do with Ukrainian cultural activities, like the Prosvita [enlightenment] society in the city of Kamenets-Podolsk (Kamianets-Podils'k), where they were students. Rather, he associated with "foreigners," Russians and Jews, and was rapidly drawn into the revolutionary socialist movement.[20] The basis for a choice in this generation of young intellectuals appears to have been chance, or the psychological make-up of the individual, which was reinforced increasingly by the cumulative impact of associations formed after the initial choice was taken. Thus by the time the revolutionary conflicts drew to a close the educated classes in the Ukraine were deeply split. Even more divided was the real foundation of any independence movement, the peasants. They—or at least those who were somewhat more prosperous than the average—had initially welcomed the Ukrainian governments. The increasing impotence of the new regimes and their preoccupation with factional strife and unrealistic programs instead of practical measures caused much indifference or disaffection among the peasants. In the judgment of one of the ablest students of the revolutionary period, however, the Ukrainian peasant preferred a nationalist government to either a Red or a "White" administration supporting a central regime.[21]

That the Communists were victors in the physical struggle is no proof of greater popular support, for much of their strength came from the Russian workers of the cities, or from outside the Ukraine. Nevertheless, the Ukrainian government under Petliura was to a considerable extent discredited, because it had failed to devote sufficient attention to the needs of the peasantry and to establish law and order. Moreover, by an eleventh-hour alliance with Poland, it had compromised its claim to represent the entire Ukrainian nation. This resulted from the fact that Galicia, which upon the dissolution of the Hapsburg monarchy had formed its own West Ukrainian Republic, was surrendered to the Warsaw regime as a price for aid in the east, a solution in which most Galicians refused to acquiesce. Nevertheless, Poland and the Soviet Union made peace, and shortly afterwards the remnants of the Ukrainian

---

[20]Vyktor (Victor) Prykhodko in *Krakivs'ki Visti*, January 18-19, 1942, p. 2.

[21]William H. Chamberlin, *The Ukraine: A Submerged Nation* (New York: The Macmillan Company, 1944). Moreover, one of the best Communist historians of the revolutionary period in the Ukraine, M. G. Rafes, a former adherent of the Jewish Bund, says the "natural" development of the peasants (and workers, especially in the sugar refineries in the small towns) was to "national socialism," "the Ukraine for the Ukrainian peasants," although he of course adds that they were inspired by the "reactionary bourgeois intelligentsia"; see *Dva goda revoliutsii na Ukraine: Evoliutsiia i raskol "Bunda"* (Two Years of Revolution in the Ukraine: The Evolution and Division of the "Bund") (Moscow, 1920), p. 8. See also the comprehensive analysis by Borys, *The Sovietization of Ukraine*, especially pp. 57-72 and 164-70.

army and bureaucracy retreated across the border for internment in Poland. From this sanctuary a group of a few hundred under Colonel George Tiutiunnyk sortied in October, 1921, for a last desperate raid into the Soviet-occupied Ukraine.[22]

After that the East Ukraine lay under Communist rule, which could no longer be challenged by military force. For a time, however, it appeared as if the rising tide of nationalist sentiment—it rose even among those who had long been adherents of Marxist doctrines—might bring about what arms had failed to accomplish. To understand this situation it is necessary to recall that the Communists under Lenin had modified their original stand in order to appeal to the nationalism of the non-Russians. In January, 1918, soon after the Bolsheviks came to power, the Third Congress of Soviets asserted a theoretical right of all the nations of the tsarist empire to go their several ways, to secede from the Bolshevik government in Moscow. At the same time, it deprived this right of any content by insisting that it be exercised only by the "toiling masses." Although the Communist Party's stand was more ambiguously phrased, its insistence that the interests of the toilers were represented only by the Communist Party and that the non-Russian Communist Parties formed inseparable parts of the central Bolshevik organization, in fact rendered self-determination a fiction. During the following years, the central Party leadership used armed force when possible to insure that these local Communist parties, thus reduced to mere branches of a unified Party, should "rule" within each smaller nation which had formed part of the tsarist empire.

Having provided for the initial objective of substantial Communist control, however, the Bolshevik leaders made sweeping statements against "Great Russian chauvinism," and directed that the culture of each nation be "national in form, socialist in content." Encouraged by this apparent desire for development of the national culture at the expense of the Russian cultural supremacy, which had been grafted on their peoples in tsarist days, many of the Communist leaders of the non-Russian nations set about vigorously promoting an independent cultural life as soon as Communist control was established. In the Ukraine, the major leader in the effort during the early twenties was the commissar of education, Alexander Shums'kyi; after his deposition in 1927 he was succeeded by Nicholas Skrypnyk, an even more devoted Communist, but a firm adherent of Ukrainian cultural nationalism.[23] To what extent these men were sincere adherents of Ukrainian nationalism and to what extent the favor

---

[22]Mazepa, *Ukraïna v ohni i buri revoliutsii*, Vol. III, pp. 96-105. On the West Ukrainian struggle, see Lev Shankovs'kyi, *Ukraïns'ka Halyts'ka Armiia* (Winnipeg: D. Mykytiuk, 1974).

[23]In the past forty years a considerable number of major scholarly works on various aspects of Soviet rule in the Ukraine prior to the Second World War have appeared. The most important are Borys, *The Sovietization of the Ukraine*, in many respects the best single work on the Soviet Ukraine in that period; Robert S. Sullivant, *Soviet Politics and the Ukraine, 1917-1957* (New York: Columbia University Press, 1962); George S. N. Luckyj, *Literary Politics in the Soviet Ukraine, 1917-1934* (New York: Columbia University Press, 1956); Basil Dmytryshyn, *Moscow and the Ukraine, 1918-1953* (New York: Bookman Associates, 1956); Hryhory Kostiuk, *Stalinist Rule in the Ukraine* (New York: Frederick A. Praeger, 1960); Bohdan Krawchenko, *Social Change and National Consciousness in Twentieth-Century Ukraine* (New York: St. Martin's Press, 1985); and *La Renaissance nationale et culturelle en Ukraine de 1917 aux années 1930* (Paris: Institut National des Langues et Civilisations Orientales, 1986). See also Jurij Lawrynenko, *Ukrainian Communism and Soviet Russian Policy toward the Ukraine: An Annotated Bibliography* (New York: Research Program on the USSR, 1953).

they extended to it was motivated by a desire to secure popular support and to curb the overweening power of Moscow in the interest of an internationalism which, to them, was in closer accord with original Communist ideology, it is hard to say. At any rate, they went to very considerable lengths to encourage specifically Ukrainian traits and traditions, especially in scholarship, literature, and the schools. While these Communist supporters of Ukrainian nationalism always formed only one segment of the ruling group in the Ukraine, and hence could not completely eradicate Russian permeation of Ukrainian cultural life, they nevertheless developed a generation of young people who were accumstomed to think and write in the Ukrainian literary language, although many continued to regard the use of Russian as a sign of culture.

Perhaps the Communists of the Skrypnyk group remained at heart more devoted to Communism than to nationalism. Such was certainly not the case with a very large group of intellectuals, some from the rising generation, others from the group which had supported the national governments of the revolutionary period but later accepted the Soviet regime. Foremost among the latter was Michael Hrushevs'kyi; although he had served for a time as president of the Rada, he decided to return to the Soviet Ukraine when it appeared to offer an outlet for nationalist activity. For him and his group, which consisted predominantly of scholars and men of letters, the real aim was to reverse the Communist prescription by building a culture "socialist in form, national in content." Thus Hrushevs'kyi, who had always accepted a certain amount of socialist doctrine as the basis for needed reforms in the Ukraine, occasionally made room for Marxist ideology in his historical writings but left it clear that the real apex of his values was the Ukrainian nation. Moreover, he and his group persistently maintained that historical and economic links bound the Ukraine more closely to Western Europe than to Russia.

From the Communist point of view, such ideas were dangerous enough in themselves; while Communism could tolerate for a time basically antipathetic forms, it could not allow its own forms to be used as a cover for developing an independent ideology. It appears that Stalin, the most ruthless insister on conformity, moved to crush the "national deviation" of the Ukrainians as soon as his power was sufficient; indeed, the first steps in this direction were taken as early as 1927. The great attack came in 1930, however, with the dismissal of Hrushevs'kyi from his academic post and the suppression of his scholarly organ *Ukraïna*. Along with this attack, which was carried out against all elements of intellectual life—including some obviously devout Marxists like the historian Iavors'kyi—which favored independent development of the Ukraine, went trials of suspect scholars who were accused of having belonged to a subversive League for the Liberation of the Ukraine.[24] That this campaign of suppression coincided with the drive for the collectivization of agriculture in the Ukraine is hardly coincidental. In many respects the Ukrainian peasant

---

[24]See especially Kostiuk, *Stalinist Rule in the Ukraine*, pp. 86-89, who argues convincingly that this organization and the related Union of Ukrainian Youth may never have existed at all. See also Luckyj, *Literary Politics in the Soviet Ukraine*, pp. 154-55; John S. Reshetar, "National Deviation in the Soviet Union," *American Slavic and East European Review*, XII (April, 1953), 162-74; T. Skubyts'kyi, "Klassovaia bor'ba v ukrainskoi istoricheskoi literature" (The Class Struggle in Ukrainian Historical Literature), *Istorik-Marksist*, No. 17 (1930), pp. 27-40; and Boris Krupnyts'kyi, "Die ukrainische Geschichtswissenschaft in der Sowjetunion 1921-1941," *Jahrbücher für die Geschichte Osteuropas*, 1941, pp. 125-51.

was much more profoundly affected by the establishment of the kolkhoz (Ukrainian *kolhosp*), or collective farm, than was the Russian. The former was frequently more prosperous, hence had more to lose; moreover, the lack of a traditional communal agricultural organization in the Ukraine made the new system more alien and repugnant.

It appears certain that the Ukrainian peasantry formed a disproportionate, if not predominant, part of the hapless millions deported as "kulaks" to Siberia or Kazakhstan or driven by famine to the primitive slums of the expanding Soviet cities. Very probably this situation created a potential basis for a national rebellion based on economic and social oppression by alien rulers, just as had the Polish and Russian preponderance in governmental and landowning groups before the war. The Communists were frequently forced to use non-Ukrainians, Russian and Jewish intellectuals, workers from the towns, where they had real support, or persons imported from Russia itself, in order to carry out collectivization. Consequently, it is probable that the suppression of the nationalist intelligentsia at this time was at least in part a precautionary step to destroy a group which was of limited danger in itself yet might have presented a real threat to the Communists if it could have utilized the discontent of the peasants to turn them to nationalism. To what extent the Soviet regime succeeded in eliminating the nationalist intellectuals is one of the principal topics which will be dealt with on the basis of the evidence provided in this study. It should be noted at this point, however, that their resistance was undoubtedly crushed between 1930 and the closing series of purge trials in 1937-38.[25]

While articulate nationalism was being crushed in the Soviet Ukraine, a somewhat different development was taking place in the West Ukraine. In Poland the extreme policy of the ruling nationality, which had been chauvinistic enough under the Austrian empire, became still more violent toward the Ukrainians after the reestablishment of the Polish national state. As was previously noted, Petliura's agreement with the Poles had been deeply resented by the Galician Ukrainians. While most nationalists endeavored to smooth over criticism of Petliura personally, especially after his assassination in Paris in 1926, most West Ukrainians gave no support to the émigré UNR government. The West Ukrainians, on the contrary, tried their own approaches to the problem of carrying on Ukrainian life under conditions of oppression by nontotalitarian, but intolerant, alien nationalist governments.

One attempted solution was the formation of legally recognized parties which carried on electoral campaigns and sent representatives to the Polish Sejm or parliament where they attempted to protect the interests of their group within the framework of means permitted by the ruling nationality. This type of political activity, together with a wide variety of cultural work aimed at developing Ukrainian culture and maintaining the national distinctiveness of the masses, absorbed the efforts of a very large proportion of the West Ukrainian intelligentsia during the twenties and thirties. In particular, most of the

---

[25]Robert Conquest, *Harvest of Sorrow: Soviet Collectivization and the Terror-Famine* (New York: Oxford University Press, 1986); Dmytro Zlepko, *Der ukrainische Hunger-Holocaust* (Sonnenbühl: Helmut Wild, 1988), based on Auswärtiges Amt documents; and U.S. Congress, Commission on the Ukraine Famine, *Report to Congress* (Washington: Government Printing Office, 1988).

older generation which had been reared under the relatively peaceful and stable conditions of Austrian rule, circles closely associated with the Greek Catholic Church, and most of the liberal professions engaged in this activity. Although there were a number of minor parties, some of which had authoritarian leanings, the majority of this segment of Ukrainian political workers was grouped in the Ukrainian National Democratic Union (Ukraïns'ke Natsional'ne Demokratychne Ob"iednannia—UNDO), which was definitely democratic in character, with varying amounts of Catholic, liberal, and socialist ideology embodied in its program. Its efforts met with very uncertain success, fluctuating from periods of relatively satisfactory cooperation with the Poles to embittered boycott of an unbearably oppressive regime.[26]

Some West Ukrainians soon rejected the road of accommodation to the Polish government; in the early twenties they turned to Communism as the champion of both nationalist aspirations and social needs. While the Ukrainians of Galicia were not so badly off economically as were those in the East Ukraine before and after the war of 1914, they suffered from a high ratio of population to available land, from inadequate agricultural productivity, and above all from the fact that the vast majority of bureaucratic and urban jobs which would have served as the natural outlets for their sons, compelled by ambition or lack of employment to leave the land, were absorbed by Poles and Jews. In Volhynia, conditions were much worse; probably they were as bad, as far as purely economic circumstances went, as those within the Soviet Ukraine prior to 1930. Consequently, a broad economic basis for Communist propaganda existed; under the circumstances in which a nationalist Ukrainian Communist regime appeared to be taking form in Kiev, this propaganda appealed strongly to the nationalist element among West Ukrainians as well. As a result, two Communist-front organizations, the Ukrainian Party of Labor (Ukraïns'ka Partiia Pratsi) and the Peasants-Workers Association (Selians'ko-Robitnycha Partiia—Sel-Rob) had considerable success, especially in Volhynia. More serious from the strictly nationalist point of view, many students, the backbone of the new generation which would have to carry on national life, were attracted to the Communist program.[27]

At the same time, an extreme movement of a different type attracted wide support. The movement which is commonly known in American scholarship as "integral nationalism" arose in Western Europe at the close of the nineteenth century, considerably before Communism became a factor of any real political importance. It is generally recognized that one of the first exponents of the ideology was Charles Maurras, who, together with a group of extreme French nationalists and advocates of political reaction, established the Action Française at the turn of the century. Integral nationalism never had much appeal in France or other Western European countries, but in modified forms it became a dominant force in the "dissatisfied" countries of Central and

---

[26]See Raymond L. Buell, *Poland: Key to Europe* (3rd ed.; New York: Alfred A. Knopf, 1939).

[27]Stepan Baran in *Krakivs'ki Visti*, January 18-19, 1942, p. 2; Alexander J. Motyl, "The Rural Origins of the Communist and Nationalist Movements in Wołyń *Województwo*, 1921-1939," *Slavic Review*, XXXVII (September, 1978), 412-20; E. M. Halushko, *Narysy istoriï ideolohichnoï ta orhanizatsiinoï diial'nosti KPZU v 1919-1928 rr.* (Outline of the History of the Ideological and Organizational Activity of the Communist Party of the Western Ukraine in 1919-28) (L'vov: Vydavnytstvo L'vivs'koho Universytetu, 1965).

Southern Europe in the twenties. Here it was one element which provided an ideological platform for Mussolini's Fascism and for the rising Nazi party in Germany. Its influence was also felt strongly in the extreme nationalist parties of Poland, Hungary, Rumania, and Yugoslavia. Because integral nationalism is by definition a movement of individual nations rather than a universal ideology and because its adherents reject systematic rational programs, it is difficult to define its precise nature. The following characteristics, however, stand out: (1) a belief in the nation as the supreme value to which all others must be subordinated, essentially a totalitarian concept; (2) an appeal to mystically conceived ideas of the solidarity of all individuals making up the nation, usually on the assumption that biological characteristics or the irreversible effects of common historical development had welded them into one organic whole; (3) a subordination of rational, analytic thought to the "intuitively correct" emotions; (4) expression of the "national will" through a charismatic leader and an elite of nationalist enthusiasts organized in a single party; (5) glorification of action, war, and violence as an expression of the superior biological vitality of the nation.[28]

In the twenties these concepts came to permeate much of European—and to a much lesser extent American—thought, even when they were not accepted explicitly as a political program. Among the suppressed nations of Eastern Europe, where conditions were different from those in the Central European states in which the new ideology eventually won control, the new ideas were readily received, but in a somewhat modified form. This was the case in the West Ukraine in the twenties, where two essentially distinct groups prepared the ground for integral nationalism.[29] One drew its strength from the resentment of the Galician soldiers who had borne a heavy part of the burden of the Ukrainian struggle for liberation, only to be consigned to second-class citizenship by Poland. The most active were veterans of the Sichovi Stril'tsi (Sich Sharpshooters), a unit which had operated under Colonel Eugene Konovalets' in the East Ukraine. After the collapse of the UNR, the unit disbanded in Galicia; many of its members united in (1920) in an illegal, para-military organization known as the Ukraïns'ka Viis'kova Organizatsiia (Ukrainian Military Organization—UVO). In the bitter struggles with the Poles in the twenties, this group was harshly treated and retaliated with some deeds of violence. Basically, however, it was a military protective group rather than a terrorist underground.

---

[28] The classic discussion of integral nationalism is Carlton J. H. Hayes, *The Historical Evolution of Modern Nationalism* (New York: Macmillan, 1948). Cf. John A. Armstrong, "Collaborationism in World War II: The Integral Nationalist Variant in Eastern Europe," *Journal of Modern History*, XL (September, 1968), 396-410.

[29] Published sources include V. Martynets', *Ukraïns'ke pidpillia vid UVO do OUN: Spohady i materiialy do peredistoriï ta istoriï ukraïns'koho organizovanoho natisionalizmu* (The Ukrainian Underground from the UVO to the OUN: Memoirs and Materials Concerning the Prehistory and the History of Organized Ukrainian Nationalism) (Winnipeg, 1949); Bohdan Kravtsiv in *Ukraïnets'-Chas*, June 10, 1951, p. 4, June 17, 1951, p. 4, July 1, 1951, p. 4, and August 8, 1951, p. 5; and Vasyl' Rudko ("R. Lisovii"), "Rozlam v OUN" (The Split in the OUN), *Ukraïns'ki Visti*, May 23, 1949, p. 3. Alexander J. Motyl, *The Turn to the Right: The Ideological Origins and Development of Ukrainian Nationalism, 1919-1929* (Boulder: East European Monographs, 1980), points out that Konovalets' and Dmytro Dontsov collaborated intermittently, and contends the UVO was violent from its inception.

As a reaction to Communism, more radically nationalist groups arose. As has been noted, Communist influence threatened to win the bulk of the Ukrainian student population in the early twenties; this was true not only in the legally recognized universities, but also in the underground university established illegally in L'vov by Ukrainian scholars to give academic training to hundreds of the young people to whom the Poles denied admission to institutions of higher education. One of the principal factors in turning the students from Communism to a nationalist movement, organized in 1926 as the Union of Ukrainian Nationalistic Youth (Soiuz Ukraïns'koï Natsionalistychnoï Molodi—SUNM), was the work of Dmytro Dontsov. Dontsov, an East Ukrainian by origin, had been an active propagator of nationalism even before the First World War. By the early twenties his teachings had come to resemble those of the integral nationalists, although apparently he derived most of his ideas from the German nationalists, like Fichte and Herder, rather than from Maurras or Italians like Pareto and D'Annunzio. Space does not permit any real analysis of the ideology which Dontsov propagated with great success among the youth of Galicia. Insofar as it deviated from the general pattern of integral nationalism, however, it stressed especially the following features: (1) the emphasis on force inherent in the ideology was largely expressed, in the absence of the possibility of sustained open opposition to the dominant group, in advocacy of terrorism; (2) since a state which could be glorified as the bearer of the "national ideal" did not exist, enormous stress was placed on securing absolute adherence to the "pure" national language and culture; (3) absence of the tradition of a state which, through its institutional and legal structure, had supported the national aspirations, and opposition to existing states, led to extreme glorification of "illegality" as such; (4) in close connection with the two preceding points, the essential irrationalism of the ideology was expressed by fantastic romanticism, which was, however, among the comparatively unsophisticated Ukrainians more spontaneous and genuine than the cynical rejection of reason by Germans and Italians; (5) the failure of the efforts of the older generation, and its tendency to compromise with the Polish "occupiers," enhanced the natural tendency of integral nationalism to rely on youth and reject the moderation of its elders.

How these elements in the ideology of the dominant nationalist parties influenced the course of events during the Second World War forms a major topic of this study. Here it should be stressed, however, that integral nationalism was not the only foreign influence on the ideology of the nationalist parties between the two world wars. Also of great importance was the tradition of revolution which had its field of development so close at hand in the tsarist empire. In their terrorist underground activity during the late twenties and early thirties, which included especially assassination of Polish officials and Soviet representatives, the Ukrainian groups modeled themselves on movements like the Russian Narodnaia Volia of the 1870s. In other respects they (and indeed other integral nationalists like the German Nazis) copied Bolshevik methods, especially the organization of a secret political police to maintain the "purity" of the party and the ruthless methods of intraparty strife. The stridency and lack of regard for the truth in propaganda show similar influences. There remained, however, strong elements of liberal and democratic, as well as Christian, principles, even when the participants in the movement verbally rejected them. Formal learning, respect for established authority, individual decision, and popular choice were never completely absent from the real workings of even the most radical groups. Integral nationalism was a fever which gripped some of the most active elements of the Ukraine in the generation after 1918, but it is easier to understand and perhaps to condone in this nation than in others which have had more opportunity for self-expression through the development of a state based upon law.

During the twenties the Ukrainian Military Organization and the Union of Ukrainian Nationalistic Youth gradually won over nearly all politically active elements in the West Ukraine, except those which adhered to the moderate legal parties. Moreover, there were always close connections between the veterans' organization and the students' group; in 1929 these connections were formalized by the establishment of the OUN (Organizatsiia Ukraïns'kykh Natsionalistiv—Organization of Ukrainian Nationalists) which joined both groups into a single party which was to carry on the struggle both by political means and by force against all oppressors of the Ukrainian nation.[30] Through its appeal to the frustrated youth living under Polish rule and through its attraction for many of the embittered émigrés from the East Ukraine, the new movement rapidly attained considerable strength. For eight years it was directed by the former commander of the Sichovi Stril'tsi, Konovalets'. His assassination, almost certainly by a Soviet agent, on May 23, 1938, was a severe blow to the OUN.[31]

Before the new leadership of the organization could fairly establish itself, it was confronted with a situation which would have severely tried the capacity of a much more experienced body. The agreements made at Munich in October, 1938, had weakened the Czechoslovak republic; the Ukrainian nationalists of the small and backward province of Carpatho-Ukraine began to agitate for autonomy. In this they were encouraged by the Nazi regime, which wished to use Ukrainian nationalism as an element tending to disrupt the Czechoslovak state, facilitating subsequent domination by Germany. Apparently the Germans also wished to encourage Ukrainian nationalism in the Carpatho-Ukraine as a potential threat to the Soviet Union and to Poland. In October, 1938, the nationalists declared the Carpatho-Ukraine to be a "free, federated [in Czechoslovakia] state," and eventually Prague recognized its autonomy, although the economically most valuable part was ceded to Hungary. Local Ukrainian nationalists, most of whom were members of, or sympathetic to, the OUN, were organized and excited to more extreme action by OUN leaders who had been living as émigrés in Germany and who had been dispatched to the Carpatho-Ukraine by the OUN directory on the advice of the German

---

[30]Ukrainian writers usually reserve the term "nationalist" for the OUN alone. I use it in the ordinary Western sense, but capitalize the term when referring to the OUN exclusively.

[31]The process of organizational recombination was more complex than I can treat here; see Motyl, *The Turn*, pp. 133-44, 152. Motyl ("Ukrainian Nationalist Political Violence in Inter-War Poland," *East European Quarterly*, XIX [March, 1985], p. 51 ff.) emphasizes that a large majority of assassinations and attempted assassinations during 1930-35 were initiated by young Galician OUN members.

intelligence service.³² A major part of their activities was devoted to forming a para-military organization, the Carpathian Sich, which, they hoped, would form the nucleus of an army of an all-Ukrainian state.

When the Germans occupied Bohemia and Moravia in March, 1939, they agreed to permit Hungary to occupy the remainder of the Carpatho-Ukraine. The Ukrainian nationalists were informed of this decision and advised to submit to Hungarian rule;³³ they resolved, however, to take the desperate course of proclaiming the independence of the Carpatho-Ukraine under a government headed by a priest, Monsignor Augustine Voloshyn. This "independence" lasted only a few days, however; the Carpathian Sich was unable to offer any effective resistance to the heavily armed Hungarian forces. The first major attempt of the nationalists in nearly two decades to liberate Ukrainian soil from foreign rule had failed. It was the forerunner of many such disappointments for the OUN and for all nationalist Ukrainians.³⁴

---

³²For accounts by participants in the early development of the Carpatho-Ukrainian "state," see Vasyl' Veresh-Sirmians'kyi, "Zakarpats'ka Molod'" (The Transcarpathian Youth), *Ukraïns'ki Visti*, March 16, 1947, p. 6; Stepan Rosokha, "Karpats'ka Ukraïna v borot'bi za derzhavu" (The Carpatho-Ukraine in the Struggle for Statehood), *ibid.*; and Iurii Tarkovych, "Sontse iz zakhodu" (The Sun from the West), *Ukraïns'ki Visti*, March 17, 1948, p. 5. On the role of the OUN see also Rudko (*Ukraïns'ki Visti*, May 23, 1949, p. 3) and Seton-Watson, *Eastern Europe between the Wars*, p. 395.

³³German Consul in Hust [Carpatho-Ukraine] to Foreign Ministry, March 14, 1939, and Staatssekretär von Weizsäcker to German Consul in Hust, March 15, 1939, Germany, Auswärtiges Amt, *Documents on German Foreign Policy, 1918-1945*, ed. Raymond J. Sontag *et al.*, Series D, Vol. IV (Washington: Government Printing Office, 1953), pp. 210, 237.

³⁴Stepan Rosokha in "Karpats'ka Sich, 1938-1939" (The Carpathian Sich, 1938-1939), *Istoriia Ukraïns'koho Viis'ka* (History of the Ukrainian Army) (Winnipeg: Vydavets' Ivan Tyktor, 1953), pp. 593-603, and Roman Il'nyts'kyi, *Deutschland und die Ukraine, 1934-1945: Tatsachen europäischer Ostpolitik, ein Vorbericht*, Vol. I (Munich: Osteuropa Institut, 1955), treat the nationalist interlude in the Carpatho-Ukraine at considerable length.

II
The Ukrainians and the Polish Catastrophe

Few groups in the Europe of 1939 had more to gain from a change in the *status quo* than did the nationalist Ukrainians. All who dreamed of an independent and united Ukraine realized that it could arise only out of a series of catastrophic changes in Eastern Europe. The only event likely to initiate such upheavals was a major war.

For many years the most probable war of this nature had appeared to be one between Poland—perhaps with the backing of one or more Western powers—and the Soviet Union. Later, after Hitler's accession to power and the phenomenal increase of German strength, the likely antagonists appeared to be Germany and Poland on the one hand and the USSR on the other. Either contingency, the Ukrainian nationalists felt, would probably lead to a liberation of the Soviet Ukraine, since both Polish and German leaders had long included detachment of this area from Moscow among their major aims in the East. The end of the Polono-German *rapprochement* of the middle thirties dispelled the hope of an immediate Central European combination against the Communist oppressor, but it opened up the prospect, scarcely less attractive for many Ukrainians, of German destruction of the hated Polish state. Consequently, in spite of the severe disappointment suffered when the Germans failed to support the embryonic Ukrainian "state" in the Carpatho-Ukraine, most nationalist circles were prepared in late 1939 to go along with German policy as they had in the preceding years. While the shock of the German-Soviet nonaggression pact in August caused considerable questioning of the validity of this course, it did not deter the more active elements from maintaining their collaboration with Germany. Few, if any, could foresee that Germany would actually allow the Soviet Union to absorb the West Ukrainian lands.

Perhaps of all Ukrainian nationalist movements the least prepared to cope with the startling changes which took place after August, 1939, was that of Paul Skoropads'kyi. As was previously indicated, this movement had never been strong numerically, even in its days of dominance in the Ukraine. In emigration it was further weakened by the fact that many of its original followers had really been adherents of the Russian monarchy at heart, and saw little advantage in supporting a Ukrainian "monarch" unless he was the only ruler available. It is true that, following these defections, the Het'man and his remaining followers had become much more nationalist in their outlook; it was, however, scarcely possible for them to compete with the OUN in this respect, and they lacked the prestige of the UNR, which could claim lineal descent from those who had first endeavored to realize the dream of a modern Ukrainian state. With the exception of a small group in Great Britain, the bulk of Skoropads'kyi's émigré followers were organized in the Ukraïns'ka Hromada (Ukrainian Community) in Greater Germany, where they claimed some 3,500 members in 1940.[1] Most were middle-aged or older.

What the Het'manites lacked in numerical strength and youthful vigor they had in part made up through the prestige of their adherents. Foremost among these, until his death in 1931, was Viacheslav Lypyns'kyi, a talented historian and philosopher who is widely acknowledged to have been the most original and profound Ukrainian thinker of the post-1918 era. In the period now under consideration, his influence in the Hromada was continued by a group of able historians headed by Dmytro Doroshenko. The official ideology of the movement was a compromise between the philosophical reflections of such men and the exigencies of practical politics, particularly the need of adjustment to the emerging New Order.

A "catechism" for the Het'man followers, published in 1940, strongly emphasized the continuing theme of the movement — territorial rather than ethnic patriotism as the basis for a future Ukrainian state.[2] The Ukrainian nation was declared to be the organized collective of the Ukrainian people belonging to the "Aryan" race[3] — an ambiguous statement which was at once a concession to Nazi doctrine and a hint of willingness to accept as part of the Ukrainian nation the Russian and Polish "Aryans" living on Ukrainian soil. The remainder of the program was frankly conservative: a class society based on the orders of the "plow," the "work bench," and the "word" is advocated, with all subjects being guaranteed the right to live, to work in their proper calling, and to have due process of law.[4] The church was to be independent but allied to the monarchy.[5] It is fairly obvious that in the fierce turmoil which was to grip the Ukraine during the war years, doctrines derived from reflection on a long course of Ukrainian history would be understood and appreciated only by the most reflective members of the new generations reared under Stalinism or those attracted by the advance of extreme nationalism. The Het'manite

---

[1] See the first issue of *Ukraïns'ka Diisnist'*, November 15, 1940, p. 1, the organ of the Het'man group. For a succinct but generally accurate and penetrating summary of the position of this and other Ukrainian groups in mid-1941, see a memorandum from the files of the Reichsministerium für die besetzten Ostgebiete, Occ E-4 (5), in Yiddish Scientific Institute (hereafter referred to as Occ E-4 [5]). Since the signature is illegible, I have not been able to determine the name of the author of this memorandum.

[2] A. M. Andriievs'kyi, *Katekhyzys abo nastavlennia v derzhavnii nautsi dlia ukraïns'koho Het'mantsia-Derzhavnyka* (A Catechism or Position on State Science for the Ukrainian Adherent of the Het'man State) (Berlin, August 15, 1940).

[3] *Ibid.*, p. 3

[4] *Ibid.*, pp. 21 f.

[5] *Ibid.*, p. 23.

ideology in itself would probably have proved an insurmountable handicap to the fulfillment by the Het'man group of its aspirations for power.

Somewhat paradoxically, in the light of its ideological position, which differed fundamentally from National Socialist teachings, Skoropads'kyi's movement had many close links to the rulers of the Third Reich. There was, of course, a strong precedent for this position in the heavy dependence of the Het'man on the forces of Kaiser Wilhelm; moreover, the Het'man is reported to have been on terms of personal friendship with Hermann Göring.[6] The conservatism of the Het'manites, while differing in important respects from Nazism, was useful to the German leaders as a factor which could be used against Communism. Yet, because of its tendency to avoid violent action, it was less likely in practice to interfere with their aims than was the position of the Nationalists (OUN), which was so much closer to theirs ideologically. At times the conservative caution of the Skoropads'kyi followers almost reached the dead center of passivity. In December, 1940, for example, their organ argued that the Ukrainian question was not going to be settled at the moment and condemned "agitators" who were trying to "form ministries and imagine international combinations" in which such a settlement could take place.[7] Later this was to lead to an almost incredible complacency in the face of German ruthlessness in the Ukraine. For example, as late as August 30, 1942, Het'man Skoropads'kyi himself advised his followers to exercise caution, to collaborate with the Germans against the Bolsheviks, and to wait for peace. He concluded by asserting that "the Germans must be convinced that the Ukrainians are honest people."[8]

From the point of view of ideology and political orientation, the UNR was at the opposite pole of Ukrainian politics. In many ways, however, its development had closely paralleled that of the Het'man movement. The UNR was, of course, the "legitimate" successor of the republic of 1918-1920. As was previously mentioned, the first president, Simon Petliura, had been succeeded by Andrew Livyts'kyi, who continued to regard himself as chief of state of a government-in-exile and, consequently, above parties. Actually, by 1939 the bulk of his followers were members of the Ukrainian Social Democratic Party, though the aura of legitimacy kept many others, especially Social Revolutionaries, in loose allegiance to him. Furthermore, the ideology of the group was unquestionably socialist and democratic—though of a somewhat dated type, namely, the rather loosely formulated and Utopian theory of the pre-1917 era.

In practice, certain disquieting developments had taken place in the outlook of the UNR. Doubtless, no democratic group could survive eighteen years of émigré existence without certain signs of deterioration. The very strength of democratic government itself—frequent renewals of support through submission of policies to popular verdict and recruitment of new forces from the masses of the people—are rendered inoperative by emigration. The

---

[6]Joachim Joesten, "Hitler's Fiasco in the Ukraine," *Foreign Affairs*, XXI (January, 1943), p. 334.

[7]Editorial in *Ukraïns'ka Diisnist'*, December 1, 1940, p. 1.

[8]*Ukraïns'kyi derzhavnyk al'manakh na 1943 rik* (Ukrainian Statist Almanac for 1943) (Berlin, n.d.), p. 8. As a result of the weaknesses outlined above, the Het'man organization played a comparatively insignificant role in the development of real political forces in the Ukraine during the period of this study. Hence it will not be useful to interrupt a discussion of more important activities to mention its stand on developments.

democratic government—an essentially dynamic phenomenon—is rendered static by its severance from the masses, and its members are turned in upon themselves. Personal feuds, factionalism, and striving for outside support replace the more healthy characteristics of democratic politics. Such was the development in the UNR. When the war began, the "government" was dispersed in three European capitals. Several of the lesser ministers were in Prague, where, until a short time before, the democratic atmosphere and the encouragement of the Czechoslovak government had created a favorable climate for Ukrainian cultural development. In Paris were Viacheslav Prokopovych, prime minister, and Alexander Shul'hyn, foreign minister. The chief center, however, was Warsaw, where President Livyts'kyi and his ministers Sal's'kyi and Smal'-Stots'kyi resided.[9]

This distribution of the personnel of the government corresponded roughly to its ties with the European governments. The basic commitment was to Poland, in line with Petliura's policy in the final months of his regime. In exile, the government's ties with the Polish state had become still closer.[10] At the outbreak of the war a considerable number of former officers of the Ukrainian Republican Army were serving as professional soldiers ("contract officers") with the Polish army. Moreover, the Promethean movement, which had been founded by Ukrainians in the twenties and was headed by Smal'-Stots'kyi, leaned heavily on Warsaw. This movement, which endeavored to unite the émigré leaders of the non-Russian nationalities of the Soviet Union, played a large part in Polish aspirations for the development of a bloc of states in Eastern Europe, stretching from Finland to the Caucasus, in which Poland could become a true great power by exercising her "natural" position of leadership. The Ukrainian leaders of the Promethean movement were, of course, aware of the Polish aims, but in their overwhelming desire for liberation of their peoples from the Communist yoke they accepted the assistance of the Warsaw government.[11]

From the point of view of practical politics, the dependence of the UNR leaders upon Poland is readily understandable. Unfortunately, the Polish environment did much to accentuate the naturally unwholesome condition of exile. The tendency to chauvinism in the Polish state, its rapid abandonment of democratic principles in the thirties, and the atmosphere of military factionalism were reflected to some extent in the parallel development of the Ukrainian movement.

As corollaries of their ties with Poland, and also of their democratic ideology, the UNR leaders preferred to carry on their activities in France and Rumania where they received some encouragement from official circles. There

---

[9] Roman Smal'-Stots'kyi is well known in the United States as Smal-Stocki, a Polish form of transliteration of the Ukrainian; Shul'hyn is equally well known under the Russian form of his name, Shul'gin.

[10] At least they had become closer after Petliura's assassination. As noted previously, he had left Poland because of the difficulty of his position in a country which stifled Ukrainian life within its borders. Livyts'kyi, however, found it possible to continue to reside in Warsaw, and the resultant hostility of the Galician elements drove him still closer to the Polish regime.

[11] For a sympathetic account of the Promethean movement by its leader at the outbreak of the war, see Roman Smal'-Stots'kyi, "The Struggle of the Subjugated Nations in the Soviet Union for Freedom: Sketch of the History of the Promethean Movement," *Ukrainian Quarterly*, III (Autumn, 1947), pp. 324-44.

was a large group of republican émigrés in Rumania, but the political environment deteriorated rapidly there in the same fashion as in Poland. Conditions in France were far more favorable, and the Ukrainian republican community there, which included a number of persons who had been prominent in the UNR government, remained basically democratic in its outlook. The Franco-Soviet pact appeared to destroy any hope of real assistance from France, however. At the same time, as has been noted, the prospect of Polono-German cooperation against the Soviet Union was strengthened. This prospect was so attractive to the UNR leaders that many, including, it is said, President Livyts'kyi, refused to accept the reality of the deterioration in German-Polish relations as late as the summer of 1939, and hoped desperately for a reversal of the German policy even after the Molotov-Ribbentrop pact was announced.[12]

When war broke out dozens of Ukrainian officers faithfully carried out their assignments in the hopelessly outmatched Polish army. In return, the Polish government apparently gave little attention to the safety of the UNR members in Warsaw. Nevertheless, Livyts'kyi was finally able to leave the city and to reach the Ukrainian ethnographical area of Poland. There his party received news of the rapid approach of Soviet forces which were cutting across eastern Galicia between them and the Rumanian border. They decided that German captivity was preferable to falling into the hands of their archenemies. Before surrendering to the Germans, however, the President was able to send word to Prokopovych that, in accordance with the constitution, he should assume the office of president, and that Shul'hyn should in turn become premier.[13] The Prometheans, headed by Smal'-Stots'kyi, had reached L'vov (L'viv), and were in even greater peril from the Soviet approach, but they, too, succeeded in reaching the German lines and were safely evacuated, probably through special efforts of Admiral Canaris, the German chief of intelligence, who hoped to preserve the group for future use against the Soviet Union.[14]

Once they had reluctantly accepted the protection of the German forces, the Ukrainian republicans were treated as enemy prisoners. Their organization was declared illegal, and the leaders were subjected to close surveillance and restriction of movement. Their treatment, however, was soon made less severe. A number of the "contract officers," while nominally prisoners of war, were allowed to move about in German-occupied Poland, while several political leaders were even given employment in writing studies on the Ukraine for the Germans. Undoubtedly this moderation was in part facilitated by the willingness of Livyts'kyi and other leaders to maintain unofficial contacts of a friendly nature with German representatives. As will be shown, however, they were by no means willing to become pawns of the Germans and took what occasions arose to endeavor to regain their freedom of action.[15]

For a certain time, the "successor government" in Paris was able to pursue an independent policy. Prokopovych and Shul'hyn were active in aiding the Allied cause, especially in efforts to secure the enlistment of the considerable

---

[12]Interview 14.

[13]Interview 23; *Nastup*, March 9, 1940.

[14]Cf. Karl Abshagen, *Canaris, Patriot und Weltbürger* (Stuttgart: Union Deutsche Verlagsgesellschaft, 1949), p. 217; Interview 14.

[15]See Chapter IV.

number of workers of Ukrainian origin for a hoped-for legion to aid Finland in her struggle against the Soviet Union. Before these plans could materialize, the rapid German invasion of France also enveloped them. Shul'hyn was sent to a concentration camp, Prokopovych died a few months after the French surrender, and all significant activity in this quarter ceased.

The OUN, which had rapidly increased in influence in the thirties, followed a still different course. The assassination of Konovalets' was a severe blow, but its most injurious consequences were not felt immediately. Soon afterwards the OUN was deeply involved in the attempted formation of the Ukrainian "state" in the Subcarpathian province of Czechoslovakia. The collapse of this project in March caused extreme disappointment. It did not, however, discredit the OUN in the eyes of most nationalist Ukrainians. After all, they pointed out, the Ukrainians had put up a determined, if brief, struggle against overwhelming odds, while the other nationalities of the Czechoslovak republic had submitted to the dictates of the surrounding powers without offering any resistance at all. Thousands of young Carpatho-Ukrainians went into exile (mostly to Greater Germany), thus expanding the ranks of the OUN. The Carpathian Sich, the military organization which fought the Hungarians, took its place in the Ukrainian legend along with the Zaporozhian Cossacks, the Sichovi Stril'tsi, and Tiutiunnyk's band. The net result was an immediate increase in the prestige of the organization, although doubts of the wisdom of the course it had followed were to come to the surface later.

At the outbreak of war, the leadership of the OUN was very much the same as it had been prior to the death of Konovalets'. Aside from its chief, Andrew Mel'nyk, there were eight members of the Provid, or directorate. The importance of these men in the events which are to be described warrants a somewhat detailed consideration of their backgrounds and personalities. Two were generals of the revolutionary period; the OUN, like most Ukrainian organizations, felt it desirable to ornament its directing organ with personalities who recalled the days of the active struggle for liberation, thus serving to connect the organization more closely with the nationalist myth. General Kurmanovych's role seems to have been largely confined to this contribution of prestige; the same cannot be said concerning General Kapustians'kyi, who was to play a courageous and active role in nationalist organization in the East Ukraine after June, 1941. Neither, however, appears to have exerted major influence on the development of the policy of the organization. Also of limited importance in policy formation were two of the younger members of the Provid, Iaroslav Baranovs'kyi and Dmytro Andriievs'kyi. Baranovs'kyi, only thirty-three when war broke out, was of a different generation from that of most of the members of the Provid. Of Galician background, he had been an active member of the underground student organization in L'vov and had been imprisoned by the Poles. Later he continued his law studies in Austria.[16] His age and background would seem to have made him a natural link between the Provid and the Galician nationalist youth, and indeed, up until 1940 his influence in the latter group was considerable. Unfortunately for him, his reputation was in constant danger of being brought into question by the fact that his brother, Roman, had acted as an agent for the Polish police, although Iaroslav

---

[16]Obituary in *Nastup*, May 30, 1943, p. 5.

was from all evidence, quite innocent in this connection.[17] Andriievs'-kyi, though only a few years older than Baranovs'kyi, had quite a different background and function in the organization. He had left the East Ukraine as a young man, had followed a brief career in the diplomatic service of the republic, and then had been trained as an engineer in Belgium. Joining the movement, he took over a considerable part of its external relations, though the chief contacts were carried on with Germany through other channels. His moderation and talent as a writer made him a valuable asset to the organization.[18]

Next in scale of importance in the Provid were two military men, much younger and more active, however, than the generals previously referred to. Richard Iarii was unique among members of the Provid in that he was Ukrainian only by adoption. It is uncertain whether he was of Czech or German origin; he had served as an officer in the Austro-Hungarian army, along with numerous Galician Ukrainians, and upon the dissolution of that force had cast in his lot with the struggling Ukrainian Republican Army. He served loyally and well and, after the failure of the Ukrainian efforts, continued to collaborate with his comrades in the UVO. As Germany became stronger, he established close ties with German military intelligence circles. To the other members of the Provid he was a good comrade, a talented supporter of a cause desperately in need of help, and a welcome intermediary in dealing with the Germans. At the same time, he was regarded as ambitious, and it has been suggested that he was not overscrupulous. Some of his associates felt that his allegiance was not wholeheartedly to Ukrainian nationalism.[19] Colonel Roman Sushko, like Iarii, had served in both the Austro-Hungarian and Ukrainian armies. Although discredited in Nazi circles, he, too, was in close contact with the Abwehr. Unlike Iarii, however, he was a typical West Ukrainian of Galician peasant stock.[20]

Of greatest influence were Nicholas Stsibors'kyi and Omelian Senyk. Stsibors'kyi was born in Zhitomir in 1897, the son of a tsarist army officer, and spent his youth in Kiev. Thus he was familiar with the East Ukraine as it had existed prior to the Revolution. After serving in the Ukrainian army, he had emigrated to Prague, where he studied engineering and economics.[21] Joining the UVO and the OUN during this period, he rapidly rose to the position of official theorist of the latter group; in this capacity, he exerted great influence. Senyk, in contrast to Stsibors'kyi, was the practical organizer of the party. Of Galician origin (his father was an official in L'vov), he was also a veteran of the revolutionary struggle, as well as of the Austro-Hungarian army.[22] He had taken part in underground work in Poland in the twenties, but was generally regarded by the younger generation as too moderate and too conservative. He appears, however, to have enjoyed the confidence of Konovalets' down to the

---

[17]Interviews 52, 75; Bohdan Mykhailiuk, *Bunt Bandery* (Bandera's Rebellion) (1950), p. 50.

[18]Interviews 48, 67.

[19]Interview 67.

[20]Obituary in *L'vivs'ki Visti*, February 2, 1944, p. 2; letter to Reinhard Heydrich, Aussenpolitisches Amt der NSDAP, Reichsleitung, September 18, 1940 (T 454, Reel 92).

[21]Obituary in *Nastup*, September 27, 1941, p. 1.

[22]*Ibid.*

latter's death, and he took over practical direction of the organization immediately after this event. In this capacity, he was instrumental in carrying out the transfer of authority to Colonel Andrew Mel'nyk.

Mel'nyk was in a position to assume a role of unique importance in the Ukrainian Nationalist movement. In many respects his natural qualities admirably fitted him for this role. He was a man of fine bearing, dignified yet friendly, exceptional in his moderation and composure among a group where dignity and balance tended to be submerged by bitterness and extremism. Born of peasant parents in Eastern Galicia, he was somewhat older (forty-eight) than most of his colleagues. After receiving an engineering degree in Vienna in 1912,[23] he had served in the Austro-Hungarian army. There, it is said, he was referred to by his brother officers, Austrian and Ukrainian alike, as "Lord Mel'nyk"—this not in sarcasm, but as a sincere tribute to his embodiment of the English concept of the gentleman, then still an ideal in Central Europe.[24] His later career, while not exceptionally distinguished, did nothing to impair this reputation. He was chief of staff under Konovalets' in the Sichovi Stril'tsi, and later served a term in a Polish jail for activity in the UVO. In contrast to most of the other leaders, however, his career in the thirties was placid. Pursuing his profession of engineer, he worked as director of forests on the huge estates of the Metropolitan of L'vov.

Whether it is accurate to describe Mel'nyk as a devout Catholic may be questioned, but there is no doubt that he was far more friendly to the church than nearly all of his associates. For a number of years prior to Mel'nyk's assumption of leadership, he was chairman of the Catholic youth organization in Galicia, Orlo,[25] which was regarded as anti-Nationalist by the great bulk of the OUN youth in that area. It seems probable that his elevation to the post of director of the Provid was very gratifying to Greek Catholic church circles, which thereby hoped to dispel the anti-clerical tendencies of the OUN and to prevent further unfolding of the anti-Christian elements in its ideology. At the same time, Mel'nyk's church ties and moderate attitude were doubtless welcome to many members of the Provid, especially to Senyk. Conditions inside Poland were highly unfavorable to the development of a secure base for a Ukrainian nationalist party, regardless of its ideology. The terroristic response to drastic and bloody Polish suppression of all national aspirations was understandable. It was adopted from time to time by all elements in the OUN and countenanced by even broader circles of Galician society. Over a period of years, however, this tactic tended to get out of hand, to defeat the purposes of the organization by inducing still harsher repression and by alienating those members of the Ukrainian community who still hoped to lead normal lives. The latter danger was becoming especially acute during the late thirties when the legal Ukrainian parties in Poland were tending more and more to separate themselves from the underground and were attempting to normalize their relations with the Polish government. To stem this tendency, more prudent and

---

[23]*Nastup*, December 12, 1940, p. 3.

[24]Interview 62.

[25]*Entsyklopediia Ukraïnoznavstvo* (Encyclopedia of Things Ukrainian), eds. Volodymyr Kubiiovych and Zenon Kuzelia (Munich: Naukove Tovarystvo im. Shevchenka, 1949), p. 959.

moderate leadership was needed in the OUN; connections with the church, especially the influential Metropolitan Sheptyts'kyi, could be invaluable.[26]

The real difficulty in this approach was that it was fundamentally incompatible with the development and ideology of the OUN. Officially, the Provid adhered to a credo of integral nationalism. In the political context of Central Europe in the 1930s, this meant that it was strongly attracted by Fascist totalitarianism. The totalitarian element in the ideology of the OUN consisted in its emphasis on the nation as an entity valued above all others, to be served by whatever means might be required. OUN adherents maintained that the state was merely the most convenient form of national life, not an absolute value in itself, as was the nation.[27] This position was necessary tactically in order to distinguish sharply the OUN from the Het'man movement. Putting the state in a secondary place, however, tended to drive the movement still further in the direction of deification of the mystic concept of the nation, even to the point of racism. "Nationalism is based on feelings, which are carried by the racial blood."[28]

The incompatibility of such doctrines with Christian teachings could not be concealed, even in the atmosphere of misty romanticism prevalent in many Nationalist circles. Thus, the Catholic leader of the Carpatho-Ukraine, Monsignor Voloshyn, in praising Mel'nyk, pointed out that he was a man of typically European culture, with an ideology based on Christianity and differing from that of many Nationalists who placed the nation above God.[29]

This statement was probably true, but it made Mel'nyk's position still more anomalous. He was the leader of a movement whose official ideology was totalitarian; moreover, all the circumstances of the period and of the movement itself tended to intensify the totalitarian element. He was trying to work against this tide, to moderate, even if only slightly, its violent philosophy. To be successful, he was compelled to assert his authority as autocratic director of the movement. Now, it may be true historically that totalitarianism

---

[26]This analysis is a deduction from the circumstances of the OUN and from the backgrounds and connections of the persons involved. It cannot be documented directly, but appears to fit all the known facts. For comments on the suspicions raised by Mel'nyk's association with the church and Senyk's sponsoring of him, see Vasyl' Rudko ("R. Lisovyi"), "Rozlam v OUN" (The Split in the OUN), *Ukraïns'ki Visti*, May 23, 1949, p. 3. It should be noted that several critics of the first edition of this book have objected to the assertion that the younger generation of the OUN tended to be anti-clerical, though others have agreed with this interpretation. Aside from Ukrainians, the weightiest objection was by Hans J. Beyer in *Historische Zeitschrift*, CLXXXVI (October, 1958), pp. 422-24. While the matter can probably never be settled definitively, I remain convinced that my first interpretation is substantially correct. For corroboration see Lev Shankovs'kyi, *Pokhidni hrupy OUN* (March Groups of the OUN) (Munich: Vydavnytstvo "Ukraïns'kyi Samostiinyk," 1958), p. 36.

[27]"Maksym Orlyk" in *Nastup*, August 17, 1940, p. 2. For the most part I have relied on periodicals of fairly large circulation (about 6,000 in the case of *Nastup*) as the principal sources for ideology of the OUN in this period. The more philosophical treatises of Dontsov and especially of Stsibors'kyi (*Natsiokratiia*) are of a great deal more interest to the student of political theory. For the purposes of this study, however, it seems preferable to utilize sources which, though less profound, had a more immediate impact on the rank and file of the membership and followed the currents of changing ideological emphasis.

[28]"Sigma" in an editorial in *Nastup*, March 23, 1940, p. 1.

[29]Interview for *Nastup*, December 21, 1940, p. 3.

and autocratic authority are separable. In the Central Europe of 1939, however, it was difficult to maintain the distinction.

As a matter of fact, Mel'nyk himself was reluctant even to attempt to assert a claim to dictatorial power. Writings which deal with him primarily, and which he may be assumed to have controlled, refer to him more frequently as "director of the Provid" than as "leader." Attempts to build Mel'nyk up as a mystic exponent of the national will are present, as in a reference to the leaders who embodied the genius of the nation—"Shevchenko, Konovalets', and now Mel'nyk"[30]—and in one to Mel'nyk's "monolithic character."[31] On the whole, however, the more prominent theme is that of military subordination to a *body* of hierarchical superiors, rather than unrestrained submission to the will of a charismatic leader.

> The leadership [Provid] bears a responsibility to history, to future generations, to the nation (including those who were and are to be), to God, but never to its subordinates! This would lead to anarchy as surely as would questioning of orders in an army.[32]

As the need for suppressing factionalism grew stronger, however, this more moderate position tended to be abandoned in favor of outright adherence to the *Führerprinzip*.

It is evident from the above discussion that there was a deep conflict between the "natural" tendencies of the ideology of the movement and the personal temperament and conviction of its chief. Had the matter been confined to the émigré section of the OUN, a compromise might have been reached, or Mel'nyk might have even come out the victor. It will be noted that of the nine members of the Provid (including Mel'nyk himself), all but two had been military officers. Moreover, the great majority of them had served not only in the somewhat irregular Ukrainian army, but also in the tightly disciplined officer corps of the Russian or Austro-Hungarian Empires. Standards of military discipline and honor prevented them from fully subscribing to the principle that all means are legitimate, at least when this principle was to be applied in factional struggles within their own group against their acknowledged superior. Moreover, with the exception of Baranovs'kyi, all were past forty, and it may be supposed that the passage of years had immunized them against impulsive and violent action.

If, however, the OUN had been confined to the emigration, it would have had scarcely greater influence than the UNR or the Het'man group. As a matter of fact, unlike these two groups, it was predominantly West Ukrainian in membership. It is true that of the nine Provid members, three were East Ukrainian émigrés. Of these, however, two had very limited influence, while Stsibors'kyi owed his prominence primarily to his ability as a theoretician. Moreover, the Provid did not accurately reflect the composition of the rank and file of the membership. In the first place it provided no representation for the very important groups of OUN members in or from Volhynia, the

---

[30]*Ukraïns'kyi Visnyk*, February 1, 1941, p. 2.

[31]*Nastup*, December 14, 1940, p. 1.

[32]Editorial in *Nastup*, February 1, 1941, p. 1.

Carpatho-Ukraine, and Bukovina.[33] More significant was the difference in age; the great bulk of the membership, and its most active component, was drawn from the youth of Galicia. As discussed in the preceding chapter, this generation, living double lives, studying in the underground university, liable to arrest by the Polish authorities at any moment, had had recourse to violence, and many had suffered terribly for their deeds. There was a constant tendency to suspect that the émigré leaders were shirking the hardships and dangers of the fight, or at least were unable to understand its demands.

This feeling was greatly accentuated by the age difference between the leadership and the bulk of the members in Galicia. There was a gap of about ten years between the average member of the official émigré leadership and the average unofficial leader at home; the rank and file members in Galicia were still younger. In itself, this difference was significant enough; lack of maturity was bound to lead to extremism among members of an organization like the OUN. There were, however, additional factors of great importance. The younger group had lacked the experience of growing up in a stable, prewar society. Furthermore, the older generation had had an opportunity to fight for Ukrainian statehood openly and in a recognized manner. In establishing a state and an army, if for only a brief period, it had escaped from the frustrating sense of inferiority which was the result of living in a state governed by another nationality. While the older generation had had its peaceful years, followed by a retrospectively glorious fight, the younger generation had known only the bitter, ambiguous struggle against Polish repression. Thus, the latter harbored a feeling of tension, a sort of inferiority complex vis-à-vis the formal leadership.

Nor was the directorate entirely guiltless in this situation. It is true that most of its Galician members had shared the hardship of the struggle against Poland (three had been imprisoned) and that a life of exile is not much preferable even to underground existence in one's native country. The generation which had come to maturity during the war, however, tended to view itself as a closed elite, entrance to which was unattainable by the younger men. The unwillingness to permit full participation in this elite may be understood from the following expression: "I don't mind playing politics, but I object to playing it with my children." In this connection a ready, if understandably infuriating, device was at hand: the constant use of the military titles acquired during the war, and hence not attainable by the younger men, whose only military service (when it could not be avoided) was as conscripts in the Polish army.

While Konovalets' lived, his great authority and, it is said, his skillful handling of the problem of the different generations had prevented it from assuming serious proportions, although there were rumblings of protest from the younger group. Mel'nyk was faced with a far more difficult set of problems: he had to try to unify the Ukrainian population of Galicia behind the organization, but any modification of ideology or tactics would be regarded as treason by the younger men; he had to try to bargain for Ukrainian ends with powers which were enormously superior, a process in which any yielding to

---

[33] It should be pointed out that there were several other leaders (of the older generation) whose influence probably exceeded that of some members of the Provid. In these unofficial groups the Carpatho-Ukraine (but not Volhynia and Bukovina) was adequately represented. East Ukrainians were considerably overrepresented in proportion to their number among the rank and file.

impulsive action might be fatal. In addition, the very factors which inclined Mel'nyk to exercise a moderating influence in the OUN made him incapable of keeping the revolutionary youth in hand. His association with the church was like a black flag to their anti-clericalism. His calmness and dignity made little impression on men whose ideal leader was an iron-willed conspirator. His refusal to raise the nation to the level of the absolute was simply taken as a sign of weakness, if it was comprehended at all. In a stable community, Mel'nyk would doubtless have been a highly useful citizen, or even a successful statesman, but his character ill equipped him to become the leader of a terroristic conspiracy. Thus, the basis was laid for a catastrophe within the most powerful Ukrainian organization.

First, however, came the greater catastrophe of war. For many years the OUN had been closely tied to German policy. This alignment was furthered by the semi-Fascist nature of its ideology, and in turn the dependence on Germany tended to intensify Fascist trends in the organization. All considerations of power politics led the OUN to seek German aid, since Germany was the only power which had either the will or the means to attack its archenemies—Poland and the Soviet Union. The great problem, as was hinted in the previous paragraph, was that of dealing with the Germans without becoming their helpless puppet, since the disparity of strength between the parties was obviously enormous.

Up to 1939 the Ukrainian Nationalist leaders had been confident that Germany was really interested in securing the independence of the Ukraine, and felt that she would deal fairly with them. To an extent, however, they were less dependent on Germany than this trustful attitude might have implied. Unlike the Het'man group, which was concentrated largely in the neighborhood of Berlin, the OUN was more evenly spread over most of Central and Western Europe. Both Konovalets' and Mel'nyk traveled frequently and avoided settling within the German-dominated area. Nevertheless, in Richard Iarii they had a constant channel of communication to that section of the German regime which was represented by Admiral Canaris and the Abwehr. In the summer of 1939, Colonel Sushko was also collaborating closely with the Germans, preparing a group of some two hundred men in Wiener-Neustadt, Austria, to act as an auxiliary to the Wehrmacht in its approaching attack on Poland and to provide an armed nucleus for an uprising which the OUN hoped would lead to independence for the Ukrainians in that country.[34] Moreover, *de facto* dependence of the OUN on Germany had been greatly increased by the large immigration of its members to German territory in 1939, especially to the "Protectorate of Bohemia-Moravia," where a major center of the Carpatho-Ukrainians with the important pro-OUN organ *Nastup* was soon to be established.[35]

---

[34]Liubomyr Ortyns'kyi, "Druzhyny Ukraïns'kykh Natsionalistiv (DUN)" (The Brotherhoods of Ukrainian Nationalists [DUN]), *Visti Bratstva kol. Voiakiv 1. UD UNA* (June-July, 1952), p. 4; Abshagen, *Canaris*, p. 217.

[35]*Nastup* had actually been founded in the Carpatho-Ukraine by Dr. Stephen Rosokha, but after the destruction of the Ukrainian government there Rosokha proceeded to Prague, where he was able to begin publishing around the beginning of 1940. Though not himself a member of the OUN, he was a fervent supporter and admirer of Mel'nyk, and his pages were always available to OUN writers. In addition to this paper, which labored under a comparatively mild German pre-censorship until its suppression in 1943, there was *Ukraïns'kyi Visnyk* in Berlin which, as it

In spite of these growing ties of dependence, when the Provid decided to hold the Second Congress of the organization in August of 1939, Rome instead of a German city was chosen as the meeting place. At this congress it was decided that Mel'nyk should maintain his headquarters in Switzerland, and a policy generally cautious in regard to Germany was envisaged.[36] Shortly after its adjournment came the impact of the news of the Molotov-Ribbentrop pact, with its implications of concessions to the Soviets in the offing. The agreement was openly denounced by the official organ of the OUN.[37] With war actually beginning almost at the same time, however, it was impossible, even had the Provid so desired, to withdraw from the arrangement for military collaboration with the Germans.

After a period of hesitation arising from his uncertainty concerning Soviet intentions in eastern Poland,[38] Canaris permitted Sushko's group to proceed from its base in Slovakia as far as the Ukrainian ethnographical territory on the San River, but at this point it was obliged to turn back because of the advance of Soviet troops.[39] Within Galicia proper, at least one small uprising, doubtless inspired by Nationalists, occurred against the Polish regime.[40] From the OUN point of view, the one advantage of the Sushko expedition was that it served as an armed escort for Iaroslav Baranovs'kyi, who came as a delegate from the Provid to the local groups. His mission was to give the latter information on the delicate situation arising from the Soviet occupation and to warn them to exercise caution in coming out into the open.[41] This was undoubtedly necessary since, had rebellions been carried out on a large scale, they would have served no purpose in destroying the tottering Polish authority, while they would have revealed the identity of the underground members to the approaching Soviet forces.

One further result of the brief Polish campaign, of still greater significance for the development of the OUN, must be mentioned. As the Germans closed in on Warsaw, the Polish authorities were confronted with the problem of disposing of the political prisoners, especially the Ukrainians, whom they held there. After various efforts to evacuate them, the most important prisoners were allowed, either through deliberate intent or through the humane

---

nominally was not a newspaper but a bulletin for members of the Ukrainian National Union in Germany, escaped pre-censorship. Like *Nastup*, it was officially non-OUN but followed the OUN line closely and appears to have been more influential than the formal organs of the OUN which, however, are now largely unavailable for the war period.

[36] In addition, he himself was confirmed as head of the Provid, and its membership was ratified. Interviews 61, 67.

[37] *OUN u Viini* (The OUN in the War), Information Section of the OUN (UNR), April, 1946, pp. 24-28, citing *Natsional 'na Presova Sluzhba* (an OUN "press release" service not available to me) for September 1, 1939.

[38] Abshagen, *Canaris*, pp. 208-9.

[39] Interviews 8, 14, 67; Nykon Nalivaiko, "Legioni v natsional'nykh viinakh" (Legions in National Wars), *Narodna Volia* (October 27, 1949), p. 2.

[40] *Nastup*, March 16, 1940, p. 3, describes the formation of a group of three hundred partisans near L'vov in the week of September 11-17 to fight Polish police who had been committing atrocities and to drive off Polish partisans and troops.

[41] Interview 67.

action of their guards, to go free.[42] Thus the leaders of the Galician group, embittered by years of confinement, were once again free to pursue their activities.

The brief Polish war, which was the opening chapter of a struggle of tremendous consequences for the world at large, was of great indirect importance for Ukrainian national life. For the first time in modern history, the Galicians were really united with the East Ukrainians in a single state. However, this state was the most dreaded enemy of the Ukrainian nationalist movements. These circumstances were bound to have a considerable effect on the development of the nationalist movements, and in fact a radical process of realignment of the Ukrainian forces was already under way; during the twenty months following the Polish collapse this intraparty conflict was to occupy almost as much attention in the Ukrainian émigré community as did the larger events of world politics.

---

[42] For an interesting description of the way in which some of these Ukrainians secured their freedom, see Mykola (Nicholas) Klymishyn, "Smertnyi pokhid" (The Death March), *Nastup*, February 24, 1940, p. 3; this account was confirmed by Interview 76.

III
Retrenchment and Revolt

By the end of September, 1939, it appeared that Germany had definitely abandoned the Ukrainian nationalists. The agreement which allowed the Soviet Union to occupy the territory of Poland up to the line of the Bug and the San meant in effect that the compact Ukrainian area in Galicia, the Ukrainian land which possessed the strongest nationalist feeling, had passed under the control of the Soviet regime. Some Nazi circles secretly argued that OUN organizations in Soviet-occupied areas be dissolved.[1] A few small areas of Ukrainian settlement remained under German control in what was now designated as the Generalgouvernement Polen, however. Aside from minute border districts, these were the Chelm (Kholm) region and the Lemko region, a rugged stretch on the northern slope of the Carpathians from Przemysl (Peremyshl') almost to Cracow. Most Lemkos were hardy but impoverished mountaineers with their own dialect of Ukrainian. Under the Polish regime they had been subjected to the same repression which was directed against the eastern Galician Ukrainians, but the low economic potential of the Lemko area discouraged significant Polish settlement there.

In the Chelm district, a violent denationalization policy had been carried out. Its mixed ethnographic composition was complicated by changes in religion. Originally much of the Chelm population, including a large majority of its Ukrainians, had been Greek Catholic like the Galician Ukrainians. Under Alexander II, a harsh policy of repression aimed to strengthen the Orthodox Church by destroying the Greek Catholic Church. Numerous Greek-rite parishes were forcibly transferred to the Orthodox Church, and a number of Latin rite churches which were accused of ministering to Greek Catholics who resisted transfer to Orthodoxy were also seized. Either because they originally had some sympathy for Orthodoxy, or because they became accustomed to it over the decades, many of the "converted" congregations had retained some ties with it after the area had become a part of Poland. Stimulated by part of the Latin clergy (the Greek Catholic hierarchy opposed the step), the Polish

---

[1]Letter from Aussenpolitisches Amt der NSDAP to SS Deputy Chief Heydrich, September 18, 1940, referring to the OUN as "no more than a national Galician offshoot of the fallen tree of the Great Russian social revolutionary movement" (T 454, Reel 92).

government seized many of the churches or, in some cases, even burnt them to the ground. The Orthodox priests were expelled and replaced by Catholic pastors of the Latin, not the Greek, rite. The small supply of intellectuals made it difficult for other Ukrainian communities to aid the Ukrainians of Chelm, and, as a result, the policy of denationalization had considerable success.[2]

For over twenty months these small and handicapped areas were to serve as the principal territorial base of Ukrainian nationalist efforts. The reason that they were able to fulfill this function arose from the deliberately ambiguous nature of German policy toward the Ukrainian movements during this period. The Molotov-Ribbentrop pact, which was a formal barrier to the use of Ukrainian nationalist sentiment to disrupt the Soviet Union, was, indeed, merely regarded as a truce by the Nazi leaders, but the duration of the truce was viewed as indefinite. Any overt encouragement of the Ukrainian nationalists would be looked upon by the Soviet Union as an unfriendly gesture, if not as preparation for an attack; consequently, Hitler was determined to use extreme caution in dealing with the Ukrainians as long as he felt that amicable relations with the Soviet Union were in his interest.[3] At the same time, the Machiavellian strain in Nazi thinking impelled the German rulers to regard Ukrainian nationalism as an ace in the hole for future contingencies. In order to maintain its vigor, it was necessary to give it a certain minimum of encouragement, however indirect and covert.

Moreover, the presence of several hundred thousand Ukrainians in the Generalgouvernement offered the opportunity to put into practice another favorite maxim of the Florentine theorist: *Divide et impera*.[4] The aim of this principle as adapted to Nazi policy was the destruction of the national consciousness of the peoples of the Generalgouvernement, so that they might be absorbed in the "higher" German nation if "racially suitable" or maintained as docile Helots if they were "biologically inferior." The first step in this policy was to splinter the nationalities by promoting a feeling of ethnic distinctiveness in each subgroup and by favoring the smaller groups in the appointment of

---

[2]Adrien Boudou, *Le Saint-Siège et la Russie: Leurs Relations Diplomatiques au XIXe Siècle*, Vol. II (Paris: Editions Spès, 1925), p. 440. See also Hugh Seton-Watson, *Eastern Europe between the Wars, 1918-1941* (Cambridge: Cambridge University Press, 1940), p. 335; Raymond L. Buell, *Poland: A Key to Europe* (3rd ed.; New York: Alfred A. Knopf, 1939), p. 279n; and Volodymyr Kubiiovych, "Die ukrainische Volksgruppe," *Das Generalgouvernement*, I (December, 1940), pp. 14-19.

[3]This is shown not only by Hitler's express order to exercise caution in dealing with the Ukrainians in the Generalgouvernement in order to avoid difficulties with Russia (Memorandum for the files concerning the session of the RVA [Reichsverteidingungsausschuss], Warsaw, March 2, 1940, EC 300; hereafter referred to as EC 300), but also by the fact that even much later he requested Bormann to see that Leibbrandt's work *UdSSR* (which was strongly pro-Ukrainian) not be spread even among Nazi members, since it might fall into the wrong hands with bad results for German-Russian relations (Bormann to Rosenberg, November 25, 1940, CXLIII 258, Centre de Documentation Juive Contemporaine; hereafter referred to as CXLIII 258).

[4]The exact phrase employed by Governor Frank to describe his policy toward the nationalities in the Generalgouvernement (extracts from the diary of Hans Frank, Abteilungsleitersitzung, Cracow, April 12, 1940, p. 6, USSR Exhibit 223; hereafter referred to as USSR Exhibit 223).

local civil and police authorities.[5] In line with this policy, the small Ukrainian group in the Generalgouvernement was to be favored at the expense of the Poles, who were regarded as the most dangerous opponents of German interests in this area. In March, 1940, Hitler expressed his personal eagerness to utilize the anti-Polish attitude of the Ukrainians. In order to avoid difficulties with the Soviet Union, however, he directed that no "Ukrainian national party" or similar wide representation be formed but that their role be confined to a consultative one within the Generalgouvernement.[6] In line with this dictum, Frank, the chief of the Generalgouvernement administration, told his subordinates a month later that, while he would by no means permit the foundation of an extensive national community organization by the Ukrainians, he could allow the formation of a self-help and welfare organization.[7]

The Nazi tactic envisaged using Ukrainian national feeling as a counterweight to Polish sentiment to bolster German rule in the Generalgouvernement. After the Poles had been destroyed as a national entity, then the Ukrainians, too, would be absorbed by the Germans or reduced to Helot status. Because the first stage of the process required a lenient attitude toward the Ukrainians, however, it was possible for nationalist groups in the Generalgouvernement to carry on limited but significant activity. Several months before Hitler had made his decision concerning the formation of a Ukrainian welfare body, the Ukrainians of the Generalgouvernement themselves proceeded to create a rudimentary national organization. This step was not prevented because a number of the subordinate officials, particularly Dr. Fritz Arlt, the chief of the nationalities section in the Generalgouvernement, realized the need for securing the friendship of the Ukrainians and endeavored to use their superiors' purely tactical leniency toward this group to grant the Ukrainians a measure of national expression.[8]

The organizational work was begun with the construction of a wide variety of community organizations wherever considerable numbers of Ukrainians were found. For example, a Ukrainian National Council was formed in the San River area, a Ukrainian National Committee in Jaroslaw (Iaroslav), and a Ukrainian Central Committee in Chelm.[9] At first there appeared to be a certain amount of rivalry between these centers, which were evidently improvised by local groups without much consideration of broader political interests.[10] The more far-sighted elements of the Ukrainian group in the Generalgouvernement were anxious, however, to establish as strong a position as

---

[5]Memorandum containing the general policy outlined by Himmler and approved by Hitler on the treatment of the Eastern Peoples, May, 1940, NO 1880 (hereafter referred to as NO 1880). Actually, Himmler wanted to split the Lemkos off from the main body of Ukrainians; there is no evidence that any substantial effort was made to do so, however.

[6]EC 300.

[7]USSR Exhibit 223.

[8]This statement is based on interviews with German officials concerned and with Ukrainians who were the beneficiaries of their temperate policy toward the Ukrainian community. Interviews 8, 11, 36, 46.

[9]*Krakivs'ki Visti*, March 29, 1942, p. 3.

[10]I have no substantial evidence that the incipient conflict in the OUN created any difficulties at this stage of the development of community organization.

possible, and realized that unity was necessary. Various elements cooperated in working toward this unity, including members of parties such as the Ukrainian National Democratic Union, which had been prominent in legal life under Poland, and persons who had previously played no active part in politics. Among the latter was Dr. Volodymyr Kubiiovych, recognized as a leading geographer and ardent patriot, but unfamiliar with politics. In addition to these elements, however, the OUN also played a prominent part. Its chief representative was Colonel Sushko, who, after his forced retreat from the San, remained in the German-occupied part of Poland where he continued his collaboration with Wehrmacht authorities, especially in the development of police units. Through the efforts of these disparate groups, a meeting of the community organizations was held in Cracow in mid-November, 1939. This conference sent a delegation to Governor Frank.[11]

Kubiiovych was the natural leader of this mission. While he was politically inexperienced, he had enjoyed excellent contacts with German scholars before the war and spoke fluent German. Unlike many of the other leaders, he was not a refugee from the Soviet-dominated territories but a native of the Lemko area, hence one of the few available Ukrainians who would not afford grounds for Soviet protest. Most important, he was able to maintain his initial prestige as a patriot standing above parties because of his tact, moderation, and good judgment, and was also to carry out the difficult task of negotiating with the Germans without losing his — and his fellow Ukrainians' — self-respect. At this stage, however, it is doubtful whether the project of forming a unified organization could actually have been carried through, in spite of Kubiiovych's ability, had it not been for the support of Colonel Sushko, with his Nationalist organization and his close relations with the German authorities.

At any rate, it was Kubiiovych and Sushko who secured permission for the establishment of an association headed by a central committee.[12] The process of organizing the Ukrainian groups into one association lasted a considerable time. This was due probably to the natural difficulties encountered by the Ukrainian leaders in working out a complex organization after twenty years of near-exclusion from public administration, as well as to delay in securing the approval of Frank and Hitler. On April 13-15, 1940, however, representatives of Ukrainian groups met openly in Cracow as a steering committee, and in early June this body was formally recognized by Frank as the Ukrainian Central Committee.[13]

The accomplishment was a considerable one, although on paper the new body was extremely limited in its function which, in accordance with Hitler's injunction, was defined as the improvement of the welfare of the Ukrainian population of the Generalgouvernement. For this purpose, the committee was granted the right to prepare a budget covered in part by allocation of funds from the treasury of the Generalgouvernement and was allowed to direct a network of Aid Committees throughout the Ukrainian ethnographical area.

---

[11]*Krakivs'ki Visti*, March 29, 1942, p. 3.

[12]*Ibid.*; Interview 9.

[13]*Entsyklopediia Ukraïnoznavstva* (Encyclopedia of Things Ukrainian), eds. Volodymyr Kubiiovych and Zenon Kuzelia (Munich: Naukove Tovarystvo im. Shevchenka, 1949), pp. 580-82.

Among the more important formal functions of the organization was the distribution of aid received from philanthropic agencies in the United States and from the International Red Cross.[14] As is usually the case with Ukrainian organizations working under the shadow of arbitrary foreign regimes, however, the formal aspect of its activity was not the most important. Officially, the committee had no control over education, but through its relations with the German authorities it was able to exert great influence on the selection of teachers and the provision of instructional facilities. Through its control of welfare funds, it was able to facilitate the attendance of numerous children at the Ukrainian schools.[15] Thus it rendered an important contribution to the reinvigoration of Ukrainian cultural life throughout the area.

This educational activity was carried on in close connection with the development of a Ukrainian press. The November conference, in addition to laying the groundwork for a central representative body, had founded (also under Dr. Kubiiovych's direction) a large-scale publishing agency which issued a series of new school texts in Ukrainian, as well as popular editions of Ukrainian works.[16] Still more important, it began the publication of a newspaper which stood head and shoulders above any other Ukrainian publication in the German-dominated areas. *Krakivs'ki Visti* (Cracow News, as it was named after the Germans forbade the use of "Ukrainian" in the title) was one of the few papers which did not become a party organ but consistently served as a forum for a broad variety of Ukrainian viewpoints. Moreover, it was the only paper of this nature which possessed considerable material resources and attracted numerous contributions from writers of real talent. It was subjected to a censorship stricter than that inflicted on Ukrainian papers in Greater Germany (although much less severe than that of the papers later established under German rule farther east); nevertheless, it was able to reflect a considerable range of Ukrainian life and thought. As a result it is an invaluable witness of the events of the war years.

From the standpoint of Ukrainian national interests, the favorable policy of the Germans toward the group's cultural development was particularly valuable in enabling it to regain some of the ground lost under the Polish repression. It would take a lengthy volume to detail the ways in which the Ukrainians were able to improve their situation in this respect during the early war years. A single statistic will suffice, however, to indicate the general nature of the gains made. In the school year 1942-43 there were 4,173 Ukrainian-language schools in the Generalgouvernement,[17] while on the corresponding territory before 1939 there were only 2,510—of which only 457 were exclusively

---

[14]*Ibid.*

[15]Interview 9.

[16]*Krakivs'ki Visti*, January 2, 1942, p. 3.

[17]This refers of course to the enlarged Generalgouvernement, which included eastern Galicia. It is, however, indicative of an extension of the Ukrainian educational system which was if anything even more pronounced in the areas west of the San and the Bug. For additional details on cultural and organizational developments see Roman Il'nyts'kyi, *Deutschland und die Ukraine, 1934-1945: Tatsachen europäischer Ostpolitik, ein Vorbericht*, Vol. I (Munich: Osteuropa Institut, 1955), pp. 253-58.

Ukrainian.[18] The most marked advance took place in the Chelm area, where, in the autumn of 1939, a large influx of intellectuals fleeing Soviet rule in eastern Galicia brought a new vigor to the cultural life of the Ukrainian community.[19]

To round out the picture, however, one must add that the methods employed by the Ukrainians to win ground back from the Poles were not limited to cultural development. In line with the policy described above, the Germans frequently appointed mayors of ethnographically mixed towns from among the Ukrainian element, thus giving the latter a decided advantage in the civil administration. The separate police system was also staffed in a manner favorable to the Ukrainians, although the Germans closely supervised this force. Nevertheless, in numerous cases their position in the police detachments enabled the Ukrainians to harass and even to attack the Poles.[20]

While the Ukrainian nationalist forces were being strengthened by the creation of a new base in the Generalgouvernement, the OUN was being gravely weakened by a fierce internal conflict. The fundamental causes of this conflict have been examined in the preceding chapters. Its catalytic element was the liberation of the most active leaders of the younger generation from the Polish prisons.

In Cracow, where most went, they came into contact with the comrades with whom they had fought and suffered before their imprisonment, and a new grouping rapidly coalesced. The nominal leader was Volodymyr Lopatyns'kyi, who was the official director of the *krai* OUN—i.e., the organization on Ukrainian ethnographical territory in Poland.[21] Along with him came other young men who had long been active in the struggle against the Polish authorities—John Gavrusevych, Iaroslav Horbovyi, Leo Rebet, and many others. For the most part these men, vigorous as they were, had been confined, by the nature of their conspiratorial work, to Poland, and consequently were not very familiar with the broader aspects of the OUN. They were a hardened group of rebels, remarkably courageous and inured to a life of insecurity, but deprived by this very training of the opportunity to consider theoretical and complex questions. There were among them, however, two young men who had recently had the opportunity of observing the workings of the organizational headquarters at first hand. One was Dmytro Myron, who

---

[18]P. Isaïiv, article on Ukrainian schools in the Generalgouvernement during the Second World War, *Entsyklopediia Ukraïnoznavstva*, p. 952; Buell, *Poland*, p. 279. The remainder were "mixed" schools given over, Buell says, to Polish teachers.

[19]Iurii (George) Tarkovych, "Zabuti Zemli" (Forgotten Lands), *Krakivs'ki Visti*, May 10, 1942, p. 1.

[20]Activity report of the chief of the Ordnungspolizei, November 11, 1940, Occ E-2 (11), in Yiddish Scientific Institute (hereafter referred to as Occ E-2 [11]). This German official reported that "lack of proper training" enabled the Ukrainian auxiliary police to take a partisan, even a vicious attitude toward the Poles, and gave as an example the necessity of arresting two Ukrainian officers who had failed to hinder attacks on Poles by armed Ukrainians. These remarks apply to the situation in the mixed Polish-Ukrainian ethnic territories (especially Chelm) *before* large-scale violence occurred, as outlined in Chapter VI.

[21]Interviews 24, 75.

was later to prove to be a talented organizer of undergrounds in the East Ukraine. The other was Iaroslav Stets'ko.[22]

Among the entire group, Stets'ko (a priest's son) was distinguished by his quick intelligence and ability to generalize his experiences in the form of political prescriptions. Like most of the others, he had been sentenced to imprisonment in connection with the mass trial of OUN members in 1936. However, he had not been proved to have been as deeply implicated as many, and consequently was released before the outbreak of war. Taking an active part in the organizational work of the OUN, he was called to Rome by Mel'nyk in the summer of 1939 to help in preparation of the Second Congress. Stets'ko's role in Rome is not entirely clear. According to one version, he was relieved of his preparatory duties by Stsibors'kyi when he proved unable to carry them out satisfactorily;[23] if this is true, the implied rebuke was hardly likely to increase his love for his supplanter, and might indeed have sown a seed of resentment against the entire leadership. At any rate, it appears clear that the Provid was not prescient enough to seize the opportunity to secure the lasting loyalty of this brilliant young OUN member.

In retrospect, at least, Stets'ko was doubtful of the wisdom of the policy he saw being implemented by the older men. It was a cautious policy, and a particularly distasteful aspect of its caution, according to Stets'ko, was the care taken to maintain good relations with Germany, in spite of the repeated disappointments which that power had inflicted on the Ukrainians. Before the close of the Rome meeting, however, Stets'ko had a reassuring conversation with Mel'nyk; after this, he temporarily threw his support behind his chief. Mel'nyk might have had some qualms about exalting himself as the chief of the Provid. In his youthful enthusiasm Stets'ko was willing to accept—at least in theory—the full implications of the authoritarian strain in OUN ideology. In an enthusiastic speech he praised Mel'nyk as a great leader, a heroic fighter, and called for unswerving loyalty to him such as had been accorded Konovalets'—"The leader is dead, long live the leader!"[24]

By the beginning of 1940, Stets'ko, under the impact of the fresh defeat of the OUN policy of alignment with the Germans and the stimulation of more impatient members of his group, had begun to express grave doubts concerning the official leaders of the party. His abilities made him a valuable member of the emerging faction, but it was not the kind of body which seeks its leader among intellectuals. The basic charge which it made against the older generation was that it was timid, lacking in determination; consequently, it was fitting that the rebel group chose a leader who possessed to an unusual degree the qualities of inflexible will and readiness for desperate action. This leader was found in the chief of the terrorist group which had carried out the attacks on the Polish officials—Stephen Bandera.

---

[22]Jaroslaw Stecko.

[23]Interview 67.

[24]Text in *Nastup*, December 13, 1941, p. 3. This article was of course published long after the break, in order to discredit the Bandera followers. There is no doubt that an article of this general tenor was written, however. The discussion of this opening phase has been based primarily on interviews (24 and 67) with Ukrainian leaders particularly well acquainted with both sides of this early stage of the controversy.

By January, 1940, the new alignment was sufficiently solidified for Bandera and Lopatyns'kyi to be able to go to Mel'nyk in Rome with a series of demands.[25] It is not clear precisely what these demands were, for the participants in the clash have held to opposite versions. According to Bandera's supporters, the kernel of their declaration was a demand for a change in orientation of OUN policy to make it less dependent on the Germans. In particular, they say their leaders demanded that Mel'nyk take the headquarters of the organization to a neutral state, and from this vantage point bring about cooperation between the OUN and the Western powers in forming a legion composed of Ukrainians in France to aid Finland in her defense against Soviet attack.[26] While these contentions have a certain air of plausibility, in view of the past and future collaboration of the group around Mel'nyk with the Germans, the adherents of the official leader point out that Bandera himself cooperated with the Germans when it suited his purpose and that Mel'nyk followers in France worked with zeal for just such a legion as Bandera's supporters assert *they* proposed.[27]

While the content of many of the demands presented by Bandera and Lopatyns'kyi is disputed, it is generally agreed that the most precisely formulated item concerned a change in the composition of the Provid. The *Krai* leaders demanded the dismissal of Baranovs'kyi,[28] Senyk, and Stsibors'kyi. Because of the influence exercised by the two last-named leaders, compliance with this demand would have meant a real revolution in the direction of the OUN, especially since Bandera and his companion urged that they be replaced by adherents of the younger group. Aside from the intrinsic importance of this element of the dispute, however, the reasons presented by the two emissaries do much to reveal the psychology of the young rebels.

The charge made against Senyk harks back to the earliest stages of dissension between the two generations in the Nationalist organization. When Bandera, Stets'ko, and the other Galician terrorists were arrested for attacks on Polish government officials, they were confronted with a mass of written evidence of conspiracy which made their defense hopeless, under the conditions prevailing in Poland. This material was obtained by the Poles from Czech officials, who had in turn obtained it in some unknown manner. What is clear, however, is that Senyk, in his capacity as administrative assistant to Konovalets', had initially prepared the documents. The *krai* group was bitter over this occurrence, attributing it to Senyk's negligence in preparing such dangerous documents and then in failing to safeguard them properly. Whether they were correct in this judgment is hard to determine, but one can readily understand how such a feeling could develop into hatred during the harsh years in prison. More fundamentally, however, the accusation indicates the difficult position of those who endeavor to direct a fanatic underground

---

[25] Stepan (Stephen) Bandera, "V desiatu richnytsiu stvorennia Revoliutsiinoho Provodu OUN" (On the Tenth Anniversary of the Creation of the Revolutionary Directorate of the OUN), *Surma* (February-March, 1950), p. 6.

[26] Unlike the projected UNR legion mentioned in the preceding chapter, the OUN plan called for an armed unit entirely separate from the émigré Polish forces.

[27] Interview 52.

[28] For the involved charges against Baranovs'kyi, see *OUN u Viini* (The OUN in the War), Information Section of the OUN (UNR), April, 1946, p. 37; Interview 75.

movement from outside the country where the movement must exist and suffer. It also sharply illuminates the basic tension between the man of action, of revolutionary *élan*, and the administrator who is never quite regarded as pulling his share of the load.

The accusation against Stsibors'kyi is even more revealing. Several years previously, when he was an editor of *Ukraïns'ke Slovo*, the OUN organ in Paris, Stsibors'kyi had been approached in the newspaper office by a Communist agent who tried to persuade him to betray the national cause. Instead of throwing the man out, so the story goes, Stsibors'kyi had engaged him in an ideological debate. The Bandera group now alleged that Stsibors'kyi had failed to act promptly because he was really considering the Communist's proposal, and bolstered their charge by asserting that the presence of Stsibors'kyi's sister in Kiev gave the Soviet network a grip on him. In view of Stsibors'kyi's vigor in the anti-Communist cause, before and after the incident, this accusation appears highly implausible. The emphasis on the culpability of his arguing with the Communist is, on the other hand, highly illuminating. As has been indicated, Stsibors'kyi was a born theorist, a man who served the movement primarily by words. Paradoxically, his own theory emphasized will, the need for action, and the primacy of the *Volkgeist*. It remained — a sort of poetic retribution — that his most extreme disciples, trained to condemn the rationalist, turned first against his reputation, and then in deadly earnest against his person.[29]

Whatever discussion may have taken place over the *krai* representatives' other proposals, there is no question but that Mel'nyk firmly rejected the demand to dismiss his colleagues. His critics assert that this action is evidence of his inflexibility, or even of his haughty attitude toward the younger members of the organization. His admirers maintain that it is convincing proof of his devotion to principle, his loyalty to faithful companions. Whichever judgment is correct, the failure to reach an agreement soon led to open conflict. Bandera and Lopatyns'kyi returned home, and on February 10, at a secret conclave of the Galician youth leaders in Cracow, Bandera was designated the chief of a new, "revolutionary" Provid.[30]

Most of the remainder of 1940 was spent in a sharp struggle of the opposing factions to consolidate positions and win over uncommitted elements.

---

[29]The preceding discussion of the reasons for the split has been based primarily on interviews (especially 24, 52, 67, 75) with several of the principal protagonists and their close adherents. Published sources which deal with the controversy include Bandera in *Surma* and *OUN u Viini*, pp. 34-35, which represent the opposing viewpoints. Somewhat more impartial (though leaning toward the Mel'nyk side) is Vasyl' Rudko ("R. Lisovii"), "Rozlam v OUN" (The Split in the OUN), *Ukraïns'ki Visiti*, May 23, 1949, p. 3, and October 27, 1949, p. 3. Rudko also avoids attributing too much importance to the ostensible grounds of the split emphasized by both sides and correctly stresses that the principal source of conflict was a difference in temperament and background between the two generations. Il'nyts'kyi insists that the real reason for the split was the desire of the younger group to avoid alignment with Germany and to seek the support of the Western Allies (pp. 266 ff.). On pp. 363-67 Il'nyts'kyi prints a statement called "Stephen Bandera's demands on Andrew Mel'nyk, 1940," followed by Bandera's "account" of Mel'nyk's reply. In view of the lack of a specific date I suspect that the whole passage is based on Bandera's biased recollection rather than on a contemporary document. On p. 271 Il'nyts'kyi admits that there was no contemporary published material to support this argument, which appears to me (like many of Il'nyts'kyi's contentions) to be highly partisan.

[30]Bandera in *Surma*, p. 4.

At first the contest was conducted with some restraint on both sides. There remained some possibility of reconciliation.[31] Antagonism between the rival factions was greatly exacerbated, however, by efforts of the *krai* group to win over some of the senior members of the organization. Nearly all of the latter felt it was the height of presumption for the younger men to form a counter-directorate. Moreover, they asserted that the attempts of the Bandera followers to gain their sympathy amounted to urging them to betray their comrades; thus they felt the proposals were dishonorable as well as impertinent.[32] On the other hand, the young generation felt that it was merely attempting to overthrow an inflexible and arbitrary leadership in order to carry out the true aims of the organization. Consequently they bitterly resented the scornful rejection accorded them by the older men.

Matters came to a head with a series of coups and counter-coups in midsummer. For example, a group of young Bandera adherents tried to take over the headquarters of the Ukrainian Central Committee in Cracow. The administrative officials, most of whom were not affiliated with the OUN, regarded them with more annoyance than outright hostility, but when Colonel Sushko returned he quickly ejected them.[33] Then, in August, he led a small group of his followers, probably drawn from the auxiliary police units in which he was active, in a raid on the Bandera headquarters in Cracow, which resulted in the disruption of their clandestine press and the seizure of a number of documents.[34] By that time all negotiations for reunion had been broken off, and by November the conflict flared up in open violence in the streets of Cracow. As noted earlier, Nazi circles scorned the OUN generally, and particularly distrusted Sushko. Military intelligence (Abwehr) officers, on the other hand, urged the Bandera faction to reconcile with Mel'nyk, as they wished to avoid further splintering of Ukrainian political groups.[35]

In Greater Germany itself all Ukrainians, except the adherents of the Het'man's Hromada (mostly East Ukrainians) were supposed to be joined in the UNO (Ukraïns'ke Natsional'ne Ob"iednannia—Ukrainian National Union), accorded semiofficial recognition by the German authorities. Officially nonpartisan, the UNO nevertheless recognized nationalism as the guiding ideology, and acted as a social and welfare adjunct of the OUN.[36] Its head, Colonel Tymosh Omel'chenko, was a strong supporter of the "legitimate" OUN Provid under Mel'nyk. After the younger generation broke away to join Bandera, Omel'chenko and his lieutenants ordered all UNO members to report attempts at "disruptive work" and eventually cleansed their organization of active Bandera supporters.[37] In June, 1941, Omel'chenko joined Kubiiovych in urging German authorities to support an independent Ukraine,

---

[31]*Ukraïns'kyi Visnyk*, October 19, 1941, p. 2; Bohdan Mykhailiuk, *Bunt Bandery* (Bandera's Rebellion) (1950), pp. 52 ff.

[32]*OUN u Viini*, p. 37.

[33]Interview 9.

[34]*OUN u Viini*, p. 33n; Zynovii Matla, *Pivdenna pokhidna hrupa* (The Southern Task Force) (Munich: Tsitsero, 1952), p. 4.

[35]*Nastup*, November 16, 1940; *Ukraïns'ka Diisnist'*, December 1, 1940, p. 1.

[36]*Ukraïns'kyi Visnyk*, September 10, 1940, p. 2, and January 10, 1943, p. 3.

[37]Cf. Occ E-4 (5).

with vastly expanded geographic limits, under Mel'nyk, "who today undoubtedly enjoys the greatest prestige among Ukrainians ... the only man worthy of being entrusted with leadership of the Ukrainian nation."[38]

The stand of the UNO leaders was important, for it was constantly growing in numbers and strength, due to the heavy influx of Ukrainians from areas occupied by Hungary and the USSR. Whereas in 1937 the UNO had only a few score members, nearly four hundred were added in 1938, about 2,000 in 1939, and almost 11,000 in 1940.[39] Since the Ukrainian immigrants were largely factory and agricultural workers, branches were formed in numerous towns throughout Germany proper, the Protectorate, and the districts newly annexed from Poland.[40] As they were unable to control the UNO, however, Bandera's supporters rapidly set about forming cells of their own. Thus in 1941 there were parallel and antagonistic centers of Ukrainian life in many towns and industrial establishments in Greater Germany.[41]

In their efforts to win control of the nationalist movement, both parties resorted to arguments as well as organizational pressure. Much of this was oral, especially on the part of the *krai* group, which, in comparison with the Mel'nyk following, possessed neither the physical plant nor the experienced polemicists for a press contest. They stressed the hesitancy and failures of the older Provid, argued that it was dependent on foreigners, and asserted that the other generation of leaders wished to revert to a purely military, tactical organization of the UVO type, leaving political and ideological questions to the legal parties like the UNDO.[42] Fundamentally, however, as previously indicated, the rebels' appeal was to youth, will, action.

The rebuttal offered by Mel'nyk's supporters is easier to follow because it could be expressed in openly published periodicals, although in a somewhat veiled form. Part of the defense was provided by non-members, especially by church leaders. Bishop John Buchko, who was considered to be a close associate of Sheptyts'kyi, and who later headed the entire Ukrainian Catholic Church, was vigorous in his praise of Mel'nyk. The bishop was at the time in America, where he was making a pastoral visit to Ukrainian immigrants; in an interview in New York he was reported to have declared that the Ukrainian Nationalists represented the flower of the nation and to have said they possessed in Mel'nyk an outstanding personality as leader.[43] As previously noted, Monsignor Volyshyn likewise chose this time to praise Mel'nyk above other Nationalist leaders. In spite of the prestige of their authors, however, it is questionable whether such statements were conducive to strengthening

---

[38]Memorandum from Omel'chenko and Kubiiovych, Aussenpolitisches Amt, der NSDAP, Reichsleitung, June 10, 1941 (T 454, Reel 92).

[39]*Ukraïns'kyi Visnyk*, January 10, 1943, p. 8.

[40]That is, Posen and West Prussia; the UNO did not exist in the Generalgouvernement.

[41]As was indicated somewhat later by the ability of Bandera's followers to obtain numerous petitions for his release from imprisonment from groups of Ukrainians working in Germany. See Occ E-4 (9), in Yiddish Scientific Institute (hereafter referred to as Occ E-4 [9]), and the denunciation of "diversive work" among Ukrainian workers in Germany in *Ukraïns'kyi Visnyk*, March 30, 1941, p. 1.

[42]Bandera in *Surma*, p. 2. Substantially the same arguments are presented in a clandestine publication of April, 1942 (*Biuleten'*, No. 4, pp. 5-7).

[43]*Nastup*, October 19, 1940, p. 3.

Mel'nyk's position in view of the pronounced anti-clericalism of the youthful circles.[44]

A major part of the Mel'nyk adherents' arguments, however, consisted of emphasis on the duty, in an authoritarian organization such as the OUN, of subordination to the leadership. As has been shown, Mel'nyk's own character and views rendered this line somewhat ineffective. Nevertheless, the party organs came to carry more and more eulogies of the director, and theoretical discussions of the nature of his position became more frequent.[45] A major problem for any authoritarian organization is the establishment of the legitimacy of the leader. If force cannot quell doubts, appeal must be made to his sanction by some figure of the past who is held in veneration by all. Therefore it was firmly asserted that Konovalets' had designated Mel'nyk as his successor, and that Mel'nyk had called the Rome congress in compliance with the assassinated leader's long-range instructions.[46] Those "calling themselves nationalists" yet falling into the "democratic-liberal vices" of individual defiance of authority and party intrigue were roundly denounced.[47] Somewhat later, in stressing the military duty of members of the OUN to observe discipline, one spokesman of the "legitimate" group declared that exclusion from the organization meant "moral death."[48]

There remained yet another area in which the struggle for power was waged. It has been noted that nearly all of the influential older members rejected the proposals of the Bandera group for alliance. There was one exception: Iarii. The adopted Ukrainian had for some time been at odds with Mel'nyk concerning, it is said, financial accounting and his own desire for freedom from Mel'nyk's control in negotiating with the Germans.[49] In the emergence of a new center Iarii evidently saw an opportunity to escape distasteful subordination to what he considered an émigré clique which was hopelessly confused as to its real aims. Consequently, he broke completely with the old Provid and brought his valuable contacts to the *krai* group, in whose youthful energy he saw the only hope for developing a liberation force.[50] In so doing, however, he helped turn many Ukrainian elements against the new movement, for it appeared strange that among members of the Provid the foreigner alone should have joined Bandera's group. Almost from the beginning this circumstance appears to have given rise to the suspicion that foreign powers—the Soviet Union as well as Germany—had inspired the rebellion to

---

[44]Other influential elements supported Mel'nyk, or at least condemned the tactics of Bandera's followers. In addition to Omel'chenko's and Kubiiobych's memorandum to the Germans, the latter supported Mel'nyk more obliquely in an article deploring the political rashness and violence of youth (*Ukraïns'kyi Visnyk*, March 30, 1941, p. 1). A little later (*ibid.*, April 10, 1941, p. 1) several professors urged Ukrainian youths in higher schools in Greater Germany to put national unity above party interests.

[45]E.g., on December 14, 1940, *Nastup* devoted the entire first page to Mel'nyk on the occasion of his birthday; again, on December 23, almost all of page 1 was devoted to him.

[46]*Nastup*, October 5, 1940, p. 1.

[47]*Ibid.*, October 12, 1940, p. 1.

[48]*Ibid.*, May 24, 1941, p. 4.

[49]Interview 67.

[50]According to a letter which Iarii wrote to me, dated Easter, 1953.

weaken the Nationalist movement.⁵¹ Whether Iarii was a mere tool of the Abwehr, or was trying to use the Germans to attain Ukrainian nationalist goals, is hard to determine; but it appears fairly certain that rumors that he was connected with the Communists are unfounded.

Such suspicions did not, however, prevent the *krai* group from proceeding with its organization. As will be shown, a strong network of underground workers was maintained in Soviet-occupied Galicia under authority of the insurgent Provid. In the Generalgouvernement, too, considerable progress was registered. In March, 1941, a general conference of the OUN-B[andera] was held in Cracow, called, in rejection of the Rome conference, the "Second Congress of the OUN."⁵² By this time, a large part of the younger generation was included in the new movement, and already subfactions were beginning to appear. On the one hand, the "activists," Bandera and his first lieutenant, Stets'ko, remained in complete control of the organizational framework. They were powerfully aided by Nicholas Lebed', one of the original group of *krai* leaders, who was now confirmed as third in command. More important, Lebed' began the organization of the Sluzhba Bezpeky, the security service. Like all organizations, be they underground or in full power, which demand monolithic conformity to a leader and a casting aside of scruples in the choice of means, the OUN-B was obliged to have its secret police. In Lebed'—small in stature, quiet, yet determined, hard—the S.B. found a well-qualified leader, but one who was to acquire for himself and his organization an unenviable reputation for ruthlessness.

Apparently somewhat apart from the leading group stood a number of young men whose chief interest in the organization was military. They were not yet very important, but their most typical representative, Roman Shukhevych, was later to rise rapidly. Still farther from the guiding nucleus was a group whose aims tended to include social as well as national aspects of the hoped-for revolution. Their leader was John Mitrynga, son of Galician peasants, who had been designated by Konovalets' as a special "referent" for social questions. He and his companions were too obscure to secure a place of power in the organization, but it is claimed that they exerted a certain influence on the formulation of its platform. This program, indeed, while it reiterated the "voluntarist" elements of will, action, discipline, contempt of reason and the "nationalist" element of supremacy of the nation (the decalogue of the movement is said to have required its members to place the interests of the Ukrainian nation above all else), gave some room to consideration of social matters.

---

⁵¹*Ukraïns'kyi Visnyk*, September 10, 1940, p. 2.

⁵²Mykola (Nicholas) Lebed', *UPA: Ukraïns'ka Povstans'ka Armiia* (UPA: The Ukrainian Insurrectionary Army) (Presove Biuro UHVR, 1946), p. 14; Petro Mirchuk, *Akt vidnovlennia ukrains'koi derzhavnosty, 30 chervnia 1941 roku* (The Act of Renewal of Ukrainian Statehood, June 30, 1941) (New York: Holovna Uprava Organizatsiï Oborony Chotyr'okh Svobid Ukraïny, 1952), p. 17.

While the Communist system was denounced, liberal capitalism was condemned and an ill-defined socialism advocated.[53]

While the strongest Ukrainian party was being torn by factional conflict, its members, along with those of less authoritarian groupings, were trying to maintain a vestige of independent life in the areas acquired by the Soviet Union. Galicia, the real base of organized Ukrainian nationalism, had passed under Communist control in September, 1939. At first the leaders of the legal parties appeared not to realize the full implications of this transfer. Most of them had been brought up under the relatively tolerant Austrian regime, and even under Poland they had been able to maintain a position of strained association with the sovereign power. A considerable number of them felt, or at least hoped, that this might also be possible under the Soviet regime. It must be emphasized that they were thoroughly anti-Communist; most of them had fought Communism when it was a strong force in Galicia in the twenties. The party they knew then, however, with its emphasis on Ukrainian nationalism and its still incomplete totalitarianism, represented an entirely different opponent from the Communist Party which ruled the Soviet state in 1939.

On September 22, as the Soviet troops approached L'vov, the octogenarian Constantine Levits'kyi, once a major leader of the West Ukrainian Republic, began the formation of a Ukrainian nonpartisan committee to deal with the occupier. With the help of Dr. Stephen Baran, a prominent leader of the UNDO, whose account furnishes most of the details of this episode, some twenty community leaders were brought together. This group chose a seven-man delegation to deal with the Red Army. It was two days before they could obtain an audience with General Ivanov, the Soviet commander, who received them courteously but referred them to one Mishchenko, "director of civil affairs on the western front."[54] The latter spoke fair words in fluent Ukrainian; he promised that there would be no repression, that all that had taken place before the Soviet occupation would be left in oblivion. When it came to detailed requests, however—the emissaries were especially concerned to secure the safety of the cultural society Prosvita and the Greek Catholic Church— Mishchenko referred them to the specialized officials charged with these "details."

The aged Dr. Levits'kyi returned home, evidently satisfied that his mission to the new *okkupant* had been successful. His more cautious aide, Dr. Baran, however, in his capacity as a director of the largest Ukrainian newspaper, *Dilo*, went with the editor of *Novyi Chas*, Zenon Pelens'kyi, to confer

---

[53]Borys Levits'kyi, "Istorychne znachennia rozlamu v OUN" (The Historical Significance of the Split in the OUN), *Vpered*, No. 2 (11) (1950), pp. 5-6. The discussion of the trends and personalities in the newly formed OUN-B has been based primarily on interviews (24, 31, 75, 76) with several of its most active members. Lebed's associates deny that he played a major part in the S.B., however. But see Iaroslav Stets'ko, *30 chervnia 1941: Proholoshennia vidnovlennia derzhavnosty Ukraïny* (June 30, 1941: Proclamation of the Renewal of Statehood of the Ukraine) (Toronto: League for the Liberation of Ukraine, 1967), who lists (p. 184) Lebed' among the builders of the S.B.

[54]There were at least three high-ranking officials of this name in the Ukrainian Communist Party at that time. The most valuable work on Soviet rule in the West Ukraine in 1939-41 is a very extensive collection of eyewitness accounts assembled during the German occupation by Milena Rudnyts'ka, *Zakhidnia Ukraïna pid Bol'shevykamy* (The West Ukraine under the Bolsheviks) (New York: Naukove Tovarystvo im. Shevchenka v Amerytsi, 1958).

with A. T. Chekaniuk, head of the newly installed press affairs office, concerning continuation of Ukrainian journalistic activities.[55] Then the true nature of the Soviet conquest began to reveal itself. Chekaniuk was already installed in the editorial offices of *Dilo* and evidently perfectly acquainted with the views and backgrounds of his petitioners. He showed them a staff of twenty newly arrived Soviet journalists who were already preparing the publication of *Dilo*'s successor, the Communist *Vil'na Ukraïna*. Then he made it perfectly clear to his "guests" that while some use might be found for their talents if they were properly directed, the direction itself was already, and would remain, completely in the hands of the Communists.[56]

Within a week, several leading figures in the Ukrainian community, including Constantine Levits'kyi and the secretary of the representative committee, John Nymchuk, had been arrested. For the time being, however, the actual members of the delegation to Soviet headquarters were spared, and several managed to escape to German-occupied territory.[57] The leaders of the UNDO were also arrested; Dr. Dmytro Levits'kyi, the head of the party and of the Ukrainian delegation in the Polish parliament, was arrested on September 28 and so were his most important colleagues about the same time. The arrested leaders were sent to Moscow—it is said to the infamous Lubianka prison—and with rare exceptions have not been heard of since.[58] The Communists, after getting rid of the principal nationalist politicians, quickly proceeded with their own political organization of Galicia and Volhynia. Even the official Soviet version indicates that a minimum time was allotted to the process of registering "popular approval" for incorporation of the occupied lands in the Soviet Union. A "Ukrainian National Congress," "elected" immediately after the Soviet invasion, met on October 26; on November 1 the head of its plenary committee, M. I. Panchyshyn, sent a request for admission to the Ukrainian Soviet Republic; on November 15, the Verkhovna Rada (Supreme Soviet) of the latter division of the Soviet state approved the request; thus East and West Ukraine were "united."[59]

In spite of the complete replacement of independent press and political organizations by Communist agencies, however, a strong effort was made in the early months to attract support for the new regime. Perhaps one reason for this attempt was the desire to influence Ukrainians still outside the enlarged

---

[55]Chekaniuk, a specialist in political journalism, was editor of the major Kiev newspaper *Komunist*, and in 1940 became a candidate of the Central Committee of the Communist Party of the Ukraine.

[56]The preceding paragraphs are based largely on Stepan Baran's article, "Zustrich z bol'shevykamy" (Encounter with the Bolsheviks), *Krakivs'ki Visti*, April 12, 1942, p. 2, and April 14, 1942, p. 2, confirmed in all essential aspects by Interviews 41, 78.

[57]Baran, "Zustrich," *Krakivs'ki Visti*, April 12, 1942, p. 2.

[58]*Krakivs'ki Visti*, March 22, 1942, p. 4. In one town at least, participants in the revolutionary struggle for Ukrainian independence also seem to have been singled out for arrest or execution (*Krakivs'ki Visti*, August 3, 1941, p. 2).

[59]S. M. Belousov and O. P. Ohloblyn, *Zakhidna Ukraïna* (The West Ukraine) (Kiev: Akademiia Nauk URSR, Instytut Istoriï Ukraïny, 1940), pp. 108 ff. Panchyshyn was apparently selected by the Soviet authorities because he was a respected L'vov physician, rather than as a Communist sympathizer. See Kost' Pan'kivs'kyi, *Vid derzhavy do komitetu* (From State to Committee) (New York: Zhyttia i mysli, 1957), p. 23.

Soviet Ukrainian Republic, especially in the Generalgouvernement. In a protocol to the German-Soviet Boundary and Friendship Treaty of September 28, 1939, which had defined the frontier between the parts of Poland annexed by the two totalitarian powers, it was provided that the government of the USSR should place no obstacles in the way of migration of ethnic Germans from eastern Poland to Germany. This secured for the Nazis the right to "bring home" the tens of thousands of German-speaking Volhynians. In return, Germany acknowledged an equal right of Belorussians and Ukrainians to migrate to the Soviet Union.[60] In accordance with a further provision of the protocol, a Soviet "repatriation" commission was allowed to travel through the Lemko region in early 1940;[61] by the end of June, it had induced only thirty-five hundred Ukrainians to cross the border into the Soviet Union, however.[62]

The campaign to win friends in Galicia and Volhynia was in part negative; measures which were most likely to inflame anti-Soviet sentiments were avoided. The church was not entirely suppressed, though it was sharply criticized.[63] Its real property was confiscated and the religious orders disbanded.[64] The Soviet authorities weakened the influence of the church on the youth by liquidating the Catholic school system and forcibly inducting the children into Communist organizations.[65] However, the person of Metropolitan Sheptyts'kyi was respected.[66] The part of the intelligentsia which was not prominent in politics was allowed to remain at large, although persons in callings such as the law sometimes found it necessary to turn to nonprofessional work.[67] On the more positive side, the Ukrainian language was given a far greater scope than it had enjoyed under Polish rule. In particular, the University of L'vov was formally Ukrainized in language and personnel, although it is said that the

---

[60]Germany, Auswärtiges Amt, *Nazi-Soviet Relations, 1939-1941: Documents from the Archives of the German Foreign Office*, eds. Raymond James Sontag and James Stuart Beddie (Washington: Department of State, 1948), pp. 104-5.

[61]*Krakauer Zeitung*, February 18-19, 1940, p. 6, reports the departure of one thousand Ukrainians from this area after a visit of the Soviet commissioners.

[62]According to *Nastup*, June 29, 1940, pp. 2-3. In an article which was remarkably hostile to the Soviet regime, in view of the latter's publicly cordial relations with Germany at that time, the Nationalist paper stated that the "intensive propaganda" of the Soviet commission, aided by "the pro-Russian intelligentsia" but combatted by "healthy Ukrainian elements," had resulted in the meager migration cited. Either this is one of the not too infrequent examples of ability of the Prague publication to print items contrary to German policy, or someone in authority gave the signal for an anti-Soviet attitude even at that early date. In the latter case it may have been a subtle riposte in the hidden conflict over Soviet demands for Bukovina. On the other hand, as early as March the *Krakauer Zeitung* printed a report by a German who had visited the villages of the Lemko area. He praised the young Ukrainians, noting that they wore the national blue and yellow colors and greeted him with "Heil Hitler!" and "Slava Ukraïna!" (Glory to the Ukraine) (*Krakauer Zeitung*, March 7, 1940, p. 5).

[63]See F. Iastrebov, "Uniats'ke dukhovenstvo na sluzhbi u polskoho panstva" (The Uniate Clergy in the Service of the Polish Aristocracy), *Komunist*, October 9, 1939, p. 2.

[64]"Die Tragödie der ukrainisch-katholischen Kirche," *Ukraine in Vergangenheit und Gegenwart*, January, 1952, p. 14.

[65]*Krakivs'ki Visti*, March 18, 1942, p. 4; Stepan (Stephen) Baran, *Mytropolyt Andrei Sheptyts'kyi* (Metropolitan Andrew Sheptyts'kyi) (Munich: Vernyhora Ukraïns'ke Vydavnyche Tovarystvo, 1947), p. 112.

[66]*Ibid.*

[67]Interview 36.

resistance of remaining Polish professors to lecturing in Ukrainian was not harshly dealt with.[68] Students from the East Ukrainian universities were brought on tours to the West Ukraine, and L'vov students made Communist-sponsored trips to Kiev.[69] Other elements of the Galician population—teachers, physicians, artists—were brought to Kiev to participate in Ukrainian cultural activities.[70]

After a comparatively short time, however, the Soviet administration appears to have become convinced that this "generous" treatment of Ukrainian national aspirations was unrewarding. About the middle of 1940, the Ukrainian occupation troops, which had evidently been on too friendly terms with the local population, were withdrawn and replaced by units recruited in Central Asia.[71] A strip along the border with the Generalgouvernement was cleared of its population to a depth of several miles, and crossing was made almost impossible.[72] A start was made in the collectivization of agriculture.[73] No less important than these deliberate measures perhaps was the sending of tens of thousands of "carpetbagger" Soviet state, party, and army officials to the West Ukraine, where by their alien aspect (many were Russian) and their sheer numbers they severely irritated the local population.[74]

While it is impossible to know what the Soviet motives for introducing a harsher policy were, one may guess that the negative reaction of the population to the "tolerant" epoch played a part. The Soviet authorities probably discovered soon that the student exchanges had an effect opposite to that intended, for the West Ukrainian students were disagreeably surprised by the material poverty of the East Ukraine and the predominance in many nominally

---

[68]For the official Soviet version see M. Marchenko (the new rector of the University of L'vov), "L'vivs'kyi Universytet na novykh shliakhakh" (L'vov University on New Paths), *Kommunist*, December 16, 1939, p. 2. But Polish *Communists* (including Władysław Gomułka) carried on active propaganda in L'vov. Pavlo Kalenychenko, *Pol'ska prohresyvna emigratsiia v SRSR v roky Druhoï Svitovoï Viiny* (The Polish Progressive Emigration in the USSR in the Years of the Second World War) (Kiev: Vydavnytstvo Akademiï Nauk Ukraïns'koï RSR, 1957), p. 28.

[69]Interview 51; *Krakivs'ki Visti*, September 17, 1943, on a trip of about forty students of the L'vov veterinary school to Kiev in the spring of 1940.

[70]Arthur W. Just, in *Krakauer Zeitung*, August 12, 1941, p. 5.

[71]Mykhailo Kohut, "Iak zhylo halyts'ke selo pid bol'shevykamy" (How a Galician Village Lived under the Bolsheviks), *Krakivs'ki Visti*, March 1, 1942, p. 6; Report of interview with Dr. H. J. Beyer (a German official who had been active in Galicia), *Ukraïns'kyi Visnyk*, July 16, 1941, p. 3.

[72]*Nastup*, June 29, 1940, p. 3; *Krakivs'ki Visti*, November 10, 1940, p. 3, based on an article in the *Frankfurter Zeitung*.

[73]Kohut in *Krakivs'ki Visti*, March 1, 1942, p. 6; *Krakivs'ki Visti*, November 25, 1941, p. 2, and May 17, 1942, p. 4. See especially Rudnyts'ka, *Zakhidnia Ukraïna pid Bol'shevykamy*, pp. 333 ff.

[74]*Krakivs'ki Visti*, January 13, 1942, p. 4, states that, due to the influx of Polish refugees from the German military campaign and the arrival of Soviet officials, the population of L'vov increased from 318,000 to 450,000 under Soviet occupation. On August 14, 1941, it printed a letter from L'vov stating that Soviet officials and their families in L'vov had numbered 100,000. Just (*Krakauer Zeitung*, August 12, 1941, p. 5) concludes from the number of votes cast in the Soviet election in Stanislav in the summer of 1940 that the population of that city must have increased by over 40,000, 1,000 of whom, he says, were NKVD officers. Rudnyts'ka, *Zakhidnia Ukraïna pid Bol'shevykamy*, p. 94, estimates the total influx at 200,000. For more details, see John A. Armstrong, *The Soviet Bureaucratic Elite: A Case Study of the Ukrainian Apparatus* (New York: Frederick A. Praeger, 1959), Chapter 8.

Ukrainian places of the Russian language and culture.[75] East Ukrainian students coming to L'vov, on the other hand, had their first opportunity to become infected with the "virus" of "bourgeois nationalism."[76] Aside from producing these undesired ideological results, the earlier policy failed to prevent underground work by the Nationalist youth of Galicia.

Most of the members of the OUN were not able, of course, to leave the Soviet-occupied area. It is impossible to secure reliable evidence concerning the exact extent to which those who remained could carry on their activities, but it is certain that they carefully refrained from open opposition. Nevertheless, late in 1940 the NKVD succeeded in tracking down a large number of Nationalists; they were sentenced to death or prison after a proceeding in L'vov known in the OUN accounts as the "trial of the fifty-nine." Among those sentenced to death was Krymins'kyi, the chief of the OUN movement in Soviet-occupied territories.[77] In all likelihood, he and his companions had sided with Bandera in the dispute with Mel'nyk. Certainly, the remaining members who, in spite of severe losses, were able to continue as an organized underground, were firm adherents of the new leader. The new underground director, John Klymiv, was in fact one of the most fanatical supporters which this fanatical movement of the younger generation could boast.[78] While there were undoubtedly many supporters of Colonel Mel'nyk in Galicia, it is doubtful whether they were active—or rash—enough to form what could be called an underground, although apparently agents kept up sporadic contacts with headquarters in the Generalgouvernement.

The situation in Volhynia was less favorable to Nationalist activity than that in Galicia, since the OUN had never enrolled such a high proportion of the youth there. Throughout most if not all of the area, Mel'nyk and Bandera apparently had no organizations, though agents were probably present.[79] The UNR, on the other hand, as will be described, was able to establish loose connections with a group which had been formed by nationalist youths in the remote Kostopol' (Kostopil')-Liudvipol' (Liudvypil') area near the former border between Polish and Soviet Volhynia.

The situation in Bukovina prior to June, 1940, had in many respects closely paralleled that which existed in Galicia before September, 1939. The small Ukrainian population (about one quarter of a million persons) was subjected to a denationalizing policy by the Rumanian government, which included severe limitations on the use of Ukrainian in education and restriction of the press and of cultural activities. As in Galicia, there was a legal press and party, however, which endeavored to work within the scope permitted by the

---

[75]*Krakivs'ki Visti*, September 17, 1943, p. 3.

[76]Interview 51.

[77]See, for example, Mykhailiuk, *Bunt Bandery*, p. 4. Cf. *Ukraïns'kyi Visnyk*, August 17, 1941, p. 4, reprinting an article from *Ukraïns'ki Shchodenni Visti* (L'vov).

[78]Interview 43.

[79]Mel'nyk adherents have since claimed that their organizers who had been in Volhynia for a considerable time were killed by Bandera followers shortly before or after the outbreak of the German-Soviet war; see Mykhailiuk, *Bunt Bandery*, p. 88; O. Shtul', *V im'ia pravdy: Do istoriï povstanoho rukhu v Ukraïni* (In the Name of Truth: On the History of the Insurrectionary Movement in the Ukraine) (Rotterdam, 1947), p. 10.

Rumanian authorities. There was also a fairly large section of the OUN, working underground. Corresponding—less closely—to Volhynia, was a considerable area of Ukrainian settlement in southern Bessarabia. This section of the Ukrainian ethnic group, however, was so backward culturally and so cut off geographically from contact with districts in which nationalism was strong that it appears to have played almost no role in the nationalist movements of the war period.

In June, 1940, while Germany was still occupied with the final phases of the French campaign, the Soviet Union began to press claims for territorial cessions from Rumania. It had long been recognized that Moscow would seize the first favorable moment to secure the retrocession of Bessarabia, the annexation of which by Rumania it had never recognized. Demands for Bukovina, however, apparently came as something of a shock to the German negotiators who were preparing a settlement of the Russian demands. They objected on the grounds that Bukovina had never been a part of the Russian Empire and that it contained a large German colony. Molotov countered that it was the last "missing piece" of the Ukraine, though he agreed to limit his demands to the northern, predominantly Ukrainian part and offered to permit the repatriation of the ethnic German minority.[80]

Germany was not ready for a break with the USSR; consequently Rumania was forced to give way. On June 28, her forces evacuated Chernovtsy (Chernivtsi),[81] the Bukovinian capital, and the Red Army took over. The sequence of events was similar to that which had occurred nine months previously in L'vov, but the tempo was quicker. The leading newspaper, *Chas*, was Sovietized and a new Communist organ, *Nova Rada*, founded, though a number of Ukrainian books forbidden under Rumanian rule were authorized.[82] The Ukrainian People's House and other national cultural societies were closed. At the same time, the Soviet press assailed the repressive measures which the Rumanians had taken against Ukrainian cultural life. Soviet writers were indignant at the difficulties experienced by the Ukrainian intelligentsia in Chernovtsy, although they denounced the Petliurist elements among them.[83] Numerous leading Ukrainians were not allowed to enjoy their new "intellectual freedom," but were arrested or shot as nationalist "counterrevolutionaries." It is said, however, that the German consul and the commission for evacuating the ethnic Germans succeeded in taking out numerous Ukrainian political leaders and priests of the Orthodox Church.[84] In any case, many thousands of refugees, mostly young people, found their way to Germany, where a large proportion provided an invigorating element for the segment of the OUN which had remained under Mel'nyk.[85]

---

[80]Ambassador von der Schulenburg in Moscow to Auswärtiges Amt, June 26, 1940, *Nazi-Soviet Relations*, p. 159.

[81]Rumanian Cernăuți; German Chernowitz.

[82]*Nastup*, August 3, 1940, p. 3.

[83]"Besarabiia i pivnichna chastyna Bukovyny" (Bessarabia and the Northern Part of Bukovina), *Komunist*, June 30, 1940, p. 2; S. Zhurakovych and Ie. Patner, "Misto pod Prutom" (City on the Pruth), *Komunist*, July 5, 1940, p. 3.

[84]*Krakivs'ki Visti*, September 7, 1941, p. 3.

[85]See Chapter IV.

The subjection of the West Ukraine to Soviet rule brought death or imprisonment to a considerable number of prominent Ukrainians; the entire population was oppressed by a heavy weight of fear and by severe limitations on its freedom. These factors were to be of great importance, for they created a state of mind in which the Ukrainians of the area would at least initially welcome any force which opposed the Soviet Union, without close examination of its nature. Soviet occupation covered a relatively short period of time, however, and the policies prescribed by Moscow were tempered in the first months by a desire to avoid alienating the inhabitants. Consequently, the severity of the Communist rule was not sufficient to destroy the material or psychological base for future revival of nationalist strength. In this respect, the severe factional strife which had arisen during the same period in the areas subject to German control was more important, for it meant that at a decisive moment in their history the Ukrainian nationalists could not speak with a single voice.

IV
The Opening of the Ukraine

Long before the Western world guessed his intentions Hitler had begun preparations for a campaign against the Soviet Union. As early as 1940 the Germans surreptitiously formed military training units for Ukrainians. Their enlistment was concealed by official statements that the units were for *Volksdeutsche* (ethnic Germans) only, and the purpose of the units was disguised by designating the Reichsarbeitdienst (Reich Labor Service) to be the supervising agency in the Generalgouvernement. Years later, a Ukrainian informant mentioned—and his report was transmitted by field intelligence without correction to the high-level intelligence agency Fremde Heere Ost (Foreign Armies, East)—that "fifteen thousand Ukrainians served in the German army in 1941 as scouts, parachutists, saboteurs, and interpreters." Many were also trained for police duties.[1] At first, the chief Ukrainian organizer of this army training was Colonel Sushko, and the training units were under the influence of the Mel'nyk group. After the split had fully developed, however, Bandera elements secured the upper hand in many of the groups, which were predominantly composed of young men fitted for active field service.[2]

For this reason, or because they were dissatisfied with the previous efforts of the OUN-M (Mel'nyk group) to pursue a somewhat independent course, the Germans turned more and more to the insurgent faction. This was especially the case when, in the early spring of 1941, the comparatively unconcealed development of Ukrainian units was begun by the Wehrmacht. The first such unit was known by the code name "Nachtigall" and was organized in the Generalgouvernement. Nominally, only its enlisted personnel were Ukrainian, while all officers were German. Actually, as the Germans well knew, there was a whole staff of "unofficial" Ukrainian officers, headed by the leader of the "military tendency" in the OUN-B, Roman Shukhevych. At first "Nachtigall"

---

[1] Abwehrabteilung III/Walli III, April 22, 1944 (T 78, Reel 575—*Litopys*, Vol. VI, p. 130), transmitting "On the Question of the National Movements in Galicia"; Stepan (Stephen) Huliak, "Polk im Kholodnoho Iara v Rivnomu" (The Kholodnyi Iar Regiment in Rovno), *Visti Bratstva kol. Voiakiv I. UD UNA* (August-September 1952), p. 7.

[2] Abwehrabteilung III/Walli III, cited above, and MS D.

had only about one hundred and fifty men, but at the outbreak of war it was expanded to battalion strength.³

A second unit, larger but of less political significance, was formed in Austria. Ukrainians were allowed a greater degree of formal authority than in "Nachtigall." In *de facto* command was Colonel Iarii, the dissident member of the old Provid, who was at once highly esteemed by his young subordinates and on the closest personal terms with the Abwehr officers charged with the formation of the units. John Gavrusevych, one of the top leaders of the Bandera group, was in charge of recruitment; his source of manpower lay in the large Ukrainian colony in Austria. Up to 1940, the chief Ukrainian organization in the latter territory was the student Sich in Vienna, which was dominated by the OUN. This association continued loyal to Mel'nyk, but most of the numerous Ukrainian factory workers turned to the new movement. It was among the latter that Gavrusevych secured the majority of his recruits, although about one quarter were secured from among the students, particularly those in the medical school in Graz. Care was taken to keep the force — which was called by the organizers Druzhyny Ukraïns'kykh Natsionalistiv (Brotherhoods of Ukrainian Nationalists) — in the hands of the Bandera group, although only half of the members actually belonged to the new party. Unlike "Nachtigall," which was clad in Wehrmacht *feldgrau*, "Roland," as the military unit composed of the Druzhyny was called, wore uniforms similar to those of the Galician section of the Ukrainian army of revolutionary days.⁴

As is apparent from the above description, the Wehrmacht units were prepared on a rather *ad hoc* basis, with the active cooperation of several important leaders of the OUN-B but without the utilization of the organizational framework of this group. However, Bandera and his principal lieutenants were well aware of what was going on; they approved of the formation of the units as a means for enhancing the power of their movement.⁵ Moreover, it appears that in the spring of 1941 an understanding was reached between the directors of the OUN-B and certain Wehrmacht officers especially concerned with the utilization of Ukrainians in the coming war. This agreement was extremely vague and informal. As far as can be determined from cursory mention in a contemporary German document and from the accounts of Ukrainians and German officers involved in the arrangement, it provided that the Germans would allow the Bandera party to carry on political activities in the Ukrainian areas which were to be conquered, while the Reich would be left completely free to organize the economy of the region in accordance with the needs of its war production.⁶

---

³Nykon Nalyvaiko, "Legiony v natsional'nykh viinakh" (Legions in National Wars), *Narod'na Volia* (October 27, 1949), p. 2.

⁴Liubomyr Ortyns'kyi, "Druzhyny Ukraïns'kykh Natsionalistiv (DUN)" (The Brotherhoods of Ukrainian Nationalists [DUN]), *Visti Bratstva kol. Voiakiv l. UD UNA* (June-July, 1952), p. 4; MS A. Roman Il'nyts'kyi, *Deutschland und die Ukraine, 1934-1945: Tatsachen europäischer Ostpolitik, ein Vorbericht*, Vol. II (Munich: Osteuropa Institut, 1956), pp. 140-42, maintains that Shukhevych held the rank of lieutenant in the Germany army. Il'nyts'kyi also asserts that a large portion of both units consisted of former members of the Carpathian Sich, and that non-OUN-B members were admitted only in exceptional cases.

⁵Interviews 24, 76.

⁶The whole question of an "agreement" between the Germans and the Bandera group is hotly disputed, with some OUN leaders denying that any real agreement took place and the Germans

Aside from the difficulty of defining economic and political spheres, this rudimentary agreement was vitiated by several misunderstandings. Bandera's followers, untutored in legal formulas, and indeed lacking experience in precise formulation of any kind, assumed that they had been granted a free hand in the political realm. The Wehrmacht representatives evidently believed that Germany really would support Ukrainian independence, but the Nazi leadership which controlled them never envisaged such a course. On the other hand, the army officers felt that they could control the new Ukrainian party at least as long as hostilities lasted, and saw political activity by the Bandera party as occurring only in a local, auxiliary fashion until the fighting ended.

When war broke out, the fragility of these arrangements was quickly demonstrated. The news of the outbreak of hostilities had scarcely reached Cracow when the Bandera followers organized a Ukrainian National Committee to serve, according to their proclamation, as an instrument for organizing all Ukrainian national forces for the liberation of the homeland. A highly respected former officer of the UNR army, General Vsevolod Petriv, was designated president; prominent members of most of the Ukrainian parties were secured as members, along with representatives of the OUN-B itself, headed by Dr. Horbovyi.[7] This startling emergence of the new party as the leader in consolidating Ukrainian forces in the Generalgouvernement was due to two factors: its unhesitating determination to take command, implemented by speedy action; and the widespread impression that the Germans were supporting it. The real plans of the directing group were not disclosed, however, to the more prominent Ukrainians who trusted to its guidance.[8]

Having secured a semblance of broad backing in the emigration, the Bandera group rapidly advanced toward its goal of "organizing" the territories being conquered by the German armies. Meanwhile, however, fearful events were taking place beyond the Soviet border. In the first hours after war broke out, the underground rose in a number of places and secured distinct successes against Soviet forces in some of the more remote districts where the difficult terrain made it possible for lightly armed guerrillas to act effectively against Soviet security units. Such uprisings took place in the Sambor (Sambir) area within forty-eight hours after the war started, and farther east, in the Podgaitsi (Pidhaitsi) and Monastyris'ka districts, Ukrainian militia took over police

---

insisting that the Ukrainians broke their word by proclaiming their "government" in L'vov (Interview 62). A contemporary German police report, which may be judged to be comparatively disinterested in making such an assertion, maintained that an agreement embodying the conditions cited in the text had been made (Activity and Situation Report of the SP and the SD in the USSR, January-March, 1942, PS 3876; hereafter referred to as PS 3876).

[7]Petro Mirchuk, *Akt vidnovlennia ukraïns'koï derzhavnosty, 30 chervnia 1941 roku* (The Act of Renewal of Ukrainian Statehood, June 30, 1941) (New York: Holovna Uprava Organizatsiï Oborony Chotyr'okh Svobid Ukraïny, 1952), pp. 18-20. It is claimed, however, that Petriv did not even know about his appointment as he was in the Protectorate at the time; cf. G. Polykarpenko, *Organizatsiia Ukraïns'kykh Natsionalistiv pidchas Druhoï Svitovoï Viini* (The Organization of Ukrainian Nationalists during the Second World War) (4th revised ed. of *OUN u Viini*, ed. B. Mykhailiuk) (Canada, 1951), p. 69. Il'nyts'kyi, *Deutschland und die Ukraine*, Vol. II, p. 145, describes how the OUN-B began to organize the Committee in April, though the formal foundation was on June 22, 1941.

[8]Interview 24.

functions and dissolved the kolkhozes before the German arrival.[9] In the less sheltered districts, however, Soviet repression was horrible. A military field police unit which entered L'vov while the city was still on fire dispatched the most graphic and circumstantial report. Corpses were found four or five deep in the cellars of the principal NKVD political prison; many of the estimated 3,500 victims must have been killed shortly before war began. In a second prison many victims from the surrounding countryside appeared to have been killed by blunt instruments a few days before L'vov was captured. Although the dispatch had a strong anti-Semitic tone, it admitted that a small minority of the prisoners killed before the NKVD fled were Zionists, and remarked that "it is not clear that the GPU paid any attention to nationality." The overwhelming majority were, to be sure, members of the Polish and the Ukrainian intelligentsia, including women and children. The German report sharply criticized the reliability of the Ukrainian interpreters with the unit, alleging that they were so overcome by emotion that they insisted *all* victims were Ukrainians, insulted any Poles they encountered, and demanded that "all Jews must be immediately killed."[10]

The SS *Einsatzgruppen*, on the other hand, were concerned with promoting ethnic strife rather than restoring order for military purposes. Their reports confirm the extent of NKVD summary executions in L'vov, and their own appalling murders of Jews in smaller towns. In several places the SS took great satisfaction in inciting local Ukrainians to participate in these lynchings.[11] As a result, a considerable portion of the large Jewish population of Galicia, as well as tens of thousands of Soviet officials and their dependents, streamed eastward to escape massacre by the German totalitarians.

On June 30, in the midst of the disorganization caused by these atrocities, the first groups of Bandera's followers reached L'vov. Some, like Iaroslav Stets'ko, came illegally, although with incidental assistance from German front-line units. Others arrived in "Nachtigall," which was among the advance Wehrmacht units. Accounts sponsored by the postwar Polish regime have quoted alleged eyewitness assertions that "Nachtigall" members participated in anti-Jewish atrocities.[12] Since, however, the numerous Ukrainian interpreters

---

[9]*Krakivs'ki Visti*, August 6, 1941, p. 3; *Nastup*, August 30, 1942, p. 2, quoting *Sambirs'ki Visti*, August 10, 1941; Il'nyts'kyi, *Deutschland und die Ukraine*, Vol. II, pp. 167-73. A Soviet account, N. K. Popel', *V tiazhkuiu poru* (A Troublesome Time) (Moscow: Voennoe Izdatel'stvo Ministerstva Oborony Soiuza SSR, 1959), pp. 6, 47-48, admits that there were strong "Banderist" rebellions in L'vov and elsewhere in Galicia both immediately before and after the outbreak of war with Germany.

[10]454th Security Division, Ia, Kriegstagebuch, September 22, 1941, Anlage 95, report of Geheime Feldpolizei, Gruppe 711, July 7, 1941 (T 315, Reel 2215).

[11]Chief of the SP and the SD, Report on Events in the USSR, No. 20, July 12, 1941, and No. 23, July 15, 1941 (T 175, Reel 233). In his exhaustive study, *The Destruction of the European Jews* (Chicago: Quadrangle Books, 1961), p. 350, Raul Hilberg shows that Ukrainians were involved in violence against the Jews of Galicia (see also Chapter VII, p. 130).

[12]Alexander Drożdżyński and Jan Zaborowski, *Oberländer: A Study in German East Politics* (Poznan: Wydawnictwo Zachodnie, 1960). As the title indicates, this work was designed to discredit the German officer, Theodor Oberländer, who had supervised "Nachtigall," and at the time of publication was a member of the cabinet of the Federal Republic of Germany. I have not been able to find any corroborating evidence indicating involvement of "Nachtigall" members, specifically, in anti-Semitic atrocities.

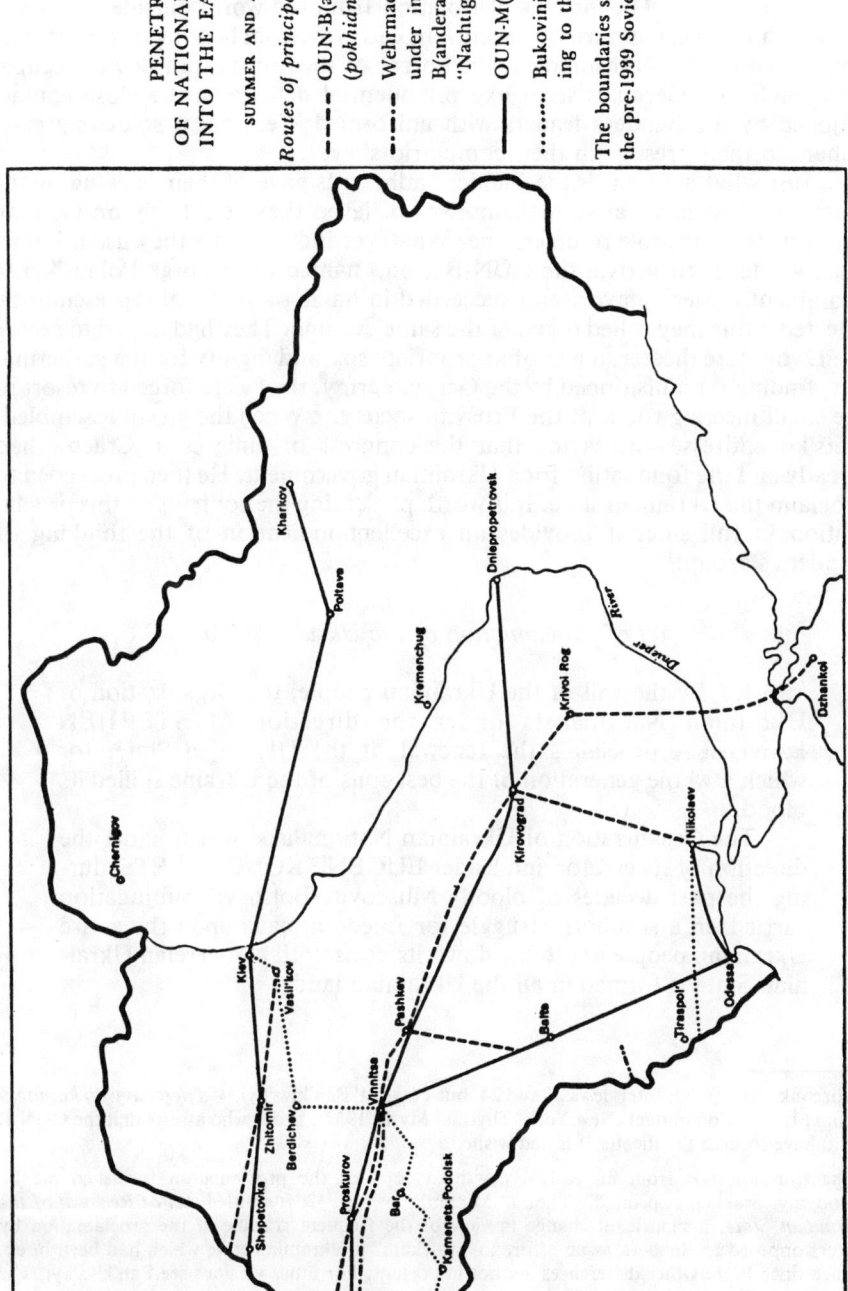

PENETRATION OF NATIONALIST GROUPS INTO THE EAST UKRAINE

SUMMER AND AUTUMN, 1941

Routes of principal groups:

---- OUN-B(andera) task forces (pokhidny hrupy)

-·-·- Wehrmacht auxiliary units under influence of OUN-B(andera) ("Roland" and "Nachtigall")

——— OUN-M(el'nyk) groups

·········· Bukovinian groups adhering to the OUN-M(el'nyk)

The boundaries shown are those of the pre-1939 Soviet Ukraine.

for German formations like the military field police team referred to above wore similar uniforms, they may well have been the real culprits.

Bandera followers in "Nachtigall" and their clandestine OUN-B associates like Stets'ko were intent on other objectives: taking advantage of the confused situation in the Galician capital to attain a commanding position for the OUN-B program. The months of isolation from the world outside the Soviet Union had prevented most of the citizens of L'vov from hearing of the internal conflict of the OUN. Moreover, the horror of the last days of Soviet occupation made the Germans seem like providential deliverers; the close contact enjoyed by the Bandera leaders with uniformed Wehrmacht soldiers greatly enhanced their prestige in their compatriots' eyes.

Just what assurances the Bandera adherents gave of their backing by the Germans, just how far they themselves believed they could rely on German support, is impossible to determine. Whatever inducements they used, immediately after their arrival the OUN-B group named Dr. George Polans'kyi, a prominent citizen, mayor, and succeeded in having a national representation "elected"; this they called together the same evening. They had hoped to secure the L'vov state theater, a hall of appropriate size and dignity for the gathering, but, finding it requisitioned by the German army, they were forced to resort to the small meeting room of the Prosvita society.[13] When the group assembled, Stets'ko addressed it, saying that the congress of émigrés in Cracow had already laid the foundation for a Ukrainian government. He then proceeded to proclaim the Ukrainian state. It is worth presenting the contents of this proclamation in full since it provides an excellent indication of the thinking of Bandera's group.[14]

Act of Proclamation of the Ukrainian State

1. By the will of the Ukrainian people, the Organization of Ukrainian Nationalists under the direction of STEPHEN BANDERA proclaims the renewal of the Ukrainian State, for which a whole generation of the best sons of the Ukraine spilled its blood.

The Organization of Ukrainian Nationalists, which under the direction of its creator and leader EUGENE KONOVALETS' during the past decades of bloody Muscovite-Bolshevik subjugation carried on a stubborn struggle for freedom, calls upon the entire Ukrainian people not to lay down its arms until a Sovereign Ukrainian State is formed in all the Ukrainian lands.

---

[13]Mirchuk, *Akt*, p. 30; Interviews 21 and 24; but cf. Kost' Pan'kivs'kyi, *Vid derzhavy do komitetu* (From State to Committee) (New York: Zhyttia i Mysli, 1957), p. 55, who asserts that the OUN-B could have secured the theater if it had wished.

[14]The translation is from an early typewritten copy of the proclamation furnished me by Volodymyr Stakhiv. A printed version in Mirchuk, *Akt*, p. 32, is entitled *Act of Renewal of the Ukrainian State*, a significant change in view of the frequent ridicule of the proclamation by writers opposed to Bandera as an effort to "proclaim" a Ukrainian state which had been in existence since 1918. Other differences are not important. For other versions see Pan'kivs'kyi, *Vid derzhavy do Komitetu*, pp. 111 ff.

The sovereign Ukrainian government assures the Ukrainian people of regularity and order [*lad i poriadok*], multi-sided development of all its forces, and satisfaction of its demands.

2. In the western lands of the Ukraine a Ukrainian government is created which will be subordinated to a Ukrainian national administration which will be created in the capital of the Ukraine—Kiev.

3. The Ukrainian national-revolutionary army, which is being created on Ukrainian soil, will continue to fight against the Muscovite occupation for a Sovereign All-Ukrainian State and a new, just order in the whole world.

Long live the Sovereign Ukrainian State!

Long live the Organization of Ukrainian Nationalists!

Long live the director of the Organization of Ukrainian Nationalists—STEPHEN BANDERA!

> The City of L'vov, June 30, 1941, 8 P.M.
> Head of the National Congress
> Iaroslav Stets'ko

The meeting at which the *akt*—as this proclamation has come to be known in Ukrainian polemics—was made was of comparatively small importance because of the hasty manner of its calling and the small number of people present. Nevertheless, the gathering was immediately dignified by the title of "National Assembly." Considerably more important than the initial proclamation was the fact that, in the confusion attendant upon the Red army's withdrawal and the German entry, the Ukrainians had been able to secure access to the L'vov radio station.[15] Consequently, soon after the *akt* was proclaimed, Stets'ko was able to broadcast it. Moreover, during the day, Stets'ko and a few followers, including in particular the Reverend John Hryn'okh, chaplain of "Nachtigall," had been able to gain access to the bedridden Metropolitan. Without going into details concerning their relations with Mel'nyk (they later asserted that Metropolitan Sheptyts'kyi "must" have known about the conflict), they informed him of their plans for proclaiming the Ukrainian state and asked his support.[16] Apparently convinced that the group had the backing of the Germans, and hoping for a quick establishment of Ukrainian independence, the Metropolitan wrote a pastoral letter in which

---

[15]Interviews 21, 24, 63; Mirchuk, *Akt*, p. 30; Vasyl' Rudko ("R. Lisovii"), "Rozlam v OUN" (The Split in the OUN), *Ukraïns'ki Visti*, November 3, 1949, p. 3. See especially the summary of events in Auswärtiges Amt, July 21, 1941, Series 5081, E 292424, "Ausrufung der 'ukrainischen Staatsgewalt'" (T 120, Reel 2532), which confirms many details.

[16]Interviews 24, 63. They base their statement on the fact that Sheptyts'kyi was in close touch with Klymiv, the OUN-B chief in east Galicia. But Iaroslav Stets'ko, *30 chervnia 1941: Proholoshennia vydnovlennia derzhavnosti Ukraïny* (June 30, 1941: Proclamation of the Renewal of Statehood of the Ukraine) (Toronto: League for the Liberation of Ukraine, 1967), p. 189, admits that he did not discuss the conflict in the OUN with Sheptits'kyi or Slipyi.

he exhorted the people to support the newly proclaimed government, saying that "the sacrifices which the final attainment of our goals require demand above all dutiful obedience to the just orders of the government which do not conflict with God's laws." Moreover, he declared: "We greet the victorious German Army as deliverer from the enemy. We render our obedient homage to the government which has been erected. We recognize Mr. Iaroslav Stets'ko as Head of the State Administration of the Ukraine."[17]

The pastoral letter was read over the radio by Father Hryn'okh the same morning, apparently in the presence of Bishop Slipyi. This endorsement appears to have removed any doubts which may have been lingering in the minds of most of the prominent Ukrainians in L'vov concerning the authenticity of the Stets'ko government.

The Bandera leaders went ahead rapidly to consolidate their victory. They felt the need of a name which would carry greater prestige than that of the young enthusiast Stets'ko, who had, as Bandera's deputy, already declared himself chief of state. Consequently, they prevailed upon the aged Constantine Levits'kyi, who had been released from prison several months before the war broke out, to accept the post of president of a parliament or Council of Seniors. At the same time, the Bandera group prepared to establish a "cabinet," which was to have included men from a wide group of parties. Stets'ko himself was to be "premier," since he feared that a nonparty man might give way to German pressure. Bandera adherents were to be placed in such key posts as deputy war minister, which was to be held by Shukhevych; minister of security, to be held by Lebed'; and minister of political coordination, to be held by Klymiv.[18]

The Bandera government, however, was not to live long enough to bring these plans to fruition. The proclamation of the government in the Prosvita hall had deeply disturbed the Wehrmacht officers who had organized "Nachtigall." They knew that it would induce a violent reaction among the ruling Nazis in Berlin, whereas the Wehrmacht group had hoped that by careful procedure they could secure the gradual development of a friendly, autonomous Ukrainian regime, at least in Galicia, without high party circles' realizing what was happening. Some of them were also alarmed at the possibility that the wide publication given the *akt* might arouse Russian patriotism against German-supported Ukrainian separatism, thus strengthening Soviet resistance.[19]

The Bandera group, on their part, maintain that they anticipated an unfavorable reaction from the Germans but felt that it was necessary to go ahead with the proclamation so as to confront them with a *fait accompli*. On July 3, messages announcing Ukrainian independence were, accordingly, dispatched to the various Axis states. Banderists also felt it would be difficult for the

---

[17]This quotation is taken from a contemporary leaflet copy of the pastoral letter.

[18]Stets'ko, *30 chervnia 1941*, p. 226, Cf. Il'nyts'kyi, *Deutschland und die Ukraine*, Vol. II, p. 189; Mirchuk, *Akt*, pp. 35-36; Pan'kivs'kyi, *Vid derzhavy do Komitetu*, pp. 40-46; Interview 24. Mirchuk and Il'nyts'kyi list Petriv as war minister, while a contemporary German SD report (NO 4529) has Iarii in that post, Klymiv as minister of security. Il'nyts'kyi lists Lebed' simply as "state secretary."

[19]Interview 62. The danger of arousing Russian patriotism was especially feared by the OKW (Oberkommando der Wehrmacht) officers, according to one of Stets'ko's assistants (Interview 29).

Germans to take overt action against a widely proclaimed "Ukrainian government," since such action might lead to a great loss of support for the German campaign by the non-Russian nationalities of the Soviet Union. If suppression did occur—so Banderists later argued—these nationalities would know what to expect from a Nazi regime. As a matter of fact, Bandera and his followers appear to have had a fairly correct understanding of the attitude of the Wehrmacht officers with whom they were dealing. In spite of their dismay over the proclamation, the latter were very hesitant to take countermeasures. They "looked the other way" when possible, while quietly working to convince influential circles in L'vov of the inadequacy of the Stets'ko regime.[20]

The Bandera group, however, was quite unable to fathom the real nature of high German policy. In view of what happened later in the Ukraine, it is probable that a severe repression of any form of self-administration for the Ukraine as a whole would have been ordered by Hitler and his henchmen, regardless of whether the *akt* had been proclaimed or not. However, the proclamation immediately produced the reaction feared by the Wehrmacht group. About three days after the *akt*, an SS *Einsatzgruppe* [task force] arrived in L'vov. It was accompanied, significantly, by several Ukrainians in the role of interpreters or "political reporters," including at least one prominent follower of Mel'nyk, Chuchkevych. After a few days of feeling out the ground, this force waited upon Stets'ko and his friend Rebet when they came to the city administrative building on July 9 and placed them under "honorary arrest."[21]

About the same time, Bandera (who had never been allowed to leave the Generalgouvernement), Gavrusevych, Bandera's representative in Berlin, Volodymyr Stakhiv, and Stets'ko's assistants, Stariukh and Ilnits'kyi, were arrested.[22] All were assembled in Berlin and questioned thoroughly by both police and Wehrmacht officers. The Germans, however, were obviously proceeding with caution. They realized that at that moment considerable trouble could be caused the advancing German armies by disturbances in Galicia, which would probably be the result of drastic action against the OUN leaders.[23] At the same time, they warned the group of the possible serious consequences of their actions, and urged the leaders to withdraw the *akt* and accept a status in eastern Galicia similar to that of the Ukrainian Central Committee in Cracow. Bandera and his followers refused; however, they were not imprisoned. On the contrary, while nominally under house arrest, they were allowed to carry on their political activities in Berlin; Stets'ko was even able to go to

---

[20]Interview 62. The 444th Security Division, Ic, did not issue an order until January 13, 1942, requiring that Bandera and Mel'nyk adherents who had slipped into the occupied areas with passes falsely claiming Wehrmacht authorization be arrested and turned over to the SS *Einsatzgruppen* (T 315, Reel 2213).

[21]Stets'ko, *30 chervnia 1941*, pp. 256 ff.; Interviews 24, 36, 44, 67. Cf. Il'nyts'kyi, *Deutschland und die Ukraine*, Vol. II, p. 187, who gives the date of arrest as July 11.

[22]Mirchuk, *Akt*, pp. 38-39.

[23]As the chief of Vineta, the Propaganda Ministry's bureau for dealing with eastern affairs, later wrote: "Bandera and his closest supporters were arrested, but by clever treatment an insurrection was avoided." Taubert to Rosenberg, February 17, 1944, Occ E-4 (1), in Yiddish Scientific Institute (hereafter referred to as Occ E-4 [1]).

Cracow, where he consulted with Lebed', whom he had secretly delegated to take command of all activities in the Ukrainian lands.[24]

Meanwhile, the tide started by the proclamation was still running in Bandera's favor in Galicia. Several non-OUN administrators who had accompanied Stets'ko and Rebet at the time of their arrest were sick with humiliation to see Ukrainians, who had created the impression that they were responsible leaders acting in agreement with the Germans, thus treated as naughty boys who had stepped out of bounds.[25] The majority of the population, on the other hand, was not aware of the real nature of the departure of the Bandera party's leaders. In town after town in the eastern part of Galicia the citizens, rejoicing over the overthrow of Soviet rule, assumed that the independence of the Ukraine had really been established and greeted the new "government" with enthusiastic expressions of loyalty.[26]

From the very beginning of the war, the Bandera group had been putting into operation still another ambitious plan. Far from being content with the establishment of a government in the former Polish territories, the OUN-B was determined to extend its scope to include the East Ukraine. Bandera's followers realized that it would be an extremely slow process for the organization to spread from town to town and that in case of opposition by the Germans such a development could be quickly interrupted. Consequently, in the last months before the outbreak of war they had secretly developed a number of groups of young men (and women) to act as propagandists and organizers in the eastern area. In the final days of June these bodies, which were known as *pokhidny hrupy* (literally "march groups," but translated hereafter as "task forces") assembled (doubtless with some toleration by the Wehrmacht) at convenient points along the eastern border of the Generalgouvernement.[27]

Two of the task forces were to cross the northern Ukraine. One, under Nicholas Klymishyn, who had accompanied Lebed' in his escape from the

---

[24]Mirchuk, *Akt*, p. 39; Interviews 24, 75. Stets'ko, Bandera, and other OUN-B leaders were imprisoned on September 15, 1941. Cf. "Ausrufung der 'ukrainischen Staatsgewalt'" (T 120, Reel 2532).

[25]Interview 36.

[26]*Ukraïns'ke Slovo* (Stanislav), July 22, 1941, p. 1; *Kremianets'kii Visnyk*, August 9, 1941. These papers were furnished me by an erstwhile leader of the Bandera group, Volodymyr Stakhiv, but they appear genuine.

[27]Much the most comprehensive and useful work on the "task forces" is Lev Shankovs'kyl's *Pokhidni hrupy OUN* (March Groups of the OUN) (Munich: Vydavnytstvo "Ukraïns'kyi Samostiinyk," 1958). Il'nyts'kyi, *Deutschland und die Ukraine*, Vol. II, pp. 142-44, gives a brief account of the origin of these groups. Zynovii Matla, *Pivdenna pokhidna hrupa* (The Southern Task Force) (Munich: Tsitsero, 1952), p. 4; Mstyslav Z. Chubai, *Reid organizatoriv OUN vid Popradu po Chorne More* (The Raid of Organizers of the OUN from Poprad to the Black Sea) (Munich: Tsitsero, 1952), p. 4; "E. Pavliuk" (Ievhen [Eugene] Stakhiv, a brother of Volodymyr Stakhiv), "Borot'ba ukraïns'koho narodu na skhidno-ukraïns'kykh zemliakh, 1941-1944: Spomyny ochevydtsia i uchasnyka" (The Struggle of the Ukrainian People in the Eastern Ukrainian Lands, 1941-44: Memories of an Eyewitness and Participant), in *Kalendar Provydinnia na 1947 rik. Stovaryshennia Ukraïns'kikh Katolykiv v Amerytsi* (Calendar for 1947 of the Providence Society of Ukrainian Catholics in America) (Philadelphia: Ameryka, n.d.), p. 37; and Mykola Chartoryis'kyi, *Vid Sianu po Krym: Spomyny uchasnyka III pohidnoï grupy-Pivden'* (From the San to the Crimea: Memoirs of a participant in the southern task force) (New York: Howerla, 1951).

Polish prison convoy, had Kiev for its destination.[28] A second group under Nicholas Senishyn had Kharkov as its goal. A third task force, which was expected to break up into several subgroups, was to organize the southern Ukraine.[29] The tasks outlined for the groups were ambitious indeed. They were to proclaim the *akt* of L'vov, to organize the "state apparatus," and to construct a Ukrainian army from former soldiers of the Red and Polish armies.[30] The resources available for carrying out these projects in the vast reaches of the Ukraine were hardly commensurate with the scope of the tasks. The groups varied in size, but all could be counted in scores of men. To cover the great distances they were equipped with bicycles and wagons; a few lucky ones had motorcycles, and for the entire force there was—one automobile. Printed propaganda leaflets, which had been secretly prepared in Cracow by workers in the legal presses, were available, but hardly in the millions of copies needed.[31]

What the expeditions lacked in material resources, however, they made up for in self-assurance. After the first few days, they realized that the Germans were not going to welcome them cordially; consequently, they carefully skirted large towns and concentrations of German troops. When they were unable to avoid encounters with the latter, they adopted a bold front, in some cases even declaring that they were "emissaries of an independent Ukrainian state." The Wehrmacht commanders, like all field soldiers, were annoyed at the presence of unauthorized civilians in their zone of operations. However, most had heard of the cooperation of the youthful movement with the Germans. Moreover, in many cases they undoubtedly had real sympathy for Ukrainian nationalist aspirations, for they had seen the touching gratitude with which the Ukrainians welcomed their supposed deliverers from Soviet tyranny and their readiness to cooperate against the Bolshevik regime. Consequently, while the front-line officers told the youths to go back to Galicia, they did not invoke military law against them. The reckless young men agreed to go home—but once out of sight took other roads to the east.[32]

As a result, in the bright summer months, the little groups trudging in the wake of the mighty Wehrmacht were able to make some progress in carrying out their program. In August the northern task force reached Zhitomir, where it helped a group of local people set up a very impermanent administration, and aroused an equally transitory wave of enthusiasm among some of the younger citizens.[33] The southern force covered an even greater distance; it traveled across Galicia during July, carrying on propaganda work; reached Vinnitsa by the end of the month; and on September 2 was in Dniepropetrovsk (Katerynoslav or, more romantically, Sicheslav), five hundred miles from its starting point.[34]

---

[28]Matla, *Pivdenna pokhidna hrupa*, p. 4; Ievhen Stakhiv, "Borot'ba ukraïns'koho narodu," p. 37, says that the leader was Dmytro Myron, but Matla appears to have been in closer contact with these operations.

[29]Matla, *Pivdenna pokhidna hrupa*, p. 4.

[30]Chubai, *Reid organizatoriv OUN*, p. 6.

[31]*Ibid.*, pp. 14 ff.; Matla, *Pivdenna pokhidna hrupa*, p. 4.

[32]Chubai, *Reid organizatoriv OUN*, p. 29.

[33]Ievhen Stakhiv, "Borot'ba ukraïns'koho narodu," p. 39.

[34]Matla, *Pivdenna Pokhidna hrupa*, p. 9.

Less picturesque, but of potentially greater value, were the military units under control of the Bandera group. As was previously noted, "Nachtigall" had taken part in the occupation of L'vov, where its leaders were of great value in organizing the city for the Bandera party. Although the Wehrmacht officers accompanying the group were aware of the roles of Father Hryn'okh, Shukhevych, and George Lopatyns'kyi in the *akt*, they protected them from the arrest.[35] The unit continued eastward with the Wehrmacht, in late August reaching Vinnitsa where its members made secret contact with the southern task force.[36]

"Roland," on the other hand, had no direct connection with the activities in Galicia. Before the outbreak of war, it was sent across Hungary to the Rumanian part of Bukovina. There were considerable difficulties with the Rumanians because of efforts of the Ukrainian nationalists to establish contact with local Ukrainians who were Rumanian subjects. After the outbreak of war, however, the unit was sent with the German advance through Bessarabia, across the Dniester, and into the Ukrainian ethnographical territory north of Tiraspol' where it remained until early September.[37]

While the newest Ukrainian nationalist party was achieving widespread, though transitory successes, its chief rival was not idle. The defection of the bulk of the Galician youth had indeed dealt a heavy blow to the "legitimate" OUN under Mel'nyk. Nevertheless, it retained several very important assets. In the first place, not all of the young men had joined the rebellion; a fairly large number of the youths of Galicia and Volhynia remained with their elders, and probably a majority of the younger generation in the Carpatho-Ukraine and Bukovina did also. Secondly, the older group embodied a great deal more experience than did the young rebels; this was to be particularly valuable in operating in the East Ukraine, where most of the older men had lived during the revolutionary period, if indeed they were not natives of the area. Along with experience went contacts, for Konovalets' had managed to maintain a few tenuous lines of communication with sympathizers in the East Ukraine.[38] Fourthly, the OUN-M, although it appeared temporarily to have been replaced by its rival in the Wehrmacht's plans, never lost contact with the Germans, and was in a position to profit from this contact when the Bandera group lost favor.

On July 6, 1941, a number of the leading Ukrainian nationalists who had served as officers in the Ukrainian Republican Army joined Mel'nyk in addressing an appeal to Hitler through the Abwehr. The signers of the appeal, besides Mel'nyk, who signed simply as "retired colonel," were Generals

---

[35] Interview 63. George Lopatyns'kyi is not to be confused with his brother Volodymyr, mentioned earlier, who was killed in early 1941.

[36] *Ibid.*; Matla, *Pivdenna pokhidna hrupa*, pp. 9-10.

[37] Ortyns'kyi, "Druzhyny Ukraïns'kykh Natsionalistiv," p. 4; MS A. After the OUN-B was outlawed, these two units (under their original title of "Training Regiment 'Brandenburg'") were employed by the Abwehr for special tasks such as fighting Soviet partisans and sabotage. Chief Abwehrabteilung II (Lahousen) to liaison officers at Army and Army Group headquarters, January 16, 1942 (T 312, Reel 1698).

[38] Cf. Iurii (George) Boiko, *Ievhen Konovalets' i oseredno-skhidni zemli* (Eugene Konovalets' and the Central-Eastern Lands) (1947), pp. 34-50.

Omelianovych-Pavlenko and Kapustians'kyi, Colonels Sushko, Stefaniv, and Diatchenko, and Michael Khronoviat. Their appeal read as follows:

> The Ukrainian people, whose century-old struggle for freedom has scarcely been matched by any other people, espouses from the depths of its soul the ideals of the New Europe. The entire Ukrainian people yearns to take part in the realization of these ideals. We, old fighters for freedom in 1918-1921, request that we, together with our Ukrainian youth, be permitted the honor of taking part in the crusade against Bolshevik barbarism. In twenty-one years of a defensive struggle, we have suffered bloody sacrifices, and we suffer especially at present through the frightful slaughter of so many of our compatriots. We request that we be allowed to march shoulder to shoulder with the legions of Europe and with our liberator, the German Wehrmacht, and therefore we ask to be permitted to create a Ukrainian military formation.[39]

The willingness to hitch on to the Nazi chariot expressed in this appeal was fruitless, however, for the confident Nazi leaders were in no mood to accept allies which might prove troublesome later. Less than a month after Mel'nyk's appeal, the UNO was forced to announce that the Germans were allowing Ukrainians who had been Soviet citizens, but not those (constituting the great bulk of the emigration) who had never lived under the Soviet regime, to enter police units to serve in the east. It warned its members that some of their number who had attempted to go to the East Ukraine had been "interned" and released only by intervention of the Berlin headquarters of the UNO.[40]

Mel'nyk himself reacted to the new situation in a characteristic fashion, which revealed once more the moderate nature of his policy and the doubtful effectiveness of his approach. Shortly after war began, he addressed all "nationalists," calling for unity for the great new tasks ahead, and asking for the end of activities of "partisan factionalists." He continued by urging all to "be true to the tasks of nationalism so that a satisfactory account may be made to the Third Great Congress of Ukrainian Nationalists."[41] The last statement was an obvious hint that, however much the Bandera followers might be dissatisfied with the Second Congress, they would have another chance to carry out their program in a new meeting, if only they returned to the fold. In view of the reckless yet energetic way in which the *krai* group was pushing ahead during the first week of war, such an appeal was almost certain to be taken as a sign of weakness, rather than as the genuine expression of a desire for reconciliation which it probably was. Very likely the situation was not helped by Mel'nyk's issuing, a few weeks later, a further call to "all Ukrainians," declaring his readiness to forget all that had taken place if all would return to the OUN and demonstrate their good will.[42]

---

[39] Chief of the SP and the SD, Report on Events in the USSR, No. 15, July 7, 1941, NO 5154 (hereafter referred to as NO 5154).

[40] *Ukraïns'kyi Visnyk*, July 24, 1941, p. 4.

[41] *Nastup*, June 28, 1941.

[42] *Nastup*, July 19, 1941.

Even if such sentiments could have influenced men of the insurgents' temperament, their effect was nullified by the way in which the Mel'nyk supporters reacted to the German measures against the Stets'ko coup. It is probably true that any direct cooperation given the German police was furnished by individuals like Chuchkevych, without the assent or even the knowledge of the Provid. It is understandable, however, that the presence of such men with the *Einsatzgruppe* led Bandera's adherents to conclude that their opponents were in league with the occupying power. Moreover, if the Mel'nyk group as such did not collaborate with the Germans against the other OUN faction, it certainly rejoiced in the latter's discomfiture. On July 16, the OUN organ reprinted an account of an interview of Beyer with a *Krakivs'ki Visti* correspondent in which the German official, who had just returned from L'vov, denied reports circulated by the Ukrainian National Committee that a "West Ukrainian regional government" under Stets'ko had been formed there, and that the Wehrmacht officer, Dr. Hans Koch, had recognized "a Ukrainian administration" at a "gathering" in L'vov.[43]

OUM-M supporters also hurried to east Galicia to secure a share in the control of the area. The Bandera party, of course, rapidly lost its power in L'vov, although, as has been pointed out, the impetus of their coup was felt for some time in areas distant from the Galician capital. When it became apparent that the Germans were not really backing Stets'ko, his Ukrainian support rapidly diminished. At the end of July the Council of Seniors which he had set up was expanded by the addition of seventeen new members and renamed the National Council.[44] Apparently German influence played a part in this; along with the change of name, a certain amount of change in composition took place, Mel'nyk adherents being permitted to replace OUN-B sympathizers.[45] Constantine Levits'kyi sank into obscurity; with considerable reluctance, Dr. Constantine Pan'kivs'kyi, who had been a minor UNDO politician before the war, and was not associated with either branch of the OUN, assumed the direction of the "secretariat" which acted as executive organ.[46] Some weeks later, the organization was renamed the Ukraïns'kyi Kraievyi Komitet (Ukrainian Regional Committee) with Pan'kivs'kyi retaining direction.[47]

That its role in the reorganization of administration in eastern Galicia after the downfall of the Bandera leaders was somewhat more restricted than its part in the creation of the Ukrainian administration in Cracow in 1940

---

[43] *Ukraïns'kyi Visnyk*, July 16, 1941, p. 3.

[44] *Entsyklopediia Ukraïnoznavstva* (Encyclopedia of Things Ukrainian), eds. Volodymyr Kubiiovych and Zenon Kuzelia (Munich: Naukove Tovarystvo im. Shevchenka, 1949), p. 587.

[45] "Ausrufung der 'ukrainischen Staatsgewalt'" (T 120, Reel 2523); Chief of the SP and the SD, Report on Events in the USSR, No. 34, July 26, 1941, p. 11, NO 2954 (hereafter referred to as NO 2954). Cf. Pan'kivs'kyi, *Vid derzhavy do komitetu*, p. 72 ff., who asserts that some OUN-B members remained in the National Council. Pan'kivs'kyi also makes it clear that Levits'kyi, while he eventually went into retirement, played an important role in the transition. Both Pan'kivs'kyi and Il'nyts'kyi (*Deutschland und die Ukraine*, Vol. II, p. 216 ff.) describe at great length the controversies within the National Council concerning policy toward the German incorporation of Galicia in the Generalgouvernement.

[46] *Entsyklopediia Ukraïnoznavstva*, p. 587; *Nastup*, November 1, 1941, p. 3; Interview 36.

[47] Interview 36.

probably did not greatly disturb the OUN-M at the time, since its primary desire was to seize the long-anticipated opportunity to invade the East Ukraine. Two types of penetration were utilized. Through their long association with the Germans, the Mel'nyk followers had secured a large number of posts as interpreters, advisers, and so forth in Wehrmacht units. These posts now provided an opportunity for reaching the east in a legal manner. Because they feared that the Germans would restrict nationalist activity, however, the Mel'nyk group did not rely on legal means alone. In a fashion similar to that of the Bandera group, but evidently with greater reliance on cooperation of the German authorities, to be obtained by their contacts with the Wehrmacht, the Mel'nyk leaders organized a number of groups to go into the East Ukraine without authorization. Like the Bandera group's plan, the OUN-M project provided for three principal groups. The northern group was to go across Volhynia through Zhitomir to Kiev; ultimately, however, it was to reach Kharkov. The central group was to follow the route of the OUN-B southern task force through Vinnitsa to Dniepropetrovsk and then was to go on to the Donbas. Finally, corresponding to an OUN-B subgroup, the Mel'nyk southern group was to branch off at Vinnitsa for Odessa and Nikolaev (Mykolaïiv).[48]

All these groups, and especially the southern one, were much weaker in numbers than their OUN-B counterparts. They were handicapped by the fact that many of their members were beyond the most active age. Fortunately for the success of the Mel'nyk enterprise, however, they received an unplanned but extremely valuable reinforcement in the form of over five hundred Bukovinians, mostly young and energetic men. The OUN underground in Bukovina had become active as soon as war broke out, and, after the Rumanian and Hungarian forces freed the province, it was able to maintain an open organization until the middle of July. Then the Rumanian authorities, anxious lest their recovery of the area be threatened by a Ukrainian independence movement, repressed the nationalists with great severity. In some districts actual fighting took place between the Ukrainian nationalists and the Rumanian gendarmerie. The latter proved to be much too strong for the OUN-led forces. Many of the young men among the Ukrainian resistance groups fled to the north. Some went directly to the East Ukraine, others through Galicia to Vinnitsa.[49] Here, with the help of OUN-M members working with the Germans, a large number were recruited for the auxiliary police force; still others went on to Kiev, Zhitomir, Uman', and Proskurov, where many became cadres for pro-Mel'nyk police organizations. Another group, a much smaller one, succeeded in crossing the southwestern Ukraine to Nikolaev, where it established an OUN-M center.

The great base of the Mel'nyk party's activity in the East Ukraine in the late summer of 1941, however, was Zhitomir. The situation in Zhitomir was especially significant. The first base of OUN-M activity in the eastern Ukraine, it was also the first important city east of the pre-1939 Soviet border open to

---

[48] *OUN u Viini* (The OUN In the War), Information Section of the OUN (UNR), April, 1946, pp. 52-54.

[49] *Ibid.*, p. 51; Report No. 10 of the Representative of the Reichsministerium für die besetzten Ostgebiete at Heeresgruppe Süd, Captain Dr. [Hans] Koch, October 5, 1941, PS 053 (hereafter referred to as PS 053); Chief of the SP and the SD, Report on Events in the USSR, July 1, 1941, pp. 21-22, NO 2950 (hereafter referred to as NO 2950).

nationalist activity. The developments in Zhitomir help to explain the role of the Nationalist movement in the East Ukraine in its "honeymoon" stage.

The embryonic OUN-B "administration" was quickly set aside; apparently the Nationalist sympathizers among the townspeople who had greeted the Bandera organizers now passed over to the OUN-M without much knowledge or concern about the differences between the factions. Although Mel'nyk organizers served as the stimulating force, by far the greater part of the work of building the new administration was performed by local people, such as the head of the *oblast* (district) administration, Alexander Iatseniuk, the chief of the city administration, Pavlovs'kyi, and nearly all of his department heads.[50] A wide variety of nationalist organizations sprang up, including Prosvita, churches, and an active theater. Local artists appeared on Ukrainian programs permitted by the German-controlled broadcasting station. Schools, including two *gimnaziias* and a pedagogical institute, were reopened, and a local school administration was established.[51]

The population of the city sank to 42,000 (including 7,000 Poles and 2,000 Russians) after the deportation of the Jews. However, economic life was stimulated by the reopening of a sugar refinery and other industries; markets were reopened and private trade was encouraged.[52] One hundred and seventy-nine physicians were present, a very high number in proportion to the population.[53] An extremely active youth organization, known, like its counterparts in the West Ukraine, as the Sich, was formed; its activities included sports, choral singing, theatricals, and development of an orchestra.[54]

All of these organizations were under the control of nationalist Ukrainians, although the emphasis appeared to be on the formation of a Ukrainian territorial state which would include all persons, of whatever ethnic origin, living on Ukrainian soil. Thus one of the chief administrative officials, the head of the *raion* administration (i.e., the rural area outside the city) was a Pole, and the director of the economic section of the city administration was a Russian.[55] There appears to have been a large measure of cordiality between the local groups and the OUN representatives coming from the west. Numerous local citizens, mostly young men but including also several administrative officials, joined the Nationalist organization. Support was so strong, in fact, that a new district organization (Kraieva Ekzekutyva) of the Mel'nyk party could be formed, headed by the son of the chief of the *oblast*

---

[50]Fedir (Theodore) S. Iefremenko in *Krakivs'ki Visti*, November 1, 1941, p. 2; 454th Sicherungsdivision, Section VII, Report of October 4, 1941, NOKW 2129 (hereafter referred to as NOKW 2129).

[51]*Ukraïns'ka Diisnist'*, October 1, 1941, p. 1; Iefremenko in *Krakivs'ki Visti*, October 24 and 26, 1941, pp. 2 and 3; *Krakivs'ki Visti*, August 25, 1942, p. 5; *Nastup*, September 6, 1941, p. 5. Cf. Chief of SP and SD, Report of *Einsatzgruppen* and *Kommandos*, No. 187, March 30, 1942 (T 175, Reel 234).

[52]*Ukraïns'ka Diisnist'*, September 15, 1941, p. 1, based on *Ukraïns'ke Slovo* (Zhitomir), August 3, 1941; Iefremenko in *Krakivs'ki Visti*, October 26, 1941, p. 3.

[53]*Krakivs'ki Visti*, October 24, 1941, p. 2; many, however, were apparently Jews who were temporarily spared because of their usefulness (*Krakivs'ki Visti*, November 1, 1941, p. 2).

[54]*Krakivs'ki Visti*, October 26, 1941, p. 3.

[55]*Ibid.*, p. 2; and *Krakivs'ki Visti*, November 1, 1941, p. 2.

administration and another local leader.[56] Generally speaking, OUN-M influence was predominant in the civic life of Zhitomir as the summer of 1941 drew to a close.

The first OUN-M organizers appear to have arrived with the Wehrmacht. Foremost among them was Bohdan Konyk, a Galician, who was especially concerned with police organization. At the end of July, with the help of a young Carpatho-Ukrainian journalist, George Tarkovych, whose numerous articles are a major source for this period, he went with German authorization to a nearby camp of Soviet war prisoners and selected volunteers for the police force.[57] Zakhvalins'kyi, an East Ukrainian by origin who had once been a member of the Ukrainian Republican Army but who had lived for many years as a common worker in France, was made commander. He was an adherent of Mel'nyk. As his deputy, a local nonparty man, Kalenda, was chosen, while the commander's adjutant was a Bukovinian member of the Mel'nyk party.[58]

A major task of the police force was to prepare an organization for installation in Kiev, as soon as the capital should fall into German hands. The same purpose was evident in the formation of a newspaper, *Ukraïns'ke Slovo*; this organ was destined for transfer to Kiev as soon as possible. Consequently, the chief propaganda workers of the eastern group of the OUN-M were active in its creation. Among them were John Rohach, a Carpatho-Ukrainian, Iaroslav Chemeryns'kyi, one of the leading émigré writers, and Peter Oliïnyk. Under their direction, a number of able local journalists were recruited, though not all of them were adherents of the Mel'nyk party.[59]

All of these preparations served as a backdrop for the most important event in the development of the Zhitomir base—the arrival there of the major leaders of the party, who came to take personal direction of the campaign to win the east. Mel'nyk himself remained behind, perhaps because his departure would have aroused German mistrust, but the top level of the Provid was represented by both Senyk and Stsibors'kyi. With them came Dr. Kandyba, the son of a famous East Ukrainian poet, then still living in emigration. Kandyba, best known as "Ol'zhych," was a young man, still in his thirties. Though trained as an archaeologist, for several years he had been very prominent in the ranks of OUN leadership just below the level of the Provid. He was now placed in direct charge of all the advance groups in the East Ukraine.[60]

The three leaders had crossed Galicia in the middle of August, stopping briefly in L'vov. They were careful not to advertise their journey; apparently neither here nor in crossing the border into Volhynia—where a special pass was officially required—were they molested by the Germans. The OUN-M has always denied that there was any agreement with the latter concerning this expedition, but it is highly probable that the Wehrmacht officials in control knew about it, at least unofficially. At any rate, once they had reached

---

[56]Interviews 12, 65; cf. V. Druzhynnyk in *Krakivs'ki Visti*, October 10, 1941, p. 2; *OUN u Viini*, p. 53.

[57]Cf. Tarkovych in *Krakivs'ki Visti*, January 21, 1942, p. 2; Interview 35.

[58]Druzhynnyk in *Krakivs'ki Visti*, October 10, 1941, p. 2; Interview 65.

[59]*Nastup*, November 8, 1941, pp. 3-5; Interviews 3, 65.

[60]*OUN u Viini*, p. 54.

Zhitomir, in the last days of August, the OUN leaders acted quite openly. However, their mission came to an abrupt end.

At seven thirty on the warm summer evening of August 30, as Senyk and Stsibors'kyi, returning from a gathering of the regional police, were approaching the main street intersection of Zhitomir, a young man approached them from behind and fired two or three pistol shots. One penetrated the back of Senyk's neck; he died instantly. Stsibors'kyi was shot through both cheeks and bled to death a few hours later.[61]

The assassin was shot down by Ukrainian and German policemen as he attempted to flee; a vehicle from the German police command came up immediately afterwards and removed the body. Consequently it was difficult to determine who had instigated the murder. The man's passport, however, indicated that his name was Stephen Kozyi, and that he was a West Ukrainian.[62] Almost at once the Mel'nyk adherents accused the OUN-B of having ordered the assassination, asserting that Kozyi was a member of that group. Strong support was given to their allegation by the following circumstances: (1) the bitter attacks leveled by the OUN-B against the two murdered leaders;[63] (2) the fact, attested in a secret report by one of the most competent German specialists on the Ukraine, that Bandera followers distributed leaflets in Kiev justifying the assassinations shortly after they had occurred;[64] (3) the existence of a secret directive by the OUN-B Provid stating that Mel'nyk leaders were not to be allowed to reach Kiev. Mel'nyk adherents at the time referred to a "death sentence" passed on the two leaders "long before" by the Bandera leadership. Discussing entirely separate events, a pro-Bandera writer has recently declared that the rules of the "Second Bandera Congress" of the OUN forbade "Mel'nyk divergentists" working in the Ukraine.[65] That the OUN-M leaders knew the Bandera supporters might resort to violence is fairly certain. OUN-M sympathizers reported soon after the murders that Senyk and Stsibors'kyi had been warned by friends against the dangers from the rival faction.[66] After the war an official OUN-M source quoted a general warning issued by Mel'nyk in the spring of 1941 concerning his opponents' plans to kill OUN-M leaders.[67]

The OUN-B, on the other hand, has always denied complicity in the crime. It asserts that the deed was the work either of German agents, who intended to weaken the OUN-M by depriving it of leaders who had occasionally opposed German policies and who at the same time intended to arouse Ukrainian opinion against the Bandera group, or of Communists intent on causing conflict between the two Nationalist parties. Some credence is given to the latter theory by the fact that immediately after the event the OUN-M accounts described Kozyi as a "hardened Communist," who had, however, turned to the

---

[61]*Nastup*, September 20, 1941, p. 3; and the report of an eyewitness to the crime, Interview 35.

[62]*Nastup*, September 20, 1941, p. 3; Interview 35.

[63]An article by a "nonparty correspondent" in *Nastup*, October 11, 1941, p. 4, declared that Bandera had proclaimed long before that Senyk and Stsibors'kyi would be the first whom he would destroy "in the Ukrainian lands."

[64]PS 053.

[65]*Nastup*, September 20, 1941, p. 1; Chubai, *Reid organizatoriv OUN*, p. 54.

[66]Mykola Halahan in *Ukraïns'kyi Visnyk*, September 28, 1941, p. 2.

[67]This is quoted in *OUN u Vinni*, p. 43.

Bandera party.⁶⁸ It is difficult to tell whether there was any basis for this statement, for the Mel'nyk adherents were endeavoring to link Bandera's followers to Moscow, which, they assert, had inspired these murders as it had those of Petliura and Konovalets'.⁶⁹ Since then, however, there have been rumors that a Ukrainian who was admittedly a former Communist had been in touch with Senyk and Stsibors'kyi, leading to the suspicion that Soviet agents may have planted a betrayer in their entourage.

In view of these discrepancies, it is impossible to be sure who the real authors of the crime were. Knowing the principles and temperament of the Bandera group, however, one must admit that such a deed might not have been repugnant to them. The issuance of a categorical order like that mentioned above, in the headed atmosphere of the period, could very well have led a reckless young member of the OUN-B to the commission of murder. Whether a direct order for the act was given, or whether the consequences of the general order were envisaged by the Bandera Provid at the time it was issued, are questions which can scarcely be answered.

The bloody deed had two immediate results. In the first place it enormously increased the tension between the two factions of the OUN. The Mel'nyk group immediately launched a violent press campaign against the opposing party. It alleged that the OUN-B had carried out a whole series of assassinations of Mel'nyk members in the preceding three months. These are supposed to have included the regional director John Mitsyk and his deputy, Alexander Kuts, in Volhynia, and two leaders of the OUN-M advance groups, Shul'ha and Shubs'kyi.⁷⁰ An editorial in *Nastup* declared that "the time of amnesty for them [the Bandera adherents] is past, their sins cannot be forgiven."⁷¹ Mel'nyk, however, refused to countenance violent reprisals. In the same issue of *Nastup* he laid full responsibility for the crime on the "divergentists," but merely ordered all Ukrainians to refrain from contact with them and expressed the hope that the tragedy would purge Ukrainian life of crime and anarchy.⁷²

Whatever responsibility they may have borne for the assassinations, the Bandera followers were quickly visited with retribution. The Germans arrested all OUN-B members in Zhitomir itself, and a number were executed. During the early part of September, SS *Einsatzgruppen* arrested and executed most of the members of three of the subgroups of the southern task force, at Balta, Nikolaev, and the Crimean city of Dzhankoi.⁷³ In Nikolaev at least, the

---

⁶⁸*Nastup*, September 20, 1941, p. 3.

⁶⁹*Nastup*, October 4, 1941, p. 4; cf. Chief of the SP and the SD, Report on Events in the USSR, No. 101, October 2, 1941, pp. 3-4, NO 3137 (hereafter referred to as NO 3137).

⁷⁰*Nastup*, September 20, 1941, p. 3; *OUN u Viini*, p. 48.

⁷¹*Nastup*, September 20, 1941, p. 3.

⁷²*Ibid.*, p. 1.

⁷³Matla, *Pivdenna pokhidna hrupa*, p. 22. That the arrests were not all part of a concerted plan is indicated by the fact that part were carried out by the Rumanians in their area of occupation. The latter warned the Ukrainians to get out of this area but told them they did not care what they did on the other side of the line of demarcation (cf. Chubai, *Reid organizatoriv OUN*, p. 56). The executions in Zhitomir evidently took place immediately after the assassinations (Ie. Stakhiv, "Borot'ba ukrains'koho narodu," p. 39). On the destruction of the Crimean groups see also Activity and Situation Report No. 6 of the *Einsatzgruppen* of the SP and the SD in the USSR, December, 1941, NO 2659 (hereafter referred to as NO 2659).

OUN-M adherents denounced their pro-Bandera rivals to the Germans.[74] The expedition to the southern peninsula had been a favorite project of the OUN-B, and its complete annihilation was a severe blow to their hopes. Moreover, although some members were able to go underground, OUN-B activity in Kirovograd and Krivoi Rog (Krivyi Rih) and other places in the south-central Ukraine was seriously crippled. Still more disheartening, the sections of the northern task forces which had been heading for Kiev to "proclaim" the Ukrainian state there, as had been done in L'vov, were broken up by the Germans in Vasil'kov (Vasyl'kiv) and Fastov (Fastiv).[75] Some of the members fled to Polessia, where they hid in the forests; a few apparently slipped by secretly into the capital. Significantly for the direction of future operations, the chief remaining center of the OUN-B was in Dniepropetrovsk.

That indignation over the murders prompted this far-reaching repression of the Bandera party is improbable in view of the contempt in which the SS at least held all Ukrainians. Nevertheless, SS and security police reports for this period explicitly state that complete suppression was not undertaken until after "the murders of numerous Mel'nyk supporters" by the OUN-B.[76] Apparently the feeling that drastic action would have to be taken against the Bandera party had been building up in SS circles for some weeks. Indignation over Stets'ko's coup, openly placarded appeals of Klymiv for the secret gathering of arms to be used by a future Ukrainian army, and the stubborn persistence of the task forces in heading east undoubtedly played a role. In addition, the SS had gathered a variety of rumors concerning the group, including the plausible one that they were planning a revolt against the Germans and the implausible story that they were inspired by Communist agents. The basic reason for the occurrence of the repression at this time appears to be the desire of SS *Einsatzgruppen* to make a thorough sweep of the East Ukraine in order to bring it completely under German control and to prepare the western part for the introduction of civil administration.[77] The indignation aroused among Mel'nyk supporters by the assassinations and sympathy shown them by many other nationalist Ukrainians were in all probability merely utilized as support for the ruthless destruction of the other Nationalist party.

While the two powerful Nationalist parties were engaged in feverish activity in the newly opened Ukraine, the UNR was forced to play a secondary role. As was noted in the preceding chapter, the Livyts'kyi group had established contact with an underground group in the eastern part of former Polish Volhynia. This group, which was formed in loose association with the UNR before the outbreak of war as the Ukraïns'ka Natsional'na Vidrodzhennia (Ukrainian National Rebirth), went underground when the Soviet forces arrived. In 1940 one of its members, Taras Borovets', an operator of a stone

---

[74]The accusation to this effect in Matla, *Pivdenna pokhidna hrupa*, p. 22, is confirmed by NO 3137.

[75]PS 053.

[76]PS 3876.

[77]An analysis by the office of the Reichsaussenminister of the contents of the Activity and Situation Reports Nos. 1-5 of the *Einsatzgruppen* of the SP and the SD in the USSR, July 31-September 31, 1941, NO 2650 (hereafter referred to as NO 2650). Cf. Chief of the SP and the SD, Report on Events in the USSR, No. 81, September 12, 1941 (T 175, Reel 233).

quarry in the Kostopol' (Kostopil') area, consulted with Andrew Livyts'kyi, whom he regarded as chief of the Ukrainian state. Borovets' conferred with the president and three of his military advisers (Colonels Valiis'kyi, Sadovs'kyi, and Lytvynenko), drawing up plans for the development of a partisan organization. Borovets' was also in contact with the Mel'nyk Provid member, Colonel Sushko, who promised—despite sharp ideological differences—to direct OUN-M forces in Volhynia to cooperate with Borovets'. The latter returned to Volhynia and began preparations for active operations.[78] The little underground was to be the nucleus of a Polis'ka Sich (Polessian Stronghold) which in turn was to be a territorial subdivision of a Ukrainian Insurrectionary Army (Ukraïns'ka Povstans'ka Armiia—UPA).[79] It could not begin real activity, however, until the German advance removed the terrible burden of Soviet repression. Then Borovets'—who now assumed the *nom de guerre*, Taras Bul'ba, after the legendary leader of a Ukrainian peasant uprising—made contact with the Wehrmacht, securing authorization to develop his Polis'ka Sich as a force to combat Soviet stragglers and partisans.[80] Starting with a single company recruited in the Liudvipol' district, he rapidly developed an irregular force of some 10,000 men.

The great need was for experienced officers. Borovets' himself, like many Ukrainians of his age, had had military service in the Polish army, but only as a noncommissioned officer. Consequently, when a fellow Volhynian member of the OUN-M, Oleh Shtul', offered to arrange for trained officers, he willingly accepted.[81] Whether Borovets' secured authorization from his nominal superiors in the UNR is doubtful, but at this period tension between them and the OUN-M in Poland had greatly declined. In mid-August Borovets' and Shtul' met the OUN-M Provid members Senyk and Stsibors'kyi in L'vov, but the promised officers were slow in reaching northern Volhynia. In the meantime, as best they could, the guerrillas of the Polis'ka Sich cleared the Polessian and northern Volhynian woods of Communist supporters. Since the Wehrmacht had at this point no time to spare for this remote region, it was left almost altogether in Ukrainian hands. Generally, the Wehrmacht authorized lightly armed Ukrainian militias of up to 1 percent of the local population. Specifically, the 213th Security Division, responsible for suppressing Soviet parachutists in the Sarny district, recognized the Sich as the "District Militia

---

[78]See the works by Taras Borovets': *Armiia bez derzhavy: Spohady* (An Army without a State: Reminiscences) (Winnipeg: Volyn', 1981), pp. 273-86; ("Hrytsenko"), "Armiia bez derzhavy" (An Army without a State), *Ukraïns'ki Visti*, December 28, 1950, p. 2; *Zboroina borot'ba Ukraïny (1917-1950)* (The Armed Struggle of the Ukraine [1917-1950]) (1951), pp. 7-10; and Interview 37.

[79]Borovets' and his followers (see preceding note) have always insisted it was they who originated the term "UPA"; he showed me a pass issued by his group in 1941, bearing a stamp "Ukraïns'ka Povstans'ka Armiia." Although some Bandera followers such as Mykola (Nicholas) Lebed', *UPA: Ukraïns'ka Povstans'ka Armiia* (UPA: The Ukrainian Insurrectionary Army) (Presove Biuro UHVR, 1946), p. 26, maintained the OUN-B originated the term, at present many acknowledge the priority of Borovets' (Interview 76).

[80]Commander Army Rear Area 103, Ic, 968/41, "Besondere Anordnungen für die Behandlung der ukrainischen Frage" (T 501, Reel 5); Chief of the SP and the SD, Reports from the Occupied East, No. 4, May 22, 1942, PS 3943 (hereafter referred to as PS 3943, with the date of the individual report).

[81]Interviews 12, 72.

Command." To the Ukrainians under Borovets', the entire triangular region stretching from Pinsk to Olevsk and Mozyr was the "Olevsk Republic."[82]

In November, however, the Germans decided to send in civil administrators; they ordered the dissolution of the "Republic" and the Sich. Borovets' and his men were bitterly disappointed, but they were in no position to offer resistance. Formally, the guerrilla organization was dissolved, but the commander secretly retired with a group of a hundred or so men to his wooded home area between Kostopol' and Liudvipol'. Here an illegal camp was maintained, but evidently until well into 1942 the only overt action was against remaining scattered Soviet partisans. The Germans were aware of the existence of the band and of the fact that it was illegally gathering abandoned Soviet arms, but evidently they did not consider it worthwhile to undertake the dangerous task of entering the woods to crush it as long as it was primarily engaged in fighting their Soviet enemies.[83]

As will be described later, "Bul'ba" and his band were to play a significant role in the development of the nationalist forces at a later stage of the war. In 1941, however, few nationalists paid any attention to the tiny group of sylvan guerrillas. At that time, the only active elements appeared to be the two factions of the OUN.

---

[82]Borovets', *Zboroina borot'ba*, p. 10. Security Division 213 reported on August 25 and 31, 1941, that close cooperation with Ukrainian militia had foiled Soviet parachutists' efforts (T 315, Reel 1633).

[83]Borovets', *Zboroina borot'ba*, p. 10; Interview 12; PS 3943, No. 4, May 22, 1942.

V
Repression and Reichskommissariat

The drastic measures taken by the Germans against the Bandera forces seemingly had cleared the field for the activity of the OUN-M. Like the apparent advantage gained by Bandera's group in the early summer, this opportunity soon proved to be an illusion. For some two months, however, Mel'nyk's adherents were able to carry on far-reaching activities in the central Ukraine. Since the beginning of this period coincided with the capture of Kiev by German troops, and the Ukraine's second city, Kharkov, fell before it ended, the interlude was of great importance in enabling the OUN-M to spread the doctrine of Nationalism in the former Soviet area.

On September 19, 1941, the Germans occupied Kiev. Two or three days later, the first groups of Mel'nyk adherents arrived from the base in Zhitomir, and rapidly set about organizing national life in the city.[1] This was a difficult task at best because the Soviet forces had inflicted severe injuries on the city before leaving. A large part of this damage consisted of physical destruction, especially of industrial facilities and means of communication.[2] Even more serious from the point of view of rebuilding an anti-Communist, national civil life was the wholesale deportation of intelligentsia. For example, only five of the members of the Ukrainian Academy of Sciences were left, the others having been evacuated to what the Communist government called the "new cultural capital" of the Ukraine, Ufa, in the Bashkir Autonomous Soviet Socialist Republic.[3]

In addition to difficulties presented by the great gaps in material and human resources, there was a continued danger from the "booby traps" of hidden explosive mines and camouflaged Communist agents. The latter were not discovered for some time, but on the fifth day after the German occupation, a large number of mines blew up a considerable section of the center of the city,

---

[1]Interview 65.

[2]Leontii Forostivs'kyi, *Kyïv pid vorozhymy okupatsiiamy* (Kiev under Enemy Occupation) (Buenos Aires: Mykola Denysiuk, 1952), pp. 21-23.

[3]*Krakivs'ki Visti*, October 16, 1941, p. 2, and February 25, 1942, p. 4; *Ukraïns'ka Diisnist'*, November 1, 1941, p. 1.

thoroughly disrupting the work of the Germans and Ukrainians in reestablishing an ordered pattern of life.[4]

Immediately after arriving in Kiev, a council of the Mel'nyk leaders—Konyk and Captain Suliatits'kyi, who came in the Wehrmacht service, and Iaroslav Haivaz and Roman Bidar, who apparently came without official authorization—decided to install a *Hifsbürgermeister*, or chief of the municipal administrative apparatus. They chose Alexander Ohloblyn, a well-known historian of the Soviet period. The Wehrmacht authorities readily accepted the council's nomination,[5] an indication of the close cooperation of the OUN-M with the army authorities in the East Ukraine at that time.

Ohloblyn's authority, however, was soon to prove illusory. Volodymyr Bahazii, an instructor from the pedagogical institute, had been appointed as his deputy. Unlike Ohloblyn, Bahazii had greeted the Nationalist leaders and immediately sought to identify himself with them. They soon learned that he was highly ambitious and that he did not stop at attacking his nominal superior, whom he accused of Russophile tendencies.[6] Apparently Bahazii's loyalty to the OUN and his energy in carrying out the reorganization of city life made him indispensable. At any rate, Professor Ohloblyn was soon pushed into the background,[7] and at the end of October, after a disagreement with the German authorities concerning measures to be taken to enhance the welfare of Kiev's citizens, he resigned.[8] Bahazii then became the chief of administration.[9] Having achieved this post, he repaid the organization which had assisted him by using his influence to secure the adherence to the OUN-M of the most important officials.[10]

While most of the economic and cultural divisions of the city government were left in the hands of local men, the OUN forces took care to organize the most important branches—propaganda and police—under their own followers. Zakhvalins'kyi was brought from Zhitomir to take command of the police units, but after a short period, in which his alleged incompetence and dissolute life made him objectionable to his party, he was replaced by one of the Galician leaders, Roman Bidar. Kandyba soon arrived to take charge of propaganda activity. With him came the staff of *Ukraïns'ke Slovo*, headed by John Rohach. The newspaper was to be printed in Kiev, but the destruction of the principal press by the explosions forced the editors to continue publication for some weeks in Zhitomir.[11]

---

[4]Forostivs'kyi, *Kyïv pid vorozhymy okupatsiiamy*, p. 24; PS 053.

[5]Interviews 56, 65.

[6]Interviews 56, 65. Chief of the SP and the SD, Report of *Einsatzgruppen* and *Kommandos*, No. 191, April 10, 1942, pp. 41 ff. (T 175, Reel 235), alleges that Bahazii directed the "Jewish" school in Kiev and tutored Khrushchev's children under Soviet rule, assisted nationalists later.

[7]This is evident even in contemporary published accounts. Cf. *Nastup*, November 8, 1941, pp. 3-5, containing an article written by Petro (Peter) Oliinyk earlier in Kiev, in which Bahazii is described as the "business manager." *Ukraïns'kyi Visnyk*, October 26, 1941, p. 6, described a city administration department heads meeting presided over by Bahazii.

[8]Interview 56.

[9]Bahazii assumed the post on November 1 (*Nastup*, December 20, 1941, p. 2).

[10]Interviews 53, 65.

[11]Iurii Tarkovych in *Krakivs'ki Visti*, January 21, 1942, p. 2; *Nastup*, November 8, 1941, p. 3; Interview 65.

Having captured Kiev, the German armies rapidly pushed on to the east, taking with them most of the interpreters and advisers who had formed an essential part of the OUN-M "conquest" of Zhitomir and Kiev. By the end of October, they had reached Kharkov, where Konyk took the lead in propaganda work. He and his assistants succeeded in recruiting a considerable number of the local intelligentsia for their organization but, as will be shown later, failed in their attempt to attain a high degree of success similar to that in Kiev.[12]

Lest repeated reference to collaboration of the Mel'nyk forces with the Wehrmacht lead to an exaggerated conception of the role of the OUN-M in the operations of the German army, it should be pointed out that the latter employed many Slavic interpreters and advisers in addition to the Mel'nyk followers. Some of these were Ukrainians, of all political persuasions, including Bandera supporters. Strong efforts were made to get rid of the latter after the decision to suppress their party, but for a considerable time this aim was not fully achieved. Moreover, there were numerous Het'manites and followers of the UNR. Among the latter, for example, was Peter Sahaidachnyi, who had charge of the initial operation of the most important Ukrainian newspapers.[13] Others were Russian émigrés, and many were Baltic Germans who had a command of the Russian language. The aim of the Wehrmacht was to establish a peaceful, orderly area behind the front as quickly as possible; employment of qualified persons, regardless of their political orientation, was necessary in order to do this. It is of course true that certain individual officers favored the Ukrainians,[14] but the ascendancy of the Mel'nyk group in this period was primarily due to its ability to profit from the absence of any other organized party with regular contact with the local population.

The real fate of Nationalist activity in the Ukraine, however, was being decided in Berlin, in quarters remote from the Wehrmacht officers who pursued the policy just described. Months before the outbreak of war, Hitler had decided to form a special agency for the affairs of the territories to be conquered from the Soviet Union. This department was called the Reichsministerium für die besetzten Ostgebiete (Reich Ministry for the Occupied Eastern Territories); it was placed under the direction of Alfred Rosenberg. Rosenberg, a Balt by origin, and the principal theoretician of the National Socialist Party, had long been interested in the peoples of the Soviet Union. He was a strong believer in the policy of weakening Russia, whether it remained Communist or not. Consequently, he regarded with favor Ukrainian nationalist efforts to separate from Russia, so long as the groups involved did not threaten other German aims.

At the same time that the Ostministerium, as the new department was often called, was initiated, Hitler decided to create a number of huge satrapies in the eastern area; chief among them was the Reichskommissariat Ukraine. This region was to be under the supervision of an official with a large measure

---

[12]See Chapter X.

[13]Interview 79.

[14]Notably Dr. Hans Koch and his collaborator in the Abwehr, Professor Oberländer.

of authority, but subject to Rosenberg in matters of broad policy.[15] Rosenberg realized that this vague directive would mean little unless he could count on the cooperation of the man chosen to head the Reichskommissariat. Consequently, he voiced an alarmed protest when Erich Koch, Gauleiter of East Prussia, and already widely known for his stubbornness and brutality, was suggested for the post. Since Hitler, evidently regarding Rosenberg as an impractical dreamer, wanted a determined and ruthless man in the Ukraine, Koch was nevertheless appointed.[16]

This appointment was the harbinger of worse defeats for Rosenberg's "mild" policy toward the Ukrainians. Another aspect of Nazi policy, however, aroused immediate indignation among the Ukrainian nationalists. This was a decision to keep east Galicia in the "German settlement area," i.e., to attach it to the Generalgouvernement rather than to the future Reichskommissariat. The immediate ground for this partition of the Ukrainian ethnographic territory was the desire to maintain a direct connection between the Greater Reich and Rumania, about whose continued loyalties the Nazi leaders harbored strong doubts.[17] However, a few weeks later the "unreliable" Danubian kingdom was permitted to administer all of the Ukrainian territory between the Dniester and the Southern Bug.[18] The Rumanians obviously intended eventually to incorporate the area, which they called Transnistria, into their state. Since most Ukrainian nationalist circles already hated Rumania, it is understandable that this second amputation of Ukrainian ethnographic territory was especially painful, even though the region was near the bottom of the scale of definitely Ukrainian areas in cultural development and national consciousness.[19]

While Ukrainian territory was being partitioned, a still more serious danger for the nationalist cause was shaping up. An exception to the authority of the Ostministerium in the occupied areas was the police power, which was lodged in Heinrich Himmler's hands. From the beginning of the campaign the Reichsführer SS had been charged with "establishing order" in the conquered areas in the east. The instruments employed for this task were *Einsatzgruppen*, task forces consisting of specially selected, ruthless police officials, headed by SS officers from Himmler's inner circle. During the stabilization period, these

---

[15]Chancellery Director Lammers to Rosenberg, July 18, 1941, transmitting Führerbefehl of July 17, 1941, NG 1280 (hereafter referred to as NG 1280). For a comprehensive discussion of the evolution of German policy see Alexander Dallin, *German Rule in Russia, 1941-1945: A Study of Occupation Policies* (London: Macmillan & Co. Ltd., 1957).

[16]Memorandum, Führerhauptquartier, July 16, 1941, PS 1221 (hereafter referred to as PS 1221).

[17]*Ibid.*

[18]PS 197. At the conference of July 16 (*ibid.*) it had been tentatively decided to give Rumania only a slight territorial increase east of the pre-1939 border of the Dniester River; the decision was altered sometime within the next six weeks.

[19]On August 31, *Ukraïns'kyi Visnyk* had the temerity to attack the decision openly, raising the question, "Is it possible that Ukrainian land beyond the Dniester, soaked with Cossack blood, can be transferred to Rumanian administration?" On the same page the UNO organ criticized the annexation of Galicia to the Generalgouvernement, as not corresponding to "the principle of nationality" (*Ukraïns'kyi Visnyk*, August 31, 1941, p. 3). Within the next week, several branches of the UNO in Germany sent petitions directly to Hitler, protesting the transfers of Ukrainian territory; for petitions from the groups in Pilsen, Berlin, and Luxemburg, see Occ E-4 (8), in Yiddish Scientific Institute (hereafter referred to as Occ E-4 [8]).

commanders were given powers within the broad range of "pacifying activities" in the rear areas, superseding those of all military commanders. These activities included especially the extermination of the Jewish population and the liquidation of all Communist organizations; "kommissars" and NKVD officials were to be shot outright.

The causes for conflict between the *Einsatzgruppen* and the Ukrainian nationalists have been suggested in the preceding chapter. At first the Mel'nyk group was spared because it was thought to be politically impotent.[20] During the summer the SP claimed that "the splinter group under Colonel Andrew Mel'nyk, predominantly émigrés, no longer has any political significance," and regarded the OUN-M as a useful counterweight to Bandera's organization. By early November, 1941, however, SP reports were warning that Mel'nyk's group could become dangerous if it was left entirely unwatched because of the struggle against the Bandera party.[21] As soon as the OUN-M revealed ability to build an organization in the East Ukraine, it too was crushed.

The first major incident of repression against the Mel'nyk forces occurred on November 21, an important anniversary for Ukrainian nationalists. On that date, in 1921, Tiutiunnyk's band, one of the last important nationalist forces to penetrate the Soviet Ukraine, had made a "last stand" near the little town of Bazar on the edge of the wooded region north of the Kiev-Zhitomir line. The OUN-M now decided to make this anniversary the occasion for a great patriotic demonstration, which a participant has since described in considerable detail.[22] A large group of organizers was sent in from Zhitomir; on the appointed day many thousands streamed to Bazar for commemorative ceremonies. This demonstration of the strength of Ukrainian nationalist sentiment greatly alarmed the Germans, especially since the affair had been the work of an organized group which had secured the complete cooperation of the local Ukrainian authorities. The chief of the Bazar *raion* addressed the crowd, the police under the command of an old Ukrainian officer stood guard, and the police band provided music. All of these features must have indicated to the suspicious German police authorities that the Ukrainians had deliberately flaunted their independence. The reprisals were quick, and crushing. An inquiry was instituted at Bazar, which led to the arrest of several of the organizers; the trail led back to Zhitomir, where about two dozen OUN members, including one of the leaders of Ekzekutyva, were shot. The younger Iatseniuk and Anthony Baranivs'kyi, the remaining OUN leaders there, escaped only by fleeing to the woods. OUN-M influence in Zhitomir was sharply reduced, although few, apparently, of the administrative officials who had sympathized with it were molested.[23]

In the absence of direct evidence, it would be unsafe to conclude that the Bazar demonstration was the cause of the further attacks which were now carried out against the Mel'nyk group. At about the same time, however, drastic

---

[20] NO 2650.

[21] Chief of the SP and the SD, Report of *Einsatzgruppen* and *Kommandos*, No. 133, November 14, 1941, p. 31, NO 2825 (hereafter referred to as NO 2825).

[22] P. Dub, "V rokovyny demonstratsiï v Bazari (spomyn)" (On the Anniversary of the Demonstration in Bazar [In Memoriam]), *Za Samostiinist'* (November, 1946), pp. 8-11; see also *OUN u Viini* (The OUN in the War), Information Section of the OUN (UNR), April, 1946, pp. 69-72.

[23] Alexander Iatseniuk, for example, remained chief of the *oblast* administration.

repressions of the Nationalists occurred in numerous cities, resulting in the destruction of the small Bukovinian expedition in Nikolaev and of groups in Kamenets-Podolsk (Kam'ianets'-Podil's'k), Chernigov (Chernihiv), and Poltava.[24] The chief repressive campaign was reserved for the capital. A number of OUN-M activities there, without being considered important enough to require drastic action, had contributed to a feeling of irritation on the part of the Himmler henchmen. A famous poetess, Olena Teliha, had created an unauthorized Nationalist literary periodical, *Litavry*. A youth group Sich was considered potentially dangerous. A Ukrainian National Council (Rada) had been formed by the Mel'nyk group to act as a symbol of unity in the East Ukraine and, they hoped, eventually to become the central organ of nationalist activities. The risks involved in such activity, in view of the attitude of the real rulers of Germany, were fully understood by the Wehrmacht officers, one of whom advised the Ukrainians to transform the Council into a more innocuous Aid Committee. When this advice was refused, the Council was formally dissolved (November 17), and went underground.[25] The SP authorities were aware of the organ's continued existence, and while they regarded it as too insignificant for immediate suppression, it increased their distrust of the Nationalists.[26] With this background, one can understand why the first blow fell upon the legal, but extremely Nationalist, *Ukraïns'ke Slovo*. Its large circulation — over 50,000[27] — gave it, in the eyes of the police, the potentiality of dangerous influence. Moreover, the editorial staff of this organ, as was previously noted, was composed very largely of West Ukrainians and old émigrés; these elements were regarded as especially dangerous by the SS leadership.

Unfortunately for the Nationalist cause, during their two months' activity in Kiev the newcomers had also lost ground in local opinion. Some of the antipathy which they aroused stemmed from the fact that they were outsiders; even those who had been born in the East Ukraine or were like Kandyba, whose father had been born there, had long been out of touch with the local population. With some justification, because they were better organized, had clearer concepts of what they wanted, and were used to displaying initiative, the OUN group took a leading, occasionally a monopolistic part in municipal activities. As was inevitable, they sometimes exhibited an attitude of superiority; even when they behaved more tactfully, many local inhabitants nevertheless were inclined to suspect that they harbored such an attitude. Their presence in municipal offices, even when they were on a plane of equality with local officeholders, was bound to lead to some friction. Moreover, emphasis on the principle of integral nationalism meant the neglect of social welfare and civil rights questions which were of great concern to the local population after twenty years of Soviet rule. The "leader principle," which was expressed in the East Ukraine in as extreme terms as Mel'nyk ever permitted it in the

---

[24]*OUN u Viini*, p. 72.

[25]*Ibid.*, p. 68.

[26]PS 3876.

[27]*Krakivs'kyi Visti*, March 15, 1942, p. 5. The Reichsministerium für die besetzten Ostgebiete reported (EAP 99/63, T 454, Reel 13), probably in 1942, that the Kiev *Poslednye Novosti* was the only Russian-language newspaper in "core Ukraine," praising it for "moderation," despite "occasional Panslav tendencies."

emigration, was alien to the native inhabitants. The slogan "Petliura, Konovalets', Mel'nyk—three names, one idea" was at first meaningless to the average East Ukrainian, since the second and third of these names were unknown to him. When their meaning was explained, the phrase signified to many that after Petliura's death the nationalist movement had fallen into the hands of leaders from the half-alien West Ukraine.[28]

All of these irritations might have been accepted, however, had it not been for an ideological theme which resulted in more practical discomfort. The Nationalist creed required emphasis on the "purity" of the Ukrainian people. According to the OUN leaders' belief, this "purity" had been endangered by the intrusion of Russian elements—the physical immigration of Russians, who had become especially numerous in Kiev bureaucratic and intellectual circles, and the penetration of Russian influences into Ukrainian culture and speech. The extent of this penetration will be discussed in a later chapter; it is necessary to point out its importance here, however, in order to understand the Kiev reaction to OUN policy. The Nationalists set about radically "purging" alien aspects of life in the city. A certain number of local Ukrainians accepted this campaign enthusiastically, sometimes carrying it further than the newcomers themselves. Others, although Ukrainian by background, had long been used to employing the Russian language and associating freely with persons of Russian ethnic origin. Consequently, the "purifying" process meant in many cases serious disruption of their accepted way of living and social relationships.

Because of the extreme importance of this factor it is worth describing in some detail a case which provides a striking illustration of the Nationalist psychology during this period. It is contained in the diary of a prominent Kiev author, Arkadii Liubchenko, who was evacuated by the Soviet forces but managed to remain in Kharkov until the German arrival. He then made contact with the Mel'nyk groups (which, as was previously pointed out, pursued the same policy there as in Kiev). Always nationalist, he soon became an enthusiastic convert to the creed of integral nationalism. In December, through his association with the Nationalists, he obtained a post on the Kharkov newspaper, *Nova Ukraïna*. Shortly afterwards, a Kharkov writer named Filipov appeared in the editorial offices; he told Liubchenko that he had prepared an article on the evils of the Communist regime which he wished to publish. When Liubchenko turned it down because it was written in Russian, Filipov protested that his mother had been Ukrainian and that he would submit the article in Ukrainian, as the question of language was indifferent to him. This brought the sneering reply that real Ukrainians, such as those dominating *Nova Ukraïna*, could have nothing to do with one who could not make

---

[28]Surviving OUN-M publications of this period are rare, many existing only in private collections. *Ukraïns'kyi Visnyk* of September 28, 1941, p. 3 contains a reprint of a leaflet distributed in the East Ukraine describing Mel'nyk as the successor of Konovalets', who in turn was a successor of Petliura, "killed by the Jew Shvartsvart." For a criticism of OUN propaganda in the East Ukraine during this period, and notes on the reaction of the local population, see the account of the East Ukrainian émigré Fedir (Theodore) S. Iefremenko in *Krakivs'ki Visti*, November 1, 1941, p. 2. Iuryi (George) Boiko, *U siaivi nashoho Kyeva: "Ukraïns'ke Slovo" u Kyevi v 1941 rotsi* (in the Radiance of our Kiev: *Ukraïns'ke Slovo* in Kiev in 1941) (Munich: Tsitsero, 1955) is a substantial collection of articles reprinted from the major OUN-M organ in the East Ukraine during 1941. Probably it has been edited considerably, but some articles (for example, "In the Ukraine—Speak Ukrainian," pp. 111-12) are revealing.

up his mind whether he was a Ukrainian or a Russian, since such a person was an "internationalist" just like the Bolsheviks.²⁹ It may easily be imagined what effect such ideas had upon the rebuffed applicant. This is especially the case, since work for an organ like the newspaper was for many not merely a matter of prestige, or even of expression of opinion, but of life and death. With the rapidly deteriorating food situation in Kiev and Kharkov, employment by an agency which was recognized by the Germans, and hence able to issue ration cards and provide a small income, was indispensable for most intellectuals.³⁰

In view of these circumstances, it is not surprising that the German enemies of the Nationalist movement felt that the time was ripe to destroy its prestige by an attack on its principal organ. On December 12, 1941, the SP force seized *Ukraïns'ke Slovo* and arrested all the leading editorial workers, including Rohach, Chemeryns'kyi and Oliinyk.³¹ Kandyba, too, was arrested, but by native police in a city *raion* (ward) controlled by the OUN-M; this circumstance allowed him to escape.³²

Two days later the newspaper reappeared, as *Nove Ukraïns'ke Slovo*, but with a quite different editorial policy. The new editor was Constantine Shtepa, acting rector of the University of Kiev. Of Ukrainian origin, he had been an officer in the tsarist army and, although strongly anti-Soviet, remained a pronounced Russian patriot, desiring the acceptance of the Russian culture and language throughout the Ukraine and the maintenance of governmental ties with Moscow. Consequently, he was a bitter enemy of the Ukrainina nationalist movement.³³ The first issue of his paper contained an article, inspired by the Germans, but acceptable to Shtepa, in which the Nationalists were vigorously attacked for turning what "should have been an informational journal into an organ of their group." The Nationalists, it explained, had refused to heed German warnings that the paper must serve the whole community; consequently Shtepa had taken charge to "popularize" it. What this meant, was clarified by an article on the second page which demanded "work instead of politics."³⁴

Under Shtepa's administration, *Nove Ukraïns'ke Slovo* became extremely subservient to the Germans. In part this was due to the extreme severity and alertness of the German censorship; the editor himself was compelled to publish over his own signature articles composed by the German propaganda section, although German records show that he vigorously and courageously criticized Nazi policy in private discussions with German officials.³⁵

---

²⁹Arkadii Liubchenko, *Shchodennyk* (Diary), Vol. I, ed. M. Dmytrenko (Toronto: Novi Dni, 1951), p. 25.

³⁰Interview 59. Liubchenko himself (Liubchenko, *Shchodennyk*, p. 60 ff.), when the shoe was on the other foot and he was compelled to seek work in Kiev, found this to be the case.

³¹*OUN u Viini*, p. 73.

³²L. Dniprova in *Ukraïns'ke Slovo* (Paris), June 18, 1950, p. 3. Chief of the SP and the SD, Reports from the Occupied Eastern Territories, No. 32, December 4, 1942, p. 5 (T 175, Reel 236).

³³Record of the interrogation of an editor in Kiev, early 1943, who was a specialist in ancient history, the author of *Die Völkerwanderung* and *Das römische Recht* (CXLVa 78, in Centre de Documentation Juive Contemporaine, hereafter referred to as CXLVa 78). The only person fitting this description is Constantine Shtepa.

³⁴These articles are reprinted in *Ukraïns'ka Diisnist'*, January 5, 1942, p. 2.

³⁵CXLVa 78.

The nationalists were deeply antagonized by these articles which attacked the foundations of their movement by denying the historical equality of Ukrainian culture with the Russian. Shtepa apparently went far beyond even the Communist newspapers in this respect, reverting to the "Little Russian" tradition which was so abhorrent to all nationalist Ukrainians.[36] However sincere his Russian nationalism may have been, for a man of Ukrainian origin, writing in the Ukrainian language, in the Ukrainian capital, to denounce the Ukrainian nationalist movement could only be regarded in nationalist circles as an act of high treason.

During the late autumn, while the *Einsatzgruppen* were crushing the OUN-M groups, the administration of the Reichskommissariat was being established throughout the "Right Bank" Ukraine, while the area east of the Dnieper remained under Wehrmacht control. According to the plans laid in the Ostministerium, the Reichskommissariat Ukraine was eventually to include all of the pre-1941 Soviet Ukraine except Transnistria, Galicia, and the areas acquired by the USSR from Rumania in 1940. In addition, it was to have its boundary extended roughly due east in a line passing south of Kursk to the Volga, where it was to embrace the Volga German Autonomous Soviet Socialist Republic.[37] In the northwest the Reichskommissariat was to embrace approximately two tiers of *raions* in the southern part of the pre-1941 Belorussian Soviet Socialist Republic, including Brest, Pinsk, and the greater part of the railroad connecting these towns with Gomel.[38]

By the end of August, the process of pacifying the western part of this vast area had gone so far that a conference between Koch's and Rosenberg's officials on the one hand, and representatives of the army on the other, could plan the transfer to the Reichskommissariat.[39] This was accomplished gradually in the next three months.[40]

The introduction of the Reichskommissariat did not change the general basis of the provisional organization established by the Wehrmacht.[41] However, it introduced an entirely new spirit. It brought under strict control many

---

[36]*Biuleten'* (Bulletin), No. 9-10 of the OUN-B (late 1942), pp. 14-15. This clandestine publication was furnished me by Nicholas Lebed'.

[37]Memorandum, Die neuen Ostgebiete, June 16, 1941, PS 1033 (hereafter referred to as PS 1033); Rosenberg to Alfred Meyer, October 20, 1941, PS 1057 (hereafter referred to as PS 1057).

[38]PS 1057; Memorandum, Die Zivilverwaltung im besetzten Osten, Part II, Reichskommissariat Ukraine, PS 702 (hereafter referred to as PS 702).

[39]PS 197.

[40]Former Polish Volhynia was transferred as early as the end of August (*Deutsche Ukraine Zeitung*, January 24, 1942, p. 3). For greater detail on German policy discussed in the following pages, see Dallin, *German Rule in Russia*.

[41]There had already been set up an army administration composed of *Ortskommandanturen* (local commands) and *Feldkommandanturen* (regional commands). These military government offices had established order and begun the work of rebuilding economic and social life. Alongside them had already been installed police groups, recruited and directed by the Wehrmacht Abwehr but composed primarily of Ukrainians, as previously described. These, however, were being brought under the control of the SS police agencies. Moreover, the Wirtschaftstab-Ost had installed a Wirtschafts-Inspektion Süd, with a network of economic officers including especially the *Landwirtschaftsführer* (*La-Führer*, agricultural director) in each *raion*, who were charged with directing the economy in accordance with German needs. Cf. PS 053.

aspects of Ukrainian life in which the Wehrmacht had left a relatively free hand to the inhabitants. The entire "Right Bank" was divided into five *Generalbezirke* with headquarters in Rovno, Zhitomir, Kiev, Nikolaev, and Dniepropetrovsk.[42] Under each *Generalkommissar* were about twenty *Gebietskommissare*, each of whom governed a *Kreisgebiet*, comprising an average of four *raions*. The Ukrainian administration operated in general only at this lowest level.[43] There were elders or *starostas* in charge of each village and a Ukrainian chief of the *raion* administration. While there were Ukrainians above this level in consultative or specialist posts,[44] there was no unified framework of native administration, with the exception of the towns where there was a Ukrainian chief of administration, regardless of the size of the place involved. In the larger cities, which were not included in *Kreisgebiete*, the Ukrainian "mayors," however, were closely subjected to German *Stadtkommissare*.

Just as important as his administrative structure, was Koch's personal attitude toward the Ukrainians he was to govern. To him, they were simply an inferior race, a colonial people to be exploited for Germany's interests. "They are too inferior to be compared with Germans,"[45] and "the least German worker is worth a thousand times more than the population there"[46] are typical expressions of his attitude. Consequently, this former petty railway official felt highly offended when the Ukrainian intelligentsia endeavored to organize a national life of its own. The whole tone of his administration implied that the Ukrainians were a sort of child-people, which could not achieve any degree of culture worthy of consideration; those who endeavored to do so were simply half-educated émigré agitators who must be dealt with severely, so that the simple but useful "peasants" (i.e., all non-agitators) would not be disturbed in their task of producing for the Germans.

---

[42]PS 702. The initial organization of areas west of the Dnieper included the Soviet *oblasts* of Rovno, Volhynia, Kamenets-Podolsk, Zhitomir, Vinnitsa, Kiev, Kirovograd, and parts of Nikolaev, Dniepropretrovsk, Poltava, Zaporozh'e, Pinsk, and Brest. On September 1, 1942, the remaining parts of the Dniepropetrovsk, Poltava, and Zaporozh'e *oblasts* east of the Dnieper were transferred to the Reichskommissariat. Somewhat earlier a sixth *Generalbezirk*, Taurien, had been formed, to include the southern parts of the Zaporozh'e and Nikolaev *oblasts* (cf. *Deutsche Ukraine Zeitung*, September 2, 1943, p. 3).

[43]There was, however, an advisory council at the *Generalbezirk* level in at least one instance— Zhitomir (cf. *Deutsche Ukraine Zeitung*, February 25, 1942, p. 2).

[44]The adjective "Ukrainian" is used by the Germans to describe these officials, but it refers merely to persons resident within the territorial limits of the Ukraine. Actually, many were Russian, and a special effort was made by the Wehrmacht to recruit ethnic Germans (PS 197; Extracts from the Situation Report of the commander of Heeresgebiet B, Abteilung VII, October 10, 1942, PS 051; hereafter referred to as PS 051), although the latter turned out frequently to be Communist spies deliberately left behind by the Soviet regime (Report of the representative of the Reichsministerium für die besetzten Ostgebiete at Heeresgruppe Mitte, December 15, 1941, PS 1682; hereafter referred to as PS 1682). Even when the *Volksdeutsche* were anti-Communist, they were frequently disliked by the Ukrainian Nationalists as Russophiles.

[45]Koch to Rosenberg, March 16, 1943, PS 192 (hereafter referred to as PS 192).

[46]Report of Oberkommando der Heeresgruppe B to Oberkommando des Heeres, Generalstab des Heeres, Generalquartiermeister, Abteilung Kriegsverwaltung, April 1, 1943, PS 1130 (hereafter referred to as PS 1130), is based on an oral report of Oberkriegsverwaltungsrat Dr. Classen who was present at the Nazi Party meeting in Kiev (March 5, 1943) in which Koch made the remark.

One of the first results of Koch's determination to crush all centers of autonomous life was the destruction of the Nationalist forces remaining "above ground" in Kiev. After the suppression of the West Ukrainian force, there was still a large group of East Ukrainian supporters of the Mel'nyk organization who openly carried on a limited activity. Its chief, Bahazii, was just as nationalist as the arrested West Ukrainians. A characteristic instance of his enthusiastic lack of caution occurred about the time that he became mayor. A group of foreign journalists, including several Germans, visited Kiev. In their presence, he expressed his loyalty to the OUN, praising Konovalets' and Mel'nyk as totalitarians, and saying, "The eyes of all Ukrainians are turned toward Mel'nyk." A German officer who was present begged the journalists not to report this remark, knowing it would inflame the Nazi chieftains.[47]

Although Erich Koch and his assistants were in many respects ridiculously ignorant of the true nature of Ukrainian life in Kiev, in view of Bahazii's frankness it was inevitable that they should come to see that he was working for Ukrainian ends, rather than docilely following German orders. Very probably the anti-Nationalist forces on the staff of *Nove Ukraïns'ke Slovo* played a part in stirring up antagonism to the city administration. For example, the paper printed an article by an employee of a municipal office criticizing the émigrés who had returned to Kiev. He complained that thirteen out of forty employees in his section were émigrés who were paid higher salaries than the local officials, although the former were no better qualified and had smaller families.[48] In view of Koch's and his minions' bitter hostility toward émigrés, such remarks must have encouraged them to feel that the Germans would lose no popularity by extinguishing the remaining outside influence in Kiev life.

They were, however, scarcely the real motives behind Bahazii's arrest in early February, 1942. Apparently the German official responsible for the Ukrainian leader's downfall was Generalkommissar Magunia, one of Koch's closest collaborators among the officials of the Reichskommissariat. He worked, of course, in close coordination with the *Sicherheitspolizei*; the charges against Bahazii in the police report revolve entirely around his nationalist activities.[49] For example, the head of the section on Religious Confessions is alleged to have threatened the Russophile bishop of Kiev, Panteleimon. Another charge concerned Bahazii's "misappropriation of German property," but the specific act seems to have been his sale of petroleum products (probably of Soviet origin, confiscated by the Germans) to aid the nationalist cause. He was charged, correctly, with being a leader of the underground. OUN-M, and a number of organizations controlled by the Nationalists were declared, also with apparent accuracy, to be working under his direction. Probably the charge which carried the greatest weight in the minds of the German officials, however, was that he had endeavored to secure control of the Ukrainian

---

[47] Whether they ever actually saw the report is questionable since it was apparently printed only in an Italian paper and by the Ukrainian press (*Nastup*, December 6, 1941, p. 1, quoting *La Stampa* [Milan], November 1, 1941).

[48] *Nove Ukraïns'ke Slovo*, January 3, 1942 (reprinted in *Ukraïns'ka Diisnist'*, February 1, 1942, p. 2). A major charge against Bahazii was that he maintained too large a staff in the city administration and paid them too much (PS 192).

[49] Chief of the SP and the SD, Report on Events in the USSR, No. 191, April 10, 1942, NO 3256 (hereafter referred to as NO 3256).

police. As has been previously indicated, the OUN-M did indeed control most of the Ukrainian police in Kiev, but Bahazii was scarcely responsible personally for this. Altogether, the motives behind the overthrow of Bahazii were those which prevailed everywhere in the destruction of Nationalist groups in the Reichskommissariat. The action suited Erich Koch's policy completely; he defended it vigorously against Rosenberg's criticism, displaying his own arrogant stupidity by adding a few incredible charges of his own to the grounds presented in the SP report.[50]

The repression of Nationalist forces in Kiev extended far beyond the person of Bahazii. The arrests were concentrated in two groups: the surviving literary leaders of the OUN-M League of Ukrainian Writers, headed by Olena Teliha and a young Carpatho-Ukrainian writer, John Irliavs'kyi; and the Sich, headed by a young East Ukrainian journalist, John Koshyk, also an OUN-M member.[51] Altogether, the executions (which followed quickly after the arrests in most cases) accounted for about forty persons,[52] a large number of whom were medical students organized in the Sich.[53] In addition, several of the principal agencies of national life in Kiev were forced to cease operation, including the Ukrainian National Council. Even Prosvita was suspect and was closed for a while.[54]

These arrests did not completely stamp out the efforts to develop nationalism in Kiev. The underground OUN-M (as well as remnants of an OUN-B conspiratorial group) did what they could to stimulate nationalist feeling. Likewise, the city administration was by no means so drastically altered as had been the editorial staff of the newspaper. The Germans were probably not anxious to destroy all outlets for Ukrainian nationalist aspirations. Rosenberg, in spite of his minor influence, exercised some restraint in this respect, and Koch himself denied being anti-Ukrainian.[55] Undoubtedly his contempt for all Slavs led him to place the Ukrainians and the Russians on an even plane; his favoring of the Russophile element in the journalistic field had very possibly been accidental, or at least merely an effort to establish between the groups a balance which could be manipulated by the Germans.

The drop in prestige of the OUN-M was both sharp and sustained, however, since repression of its groups continued throughout the Reichskommissariat. Moreover, as will be discussed at length later, strong Ukrainian nationalist groups opposed to the OUN ideology appeared in several places; these forces kept up the fight for development of nationalism, thus inhibiting a

---

[50]PS 192.

[51]*OUN u Viini*, p. 74; T. Iak, *Hryb* (The Mushroom), p. 43, a clandestine OUN-M brochure, probably published at the end of German occupation in the East Ukraine.

[52]Iak, *Hryb*, p. 43.

[53]Iurko Stepovyi, *Syn Zakarpattia: Ukraïns'ke revoliutsiine pidpillia v Kyievi, 1941-1942 r.* (A Son of Transcarpathia: The Ukrainian Revolutionary Underground in Kiev, 1941-42) (Munich, 1947), p. 19.

[54]PS 192.

[55]*Ibid*. Correspondence seized from John Kozmyk ("Petrenko"), a Carpatho-Ukrainian who was OUN-M propaganda director in Kiev until arrested and executed in September, 1942, indicates OUN-M opposition to Germans as well as to the Soviet regime. Chief of the SP and the SD, Reports from the Occupied Eastern Territories, No. 23, October 2, 1942, and No. 29, November 13, 1942 (T 175, Reel 236).

growth in influence by the OUN. In other areas, news of the suppression of the Kiev group—the dissolution of the National Council appears to have been especially important—caused the cautious to refrain from endeavoring to build up nationalist organizations. Consequently, after February, 1942, the work of the two OUNs was only a relatively small part of the total stream of nationalist and antinationalist forces which must be studied in their geographical, social, and ideological context rather than as parts of a developing narrative.

In order to understand the development of nationalism during the remaining twenty months of German occupation of the East Ukraine, it is necessary to give some attention to the effects of German policy on aspects of life not directly connected with nationalist feeling. A number of volumes of extremely unpleasant reading could be devoted to the misery which the blind actions of the German rulers inflicted on the long-suffering peoples of the Soviet Union. Here only an extremely brief description of four ill-conceived policies which did most to disrupt the lives of the people of the area, and in particular to affect indirectly the character of the nationalist movements, can be attempted.

The first, and in many respects the most horrible failure of German policy, resulted in the death of innumerable Soviet prisoners of war. In the summer and fall of 1941, hundreds of thousands of Red army soldiers fell into German hands. Most captures took place because of the swift German advance and the great ascendancy of German arms; but at least in part they resulted from a lack of will to fight for the Communist system and the hope that German imprisonment would soon be followed by a freer life for the Soviet peoples. The German army was quite unprepared for the extent of the surrenders. However, no amount of difficulty in caring for the prisoners can excuse the horrible consequences of their neglect which, unlike most other atrocities committed in the east, was primarily the fault of the Wehrmacht. Inefficiency or brutality of subordinate *Etappentruppen* [rear area troops] was partly to blame, but the basic ruthlessness of many higher officers also played a major role, for it placed a premium on calloused inhumanity on the part of subordinates.[56] Countless thousands of prisoners were shut in barbed-wire enclosures in the open plains. Food was so insufficient that the captives were rapidly reduced to living skeletons; by fall cannibalism had made its appearance.[57] "Gaunt yellow faces protruding from the collars of greatcoats—unabashed human misery," as a Ukrainian visitor to one of the camps put it.[58] As colder weather approached, typhus combined with starvation to bring about hundreds of thousands of deaths.

Since many of these camps were located in the Ukraine, the population soon became aware of the conditions in them, even though a substantial portion of the prisoners of Ukrainian origin were separated out and released by

---

[56]Cf. the views of high Wehrmacht commanders cited in Chapter VI in connection with suppression of partisans.

[57]Report of Armament Inspector for the Ukraine to Armament Division Oberkommando der Wehrmacht, Zur Lage im Reichskommissariat Ukraine, November 29, 1941, PS 2174 (hereafter referred to as PS 2174).

[58]Iurii Tarkovych in *Krakivs'ki Visti*, January 21, 1942, p. 2.

the Germans.[59] Moreover, the inhabitants could scarcely avoid noticing the corpses of prisoners of war shot (perhaps as "kommissars" or Communists) and left lying in the villages.[60] Consequently, a belief that the Germans intended to destroy the Slavic peoples soon became widespread.

A second German failure was less shocking than the treatment of the prisoners of war, but in the long run it had an even more deleterious effect on relations with the Ukrainian population. This was the policy in relation to agriculture. Intent on acquiring food and raw materials to increase Germany's war potential, the Nazi leadership was as determined to exploit the Ukraine's agriculture as the Soviet rulers had been in establishing collectivized farms in the 1920s.[61] The Germans were even less inclined to supply enough consumer goods to induce the individual peasant to deliver his produce, because the needs of their fighting forces required that very little production be diverted to consumer goods. Moreover, their situation was in many respects more difficult than that of the Kremlin in 1929, for the material basis for the reconstruction of individual farms—buildings, equipment, livestock—was often lacking. Under these circumstances, a return to individual operation of agriculture would probably have meant a sharp net decline in productivity and a still greater decline in surpluses available for delivery.

On the other hand, the Germans had strong reasons for favoring the dissolution of the collective-farm system, as a salient feature of the Soviet system which they affected to despise. More than any other aspect of the Soviet system, the kolkhoz appears to have been hated by large numbers of the peasants. While it is questionable whether this hatred was universally felt, it was undoubtedly a very strong sentiment among the older groups of the population, those most ready on other grounds to cooperate with the Germans.[62]

Faced with this dilemma, the German rulers followed a tactic of compromise and deceit. They promised to dissolve the kolkhoz, stipulating reasonably enough, but in opposition to the desire of the peasant for immediate acquisition of land, that the process be gradual. First, the kolkhoz was to be transformed into a *Gemeinwirtschaft* (*hromads'ke hospodarstvo*) or community enterprise; the only significant immediate effect was the increase in the *dvor* or garden allotment permitted each household. In a second stage, to follow in the near future, the *Gemeinwirtschaft* was to be transformed into a *Landbaugenossenschaft* (*khliborobs'ka spilka*) or agricultural association. At this stage each household was to receive a definite section of land, and be rewarded in proportion to the harvest from this land, although many of the

---

[59]Interview 51; Directive of Oberkommando der Wehrmacht, Abteilung Kriegsgefangene, June 16, 1941, PS 888 (hereafter referred to as PS 888); *Nastup*, July 12, 1941, p. 2; Amt Ausland Abwehr to Oberkommando der Wehrmacht, Annex, September 15, 1941, USSR Exhibit No. 338 (hereafter referred to as USSR Exhibit No. 338); Commander of Heeresgebiet Süd Rear Area, Ic, "Behandlung der aus der roten Armee desertierten Ukrainer," August 11, 1941 (T 501, Reel 7).

[60]Memorandum of First Lieutenant Oberländer, Abwehr II, Heeresgruppe Süd, November 28, 1941, USSR Exhibit No. 278 (hereafter referred to as USSR Exhibit No. 278). Oberländer points out that pro-German sentiment among the population had greatly diminished even while the Wehrmacht remained the occupying authority.

[61]Herbert J. Ellison, "The Decision to Collectivize Agriculture," *American Slavic and East European Review*, XX (April, 1961), pp. 189-202, presents strong evidence that politics rather than economic motives predominated in the Soviet collectivization decision.

[62]PS 3876.

major agricultural operations were to be performed in common to overcome the extreme dearth of draft animals, tractors, tractor fuel, and implements.[63]

Where the program was carried out without procrastination, most of the peasantry seem to have responded favorably.[64] Frustrating delays ensued throughout a large part of the Ukraine, however, especially in the Reichskommissariat. In part they were due to misplaced German thoroughness in requiring exact surveys of the land before proceeding to its division among the households in the *Landbaugenossenschaft*. More serious was the deliberate obstruction of Koch and others who, feeling that the program would leave some small segment of life free of their control, argued that it would result in reduced deliveries. As a result, only 10 percent instead of the planned 20 percent of *Gemeinwirtschaften* were converted to *Landbaugenossenschaften*.[65] In spite of the meager practical results, the de-collectivization program was a favorite theme of Koch's propaganda, doubtless because he allowed so little else of a positive nature even to be discussed. In the end, however, the constantly broken pledges unquestionably caused a loss of faith in the Germans, even a willingness to return to the known evils of the Soviet system. The peasant's saying, "A bad mother is still better than a step-mother who makes many promises," indicated his judgment of the German agricultural policy.[66]

The problem of securing agricultural supplies was closely connected with that of supplying the Ukrainian urban population with food. One way in which the Germans sought to obtain most of the farm products for their own use was to make practically no provision for feeding the city dwellers. This was especially true during the first winter. The concept was simple: the starving urban population would find some means, through barter or otherwise, of inducing the peasants to part with an extra, hidden supply of food beyond that which the Germans had been able to extract from them.[67] To a certain extent, of course, this was true. Private individuals, as in the days after the Revolution, traveled about the countryside endeavoring to get something to eat in return for whatever they had to give the peasant. The city administrations and welfare committees did what they could to secure food for their clients; indeed this was one reason the Germans allowed these suspect organizations to function at all, for they were thereby relieved of the necessity of attending to such matters. The resources at the hands of these organs were, however,

---

[63]*Deutsche Ukraine Zeitung*, February 28, 1942, p. 3. A final stage, the *Einzelhof*, or individual farm, was envisaged by the planners, but very rarely, if ever, instituted.

[64]Cf. for example Report of Ortskommandantur Melitopol', July 8, 1942, PS 1693 (hereafter referred to as PS 1693); Report No. 7 of Representative of Reichsministerium für die besetzten Ostgebiete at Heeresgruppe Mitte and Stab des Befehlshabers des ruckwärtigen Heeresgebiets Mitte Captain Müller, March 24, 1942, to Reichsministerium für die besetzten Ostgebiete, PS 1686 (hereafter referred to as PS 1686).

[65]Memorandum by Bräutigam, October 25, 1942, PS 294 (hereafter referred to as PS 294).

[66]Situation report, Wirtschaftsinspektorat Süd lc, April, 1942, NG 1089 (hereafter referred to as NG 1089); Memorandum of Generalkommissar for the Crimea, Alfred Frauenfeld, to Himmler, February 10, 1944, NO 5394 (hereafter referred to as NO 5394).

[67]PS 2174.

infinitesimal compared to the needs. This was especially true since the most valuable materials left in the cities were requisitioned by the Germans.[68]

The peasants in turn had little to sell. They had lived under the regimented planning economy of the Soviets, which prevented the individual from accumulating a private stock of agricultural products, rather than the loose system of tsarist days, when the more prosperous peasants could usually find a little more to sell if the price was attractive enough. Extremely heavy requisitions by the Wehrmacht, especially in the form of unauthorized seizures, had also depleted the supplies available. The result was a severe shortage of food in the cities, especially in the larger ones such as Kiev and Kharkov, which brought famine and the pestilences associated with it in the winter and spring of 1942.[69]

Like the agricultural policy and the starvation of the cities, the *Ostarbeiter* program was the result of ruthless efforts to increase the German war potential. Unlike the former policies, however, its evils do not even have the excuse of short-run expediency. The concept of bringing foreign workers to the armaments factories was, in itself, reasonable enough. Moreover, properly handled, it might very well have resulted in an increase rather than a decrease of popular support for Germany in the Ukraine. There is good evidence that the population was at first sympathetic to the German efforts to recruit labor voluntarily.[70] Moreover, a large number of nationalist Ukrainians supported the measure; they not only wanted to help Germany win the war against the Soviet Union, but believed that it would be a valuable cultural experience for young Ukrainians to come into contact with advanced German technology and with Western European culture in general. To them it was means of drawing the Ukrainian nation away from its too-close association with the Russians and the "Asiatics" of their empire and of establishing a European orientation for their country.[71]

Unhappily for these visions, the methods used by the Germans in dealing with the volunteer workers soon dried up the supply. They were frequently given miserable transportation and poor accommodations on arrival in Germany. Highly trained workers and professional men who had volunteered in order to increase their technical ability by experience in Germany were assigned to common labor.[72] Most important, however, the Ukrainians, like other *Ostarbeiter*, were forced to wear a humiliating badge distinguishing them from Western Europeans; they were forbidden social contacts with the latter and, in order to implement this decree, were excluded from motion-picture

---

[68]During the terrible winter of 1941-42, the social welfare department of the Kiev municipal administration dispensed only about 100,000 *karbovontsi* (i.e., rubles; nominally the equivalent of 10,000 RM or about $4,000) per month; at the time, milk was 20 *k*. a liter, potatoes about 250 *k*. a hundredweight (*Ukraïns'ka Diisnist'*, May 10, 1942, p. 1). This monetary outlay may, of course, have been supplemented by food obtained by barter. For example, a charge brought against the Bahazii administration was that it had used newsprint to barter for food with the small towns (Interview 59). Cf. also p. 84.

[69]According to Oberländer (USSR Exhibit No. 278).

[70]Report of the representative of the Reichsministerium für die besetzten Ostgebiete in Heeresgebiet B, First Lieutenant Theurer, October 7, 1942, PS 054 (hereafter referred to as PS 054).

[71]E.g., *Krakivs'ki Visti*, February 6, 1942, p. 2.

[72]PS 054.

theaters, restaurants, and other public places. The erstwhile willing worker felt that the Germans regarded him (as many did) as nothing but a Bolshevik prisoner.[73]

When this policy of segregation resulted in lack of volunteers, force was used; mandatory labor service for young men and women was officially introduced in the Reichskommissariat on September 21, 1942,[74] but in practice compulsion had long been employed. In reply to the inevitable evasion of this order, the most demoralizing of tricks—such as seizure of worshippers at church services and invitations by German authorities to theatrical performances at which all were arrested—were utilized. Force and brutal retaliation, such as burning of villages from which the potential workers ran away, were frequently applied.[75] The conscripts were sent 1,000 miles to Germany in unheated cattle cars, sealed with barbed wire. Still worse, there was no just selection of those most suited for departure, no systematic registration.[76] Mothers of small children were sometimes taken; sons and husbands who were the only support of their families were conscripted without adequate provision for the families' maintenance.[77]

The horror of such treatment was perhaps the single most important cause of popular revulsion against the Germans. In addition to all its material hardships, the mere idea of forced transportation to a distant and unknown land recalled the generations-old terror of banishment to Siberia.[78] The extent of the program was so enormous that every family was touched; it became a universal evil. Of the total population of Kiev, 38,000 persons (over 10 percent) were delivered to the *Ostarbeiter* program within the first ten months of German occupation.[79] In the southern *Generalbezirke* somewhat smaller numbers appear to have been involved[80] but in the crucial *Bezirk* of Zhitomir, 170,000 (about 6 percent of the population) were taken by mid-1943, and 30,000 more were to follow.[81] In all, as early as August, 1943, one out of every forty inhabitants of the Ukraine had been deported to Germany as forced laborers,[82] and

---

[73]Opinion report for period June 12-July 14, 1942, Auslandbriefprüfstelle, Gruppe VIII, PS 302 (hereafter referred to as PS 302).

[74]*Deutsche Ukraine Zeitung*, September 22, 1942, p. 3.

[75]Auslandbriefprüfstelle, report for September 11-November 11, 1942, PS 018 (hereafter referred to as PS 018).

[76]Landesbauernführer Körner, Die neue deutsche Ukraine-Politik, PS 1198 (hereafter referred to as PS 1198).

[77]Occ E-4 (1); PS 054.

[78]Oral report of Generalkommissar Leyser (Zhitomir) to Rosenberg, June 17, 1943, PS 265 (hereafter referred to as PS 265).

[79]Commander of the SP and the SS, Kiev, to Commander of the SP and the SS, Ukraine, July 20, 1942, NO 1603 (hereafter referred to as NO 1603).

[80]Only about 1 percent from *Generalbezirk* Nikolaev by mid-1942 (Conference of Sauckel and Reichskommissariat officials in Kiev, August 12, 1942, NO 1606; hereafter referred to as NO 1606).

[81]PS 265.

[82]According to Sauckel, director of the *Ostarbeiter* program, at a Führer Conference, August 20, 1943, NO 1831 (hereafter referred to as NO 1831).

by the end of the occupation the number of Ukrainian workers in Germany totaled 1,500,000.[83]

The suffering caused by the actions of the Germans described above did not directly affect the activity of the nationalist elements, as did their repressive attitude toward education, religion, culture, and local administration. Indirectly, however, it played an enormous part in the development of the nationalist movements in the East Ukraine during the German occupation. One effect was a general subordination of all thought, all activity, to the demands of self-preservation. The constant struggle to keep alive resulted in a reduction of the energy and attention which could be devoted to all political questions, including nationalism. On the other hand, the sheer impossibility of coming to terms with the German authority, regardless of how ready one might be to sacrifice all independence to do so, led many to seek a political movement which promised deliverance. A vast number, of course, turned back to Communism, hoping that the experience of near-defeat would lead to a modification of Moscow's policies. For others, however, the only rational solution appeared to be the nationalist parties.

Weak as they were after the waves of suppressions during the six months from September, 1941, to February, 1942, the two OUN groups endeavored to meet this challenge. Of the two factions, the Bandera group appears to have made the easiest, but not the most thorough-going adjustment. Its ability to adjust at a rather shallow level was due to several factors. The members of the OUN-B were nearly all young, and their movement placed little emphasis on systematic ideology. When they went to the East Ukraine, they carried a large number of slogans and romantic pledges as baggage.[84] These either attracted or antagonized the local population. In the latter case, the Bandera organizers frequently resorted to violent denunciations, or even force. By these tactics they alienated a large part of the intelligentsia. The latter group, moreover, tended either to form groupings of its own or to adhere to the Mel'nyk party. Hence the Bandera adherents, if they found support at all, were forced to go to the less educated classes, the workers and the peasants.[85] Thus they were brought into contact with the aspirations of the masses of the people. Since they were led by destruction of their northern forces to concentrate on the southern Ukraine, where the potentially nationalist intelligentsia was weak, this tendency was reinforced.

---

[83]PS 1198.

[84]One of these oaths, as discovered by the German police, reads:

"On my honor, for the fame of the fallen heroes, for the holy blood spilled, for my Ukrainian earth and the majesty of my Ukrainian homeland, I swear that I will struggle with all my strength and with my life for a free and Ukrainian state. With my heart, my soul, and my whole being I confess that only the Ukrainian revolution can give power to the Ukrainian state and the people. Unto death I will stand on the battlefield in order to build a national Ukrainian State. No one and nothing at all can hold me back from the path of the Ukrainian national revolution, neither difficulties nor death. I will carry out every command of my leader. I swear on the Ukraine, that I will loyally and honestly carry out all duties to the Ukrainian government which the Organization of Ukrainian Nationalists under the leadership of Stephen Bandera lays on me. I will strive with my whole strength and my life for a Ukrainian government dependent on no one, and strive for its strength and honor. Hail to the Ukraine, Hail to the Heroes!" (PS 3943.)

[85]Interviews 18, 66. Chief of the SP and of the SD, Reports from the Occupied Eastern Territories, No. 4, May 22, 1942 (T 175, Reel 235 – *Litopys*, Vol. VI, p. 45) remarks that Banderists had to rely on "simple people" because the intelligentsia was collaborating with the Germans.

Throughout this period, from the end of 1941 to the retreat of the Germans from the East Ukraine in the fall of 1943, the emphasis of the leadership of the OUN-B remained on the "voluntarist" elements of the program (underground publications of this period are filled with discussions of the role of underground movements, the nature of terrorism as a political tactic, and the role of the future Ukrainian army). At the same time, as early as April, 1942, the slogan of the *akt* — "Hail to the Ukraine, Hail to the Heroes" — was accompanied by the slogan advocated by the left group in the Bandera "Second Congress" — "Freedom for the Peoples and for the Individual."[86] Moreover, a conference of leaders in the same month decided to oppose the newly proclaimed "land reform" of the Germans.[87] Correspondingly, the underground press pointed out that the dissolution of the kolkhozes, while in line with Ukrainian nationalist aspirations, had up to then been carried out on paper only, not in reality. Therefore, it warned, with considerable perspicacity, that the whole program might be merely a device for getting more work out of the peasant. The same article advised the Nationalists to extend their work to all spheres of life, thus not falling into the error of clinging, as had the UVO, to purely military means of struggle. Significantly, a comparison from the development of the Communist Party was used; the "correct" line was likened to that of the Bolsheviks, who took a universal approach to the problem of revolution, while that of the Narodnaia Volia (of late nineteenth-century Russia) failed because it relied on terrorism alone.[88]

In the final analysis, however, the main stream of OUN-B ideology could not be diverted at this time. The leaders (those out of prison, that is) were in Galicia and Volhynia, in an environment comparatively unaffected by the Soviet stimulation to consideration of social and economic questions. The members who were in the underground in the east, and their new recruits, had rapidly changed, but they were too uninfluential and isolated to alter the body of the party. Such a change could only come about when the West Ukrainians, too, were thrown into intimate contact with reinforcements from the Soviet world.

For the OUN-M organizers in the East Ukraine, the initial process of adjustment was much more difficult because of the age of the members and the comparative depth of their ideology. Moreover, most of their recruits in the East Ukraine were intellectuals. While affected by Soviet conditions, the latter by no means represented a cross section of the Soviet world, but rather a special group which placed national above social consciousness. Eventually they did bring about a measure of change in the ideology of the party. Some new members, as was noted in the case of Liubchenko, became more violently

---

[86]*Biuleten'* (Bulletin), No. 4 (April, 1942), a clandestine publication made available to me by Nicholas Lebed'. Extracts (in German translation) of this publication appear in Chief of the SP and of the SD, Reports from the Occupied Eastern Territories, No. 14, July 31, 1942 (T 175, Reel 235 — *Litopys*, Vol. VI, p. 57).

[87]Lebed', *UPA*, p. 18.

[88]*Biuleten'*, No. 4, pp. 5-7. Other OUN-B publications of late 1942 and early 1943 (*Visnyk Ukraïns'koï Informatsiïnoï Sluzhby* [Messenger of the Ukrainian Information Service], No. 7-8, and *Ideia y Chyn* [Idea and Deed], No. 1, 1942) show considerable concern for agricultural matters, desperate living conditions, and the limitations of Ukrainian cultural and educational activities. Dontsov's "natsiokratiia" is still stressed, however, while sharp attacks are directed against "Moscophiles" and the OUN-M.

and exclusively nationalist than their tutors. Of these, a few retained their "purity" until the end of the period under consideration, and beyond. Thus one pamphlet by an East Ukrainian professor in the OUN-M underground, printed at the close of the German occupation of the East Ukraine, stressed the racial "unity of blood" in Stsibors'kyi's doctrine. Even this pamphlet insisted on the opposition of this doctrine to Fascism, and stated that Stsibors'kyi's theory is democratic in that it gives the maximum opportunity to each while demanding the maximum from him. On the social side, however, while a mixed economy of state capitalism, cooperatives, and private capital was advocated, the concept of the class struggle was denounced and the abolition of the kolkhoz demanded.[89]

Some of the OUN-M members who had first seen the East Ukraine in 1941 were inclined to go much further in forming an amalgam between their concept of nationalism and the socialistic system to which the masses of the East Ukrainians had become accustomed. On May 24-25, 1942, a conference of OUN-M leaders near Kremenets resolved to attack the German policy of colonialism. An All-Ukrainian Congress of Ukrainian Independentists was held by the organization in Kiev on August 14-15, 1942. It brought together not only OUN members from many parts of the East Ukraine, but members of many other nationalist organizations, whether or not in tune with the old ideology of the OUN. Thus the circle of experience constantly broadened.[90] Leaders like Kandyba found that their converts who had joined in the first wave of enthusiasm were essentially realists who wanted deeds not words.[91] When the Mel'nyk group could no longer present itself as the delegate of German power, its strength had to be revived by a program which contrasted with the reality of German oppression. Kandyba became convinced of the necessity of advocating the maintenance of state control of industry and commerce. Moreover, the Mel'nyk followers decided, contrary to all their preconceptions, that the only way to avoid alienating much of the East Ukrainian youth was to abandon denunciation of the kolkhoz in favor of a program which left to its members the decision to retain or abolish the collective.[92]

That such a sweeping revision of ideology was necessary for the OUN factions if they were to make converts in the East Ukraine is an indication of the great psychological differences which had developed between that region and the West Ukraine during the preceding twenty years. On the other hand, the fact that such a large segment of the party organizers, including even the older men in the OUN-M, could make the adjustment leads one to conclude that the integral nationalist ideology was not so deeply rooted in the thinking of the West Ukrainians and émigrés but that it underwent a rapid broadening of content once its adherents were brought into contact with the real conditions of the East Ukraine, and even the limited opportunities for action presented by these conditions. This does not mean, of course, that the nationalist goal was

---

[89]See the clandestine booklet by Iak (*Hryb*), and Chief of the SP and of the SD, Reports of *Einsatzgruppen* and *Kommandos*, No. 185, March 25, 1942 (T 175, Reel 234), on an OUN-M leaflet calling for a struggle for independence from the "occupier."

[90]*OUN u Viini*, p. 78.

[91]Interview 65.

[92]*Ibid.*

cast aside by those who modified their propaganda themes; the attainment of Ukrainian independence remained their central value. They realized that for the bulk of the East Ukrainian population independence could be presented as a means to the attainment of other values, but not as the ultimate value in itself. This acceptance of independence as a part rather than the whole of the nation's life was in itself the negation of the basic dogma of integral nationalism. The inherent flexibility of the Ukrainian nationalist outlook was demonstrated by the fact that it underwent a similar change at a somewhat later date under the impact of changing circumstances in the West Ukraine. To understand these circumstances, it is necessary to examine one of the most interesting aspects of Ukrainian nationalism in the Second World War — the nationalist partisan movement.

VI

From Underground to Resistance

For groups carrying on open resistance to an occupying power, the Ukraine as a whole is a highly inhospitable region; throughout most of its extent it is an open plain without natural places of concealment. Aside from the mountainous areas of the Carpathians in Galicia, the Carpatho-Ukraine, and Bukovina, which remained for a long time outside the scope of open resistance activities, sheltered retreats for bands of any considerable size are difficult to find. They are limited almost entirely to the belt of woods and swamp on the northern border. Originally, forest vegetation prevailed north of a line reaching from a point on the Polish border not far to the southwest of Kremenets almost due east, through Zhitomir and Kiev, to the boundary of the Ukraine and the Russian Soviet Republic some fifty miles northwest of Sumy.[1] In the course of the centuries, a large part of this region has been cleared for cultivation; the presence of numerous swampy areas prevented all the forest from being cut down, however, so that there are frequent wooded areas, which become more common and less separated by open spaces the farther north one goes. In the Ukraine, as it was administratively defined prior to 1941, this wooded strip rarely exceeds one hundred miles in width, although it is almost four hundred miles long. The Reichskommissariat Ukraine, however, included an additional strip annexed from Belorussia, averaging about forty miles in width, and containing still more impenetrable swamps than the more southerly wooded area. Of the forested region, the southern part, which has been partly cleared, is valuable agriculturally and is thickly settled; it forms an integral part of the historic Ukrainian lands of Volhynia, Kiev, and Chernigov. The northern part, appropriately known as Polessia, or the "forest land," is of little value for crop growing but contains the principal timber industry in the Ukraine.

As the German armies rolled into the Ukraine in 1941, they tended to advance along the main lines of communication, avoiding the difficult, swampy regions. For weeks, or in some cases even months, the less accessible areas were not brought under German control. This circumstance made possible the

---

[1] Cf. *Entsyklopediia Ukraïnoznastva* (Encyclopedia of Things Ukrainian), eds. Volodymyr Kubiiovych and Zenon Kuzelia (Munich: Naukove Tovarystvo im. Shevchenka, 1949), p. 106.

development of partisan bands which carried on resistance to the occupation authority.

Although it is certain that Soviet officials decided on guerrilla operations as soon as the extent of the German invasion became apparent, the complicated details of their planning are still not entirely clear.[2] In any event, the rapidity of German advance to the Dnieper rendered ineffective any systematic attempt to constitute a partisan movement in the Ukraine west of that river. South of the great belt of swamps and forests extending from Polish ethnographical territory into the heart of central Russia, efforts to form partisan detachments were usually unsuccessful even where more time was available. Consequently, initial endeavors produced permanent results only in the ethnically mixed East Bank *oblasts* bordering on Belorussia and Russia—Chernigov and Sumy. There Soviet state officials, NKVD officers, and Communist Party professionals like the veteran first secretary in Chernigov, Oleksii Fedorov, were able to maintain precarious continuity for Soviet power during the winter of 1941-42.[3]

Such members of the apparatus were impelled both by their interest in maintaining the Soviet *status quo* and by fear of violent death should they fall into German hands, for all "kommissars" and Communist officials were destined for execution by Hitler. So were officers of the political section of the Soviet Army. Consequently, when cut off by the German advance and driven into hiding in difficult terrain, such men had powerful incentives to gather armed bands strong enough to insure temporary survival. Their first recruits were usually rank-and-file soldiers who, with good reason, feared starvation in prisoner-of-war camps. While a high proportion of officers and soldiers alike had been stationed in the Ukraine at the outbreak of hostilities, many were not Ukrainians—for example, Alexander Saburov, subsequently an outstanding commander of guerrilla "raids" on occupied Ukrainian territory, had been born in the Urals but was an NKVD official in Kiev at the start of the war.[4]

The role of NKVD and Party *apparatchiki*, usually non-Ukrainian ethnically, was even more pronounced in the directing staffs which gradually assumed control of the scattered partisans during the winter and spring of 1942. Naturally, this applied to the Central Staff of the Partisan Movement in Moscow. But even the operational director of the Ukrainian Staff (at first also in Moscow) was a veteran NKVD official of Siberian Russian origin, Timothy

---

[2]Since the first edition of this book appeared, a great deal more information on the Soviet partisan movement has become available. Consequently, a very brief summary emphasizing ethnic elements and relations to nationalist Ukrainians appears to be sufficient here. For voluminous analyses based on German and Soviet sources, see the work by the War Documentation Project, which I edited, *Soviet Partisans in World War II* (Madison: University of Wisconsin Press, 1964).

[3]See his memoirs, *Podpol'nyi obkom deistvuet* (The Underground Oblast Committee Carries On) (Moscow: Voennoe Izdatel'stvo Vooruzhennykh Sil Soiuza SSSR, 1950), and many subsequent editions in Russian, Ukrainian, and English.

[4]Anatolii Shyian, *Partyzans'kyi Krai* (Partisan Territory) (Kiev: Ukraïns'ke Derzhavne Vydavnytsvo, 1946), pp. 19, 32. Criticizing the first edition of *Ukrainian Nationalism*, a Soviet reviewer contends that most Soviet partisans in the Ukraine were native Ukrainians and Belorussians, not Russians. But his figures relate to late 1943 and 1944, after an influx of local peasant recruits. Colonel S. Doroshenko, "O fal'sifikatsii istorii partisanskogo dvizheniia v burzhuanoi pechati" (Falsification of the History of the Partisan Movement in the Bourgeois Press), *Voenno-Istoricheskii Zhurnal*, No. 7 (1960), p. 103.

A. Strokach.[5] The key role of the Staffs was enhanced by their ability to deploy numerous light airplanes for delivering munitions and supplies to the partisan detachments and for sending in personnel expert in demolition, communication, and political control. These assets enabled the Staffs to play a primary role in political as well as military coordination—that is, to maintain a vestige of Soviet authority in areas far from direct control by the rulers in the Kremlin.

This does not imply that, in its later stages after it had been organized and developed by *apparatchiki*, the partisan movement was unable to obtain some support from the Ukrainian people. Frequently much weaker than the total forces which the Germans could employ against them, partisan detachments were obliged to obtain the aid of local people for scouting, concealment, and sabotage of German offensives. Both compulsion and persuasion were used to obtain local support. Compulsion was used to requisition food and equipment needed, to draft men into guerrilla units, and to inhibit collaboration with the Germans. Methods employed frequently included killing the families of those who entered the German police or administrative organs, as well as the collaborators themselves.[6] The mere fact that the partisans could move about in force induced the cautious peasants to believe that Soviet victory was possible and that, consequently, it would be dangerous to side with the regime's enemies. Persuasion, however, would probably have been ineffective had it not been for the atrocities practiced by the Germans, especially the *Ostarbeiter* agencies, which led thousands of persons, mostly young and fit for partisan service, to flee to the woods.[7] The German failure to carry out the land reform, by depriving the peasants of a motive for resisting the return of the Soviet forces, was also a major cause of partisan success. The partisans made strong efforts to win over the peasants, in some cases even paying for requisitioned food supplies. According to a German report, one Red partisan band even distributed land to the peasants in the area it controlled.[8]

The early development and continued strength of the Red partisans, arising in part from reinforcements sent them from the chief power base of the Soviets in the unconquered areas, enabled them to dominate the only regions suitable for guerrilla warfare east of the Dnieper. Therefore, the nationalists could not have established partisan forces there unless they had possessed overwhelming popular support.[9] The possibility of such support was decreased

---

[5]See especially the interrogation of Strokach's adjutant, Alexander Ruzanov, by Wehrmacht captain Wilfried Strik-Strikfeldt, transmitted in Reichsführer SS, Persönliches Stab, Tagebuch No. 114, October 19, 1943 (T 175, Reel 38). Contemporary propaganda versions appeared in *Der Deutsche in Transnistrien*, November 28, 1943, p. 2, and *Krakivs'ki Visti*, October 23, 1943, p. 3.

[6]Report of Gebietskommissar Steudel in Kazatin, November 8-December 28, 1943, PS 1702 (hereafter referred to as PS 1702); PS 3943, February 12, 1943.

[7]Those who obeyed the order to report for the *Ostarbeiter* program were threatened by the partisans, while the order itself often served as a pass to join a partisan unit (Occ E-4 [1]).

[8]PS 1685; PS 051.

[9]There were a few small groups. See, for example, the description of a band supposed to have been wiped out by Red partisans in the Chernigov region in early 1943, in "Persha Ukraïns'ka Partyzanka" (The First Ukrainian Partisan Group), *Vpered* (January, 1950), pp. 13-14. *Istoriia Ukraïns'koï RSR* (History of the Ukrainian SSR), Vol. II (Kiev: Vydavnytstvo Akademiï Nauk RSR, 1958), p. 553, admits that there were nationalist "pseudo-partisan" bands in the Chernigov and Kirovograd regions.

PARTISAN ACTIVITY IN THE NORTHERN UKRAINE

The following set of maps is intended to present schematically the development of partisan activity in the northern Ukraine from the beginning of the German-Soviet war until the reconquest of the major part of the area by the Red army at the end of 1943. Territorial divisions indicated, from west to east, are the *Generalbezirke* Volhynia-Podolia, Zhitomir, and Kiev, and the Chernigov *oblast* of the army rear area.

The following symbols are used throughout:

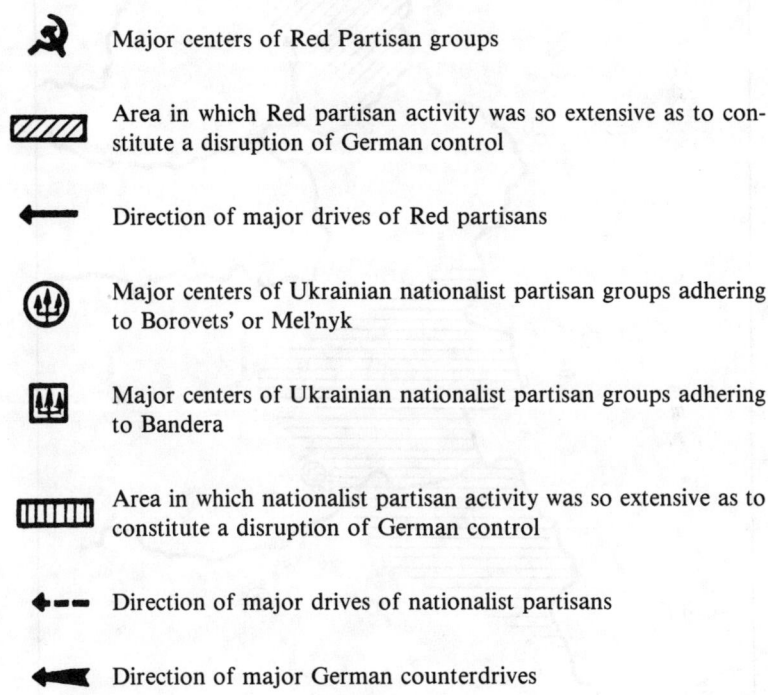

Major centers of Red Partisan groups

Area in which Red partisan activity was so extensive as to constitute a disruption of German control

Direction of major drives of Red partisans

Major centers of Ukrainian nationalist partisan groups adhering to Borovets' or Mel'nyk

Major centers of Ukrainian nationalist partisan groups adhering to Bandera

Area in which nationalist partisan activity was so extensive as to constitute a disruption of German control

Direction of major drives of nationalist partisans

Direction of major German counterdrives

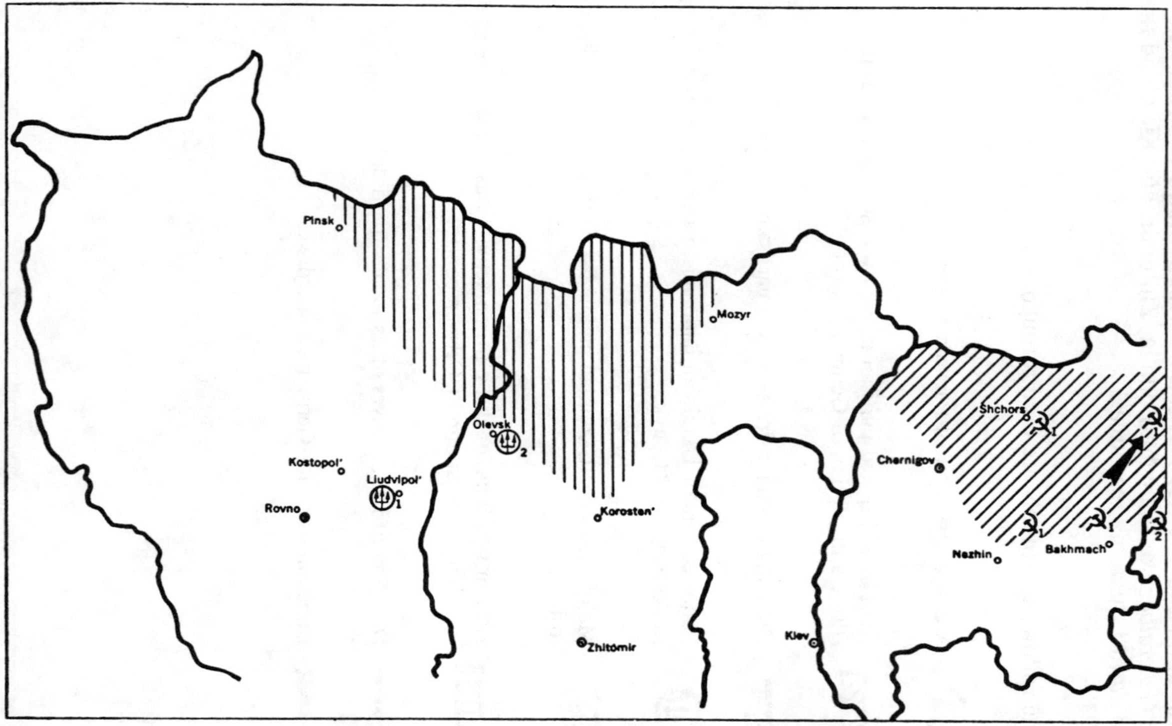

JULY, 1941–JUNE, 1942

This map represents a number of developments which were not closely related. The nationalist Ukrainian partisan groups represented were irregular forces in the German service used to combat Red partisans, rather than insurgent partisan forces, and the area represented as controlled by them is the area in which the Germans did not install a civil administration prior to November, 1941 (the "Olevsk Republic").

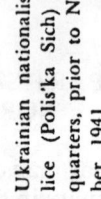 The Polis'ka Sich after it went underground in November, 1941

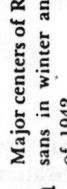 Ukrainian nationalist police (Polis'ka Sich) headquarters, prior to November, 1941

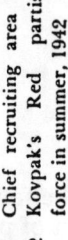₁ Major centers of Red partisans in winter and spring of 1942

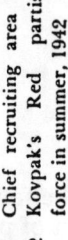₂ Chief recruiting area for Kovpak's Red partisan force in summer, 1942

FROM UNDERGROUND TO RESISTANCE / 99

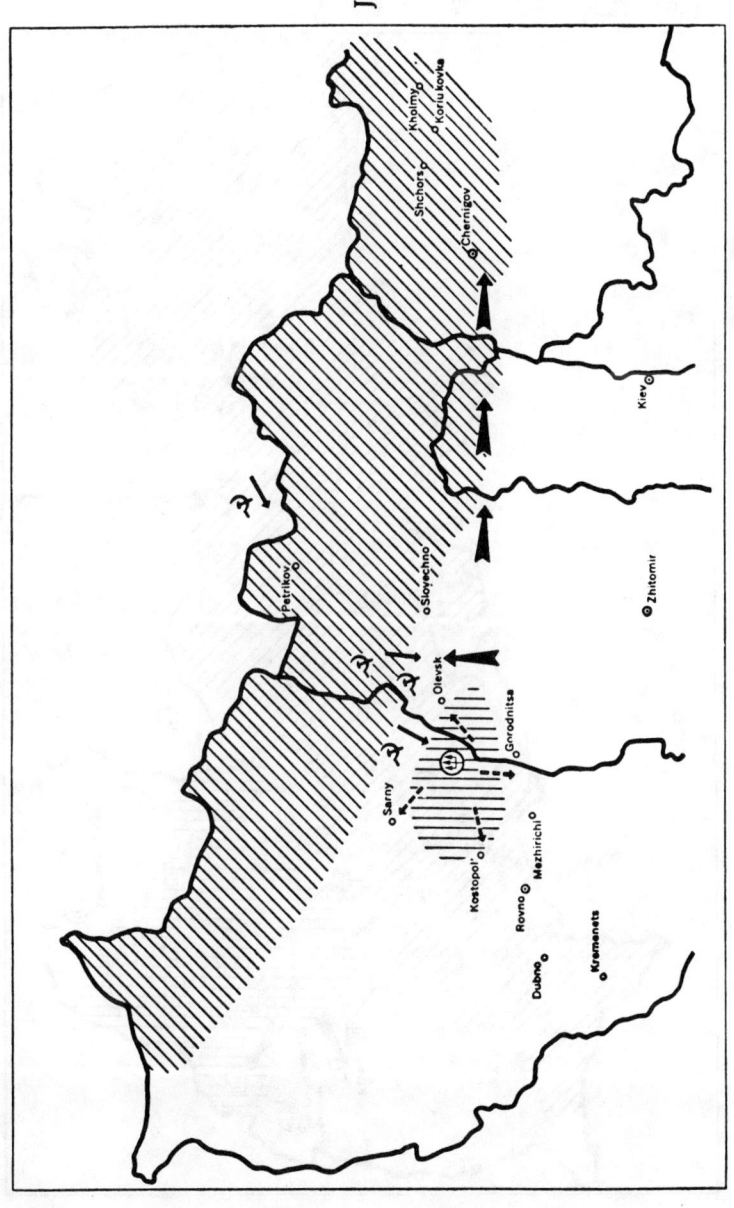

JULY–DECEMBER, 1942

JANUARY-MAY, 1943

⊞₁ Major centers of Bandera groups during the winter and early spring of 1943

⊞₂ Extension of Bandera partisan activity in April and May, 1943

⊕₁ Major centers of "Bul'ba" and Mel'nyk groups throughout the period

↗₁ Major centers of Red partisan activity in winter and early spring of 1943

↗₂ Additional centers of Red partisan activity in April and May, 1943

↓ Route of Kovpak's Red partisan band (Actually the band began its raid in November, 1942, being driven beyond the northern border of the Reichskommissariat Ukraine in December, as shown on the map, but for the sake of simplicity all of the band's activities during this first period of its invasion of the "Right Bank" Ukraine have been shown on this map.)

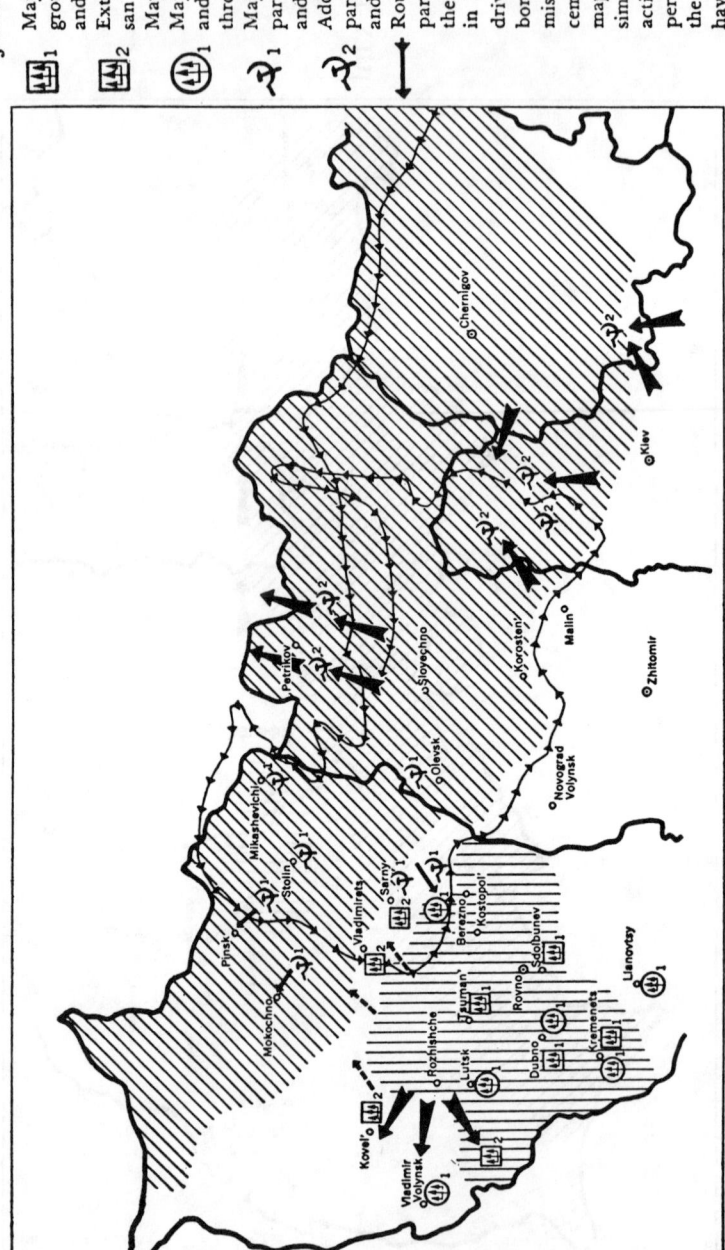

JUNE–DECEMBER, 1943

⛨₁ Major centers of Bandera partisan activity, May–July, 1943

⛨₂ New headquarters of Bandera group in late summer and autumn, 1943

⊕₁ Major Mel'nyk and "Bul'ba" bands, May–July, 1943

⊕₂ Last stronghold of "Bul'ba" group before its dissolution

⋊₁ Chief points of contact of Red partisan groups with nationalist groups, May–July, 1943

⋊₂ Route of Kovpak's Carpathian raid

⋊₃ Major areas of Kovpak's activity in Galicia, July, 1943

↓ Area to which remnants of Kovpak's band returned in September, 1943

▦ Approximate lines of combat between the Red Army and the Wehrmacht, with the Roman numerals referring to dates as follows:

I October 1, 1943
II November 12, 1943
III December 10, 1943
IV February 15, 1944

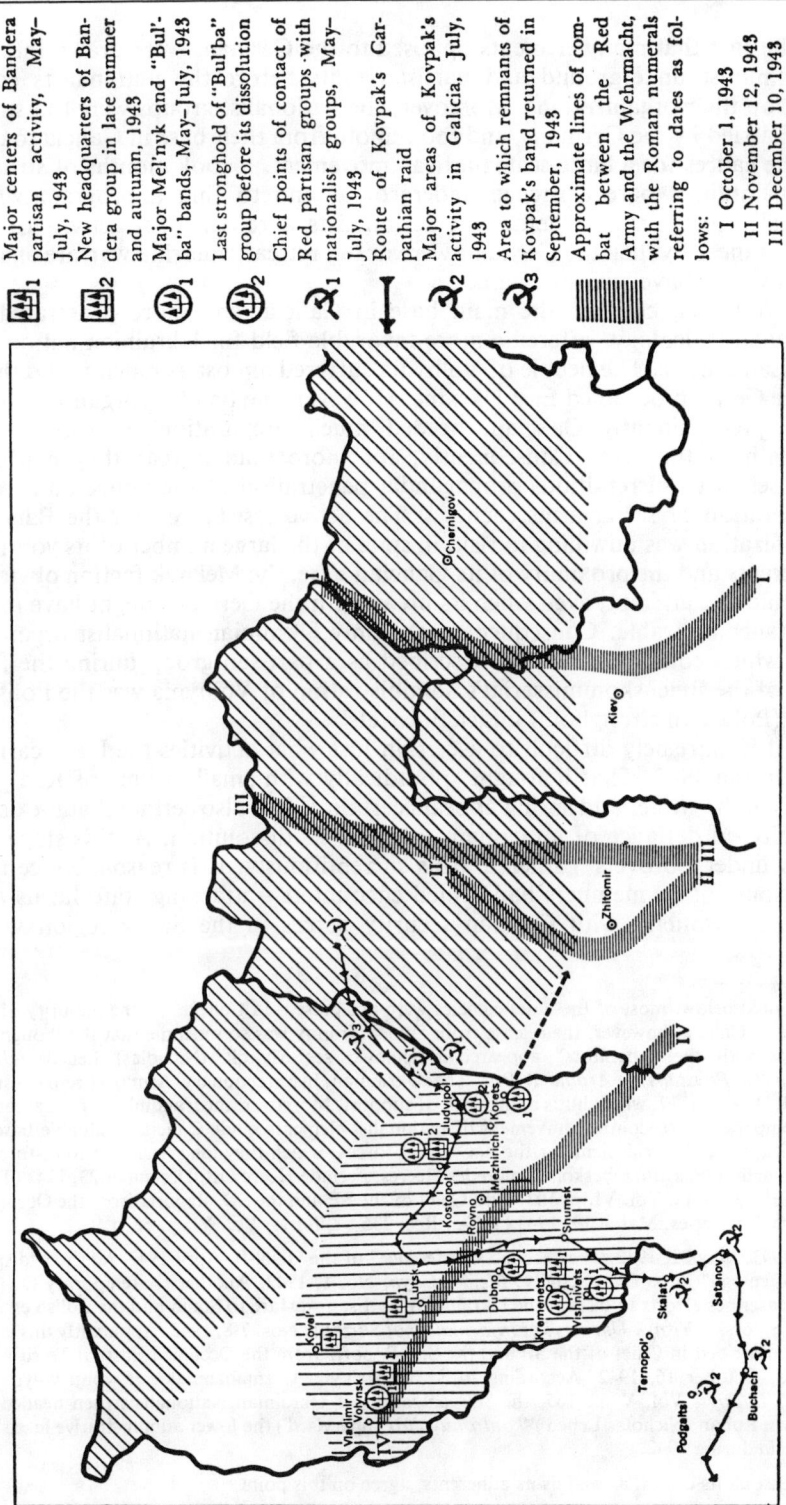

by the fact that many elements opposed to the Germans were drawn into the Communist underground and partisan units before the nationalists could develop their organizations. Moreover, the nationalist groups were too small, too harried by the Germans, and too remote from their base in Galicia to constitute cadres for a large-scale partisan movement. It took months of struggle to maintain a bare existence underground and to find a program which appealed to the masses before the nationalists were ready for activity of any importance. By then the Germans were in full retreat; guerrilla warfare against them would have had little value.[10]

Volhynia, close to the main base in Galicia, and more penetrated by nationalist ideology, offered a more favorable field for Ukrainian nationalist partisan groups. The people of Volhynia suffered almost as much as did those in the German-occupied East Ukraine. However, the Bandera organizers, who were predominantly Galician, needed much preparation to acquire real strength in the area. Consequently, for more than a year they confined themselves to surreptitious propaganda, penetration of the police units, and preparation of secret arms caches.[11] The active resistance that the Bandera organization was unwilling to risk, in spite of the large number of its youthful adherents and the proximity of its Galician base, the Mel'nyk faction obviously could not attempt, even when its break with the Germans might have made resistance desirable. Consequently, the only Ukrainian nationalist organization which could remotely be described as a partisan group during the first year of the Reichskommissariat's administration of Volhynia was the Polis'ka Sich (Polessian stronghold) under Borovets'.

It is extremely difficult to ascertain just what activities the UPA carried out during 1942. That it fought sporadically with small groups of Red partisans in the winter and spring appears certain.[12] It is also certain that it existed illegally, in defiance of a German order for its dissolution. At this stage the UPA under Borovets' gathered arms surreptitiously. It is reasonably certain that some of its members had armed encounters—attacking state farms and freeing prisoners—with German security forces in the Sarny region while

---

[10]As noted below, most of these deficiencies were not present in Galicia. To the majority of the people of Galicia, however, the release from Soviet tyranny was so welcome that the thought of conflict with the "liberators" appeared ridiculous; see Mykola (Nicholas) Lebed', *UPA: Ukraïns'ka Povstans'ka Armiia* (UPA: The Ukrainian Insurrectionary Army) (Presove Biuro UHVR, 1946), p. 17, which hints at this lack of support. Moreover, the tranquility of the area and the comparative freedom of movement of nationalist elements made Galicia a valuable base of organization and recruitment for the nationalist forces, which they long hesitated to disturb by violent action. See also Oberkommando des Heeres, Fremde Heere Ost, December 23, 1943 (T 78, Reel 565—*Litopys*, Vol. VI, p. 103); and Chief of the SP and the SD, Reports from the Occupied Eastern Territories, March 19, 1943 (T 175, Reel 236—*Litopys*, Vol. VI, p. 68 ff.).

[11]PS 3943, May 22, 1942. The "Second Conference" of the OUN-B, April 1942, rejected "dispersion of energy" in partisan activity. *Ideia y Chyn*, No. 1, 1942. Another contemporary OUN-B source ascribes efforts to disrupt the Ukraine by partisan warfare to Stalin and the Polish émigré leader Sikorski: *Visnyk Ukraïns'koï Informatsiinoï Sluzhby*, Nos. 7-8, 1942. Apparently this is the leaflet described in Chief of the SP and the SD, Reports from the Occupied Eastern Territories, No. 25, October 16, 1942. According to S. Novyts'kyi, "U zmahanniakh za voliu volyns'koï zemli," *Litopys*, Vol. V, p. 165, the "Organization of Ukrainian Nationalists then headed by Maksym Ruban (Nicholas Lebed') *'kontroliuvala'* ('supervised') the lower administrative levels" in Volhynia during 1942.

[12]At least all its critics, as well as its adherents, agree on this point.

helping peasants resist oppressive measures. But Borovets' asserted that he remained friendly to the Wehrmacht and "had spilled no German blood."[13] Hence the Germans may not have been entirely dissatisfied with the state of affairs in which this illegal band kept a region of difficult terrain and low economic potential from serving as a Red base behind the German lines. Moreover, as Borovets' himself has pointed out, it was never the intention of his movement to engage in a large-scale military campaign, but rather to retain a small staff which could draw support and recruits from the sympathetic Polessian peasantry.[14]

That the group was of some importance within these limits is indicated by the fact that in the late summer of 1942 the Soviet partisans in Polessia felt it worthwhile to send an emissary, Alexander Lukin, to negotiate for common action against the Germans.[15] The mere fact, however, that such negotiations could be undertaken is an indication of the uncertainty of the ideology and objectives of the little nationalist group. "Bul'ba" Borovets' himself, a man of little schooling, apparently was not sure what direction the movement should take, although he had a deep-rooted love for his native country. He continued to maintain ties with the UNR; there were UNR officers with the group much of the time, advising on military matters on which few of the younger members had had experience. Borovets' kept up a precarious line of communication with Andrew Livits'kyi himself through an old UNR member, Captain Raievs'kyi, who ostensibly carried on the functions of *raionchef* in the Rovno district.[16]

These connections were too discontinuous to provide much guidance, however, even if the enfeebled Warsaw headquarters had had a clear line to offer. At the same time, the group under Borovets' was acting as a refuge for extremely diverse elements seeking an escape from German suppression. As was previously described, Borovets' had made an agreement with the OUN-M by which he was to be sent a number of officers. Apparently this help was slow in arriving. By summer, 1942, however, a few men had appeared; one was the Zhitomir journalist Anthony Baranivs'kyi, who became the Mel'nyk representative at the headquarters of Borovets'.[17] Baranivs'kyi of course adhered to the OUN-M line. A quite different group consisted of the former "left-wing" of the Bandera party. Its leaders—Mitrynga, Turchmanovych, Ryvak, and Boris Levits'kyi—were with the task forces destined to proclaim the *akt* in Kiev. When these groups were broken up by the Germans before reaching their goal,

---

[13]Chief of the SP and the SD, Reports from the Occupied Eastern Territories, No. 55, May 21, 1943 (T 175, Reel 236—*Litopys*, Vol. VI, p. 75 ff.); Oberkommando der Wehrmacht, Fremde Heere Ost, May 19, 1943 (T 78, Reel 565—*Litopys*, Vol. VI, p. 74); PS 3943, May 22, 1942.

[14]Taras Borovets', *Zboroina borot'ba Ukraïny (1917-1950)* (The Armed Struggle of the Ukraine [1917-50]) (1951), pp. 10-11.

[15]Dmitrii Medvedev, *Sil'nye dukhom* (The Strong in Spirit) (Moscow: Voennoe Izdatel'stvo Ministerstva Soiuza SSR, 1951), p. 83; Taras Borovets', "Dva Khresty" (Two Crosses), *Ukraïns'ki Visti*, Christmas issue, January 7, 1948; Taras Borovets', *Armiia bez Derzhavy: Spohady* (An Army without a State: Reminiscences) (Winnipeg: "Volyn'," 1981), pp. 216-22.

[16]"Oleksander Hrytsenko" (Taras Borovets'), "Armiia bez derzhavy" (An Army without a State), *Ukraïns'ki Visti*, December 29, 1950, p. 2. Hereafter cited as "Hrytsenko."

[17]"Hrytsenko," *Ukraïns'ki Visti*, January 1, 1951, p. 4; *OUN u Viini* (The OUN in the War), Information Section of the OUN (UNR), April, 1946, p. 92.

the young men escaped arrest, but were forced to go into hiding. Then, since the whole tendency of the OUN-B indicated to them that they could no longer hope to secure the adoption of their left-wing program, all except Ryvak and Levits'kyi (who went into hiding in Galicia) fled to Volhynia, where they found a protector in the Polis'ka Sich.[18] There, apparently, they attracted to their ideology an assistant of Borovets', Leonidas Shcherbatiuk, son of one of the generals of the Republic army. With young Shcherbatiuk's support they founded in the midst of the untutored woodland peasants yet another Ukrainian party. Known as the Ukrainian Popular Democratic Party (Ukraïns'ka Narodna Demokratychna Partiia—UNDP), it advocated a program centering on maintenance of ownership of industry, means of transportation, and other large-scale enterprises by the state, with operation in the hands of the workers. At the same time, it condemned authoritarian control and violation of the rights of individuals.[19]

It was this motley group which carried on negotiations with the Soviet partisan Lukin in the autumn of 1942. While differing in details, the Soviet and the nationalist accounts of these discussions agree that the Red emissary demanded formal submission of the nationalist band to Soviet control, while Borovets' and his advisers were united in insisting on limiting an agreement to cooperation against the Germans.[20] Moreover, the Soviet sources frankly admit that the Red partisans were very weak in Volhynia at this time. They were confined almost entirely to support from the powerful Soviet bands in Belorussia. There was one band near Kovel', but it was under the command of a Pole, and apparently was composed of Poles rather than Ukrainians.[21] It is therefore quite understandable that the Soviet leadership may have wished to gain the support of the group under Borovets' until more "reliable" Soviet forces could be formed in Volhynia. It is significant that one of the alleged Communist demands was for an open campaign against the Germans, including particularly the assassination of the Reichskommisar. It is likely that the reason Borovets' gives for rejection of these demands is accurate, for it is in line with the whole tactical policy of his movement. He maintains that such action at that time would have been suicidal for the group and that it would have brought extreme suffering on the Volhynian people.[22]

When Borovets' could protract the negotiations no longer, Lukin flew back to Moscow; then the Red partisans began to move against the band they had hoped to use as an ally. In the late summer of 1942 the number of Soviet partisans sent in by air to northern Volhynia, or crossing the Pripet swamps from Belorussia, increased to the point where they became a real threat both to

---

[18]Interview 43; interview with Michael (Mykhailo) Turchmanovych, January 20, 1970.

[19]"Hrytsenko," *Ukraïns'ki Visti*, January 14, 1951, p. 2, maintains that the "proclamation" of the UNDP was made in June, 1943; other sources set the founding of the party in 1942, however, and it is certain that the group had a developed ideology before 1943. See Borys Levits'kyi, "Istorychne znachennia rozlamu v OUN" (The Historical Significance of the Split in the OUN), *Vpered*, No. 2 (11) (1950), p. 6.

[20]Medvedev, *Sil'nye dukhom*, pp. 85-86; Borovets', "Dva Khresty."

[21]G. Lin'kov, *Voina v tylu vraga* (The War in the Rear of the Enemy) (Moscow: Gosudarstvennoe Izdatel'stvo Khudozhestvennoi Literatury, 1951), p. 384.

[22]Borovets', "Dva khresty."

FROM UNDERGROUND TO RESISTANCE / 105

the nationalist group and to the German administration. By autumn the entire forest area west of the Dnieper was within their field of operation.

The unrest was soon increased by the arrival of the arch-guerrilla, Sidor Kovpak. For many months partisans in the Ukraine had been pictured in Soviet propaganda as motivated by local patriotism, and led by men described as successors of Khmel'nyts'kyi and other legendary heroes. But apparently the propagandists were increasingly under pressure to demonstrate that these leaders — in contrast to the numerous outsiders mentioned above — were really Ukrainians. Kovpak, who had become a partisan chieftain in the Sumy region, provided a welcome example. Although his enemies claimed he was a gypsy — the disarray of his bivouac led even admirers to compare it to a gypsy camp — it appears likely that he was of native Ukrainian origin, perhaps even (as he asserted) a descendant of the Zaporozhian Cossacks. He was an old Communist, a veteran of the civil war of 1918-20, but quite uneducated; his rough and earthy manner seemed to endear him to many Ukrainians, while his evident skill in partisan operations won him respect. In August Kovpak had flown from his hideout in the Briansk forest (on the border between Russia and the Ukraine) to Moscow to confer with Stalin himself. The Soviet dictator asked him — according to Kovpak's memoirs and those of other Red partisans — whether it would be possible to make a raid in force on the "Right Bank" region, west of the Dnieper. Apparently the small, scattered partisan forces there were not contributing enough to the Soviet war effort; moreover, Stalin felt the need of convincing his former subjects of the reality of Red power by sending in a force of real strength. Kovpak agreed to make the expedition, and set off late in October.[23] His passage across the Chernigov *oblast* was easy because of the strength of Fedorov's partisan forces there; on November 10 the mobile force crossed the Dnieper into the Reichskommissariat. The point at which the crossing was made was in the extreme north of Erich Koch's domain, above the confluence of the Pripet and the Dnieper,[24] in what had formed part of the Belorussian Soviet Republic. Throughout the first half of the winter, Kovpak was careful to keep within this extreme northern strip, which had the advantage of containing the most inaccessible terrain. His activities at this time could scarcely include showing the Soviet flag to a real Ukrainian population, though in late November the group penetrated southern Polessia near Olevsk, the former headquarters of the Polis'ka Sich.[25] The greatest single victory of Kovpak's group in this period was the temporary capture of the *Kreisgebiet* capital, Lelchitsi, on November 26.[26] After that, German counterattacks became extremely heavy, and Kovpak's men appear to have spent a miserable

---

[23]Sidor Kovpak, *Vid Putivlia do Karpat* (From Putivl' to the Carpathians), literary ed. Ie. Herasimov (Kiev: Ukraïns'ke Derzhavne Vydavnytstvo, 1946), p. 3 ff. Cf. P. Vershigora, *Liudi s chistoi sovest'iu* (People with Clean Consciences) (Moscow: Sovetskii Pisatel', 1951), pp. 39, 49, 181, 412.

[24]Kovpak, *Vid Putivlia do Karpat*, pp. 85-87, and map at the end of that volume. Apparently a considerable number of Red partisans were sent about the same time by air to the western region.

[25]*Ibid.*, p. 89; this corresponds with reports of a shift of Red partisan activity to the Stolin-Sarny-Olevsk triangle in PS 3943, February 12, 1943.

[26]Reichskommissar Ukraine to Reichsministerium für die besetzten Ostgebiete, December 10, 1942, CXLV 488, in Centre de Documentation Juive Contemporaine (hereafter referred to as CXLV 488).

two months evading the Germans in the frozen swamps along the middle course of the Pripet River.[27] In February, however, he headed south, cutting across a corner of "Bul'ba's" territory, then striking eastward through *Generalbezirk* Zhitomir.

While Red forces were pushing down from the northeast, the Ukrainian nationalist partisan movement was beginning to acquire real significance, although the nationalists were compelled to give some ground in northeastern Volhynia to the stronger Red partisans.[28] The SS and the Wehrmacht were agreed on the necessity of harsh measures to combat the Communist partisan threat. From the beginning, even those Wehrmacht generals who generally took a reasonable attitude toward the peoples of the east advocated the harshest measures toward partisans. For example, Field-Marshal von Reichenau based his policy on the concept that the Germans must be more feared than the partisans; he ordered that all who did not aid the fight against the latter were to be regarded as enemies, and that men who did not hinder or report partisan activities be "draconically" treated.[29] This policy was rigorously carried out in the fall of 1942.[30] The drastic reprisals carried out in western Volhynia and Polessia injured the patriotic Ukrainian peasantry as frequently as they did Communist sympathizers. Consequently, the Ukrainian police were reluctant to take part in such suppression of their own compatriots, and especially the brutal conscription for the *Ostarbeiter* program. The only alternative was desertion; in the fall thousands joined the forest refugees from burned villages and forced labor drives.[31] Unlike the latter, however, the police deserters were trained and frequently already organized by nationalists for opposition to the Germans. The command of the OUN-B in Galicia was reluctant to destroy its grip on the legal forces and risk a campaign of open resistance to the Germans at this time; but when they saw that the police units they dominated were breaking up anyway, they decided to begin a large-scale partisan movement. This step was taken in late November;

---

[27]Report of Höherer SS und Polizeiführer Russland-Süd, Ukraine, und Nordost, December 26, 1942, NO 1128 (hereafter referred to as NO 1128); PS 3943, February 12, 1943. According to one of the leaders of the Soviet partisans in Belorussia, Kovpak established an airport on one of the frozen lakes of the region. With the help of the Soviet Belorussian partisans he was able to defend it until German bombing finally broke the ice (Lin'kov, *Voina v tylu vraga,* p. 386).

[28]*Cf.* Lin'kov, *Voina v tylu vraga*, p. 375.

[29]Directive Verhalten der Truppe im Ostraum, October 10, 1941, USSR Exhibit 12 (hereafter referred to as USSR Exhibit 12). See also a memorandum by Chef des Oberkommando der Wehrmacht Field-Marshal Keitel, which stated that security troops in the rear areas would suffice only if they were allowed to proceed "draconically" without the requirement of juridical process, to convince the population that resistance would have terrible consequences (PS 459, July 23, 1941, hereafter referred to as PS 459).

[30]How drastic these measures could be in practice is shown by the reprisal burning of nine villages in the Petrikov area, leaving the peasants to shift for themselves in the dead of winter, although the Gebietskommissar himself asserted they were innocent of aiding the partisans (Occ E-4/1). The main "pacifying" campaign was carried out in Volhynia in September and early October, 1942 (NO 1128); cf. Lebed', *UPA*, p. 24, on the slaughter of nationalist adherents due to Communist provocation.

[31]Lebed', *UPA*, p. 26.

by the early part of 1943 the activity of the Bandera groups was already considerable.³²

There were two major centers of OUN-B activity. The first comprised the western part of the area which had been more ravaged by fighting between Red partisans and Germans, especially after Kovpak's passage to the southeast. Its extent may be defined by the quadrilateral formed by the towns of Kovel, Vladimirets (Volodimirets'), Kostopol', and Lutsk, although the chief operations were evidently carried out in the eastern section of this area.³³ A poor, woodland area, where the peasant population, while not extremely nationalist, appears to have viewed the nationalists with favor after the brutalities inflicted by the Communists and Germans, it made an ideal base for the nationalist activity.

A second base was established in Volhynia proper, southwest of Rovno. The activities there, however, were much more circumscribed than those farther north, because the wooded areas were smaller and the possibility of counterattack by the Germans greater. The nucleus of the Bandera forces in this area appears to have been a group of about one hundred men under a leader whose pseudonym was "Kruk." Evidently a small police unit which had broken away from its German command, it was encamped in the forest near Kremenets. Living near it on amicable terms was a group under the command of a Mel'nyk officer known as "Khrin."³⁴ Like the band under Borovets' a little earlier, both groups were really underground rather than partisan bands; they carried on such activities as raids on German convoys, "jail deliveries," and attacks on small German detachments to secure arms. It appears that they endeavored to maintain an appearance of subordination to German orders, or at least lack of hostility, for their position was too exposed to permit the luxury of open warfare.³⁵ They were of some importance, however, because they were in a section where the peasantry was very sympathetic to the nationalist

---

³²*Ibid.*, p. 24. See also the article written in the UPA underground in 1947 (reprinted in *Litopys*, Vol. III, p. 118), which indicates an insurrectionary detachment was formed in Polessia in October, 1942, to combat terrorism by Hitler's occupation forces and by Red partisans. The extent of German repression and Communist activity, which threatened to serve as an outlet for popular indignation, led the OUN-B to start operations before it really wished to do so (Interview 76). As late as October 16, 1942, Chief of the SP and the SD, Reports from the Occupied Eastern Territories, No. 25, summarized an OUN-B leaflet urging all Ukrainians to keep out of partisan activities, whether Bolshevik or Polish: "neither Stalin nor Sikorski." But follow-up report No. 29, November 13, 1942, mentions another OUN-B leaflet, in the Sarny-Kostopol area, which refers to "partisans against German and Soviet imperialism." (Both reports in T 175, Reel 236).

³³Lebed', *UPA*, pp. 24-25; PS 3943, March 19, 1943, ascribes (probably incorrectly, since the Germans were not fully informed of the nature of the nationalist bands) the attacks east of the Rovno-Lutsk road to a "Bul'bist" group. The western section of this area was partly controlled by large Polish police forces recruited to take the deserting Ukrainians' place.

³⁴The most detailed account is in MS D, which gives the strength of "Khrin's" group (with which the author of the manuscript served) as 140 in the spring of 1943, 500 in early June, and 200 a month later when Kovpak arrived. Apparently "Kruk's" group was weaker until June, when it began to forge ahead.

³⁵The nature of these groups is of course a highly controversial subject. Cf. especially O. Shtul' ("Shuliak"), *V im'ia pravdy: Do istorii povstanoho rukhu v Ukraïni* (In the Name of Truth: On the History of the Insurrectionary Movement in the Ukraine) (Rotterdam, 1947), p. 18; Oleh Lysiak, "Volyns'kyi Batalion" (The Volhynian Battalion), *Visti Bratstva kol. 1. UD UNA* (March, 1951), p. 2; Vershigora, *Liudi s chistoi sovest'iu*, p. 400.

cause, and because they formed a natural link between the headquarters in Galicia and the zones of more intense activity farther north.

In addition to the OUN-B centers just described, and the Mel'nyk group under "Khrin," there were several other small groups scattered over the area southwest of a line extending from Rovno through Lutsk to Kovel'. Little bands of Mel'nyk supporters hid in the woods near Dubno, Lutsk, and Vladimir Volynsk (Volodymyr Volyns'k); a group of dissidents who had been members of the OUN-B, known as the Front of Ukrainian Revolutionists (Front Ukraïns'kykh Revolutsionistsiv), was allied to them, while an *Otaman*, Voloshyn-Berchak, led a group of Free Cossacks in the Kremenets region.[36] By far the most important detachment, aside from the Bandera group, however, was that of Borovets', which had automatically (somewhat against the desires of its leader) swelled in numbers as the fugitives and police not affiliated with the Bandera forces sought a rallying point. Moreover, as the general confusion in Volhynia led the Mel'nyk OUN to take more open action, support from this quarter increased. One of the chief Mel'nyk leaders in Volhynia, Oleh Shtul', had for a long time been carrying on surreptitious resistance activities while ostensibly acting as an agent for a Ukrainian newspaper; now he permamently attached himself to the "Bul'ba" headquarters as representative of the OUN-M.[37] Moreover, young Iatseniuk, who had lived in Volhynia illegally for more than a year after his escape from Zhitomir, took the name "Volynets'" and formed a group operating southeast of Borovets', with a base a short distance inside the frontier east of Korets. It was the only nationalist partisan group based within the frontier of the pre-1939 Soviet Ukraine; as it was led by a man familiar with Soviet conditions who had wide connections in the Zhitomir area, it was useful for carrying out "propaganda raids" in the *Generalbezirk* Zhitomir.[38]

It was only natural that the dispersion and lack of unitary direction of the nationalist partisan forces aroused concern; the first proposal for a single command was evidently made by Borovets'. In mid-May, 1943, he had sharply rejected an SD overture to join the German police against the Bandera leaders who had "lost all moderation and goals," replying that attempts to incite hostility between Volhynians and Galicians were unacceptable.[39] The Bandera forces sent negotiators to Borovets'. Both parties were agreed that some higher center was necessary, for the lack of such authority might lead to the degeneration of the nationalist partisan movement into mere banditry. "Bul'ba" wanted the creation of an all-party front comprising UNDP, UNR, OUN-M, and OUN-B. The Mel'nyk followers agreed to his proposals, no doubt feeling that they already had the "inside track" with the partisan commander. The Bandera

---

[36] Shtul', *V im'ia pravdy*, p. 25; MS D; Interview 60. Cf. Chief of the SP and the SD, Reports from *Einsatzgruppen* and *Kommandos*, No. 187, March 30, 1942 (T 175, Reel 234), which asserts that the Free Cossacks inclined toward the OUN-B.

[37] Interview 12.

[38] *Ibid.*; Shtul', *V im'ia pravdy*, p. 27.

[39] Translations of the correspondence between Borovets' and a Dr. Pütz, Chief of the SD in Volhynia and Polessia, appear in T 78, Reel 565 (*Litopys*, Vol. VI, pp. 70-72). Later, in his memoirs, p. 33, Borovets' (*Armiia bez derzhavy*) seems to have become convinced that the Catholicism of the Galicians alienated them from Volhynians and East Ukrainians.

group, on the other hand, in accord with the guiding principle of their movement, demanded political direction by their Provid, although in return they were willing to recognize Borovets' as overall commander of military operations. They offered as ground for rejecting the proposal the obvious impracticability of associating the UNR, whose leadership in Warsaw could be reached only infrequently, in a political directorate which had to control so shifting a force as the partisans. Of equal importance—at least according to Borovets' and his supporters—was the latter's insistence on maintaining the "conspiratorial" nature of the movement, i.e., the use of a nucleus staff with most of the followers carrying on their normal activities. The Bandera group, on the other hand, unquestionably desired a large-scale movement of open resistance, which would have meant "deconspiration," the revelation of the identity of the adherents of the nationalist partisan movement. In late May, when no agreement could be reached, the negotiations were broken off.[40]

This severance of contacts, however, had no immediately serious consequences, for shortly afterwards a dramatic change in the situation in the whole western area took place with the arrival of the major Red partisan force. After he turned away from former Polish Volhynia, Kovpak pushed across the northern parts of the Zhitomir and Kiev *Generalbezirke*. Although German attacks forced him to keep on the move, the whole area north of the Zhitomir-Kiev line was so infested by Red partisans that it never again came under effective German control.[41] By May, however, Kovpak's own band was back in the northern swamp area. Then came orders from Moscow for a still more extensive operation, a penetration of Galicia.

The shortest route for Kovpak's forces lay directly across western Polessia and Volhynia, passing slightly north of Rovno. At a point in the neighborhood of Liudvipol', in the heart of "Bul'ba's" territory, however, the Kovpak group turned sharply to the northeast, traversing the Tsuman' area, which was a section dominated by the Bandera group.[42] Having reached the Tsuman' area, Kovpak turned south. His route from that point would have taken him directly through the Kremenets centers of the Mel'nyk and Bandera bands, but again he made a detour, this time to the east, skirting the Kremenets area and entering Galicia south of Ternopol' (Tarnopil').[43] The entire march across the area of operations of the nationalist partisans—over 250 miles—took the Red force about three weeks.[44]

When Kovpak's force entered Galicia in early July, it was only partially successful in achieving its primary objective, disruption of the Drohobych

---

[40]Cf. Lebed', *UPA*, pp. 41-43; Shtul', *V im'ia pravdy*, p. 20 ff.; Borovets', *Zboroina borot'ba*, p. 12; Borovets', *Armiia*, p. 50 ff.

[41]PS 265.

[42]Kovpak, *Vid Putivlia do Karpat*, map; MS D.

[43]*Ibid*. It will be noted that, although a distinct shift in route was made, the deviation was not very great—perhaps twenty miles. One source maintains that Kovpak sent emissaries to the groups at Kremenets to propose cooperation or at least neutrality, but that while they refused, the largest ("Khrin's") numbered only two hundred, and so was quite incapable of attacking Kovpak's more than two thousand men (MS D).

[44]While the force left its swamp headquarters on June 12, it evidently did not enter western Polessia until about the twentieth and was deep in Galicia by July 9 (Kovpak, *Vid Putivlia do Karpat*, p. 109, and map).

petroleum production.⁴⁵ It did, however, cause a severe disturbance of the peace of Galicia. For a long time the OUN-B had been preparing an underground armed force there. When Kovpak's arrival turned the extreme eastern part of the province into a battlefield, this organization (Ukraïns'ka Narodna Samooborona—Ukrainian Popular Self-Defense, a name chosen to conceal its identity with the Volhynian forces) came into the open to fight the Communists.⁴⁶ As they had long had numerous scores to settle with the occupation authorities, the young warriors also began sporadic fighting with the Germans.⁴⁷ What is most interesting as an indication of the state of feeling in Galicia, however, is the speed with which Kovpak's group melted away in the unfavorable environment. When the raid on the oil fields failed, the group headed for the Carpathians. It is apparent even from Kovpak's own account that the powerful force disintegrated within a few weeks of its arrival there. In the latter part of August, Kovpak himself, with part of the band, headed north, reaching the swamp region on September 1 with about three hundred men. His second in command remained behind and was killed, apparently with a majority of the band.⁴⁸ Since the Carpathians contain at least as favorable terrain for guerrilla operations as does the Polessian area, where Kovpak's group maintained itself and even grew during months of heavy German attacks, it appears that a decisive factor in the rapid destruction of the band was the hostile attitude of the Galician population.

Ultimately, an indirect but most injurious result of Kovpak's incursion was intense strife between Ukrainians and Poles in Galicia. The beginnings of fratricidal conflict between the two Slavic ethnic groups, both nationalist in their separate ways, had already been influenced by the breakdown of stable conditions in Volhynia. In principle, the German occupation authorities were more antagonistic to Poles than to Ukrainians. But the former included a far higher proportion of educated women and men fluent in German, hence more useful as a subordinate component of the occupation administration.⁴⁹ As

---

⁴⁵According to Kovpak the aim was the destruction of the oil fields around Drohobych, the second largest petroleum production center under German control (Kovpak, *Vid Putivlia do Karpat*, p. 107). While this is plausible enough, Ukrainian sources have always claimed that the aim of the expedition was disruption of the tranquility of Galicia, and especially interference with recruitment of Galician youths for the German armed forces. Probably the latter purpose occupied at least a secondary place in the minds of the Soviet leaders, since they would scarcely be willing to admit that it was necessary to send a partisan to prevent their former subjects in Galicia from joining the "fascist" forces.

⁴⁶Lebed', *UPA*, p. 49. Cf. Fremde Luftwaffen Ost, Militärpolitischer Bericht Ost, No. 1/45, January 22, 1945 (T 78, Reel 565—*Litopys*, Vol. VII, p. 150) and SS Obersturmbannführer Witiska (Slovakia) to Reichssicherheitshauptamt, January 24, 1945 (T 175, Reel 640—*Litopys*, Vol. VII, p. 154).

⁴⁷Lebed', *UPA*, p. 49; Report of "Dr. Frédéric" to Auswärtiges Amt, September 19, 1943. CXLVa 60, in Centre de Documentation Juive Contemporaine (hereafter referred to as CXLVa 60). Cf. Chapter VII below, note 27.

⁴⁸Kovpak, *Vid Putivlia do Karpat*, p. 124.

⁴⁹Borovets', *Armiia*, p. 245. A German army unit commented on language difficulties as a barrier to being sure of the loyalty of the Ukrainian auxiliary police. Oberfeldkommandantur 603, Abteilung Ia, Monatsbericht, July 16-August 15, 1943, p. 5 (T 501, Reel 217). Later, a clandestine Ukrainian publication indicated that Poles in Galicia were entering lower levels of the German service to seek revenge for Ukrainian "retaliatory actions." XXIV Panzer Korps, Ic, June 5, 1941

Ukrainian police members increasingly, during early 1943, responded to OUN-B summons to partisan activity, the Germans recruited Poles to replace them. Other Poles, however, just as much opposed to German oppressive measures as were the nationalist Ukrainians, had already constituted guerrilla bands in northern Volhynia. Some of the Polish bands cooperated— temporarily, as Borovets' had briefly considered doing—with the rapidly increasing Soviet partisan forces. Consequently, Ukrainian guerrillas came into conflict with Poles as well as with Soviet partisans. Some Poles in the occupation administration and police in Volhynia responded to Ukrainian hostility by denouncing covert Ukrainian nationalists to the Germans. Up to the summer of 1943, however, this spiral of intensifying antagonism had resulted in relatively few killings, at least among civilians.[50]

In Galicia, relations between the Ukrainian majority, relatively favored by the Germans since 1941, and the local Polish minority had been strained but largely non-violent until autumn 1943. By then, German authorities concerned with losses inflicted on the economy, where Poles played prominent roles, were warning that Kovpak's incursion had provided Ukrainian nationalists with an opportunity to settle accounts with their Polish neighbors.[51] The situation was exacerbated by Ukrainian nationalist beliefs that the Polish government in exile, in conformity with demands of the wartime coalition governments, was requiring cooperation between the Polish nationalist underground and advancing Soviet partisans and regular forces. By the spring of 1944, the German police reported widespread attacks on Polish villages in Galicia; in April, 1944, alone the UPA killed 645 Poles. Motivating these killings, the reports alleged, was a UPA order that all rural Poles were to be driven out of East Galicia—or shot if they remained.[52] Dr. Fritz Arlt, relatively well disposed toward the Ukrainian nationalists, summed up the situation as follows:

> At the same time, the Ukrainian national bands utilize the opportunity to kill, often in the most brutal manner, Poles, Czechs, and ethnic Germans living in the countryside. Furthermore, these bands

---

(T 314, Reel 212—*Litopys*, Vol. VI, p. 164). In discussing Polish-Ukrainian conflicts, I have relied almost entirely on German reports, especially by military agencies and intended for internal use, therefore relatively factual. Ukrainian nationalist postwar sources on the subject are usually reticent. As noted in Chapter VII (footnote 30), postwar publications in Poland are more abundant; but I am not competent to assess the degree to which such materials accord with a shifting official line.

[50]Oberfeldkommandantur 603, Anlage 6 (T 501, Reel 217); Abwehrstelle Ukraine, Tagebuch 16668, reporting on the "Ukrainian National Movement," September 15, 1943, that mass arrests of Ukrainians in Volhynian towns had been instigated by Polish circles (T 501, Reel 28—*Litopys*, Vol. VI, p. 95).

[51]Oberfeldkommandantur 603, Ia, Anlage 1 zu OFK 365, No. 6020/43, "Auszug aus dem Lagebericht einer Kreishauptmannschaft des Distrikten Galiziens," October-November 1943 (T 501, Reel 217); Panzer Armeeoberkommando 4, Ia, Kriegstagebuch, May 3, 1944 (T 313, Reel 391).

[52]Heeresgruppe Nordukraine, Monatsbericht, April, 1944, transmitted by Reichsministerium für die besetzten Ostgebiete representative (T 454, Reel 24—*Litopys*, Vol. VI, p. 140). Cf. prisoner of war reports in XXIV Panzer Korps IIb—No. 4019, August, 1944 (T 78, Reel 566—*Litopys*, Vol. VII, p. 128).

deliberately attack local people who are in German service or sympathize with Germany.[53]

Horrified by the fratricide, Metropolitan Sheptyts'kyi arranged with the Polish bishops of Galicia to have pastoral letters calling for peace between Ukrainians and Poles read from all pulpits on a single Sunday. Unsparing as he was of Ukrainian violations of the divine commandment against murder, Sheptyts'kyi considered that the Poles were less faithful to the call for peace, and blamed their headquarters in Warsaw for using the same methods to eliminate the Ukrainian intelligentsia in the Chelm district (435 had already been killed, he said) that the UPA employed against the Polish minority in East Galicia.[54] Ultimately, disillusion with the perfidy of the Soviet "ally" appears to have done more to bring about an armistice between the anti-Communist *Armija Krajowa* (Home Army) and the UPA than religious intervention. Negotiations between the Polish Home Army and Borovets' had occurred in early 1943; but more serious agreements appear to have been attained in November, 1944.[55]

It has been necessary, in discussing the troublesome Polish question, to jump ahead of events in Volhynia in 1943. Kovpak's force had scarcely left Volhynia before the Bandera partisans began to seize control of the nationalist resistance movement there. The failure of negotiations with Borovets' induced their commander, Dmytro Kliachkevs'kyi, to adopt the title UPA in an apparent effort to secure the prestige attached to it by "Bul'ba's" earlier start.[56] At the same time, the Bandera partisans regained the services of the most experienced of their commanders, Roman Shukhevych, who had been the chief Ukrainian organizer in "Nachtigall." After the dissolution of Stets'ko's government, this unit had been withdrawn from the front, together with "Roland." Both detachments were thoroughly reorganized, certain nationalist members were arrested and the remainder sent as a detachment to fight Red partisans in Belorussia.[57] When it appeared likely that the Germans would also suppress this anti-partisan unit, Shukhevych escaped to Galicia, arriving in L'vov in the spring of 1943. Some weeks later he became commander of all OUN-B partisan forces. According to one account, this reflected an official decision of the OUN-B Provid.[58] A German military report alleges, however, that Shukhevych's assumption of command led to a rupture with the previous director

---

[53]Reichsministerium für die besetzten Ostgebiete, Chef des Führungsstabes Politik (signed "Arlt"), November 17, 1944 (T 454, Reel 15, folder EAP-15).

[54]Frédéric report to Auswärtiges Amt (CXLVa 60) and T 454, Reel 24.

[55]Borovets', p. 240; Fremde Heere Ost to Heeresgruppe Süd, Ic, December 23, 1943 (T 78, Reel 565 – *Litopys*, Vol. VI, p. 103); Chief of Einsatzgruppe H of the SP and the SD (Slovakia), Tagebuch No. 92/44, November 21, 1944 (T 175, Reel 640 – *Litopys*, Vol. VII, p. 105).

[56]See Chapter IV, note 79.

[57]Liubomyr Ortyns'kyi, "Druzhyny Ukraïns'kykh Nationalistiv (DUN)" (The Brotherhoods of Ukrainian Nationalists [DUN]), *Visti Bratstva kol. Voiakiv 1. UD UNA* (June-July, 1952), p. 6; Lebed', *UPA*, p. 22; Chief Abwehrabteilung II (Lahousen) to liaison officers at Army and Army Group Headquarters, January 16, 1942 (T 312, Reel 1698).

[58]Interview 76.

of OUN-B activities in Galicia, Nicholas Lebed'.[59] The latter's supporters contend that Lebed' was thenceforth no longer responsible for UPA partisan activity. The issue is crucial because the UPA leaders, whoever they may have been, decided that the refusal of Borovets' and the Mel'nyk forces to accept their proposals for union required forceful action to see that the nationalist partisan struggle did not degenerate into the private enterprises of numerous *otamans* or war lords, as had the Ukrainian movement in the last days of Petliura's regime.[60]

Consequently, on July 6, shortly after Kovpak had passed through the area, "Kruk's" force suddenly appeared fully armed before the Mel'nyk detachment of "Khrin" and demanded that it submit to Bandera command. Lack of preparation made resistance impossible; apparently, too, OUN-B propaganda had prepared the ground for the coup. At any rate, the majority of the Mel'nyk group accepted the ultimatum and enrolled in the Bandera force.[61]

Shortly afterwards, Iatseniuk's group was similarly compelled to join the rival forces.[62] After these incidents, the remaining Mel'nyk and independent groups rapidly melted away; they were destroyed by Communists or Bandera partisans, or joined the latter. In mid-August, "Bul'ba's" main force, which had also been seriously weakened, in part because of continued fights with Red partisans, was attacked by an OUN-B group. Two of his principal advisers from the UNR were captured and forced to join the OUN-B group; his wife was also taken prisoner.[63] He himself, together with Shtul', Mitrynga, Raievs'kyi, and other leaders, but with only a handful of fighting men, was driven eastward into Communist-infested territory. Here in September the group encountered a stronger Red force. In the resulting fight, Mitrynga and Raievs'kyi were killed, but Borovets' and Shtul' again managed to escape.[64] Two months later they took the only course they felt remained open: they left Volhynia altogether, going to Warsaw to seek German assistance to rebuild their scattered forces.[65] Shcherbatiuk remained as commander of the tiny, demoralized group in Volhynia (which had been renamed the Ukraïns'ka Narodna Revoliutsiina Armiia—Ukrainian People's Revolutionary Army— UNRA, to distinguish it from the Bandera usurpers of the original title).[66]

---

[59] Fremde Heere Ost, November 1, 1944, "Die national-ukrainisch Widerstandsbewegung UPA," Anlage 2 (T 78, Reel 562). A note by the editors of *Litopys* (Vol. VI, p. 98) states that Lebed' remained *de facto* leader of the OUN-B "from July 1941, i.e. from the arrest of Stepan Bandera, until the Third Extraordinary Congress (Aug. 21-25, 1943)."

[60] Lebed', *UPA*, pp. 41-43.

[61] Shtul', *V imia pravdy*, p. 25; MS D; I. Hirniak, "Tse bulo 6. lypnia 1943. roku" (This was July 6, 1943), *Ukraïns'ke Slovo* (Paris), July 1, 1951, p. 3. All three sources assert that numerous Mel'nyk adherents were executed by the OUN-B.

[62] Shtul', *V imia pravdy*, p. 27.

[63] *Ibid.*; Borovets', "Armiia bez derzhavy," *Ukraïns'ki Visti*, January 14, 1951, p. 4.

[64] Interviews 50, 72.

[65] Lebed', *UPA*, pp. 41-43, confirms the general nature of the attacks on the "Bul'bist" groups, although he emphasizes their lack of organization and the "bloodless" nature of the OUN-B compulsion. See also VO Ausl. Ic, "Ukrainischer Bandenführer Taras Bulba," Führer Hauptquartier, November 22, 1943 (*Litopys*, Vol. VI, pp. 97-98).

[66] Borovets', *Zboroina borot'ba*, p. 12.

The rapid loss of strength of the Mel'nyk-Borovets' forces presents something of a puzzle. The explanation offered by the representatives of the latter is that they deliberately decided to refrain from entering into a fratricidal struggle. In part this appears to be correct. From a deeper, comparative perspective, the triumph of the OUN-B over its nationalist partisan rivals is one example of a trend which appears again and again in twentieth-century irregular warfare. The most penetrating analysis of the phenomenon was written thirty-six years ago by Franz Borkenau, on the basis of his study of Communist and non-Communist guerrillas in the Balkans.[67] Nationalist resistance forces, especially when they represent a legitimate government which preceded enemy occupation, tend to combat the latter while trying to conserve the lives and livelihood of the rural population with which they identify. However, a ruthless occupier (like the Germans) inflicts such severe burdens on the population that younger, less settled men become eager to respond drastically. The occupation forces meet such violence by extreme, often indiscriminate reprisals.

The tendency toward an upward spiral of violence may be curbed by a cautious leadership, but only if there is no competing guerrilla leadership determined to push matters to extremes, without reckoning the cost to the civilian population. If such exists, it will draw off the younger, more belligerent element of the peasant population, thus becoming stronger. In the Balkans, this extremist alternative consisted of veteran Communists under Moscow orders to strike the enemy regardless of reprisals. As indicated earlier in this chapter, similar extreme tactics used by Red partisans in Polessia and Volhynia—later in Galicia—were a major factor pushing Ukrainian nationalists toward open warfare. Borovets' and the OUN-M reacted like the Chetniks and the EDES in the Balkans, hesitating to compete with Communist "recklessness." But the Volhynian situation was complicated by a third party, the OUN-B, which had been conditioned to disregard reprisals by its extreme integral nationalist ideology and by its leaders' experience, limited to underground resistance. Hence the more moderate nationalists, caught between two extremist guerrilla forces, were probably destined to defeat regardless of their specific limitations.[68]

It is true, however, that these limitations were serious. The assertion of adherents of the defeated party that the first attacks came unexpectedly, yet resulted in complete surrender, itself implies that it was not calculated avoidance of an internecine struggle which alone led to the defeat. While the Bandera adherents were tightly organized, capable of sudden, prepared action, the other nationalist forces suffered from lack of central organization and competent leadership, since Borovets' himself was inadequately trained to conduct a campaign which required political as well as military experience and yet was unable to secure advice from a single, unified advisory body. Moreover,

---

[67]Franz Borkenau, *European Communism* (New York: Harper, 1953). I never met Borkenau, nor did I encounter his book until after the first edition of *Ukrainian Nationalism* had been published. In fact, my first version (my Ph.D. dissertation) had been submitted before Borkenau's book appeared. Consequently, the convergence of our analyses, based on entirely different case studies, heightens the plausibility of the generalized interpretation.

[68]In his memoir (*Armiia bez derzhavy*, p. 257) Borovets' emphasizes his considered refusal to match the OUN-B by mass mobilization, but notes that his younger supporters urged such a course, whereas his older officers agreed with him on avoiding mass fratricide.

the very dynamism and *élan* of the Bandera party appear to have attracted popular support; in spite of the comparative lack of military ability of "Kruk," for example, he is said to have been more popular than "Khrin." No doubt, too, their program of mass uprising, while of doubtful wisdom, was, like all forthright action, appealing to active spirits. It is noteworthy that nearly all of the members of the other partisan groups, when compelled to join the OUN-B movement, did so without taking a favorable opportunity to desert. Ukrainians in general have frequently been in the unhappy position of having to choose the lesser evil, which was unquestionably the Bandera movement, ruthless as many of its adherents were. The main concern was to fight on against the alien occupiers.[69] A third factor was the geographical location of the opposing forces. The group under Borovets' occupied excellent terrain, but an extremely exposed position, subjected to constant pressure by the Red partisans coming down from the northeast. Probably "Bul'ba" suffered as much altogether from attacks from them as he did at the hands of the Bandera partisans. The latter, on the other hand, occupied a somewhat more sheltered position in northern Volhynia and had a fairly clear line of communication to their large base in Galicia. Finally, the possession of the Galician source of manpower and leadership, very much larger than any outside source available to the rival groups, gave the OUN-B a decisive advantage, which had been consolidated by the early infiltration of the Volhynian police forces by Bandera organizers.

By fall of 1943 the Bandera group was in substantial control of the country districts of Volhynia and southwestern Polessia.[70] The Germans, of course, held the towns and with difficulty maintained movement on the principal roads, but such a large area east of Rovno was under full control of the insurgents that they set about constructing a "state" apparatus, including military training camps, hospitals, and a school system.[71] The total number of persons involved in the movement—including medical, administrative, and instructional personnel, as well as fighting men—was tens of thousands. Looked at in this fashion, the nationalist claim of 100,000 members of the UPA is perhaps not incredible, since a fairly trustworthy source describes one village in which the total personnel reached 2,000. Probably a German estimate of 40,000 (at the end of 1943) is more nearly accurate, however.[72] Included in the forces, according to nationalist accounts, were a number of non-Ukrainian elements—Jewish physicians and deserters from German police units recruited from

---

[69]This feeling was expressed in a letter from Iatseniuk to Borovets' explaining that he accepted the OUN-B coercion only so that he could continue to fight against the Soviet and German forces (Interview 50).

[70]Occ E-4 (1).

[71]Lebed', *UPA*, pp. 29-30. For confirmation of the existence of this school see Pavlo Vershigora, *Reid na San i Vislu* (Raid on the San and the Vistula) (Moscow: Voennoe Izdatel'stvo Ministerstva Oborony Soiuza SSR), p. 168.

[72]Occ E-4 (1).

prisoners of war representing many of the nations of the Soviet Union.[73] The great weakness of the movement, however, was lack of trained officers. For a long time the Bandera partisans had been forced to use as chief of staff an elderly UNR officer ostensibly in command of a Rovno police regiment.[74] Each additional UNR officer from the "Bul'ba" forces, aging though he was, was a treasure who was given a post of great importance by his new masters.[75] Similarly, Soviet officers who escaped from prisoner camps or deserted from Red forces were eagerly welcomed. The lack of trained military personnel greatly limited the partisan organization's value as a fighting force.

The weakness of the insurgent structure became apparent in February, 1944, when the Soviet army advanced into Volhynia and reached the Lutsk-Rovno line. Since there was no question of the inadequately led and lightly armed partisans offering resistance to a force which the Wehrmacht had been unable to stop, the UPA was forced to go underground until the wave of fighting had passed. Its plan was to avoid fighting with Soviet army units, but to attack NKVD units and other Soviet repressive forces after most regular Soviet military formations had left the area.[76] The UPA attempts to resume activity were severely hampered, however, by the fact that the Soviet security forces were far more capable than the Germans of organizing a network of informers which revealed the identity of the opposition group. Now "Bul'ba's" warning against "deconspiration" was proved accurate, for the organization and the individuals who had worked openly in the autumn could no longer conceal from the Communists' local agents their own affiliations.[77]

The presence of many men who had lived under the Soviet system at first acted as a disturbing influence in the UPA organization. The Bandera leadership, having carried the policy of one-party direction to a temporarily successful conclusion, was determined to maintain this position and to prevent the development of an East Ukrainian opposition, which they suspected was infected with Communist attitudes. Their instrument was the SB or Security Service, forged by Lebed' years previously, but apparently by late 1943 no longer under his direction. Though the extent of the "purges" of "unreliable elements"

---

[73] For confirmation of the presence of non-Ukrainians in the OUN-B partisan forces, see Vershigora, *Reid*, p. 262 ff. Banderists infiltrating the local administration had begun using Jews as interpreters in Volhynia because few Ukrainians were fluent enough in German. Michael (Mykhailo) Lebed', "Chasy nemets'koï Okupatsii v Matïvs'kim raioni na Volyni" (Time of the German Occupation in Matiïv *raion* in Volhynia), *Litopys*, Vol. V, p. 201. Women of various nationalities there tried to help each other against German oppression. Sofia Stepanik, "Ukraïns'ki zhinky v nimets'kykh tiurmakh Krem'iantsia i Rivnoho" (Ukrainian Women in German Prisons in Kremenets and Rovno), *Litopys*, Vol. V, p. 232 ff. V. Podliak, "Na nove zhittia" (In the New Life), *Litopys*, Vol. IV, pp. 170-74, presents the account of a Zionist physician, Kim, from L'vov, who served and died in a UPA detachment in the Carpathians.

[74] MS D.

[75] E.g., Colonel Treiko and Colonel Lytvynenko, chief adviser from Andrew Livyts'kyi to Borovets'; MS D.

[76] Lebed', *UPA*, p. 59. For an interesting Soviet confirmation of this UPA account, see Vasyl' Behma, "Zakliatye vragi ukrainskogo naroda" (The Mortal Enemies of the Ukrainian People), *Pravda Ukrainy*, November 13, 1944, p. 2. Behma, who was first secretary of the Rovno *oblast* committee of the Communist Party at the time, quoted an order of "Enei" (the pseudonym of the commander of one of the major forces of the UPA) providing that his partisans should let the Red army units pass, then attack isolated groups of military personnel, NKVD, and police.

[77] Shtul', *V im'ia pravdy*, p. 32.

(primarily East Ukrainians, but including some former Mel'nyk partisans, although apparently no old UNR émigrés) is uncertain, there is little question that it was sufficiently great to arouse extreme disaffection among the non-OUN-B elements in the enlarged partisan movement.[78] At the same time, however, the East Ukrainian elements apparently had sufficient influence — or compelling arguments — to secure the adoption of a program calculated to secure support from former Soviet citizens.[79]

As was pointed out in the last chapter, the ideology of the Bandera faction of the OUN began to change as early as the spring of 1942. The major force for change at that time was the impact of East Ukrainian conditions and attitudes upon members of the OUN-B "task forces." While this portion of the Bandera group was too small and uninfluential to bring about a fundamental change in the group's program, some new currents are clearly apparent in underground publications as early as 1942.[80] One publication (apparently issued very early in 1943) devoted much attention to the deceits and failures of the German land program, and bitterly objected to the restriction of Ukrainian education to the four-year school.[81] Exaltation of "heroism" and emphasis on Dmytro Dontsov's integral nationalism (*natsiokratiia*) remained, however.[82] Expedience counseled some reduction of the extreme ethnocentrism which had characterized the Bandera faction, but, as the following passage indicates, true tolerance was remote:

> Regardless of the negative attitude toward the Jews as a weapon of Muscovite-Bolshevik imperialism, we regard it as inexpedient at the present stage of the international situation to take part in anti-Jewish actions, in order not to become a blind tool in foreign hands and not to divert the attention of the masses from the principal enemies.[83]

A little later another underground publication condemned German racism, which had carried anthropological nonsense to the absurd.[84] In the spring of 1943 another OUN-B leaflet made the admission, strikingly novel for that period, that some Russians did not oppose an independent Ukraine, for they were born in the Ukraine and felt more bound to it than to Moscow.[85] But the same article stressed the need for upholding purity of the Ukrainian language, objecting to the "Ukrainian-Russian jargon" spoken in Kharkov,

---

[78] *Ibid.*, p. 30; MS D.

[79] See report of a press conference of the UHVR by M. Stiranka in *Ukraïns'ki Visti*, October 11, 1947, p. 3.

[80] Most of these publications were made available to me through the courtesy of Lev Shankovs'kyi for the second edition of this work. I must point out that Shankovs'kyi, in his book *Pokhidni hrupy OUN* (March Groups of the OUN) (Munich: Ukraïns'kyi Samostiinyk, 1958), using the same type of material, ascribes considerably more influence to the "task forces."

[81] *Visnyk*, No. 9, pp. 4-5.

[82] *Ideia y Chyn*, Year I, No. 1, November 1, 1942.

[83] *Ibid.* (from "incomplete" decisions of the second conference of the OUN-B held earlier in 1942).

[84] *Ideia y Chyn*, Year II, No. 2, p. 23.

[85] *Visnyk*, No. 11 (Spring, 1943).

and regretting that only the "intelligentsia" there was nationally conscious. These "conscious elements" were said to strive to "establish the Ukrainian language exclusively in the press, schools, and theater."[86] Indeed, as late as February, 1945, the German police found a UPA leaflet comparing Ukrainian antipathy toward Hitlerism to Ukrainian hatred of the "Jewish-Bolshevik dictatorship."[87] Moreover, German reports expressed surprise at how UPA propaganda, despite certain moderating trends, failed to address Russians.[88]

From the summer of 1943 on, the experience of the partisans became more and more important. The OUN-B effort to dominate the nationalist partisan groups and to secure the more or less willing cooperation of non-Galicians forced the leadership to pay more attention to the wishes of these elements. A little later, the East Ukrainians incorporated into the OUN-B dominated UPA achieved sufficient influence to inject their views directly into the stream of ideological revision. The predominantly military orientation of the OUN-B leadership in the UPA, exemplified especially by Shukhevych, was probably more open to new ideological themes than had been the fanatical Galician underground represented by men like John Klymiv (killed by the Gestapo in late 1942). At the same time Shukhevych and his lieutenants possessed far greater influence than the "task force" leaders who had been in touch with East Ukrainians in the earlier period.

Superficially, UPA organization of a "Conference of Oppressed Peoples of East Europe and Asia" (in the West Ukraine during late November 1943) suggested abandonment of ethnocentrism. But only representatives of the smaller Soviet nationalities were reported conferring with their Ukrainian nationalist hosts. The latter, moreover, were unwilling to be placed on a level with the "resistance movements" of the smaller nations, insisting (according to German reports) that Ukrainians, as representatives of a large nation, be considered a "national liberation" movement.[89]

Nevertheless, a few months earlier (August, 1943), the "Third Extraordinary Great Congress of the OUN" had demonstrated the ascendancy of new ideological influences, especially in economic matters. Apparently influenced by the reluctance of many younger East Ukrainians to see agricultural land revert completely to private ownership, the Congress made no commitment on this point, and UPA propaganda urged leaving choices on land use to the peasants. The Congress advocated that large-scale commerce and industry remain nationalized with worker participation in management. The intensive

---

[86]*Ibid.*

[87]SS office in Slovakia, III B Bo/Ak.Lf. No. 1066, February 17, 1945, transmitting UPA leaflet, "The Struggle of the Ukrainian People against the Occupiers" (T 175, Reel 640—*Litopys*, Vol. VII, p. 184).

[88]Fremde Heere Ost, November 5, 1944, based on interrogation of a Soviet lieutenant colonel (T 78, Reel 566—*Litopys*, Vol. VII, p. 86). But see Peter Potichnyi and Yevhen Shtendera (eds.), *Political Thought of the Ukrainian Underground, 1943-1951* (Edmonton: Canadian Institute of Ukrainian Studies, 1966), pp. 283-318, for a rare wartime (1943) analysis of Ukrainian-Russian relations, "Our Tactics with Regard to the Russian People," by D. Shakhai (Ukrainian version in *Litopys*, Vol. VIII, pp. 203-52).

[89]Army Leitstelle III Ost für Frontaufklärung, September 12, 1944, "Versuch einer politischen Einigung der nationalen Bestrebungen kleiner Volksgruppen" (T 78, Reel 566—*Litopys*, Vol. VII, pp. 22-27); Reichsministerium für die besetzten Ostgebiete (Arlt), November 17, 1944, "Das Wesen und Ziel der UPA" (T 454, Reel 15, folder EAP 15).

Soviet emphasis on piece-work (Stakhanovism) was rejected in favor of voluntary overtime work, while freedom in choice of jobs, profit-sharing, and free trade unions were to be guaranteed. Women were promised equality, but were to be relieved of unhealthy tasks such as work in mines. Assurances of free health service, old age pensions, family allowances, and free education at all levels indicated the concern of the OUN-B with social security measures which strongly appealed to the East Ukrainians. Political rights were by no means so closely defined. Some points of the program referred to the rights of national minorities, generally guaranteed freedom of religion, speech, and the press, and rejected official status for any doctrine. On the other hand, the ethnocentric and authoritarian elements of earlier OUN-B doctrines seemed to be reflected in the insistence on an "heroic spirit," "social solidarity, friendship, and discipline."[90] OUN-B underground publications during late 1943 and early 1944 continued to portray the glories of Ukrainian history, to stress the need for extending the use of the Ukrainian language, and to demand rigid discipline.

The mixture of social egalitarianism and romantic authoritarianism which characterized the new OUN-B ideology is most clearly apparent in the record of the last major conference (aside from those held by émigrés) for which reliable information is available. The conference was held in eastern Galicia in early July, 1944, a few weeks before the area was reconquered by the Soviet armies.[91] Although it is highly probable that the leaders of the OUN-B, who were at this time in *de facto* control of the UPA, were responsible for calling the conference, the previous claim of this faction to monolithic control of all Ukrainian nationalists was at least overtly abandoned. A considerable number of East Ukrainians in the partisan bands attended the conference and apparently were able to express views diverging from those of the Bandera faction. Moreover, a new body, known as the Ukrainian Supreme Liberation Council (Ukraïns'ka Holovna Vyzvol'na Rada—UHVR) was formed and was declared open to all parties which accepted the aim of Ukrainian national independence. The "Universal," as the proclamation issued by the new body was entitled, emphasized the following points:

---

[90]*Za Samostiinu Ukraïnu*, Year III, No. 8 (1943); English translation in Potichnyi and Shtendera, *Political Thought of the Ukrainian Underground*, pp. 333-53, with additional introductory materials. Essentially the same text of the resolutions *only* was translated into German by Wehrmachtbefehlshaber Ukraine, Ic, December 28, 1943 (T 77, Reel 856—*Litopys*, Vol. VI, pp. 106-10).

[91]The record of this conference is especially important not only because it represents a culminating stage of Nationalist ideological development, but because it is the most complete and most indisputably authentic of the OUN-B conference records. Available since the early 1960s in the Hoover Library on War, Revolution, and Peace, it can now also be found in contemporary German translation in the Arlt collection of the Reichsministerium für die besetzen Ostgebiete (T 454, Reel 15, and, with minor variations, in T 454, Reel 92—*Litopys*, Vol. VII, pp. 93-104). The original Ukrainian version is in *Litopys*, Vol. VIII, pp. 27-41, and is translated into English by Potichnyi and Shtendera, *Political Thought of the Ukrainian Underground*, pp. 355-72. Internal evidence concerning the provenance of these slightly variant but essentially identical documentary versions renders the authenticity of the OUN-B conference record above suspicion.

Representatives of the Ukrainian revolutionary liberation forces, and various political groups from all the Ukrainian lands, which have acknowledged the independence platform to be the only correct one in the liberation struggle of the Ukrainian people for an independent Ukrainian state embracing all the Ukrainian lands, have united in the Ukrainian Supreme Literation Council.

The Ukrainian Supreme Liberation Council is the supreme and only guiding organ of the Ukrainian people for the period of its revolutionary struggle, until the formation of the government of an independent Ukrainian state embracing all the Ukrainian lands.

An accompanying resolution entitled "The Provisional Structure of the UHVR" provides interesting clues to the background and outlook of the founders of the new organization, although the complex apparatus which it envisaged could scarcely have had any real existence under conditions of partisan resistance. The resolution declared the supreme legislative authority of the Ukrainian liberation movement to be the Great Assembly of the UHVR. This body was to have twenty-five members, comprising apparently the representatives of the "various political groups" who had created the UHVR.[92]

The executive power was assigned to a General Secretariat consisting of a Chairman and General Secretaries, for internal affairs, external affairs, military affairs (the commander of the armed forces), and financial and economic affairs. Additional secretaries could be named in the future. While the General Secretariat was to act in a "collegial" fashion, deciding questions by vote, the Chairman was actually given a dominant position. He was elected by the Great Assembly, and could be dismissed by it alone. The Chairman, however, was given broad appointive powers, subject only to confirmation by higher authority. He nominated all other members of the Secretariat and proposed their dismissal; he nominated the diplomatic representatives of the UHVR. Significantly, his powers extended to the legislative branch, for he could nominate new members of the Great Assembly.

Nominally an eight-man Presidium and its president occupied positions above the General Secretariat. The Presidium was an interim legislative council, the organ which "acts between sessions of the Great Assembly." It was to "advise on the political strategy, the tactics, and practical activity of all the organs of the UHVR and inform them of its supplemental decrees and proposals." Otherwise, its functions were primarily ceremonial and procedural; for example, the President was declared to "stand at the head of the UHVR and to represent it externally." The President was also to confirm officials nominated by the Chairman, except for the new members of the Great Assembly, who were to be elected by the Presidium as a whole upon the proposal of the Chairman.

In many of its functions, as well as in its title, the Presidium recalls the Presidium of the Supreme Soviet of the USSR established by the constitution

---

[92]The initial membership was not specified, very likely to gloss over the fact that the Great Assembly was self-appointed. This is one of numerous points where the UHVR proclamations are apparently intentionally obscure. On the other hand, repeated confusion in reference to the "UHVR" and the "Great Assembly of the UHVR" evidently reflects poor drafting of the documents.

of 1936. Very probably this feature of the UHVR framework was introduced by the East Ukrainian representatives at the conference who drew on their knowledge of the Soviet system. The provision of a Control Collegium to supervise the "financial-economic activity of all the organs of the UHVR, in particular ... the financial-economic policy of the General Secretariat" also suggests the influence of the Soviet constitutional structure, which until 1940 included a Commission of Soviet Control.[93]

In contrast to the Soviet constitutional provisions, though not to Soviet practice, individual officials were assigned positions of great power, however. The scope of the Chairman's authority has already been outlined. The other heads of branches of the government were given comparable, though lesser, powers. The President was given a more important position than the Soviet President, who is confined to ceremonial duties. Similarly, the Comptroller General was permitted to nominate the two other members of the Control Collegium, while the General Justice of the General Court nominated the two remaining justices. These provisions suggest that the *Führerprinzip*, the "organizational pattern that operates from the top to the bottom,"[94] had not been wholly forgotten by the nationalist leaders.

If the structure of the UHVR reflected the constitutional principles with which its members had become familiar through their association with the Nazi and the Soviet systems, the social-political principles proclaimed at the same time represented in considerable measure a reaction to these regimes. Because these principles represent a culmination of the development of the Ukrainian nationalist ideology toward greater emphasis on economic and social welfare, and upon the securing of individual rights, it is worth quoting them at some length:

(a) Assurance of popular-democratic procedures in the accomplishment of the political development of the Ukrainian State by the general assembly of the people

(b) Assurance of freedom of thought, of *Weltanschauung*, and of belief

(c) Assurance of the development of the Ukrainian national culture

(d) Assurance of a just social order in the Ukrainian State, free of exploitation of classes and suppression

(e) Assurance of the rule of law in practice, and of the equality of all citizens before the law in the Ukrainian State

(f) Assurance of civil rights for all national minorities in the Ukraine

(g) Assurance of the right of equal educational opportunities for all citizens

---

[93]On the features of the Soviet system mentioned in this paragraph see Julian Towster, *Political Power in the USSR* (New York: Oxford University Press, 1948), pp. 172-73, 263-72.

[94]Franz Neumann, *Behemoth* (London: Victor Gollancz Ltd., 1943), p. 74.

- (h) Assurance of free initiative in creative economic activity, regulated by the requirements and needs of the entire Nation
- (i) Assurance of a free form of creative use of the soil, with specification of the minimum and the maximum limits for individual use of the soil
- (j) Socialization of the principal natural resources of the country: soil, forests, water, mineral deposits; at the same time, the arable land is to be turned over to the creative peasant economy in permanent usufruct
- (k) State ownership of heavy industry and transport; turning over the right of free extensive cooperative activities by small producers to the cooperative associations in light industry and food industry
- (l) Assurance of free trade within the limits set by law
- (m) Assurance of the free development of artisanry and the right to the formation of individual artisan establishments and undertakings
- (n) Assurance of the right to free work for physical and mental workers and assurance of the protection of the interests of the workers by social legislation.

Although the above quotation indicates considerable attention to concrete problems, it must be emphasized that many practical deficiencies continued to obstruct the development of a coherent nationalist political theory. A much greater portion of the "Universal" was devoted to romanticized history and emotional appeals for action than to the proposal of clearly defined steps to be taken. The formulation of the other UHVR resolutions is frequently unclear, and the provisions are often inconsistent. These obscurities may sometimes have been inserted for deliberate tactical purposes, but in many cases, especially in the provisions for the governmental structure, they appear to have resulted from insufficient training in law and logic and from lack of real interest in constitutional questions. Moreover, it is evident that UHVR members had not undertaken the careful study on which to base real solutions to major problems, such as the agrarian quesiton. In place of carefully worked-out programs, broad principles were proclaimed which indeed pointed the way to new systems but failed to indicate how they would be implemented.

Most important, nationalism remained the central point of the ideology, about which all else revolved. As the introductory paragraph of the "ideo-programmatic principles" put it:

> The protection of the life of the nation, of national unity, and culture is the first and highest goal of every healthy national organism. The national sovereign state is the chief guarantee of the preservation of the life and the normal development of the nation and the well-being of its citizens. Therefore the Ukrainian nation must at the present time devote all its forces to obtaining and strengthening its own state.

It seems quite clear that a great many, at least of the leaders of the UHVR, like the leaders of the OUN in the East Ukraine many months earlier, were only partly convinced of the value of the new program of political, social, and economic gains. They had, however, come to see that vast numbers of East Ukrainians, by this time heavily represented in the partisan movement, would accept no ideology which failed to embrace such a program. Consequently, nationalist leaders were determined to win popular support for nationalism by presenting it as the surest road to political liberty and social welfare. Regardless of the motivations of the West Ukrainian leaders, however, it is clear that by 1944 contact with East Ukrainians had resulted in a sweeping change in the ideological position of the dominant nationalist group.

From the strictly military viewpoint, the activities of the Ukrainian nationalist partisans were of slight significance. Even from the immediate political standpoint, it is questionable whether they achieved anything of importance, for by the time the Germans were inclined to make concessions, their authority was already on the verge of being overthrown by the Red army. The "deconspiration" of the UPA undoubtedly inflicted considerable suffering upon the people of Volhynia, since it exposed the nationalist elements to the Soviet authorities. On the other side of the ledger must be placed the facts that the nationalist partisan movement undoubtedly prevented the spread of Red partisans to Volhynia and demonstrated that neither in that province nor in Galicia was there widespread sympathy for the Soviet guerrilla groups. Moreover, the fact that the Ukrainians, almost alone among east European nations, were able to carry on an armed struggle, even to a limited extent and for a comparatively short time, against both the German and the Soviet forces was an import psychological stimulus to nationalist feeling.

VII
Salvage Efforts

At the very time when partisan activity was reaching its peak in Volhynia, Ukrainian nationalist elements began the last chapter of their collaboration with the Germans. Strange as it may appear, in this final period, cooperation between these disparate forces was closer than during the abortive "honeymoon" of 1941. The key to this apparent paradox lies in the Ukrainian psychology—a better term than attitude in this case—toward the creation of a national military force and in the German policy toward securing the military collaboration of Eastern Europe.

Few political movements in this century have been as thoroughly obsessed as the Ukrainian nationalist movement with the idea of building military strength. This obsession is readily understandable as far as the OUN parties were concerned, for their ideology emphasized will, force, action. While there was a persistent trend in the senior branch of the OUN toward shaping the movement in a military mold with an emphasis on order and discipline, the younger group was inclined to cast aside all inhibitions to secure the immediate application of violence. To both, however, the army—insofar as it represented sheer power—was a high ideal. Non-Nationalist circles, such as the UNR and the legal parties in Galicia, also placed enormous emphasis upon military organization. When one reflects that in 1919-21 the nationalist movement in both the East and the West Ukraine had been bloodily suppressed by superior organized force, the roots of this concern become discernible. During the revolutionary period the lack of a substantial nucleus of trained military units, similar to those of the Poles, the Bolsheviks, and the White Russian forces had been a terrible handicap to the Ukrainian cause. In the Second World War nationalist leaders were willing to exact great material sacrifices of their people in order to overcome this critical lack.

The Ukrainian hopes for the formation in 1941 of a military force under German aegis were frustrated by the Nazi contempt for the peoples of the East. Somewhat later, even as the organized nationalist forces were being suppressed, renewed hope arose that the Wehrmacht would insist on the building of a Ukrainian army. These Ukrainian expectations were not wholly unfounded, for the bitter experiences of the winter battles around Moscow and Kharkov and the growing Red partisan threat convinced many high army commanders that if the Soviet system was to be defeated help must be secured from the Kremlin's former subjects. A leader in this group was General von

Schenkendorff, who proposed as early as March, 1942, that a national "Russian government" dependent on Germany should be formed to act as a rallying point for native armed forces.[1] With the aid of officers moved less by sympathy for the aspirations of the East European peoples than by a willingness to grasp for promising expedients, *Hilfswillige* ("Hiwis," auxiliary) units and *Ostlegionen* were recruited by the Wehrmacht from among prisoners of war to carry on service operations for the army and to combat partisans. In the late winter of 1941-42, some of these units were used as independent detachments in the front line. The success of this experiment induced Wehrmacht circles to plan extensive employment of former Soviet troops.[2]

Men from the Caucasus and Central Asia were preferred as recruits by the Germans, but Slavs were also enlisted. The chief Slavic detachments seem to have been the "Cossack hundreds." These groups were linguistically and ethnically heterogeneous, for the name appealed at once to the traditions of the Ukrainians and to the Russian-speaking Cossacks of the Don and the Kuban. News of their employment spread quickly, and by May Ukrainian circles as far away as L'vov were convinced that the Germans had employed "Ukrainian" forces in the front line on the Isthmus of Kerch and that they would soon use Ukrainian troops in large numbers.[3] Closer to the zone of operation the stories were more precise; the Ukrainian newspapers in Kiev and Mariupol' reported that several Ukrainian detachments were fighting on the Crimean front, and even mentioned the name of a commander, while they observed that preparations were being made for training 150,000 Ukrainian soldiers.[4]

The ambitious plans of the Wehrmacht group soon encountered a most formidable obstacle. Hitler had a deep-seated antipathy toward granting the "inferior" and "untrustworthy" Slavs the right to bear arms. In August, 1942, he intervened personally to limit military utilization of volunteers from the Soviet nationalities to small anti-partisan formations.[5] The Wehrmacht officers did not abandon their long-range intentions of forming an army of former Soviet soldiers to help fight Stalin, but these leaders were forced to move cautiously. In the fall of 1942, their efforts became centered around Andrew Vlasov, an officer well known among the second echelon of Soviet generals, who had been captured a few months previously. The German officers envisaged him as the spokesman of all the anti-Communist elements from the Soviet Union. For a time they were successful in securing some support for Vlasov even in the Ostministerium, although Rosenberg never fully

---

[1] PS 1685.

[2] PS 1686.

[3] Report from L'vov for week of May 22, 1942, contained in summary of Hauptabteilung Propaganda, Cracow, May 30, 1942, Occ E-2 (2), in Yiddish Scientific Institute (hereafter referred to as Occ E-2 [2]). Cf. also a citation from *Vil'ne Slovo* (Drohobych), January 15, 1942, in *Nastup*, February 15, 1942, p. 4.

[4] *Nastup*, February 15, 1942, p. 4, quoting *Nove Ukraïns'ke Slovo* for January 14, 1942; *Krakivs'ki Visti*, April 30, 1942, p. 3, quoting *Mariiupil's'ka Hazeta*, No. 32.

[5] Directive No. 46 to Oberkommando der Wehrmacht on partisan fighting, from Führerhauptquartier, August 18, 1942, PS 477 (hereafter referred to as PS 477).

trusted him, since he knew Vlasov, a Russian, would not endorse the Rosenberg plan of partitioning the Soviet state.[6]

During the winter of 1942-43 Rosenberg and the army felt, though mistakenly, that there was a chance of gradually winning Hitler's sanction for a limited program of quasi-autonomy for the peoples of the occupied USSR, a step which would secure their active support for the war against their former rulers. At the same time that he was bolstering his shaky prestige by collaboration with the Wehrmacht, Rosenberg also sought allies in the SS. His contacts there were utilized in March, 1943, in a scheme to form a "Ukrainian national representation" which, as envisaged by Rosenberg, would evidently have the dual purpose of securing greater Ukrainian support for the German war effort and preventing Vlasov's obtaining too important a role. Probably with the help of SS Brigadeführer Ohlendorf, Dr. Kinkelin, one of the higher officials of the Ostministerium, composed a list of four Kiev officials. A special effort was made to secure "pure Ukrainians" who were in close contact with the peasant. Remarkably enough, however, all four appear to have favored the Russophile element in Kiev municipal life.[7] The question of how such a "national committee" would have been received by nationalist Ukrainians went unanswered, for it remained a paper scheme. Whether its lack of reality was due to obstruction of the SS, which desired an instrument to reduce the partisan danger but continued to despise all Slavs, or whether it arose from Hitler's direct intervention is difficult to say.[8] At any rate, by the summer of 1943 the project had been dropped, along with the more grandiose plans for Vlasov's political activity.

The Ukrainians, however, who had looked with deep suspicion on the rise of Vlasov, now found in an unexpected quarter new encouragement in their hopes for a national army.[9] Although the SS continued to oppose the larger plans for arousing the Slavs against Communism, SS officers, extremely powerful in the Generalgouvernement, persuaded Himmler's coterie to authorize the large-scale recruitment of Galician Ukrainians for the Waffen SS. The continued outward loyalty of the population of Galicia, which made the province, prior to Kovpak's incursion, one of the most peaceful of Germany's conquests, was a powerful argument in favor of concessions to the West Ukrainians. Europeans classified as "Nordics" were already enrolled in special military formations under Himmler. This new departure in SS policy, made at a time when the higher SS officials were toying with the idea of

---

[6]Various aspects of the Vlasov movement have been thoroughly discussed in Jürgen Thorwald's *Wen sie verderben wollen* (Stuttgart: Steingrüben Verlag, 1952), George Fischer's *The Soviet Opposition to Stalin* (Cambridge, Mass.: Harvard University Press, 1952), and in Alexander Dallin's *German Rule in Russia, 1941-1945: A Study of Occupation Policies* (London: Macmillan & Co., Ltd., 1957). See also Catherine Andreyev, *Vlasov and the Russian Liberation Movement: Soviet Reality and émigré Theories* (Cambridge, Eng.: Cambridge University Press, 1987).

[7]They were Vadym Maikovs'kyi, Theodore Babak, Volodymyr Labuts'kyi, and George Kandiïv. Temporary list of members for a Ukrainian National Committee, by Dr. Kinkelin, CXLVa 77, in Centre de Documentation Juive Contemporaine (hereafter referred to as CXLVa 77).

[8]The latter's decision to restrict Vlasov operations was made about this time. See George Fischer, "Vlasov and Hitler," *Journal of Modern History*, XXIII (March, 1951), p. 64.

[9]*Ukraïns'kyi Visnyk*, May 30, 1943, p. 3.

backing a Ukrainian national representation, enabled the "inferior" Slavs to secure a footing in the ranks of the elite troops.[10]

The creation of SS Division Galicia, as the unit was called, was hedged about with restrictions. The word "Ukrainian" was excluded from the designation. Overt reference to "political" implications of the formation was rigorously forbidden.[11] Nevertheless, the creation of the division was supported by most of the leading elements in Galicia. Formation of the division was officially announced on May 4, 1943, when the president of the Ukrainian Central Committee, Kubiiovych, issued a proclamation urging its support.[12] While Colonel Sushko was not active in the new project,[13] General Kurmanovych spoke in favor of the division on the L'vov radio.[14] Other Mel'nyk supporters like Michael Khronoviat played leading roles in its development, and pro-OUN-M organs gave it great publicity.[15] The position of the rival nationalist group was less clear. Being illegal, the OUN-B could not take part openly in the drive to establish the military unit even had it desired to do so. Since the war, Bandera supporters have used this circumstance to maintain that they always opposed this form of collaboration with the Germans, and have denounced the other nationalist groups for supporting it. It is fairly clear that the OUN-B did not officially countenance the project in 1943. Contemporary UPA leaflets sharply attacked recruitment for the division. So did some clandestine publications from mid-1944. But other evidence suggests that, at least by then, the Banderists and the UPA did not really work against development of the division. Although a UPA leaflet of late 1944 reported that soldiers in the Galician Division had been forcibly recruited, a German secret report indicates volunteers insisted that the UPA had ordered them to enlist. Indeed, they alleged a UPA plan to have half of the Galician youth join it, but

---

[10]See Generalgouverneur Wächter to Himmler, July 30, 1943 (T 175, Reel 74), and Himmler's reply of August 11, 1943 (*ibid.*). Himmler denounced "Slavic ingratitude" of the Galician intelligentsia. Nevertheless, in a letter to Wächter of March 28, 1943 (T 175, Reel 74), Himmler agreed to an appeal to the Galician youth promising treatment for volunteers equivalent to that accorded German soldiers.

[11]Interview 70. A letter (in the possession of Dr. Liubomyr Makarushka) from Bauer to Schenk and Bisantz (all officials in the Generalgouvernement), dated August 18, 1943, states that Makarushka should be warned against ascribing political importance to the "military council" formed in connection with organization of the division.

[12]This proclamation was printed in *Krakivs'ki Visti*, May 6, 1943, p. 1. It recalled the heroic feats of the Ukrainian Galician Army and the students who defended Kiev at Kruty; at the same time it appealed to realism and national interest and emphasized the Bolshevik danger. It warned that the matter was a case of "now or never."

[13]Evidently out of pique because he was not given a leading role (Interview 36).

[14]*Nastup*, May 16, 1943, p. 2.

[15]*Ibid.*; *Nastup*, May 23, 1943, p. 6, and May 30, 1943, p. 3.

for the other half to secure German military instruction in the division.[16] Shukhevych is said to have felt that it offered a valuable opportunity for Ukrainian youths to secure military training. This would be in accord with his well-known proclivity for emphasizing the technical military needs of the nationalist movement, and it is the more plausible because just at that time his efforts to build up the UPA were being severely hampered by a dearth of young officers. In order to obtain cadres for future operations, and in order to prevent the new unit from falling into the hands of those opposed to OUN-B aims, he ordered a considerable number of his followers to enter its ranks, where they occupied prominent positions; other Bandera adherents, attracted by the opportunity for active service, joined without such authorization.

The Galician Division, however, never came under the control of either OUN party to the same extent as had the earlier German-organized Ukrainian formations. The prime organizer and highest ranking Ukrainian officer in it (the commanding staff was German) was Dmytro Paliïv, formerly a leader of one of the smaller legal parties in Poland.[17] With him were associated a large number of UNDO members like Liubomyr Makarushka,[18] while numerous old UNR officers like Generals Petriv[19] and Omelianovych-Pavlenko[20] lent their moral support.

The almost universal support given to a creation of the SS, the very organization which had done most to suppress Ukrainian nationalism, was reinforced in the spring of 1943 by the view which most Ukrainian nationalists took of the future course of events. Much as they hated the Nazis, and little as they hoped for real help from them, they hated and feared the Communists still more. That the prospects of German victory, never very high after the failure to take Moscow, were extremely remote was apparent to all after the winter of Stalingrad. Many Ukrainian leaders hoped for a protracted struggle in which both of the totalitarian powers would be so weakened that they would be forced to surrender their domination of Eastern Europe. They thought that Great Britain and the United States, in accordance with either the plain meaning of the Atlantic Charter or elementary principles of the balance of power,

---

[16]Commander of the SP and the SD (Slovakia), December 27, 1944 (T 175, Reel 567); Wehrmacht Frontaufklärungstrupp 324 attached to Hungarian First Army, "Bericht des V-Mannes 'Hirsch' über die Entwicklung der ukrainischen Frage," September 1, 1944 (T 78, Reel 565 – *Litopys*, Vol. VII, p. 18). In addition to the contemporary materials contained in these reports, *Ideia y Chyn*, II, No. 3 (about April, 1943), and *Biuleten'*, III, No. 11 (1943) appear to demonstrate that at least the Galician headquarters of the OUN-B fought the establishment of the division in its early stage. In addition to the informants cited by "Hirsch" in his report to the Germans above, a highly circumstantial memoir by Bohdan Pidhainyi, "Dva shliakhy – odna meta" (Two Routes – One Goal) in Oleh Lysiak (ed.), *Brody: Zbirnyk stattei i narysiv* (Brody: A Collection of Articles and Sketches) (Munich: Bratstva Kol. Voiakiv Pershoï UD UNA, 1951), p. 59, testifies to OUN-B involvement at least by 1944. The most important German memoir, by Major Wolf-Dietrich Heike, *The Ukrainian Division "Galicia," 1943-45: A Memoir*, ed. Yury Boshyk (Toronto: The Shevchenko Scientific Society, 1988), provides little direct evidence on UPA commanders' attitudes on this issue. However, Heike does report that Galician Division soldiers were able to visit UPA units and then return to their duties; this suggests at least tacit UPA approval of the division (p. 25).

[17]Interviews 36, 58.

[18]Interview 70; *Nastup*, May 16, 1943, p. 2.

[19]*Krakivs'ki Visti*, June 9, 1943, p. 1.

[20]Myroslav Martynets', "Gen.-Polk. M. Omelianovych-Pavlenko" (Colonel-General Omelianovych-Pavlenko), *Visti Bratstva kol. Voiakiv 1. UD UNA* (August-September, 1952), 1.

would prevent the complete subjugation of this area by the Soviet Union. What they anticipated was a period of anarchy in the area between Russia and Germany, like that of 1918, in which the nation which possessed organized military forces would be able to assert itself. Some felt that the UPA could fill this need, but many felt that in view of the UPA's low military value the nationalist movement must seize the chance to form a real army under German auspices which could later be used independently, even against its sponsors.[21]

Paradoxically, collaboration with the SS in creating a new military force was linked to an increasing conviction of German defeat and preference for the Anglo-American Allies. Apparently this widespread attitude was strongest in the OUN-B. Bandera himself assured high SS officer Gottlob Berger that Britain and the United States would win the war.[22] In October 1944 this assurance was bold, but scarcely prophetic. As early as July, 1942, however, the German police, relying on reports from Rumania, suspected the Banderists of contacts with the British secret service via a wealthy Ukrainian, Jakob Mahonin, resident in London. A more substantial link between the UHVR and Britain via Switzerland was reported in 1944. By then, a sense of desperation had helped spread wild rumors, such as the existence of a 250,000-man army of Canadian Ukrainians in Iran, dispatching parachutist detachments to the Pripet marshes.[23] In a strange mirror-image fashion, such ephemeral contacts and exaggerated hopes that a third party would enable nationalists to escape the choice between declining Nazis and still more dreaded Soviet totalitarians resembled Southeast Asian nationalist hopes that an anti-colonial Soviet intervention would rescue them from the return of European colonial rule following the brutal Japanese occupation. A German intelligence report on the UPA even indicated that some of its elements hoped for freedom on the model of what they imagined Japan had accorded the Philippines.[24] In both widely separated geographical areas, nationalists envisaged clearing the road for a

---

[21] See especially Nykon Nalyvaiko, "Legiony v natsionalnykh viinakh" (Legions in National Wars), *Narodna Volia*, October 27, 1949, p. 2, and November 3, 1949, p. 3; Ivan Hryn'okh, "Dyviziia Halychyna i Ukraïns'ke pidpillia" (The Galician Division and the Ukrainian Underground), in *Brody*, pp. 52 ff.; and the clandestine publication *Za Samostiinu Ukraïna*, No. 9, December 10, 1943, which gives the official position of the "Third Extraordinary Great Congress of the OUN [B]" on the role of Ukrainian forces in the event of German collapse. The Bandera followers stated that the Western Allies (especially Britain) wanted a prolongation of the war on the Eastern Front with mutual weakening of Germany and the Soviet Union, so that they could have a free hand on the continent. The Banderists continued that Moscow, being discredited in the eyes of the Eastern nations, could not maintain its imperialism, a circumstance which gave the Ukraine an opportunity to become the natural leader of these peoples. It is significant that, while the report of this conference called for struggle against Germany and glorified the UPA, in other places it emphasized repeatedly the need for armed forces without specifying that they be insurgent. There was no condemnation of the Galician Division.

[22] Berger to Himmler, October 6, 1944 (T 175, Reel 125).

[23] Undated memorandum (internal evidence indicates after August, 1944) from a "reliable informant,": "Über die gegenwärtige Bandenlage und die politische Stimmung in der Ukraine," Fremde Heere Ost files (T 78, Reel 565); Chief of the SP and the SD, Reports from the Occupied Eastern Territories, No. 12, July 17, 1942 (T 175, Reel 235 – *Litopys*, Vol. VI, pp. 54-55).

[24] Amt Ausland Abwehr, Abwehrabteilung III/Walli III, March 3, 1944 (T 78, Reel 565 – *Litopys*, Vol. VI, p. 118). On the comparable situation in Indonesia, see George M. Kahin, *Nationalism and Revolution in Indonesia* (Ithaca: Cornell University Press, 1952). See also Heike's memoir on Wächter's hopes, early in 1945, for acting as an intermediary between the Ukrainian Division and the Western Allied forces.

preferable third alternative by temporary collaboration with the regular military forces of the declining occupying power. Conversely, Japanese and German occupation officers hoped to purge themselves of subservience to a totalitarian regime by aiding local nationalists, thereby "buying a ticket" to the least objectionable victor. For Ukrainian nationalists, the preferred military force was, of course, the Wehrmacht. With the assistance of its defeated remnants, a strong nationalist military presence might maintain order and hold off Soviet forces until Western aid arrived. In this fantastic scenario, the Galician Division—although sponsored by the SS—represented a desperate chance for transitional alliance with Germans on the road to ultimate acceptance by the Western democracies.

The nationalist leaders were also encouraged to support the Galician Division by certain favorable conditions which they exacted from the Germans. According to Nationalist accounts, the unit was to be used only against the Soviet forces and never against the Western Allies; thus it would be in a position, they thought, to come to terms with the latter when the opportunity arose. Whether or not the Germans officially agreed to this stipulation, it was formally observed—although, as noted below, the division later fought elements which were not really Soviet-controlled. More significant, the political training and indoctrination of the soldiers, instead of being in the hands of Nazi ideologists, was left to the Nationalist leadership. Moreover, in contrast to the usual Waffen SS practice, each detachment was allowed its chaplain.[25]

The considerations just discussed played a considerable part in securing the support of both the Autocephalous Orthodox Church[26] and the Ukrainian Catholic Church for the formation of the Galician Division. Metropolitan Sheptyts'kyi had originally greeted the German army as a liberator from Communist tyranny. He soon discovered that the Wehrmacht officers, with whom he at first established cordial relations, were not the real representatives of German power. The horrible excesses of the SP, especially its massacre of thousands of Jews, caused a sharp change in Sheptyts'kyi's attitude. He was especially alarmed by the SP use of Ukrainian police for their murders, and is said to have sent a direct demand to Himmler that this practice be stopped. At any rate, a secret report to the German foreign office provides almost conclusive evidence that the Metropolitan was adamantly opposed to the Nazi anti-Semitic outrages and that by late 1943 he had come to regard Nazism as even a greater evil than Communism.[27] Nevertheless, he personally favored the

---

[25]Interviews 46, 58, 63. Ukrainian success in securing religious ministration in the Galician Division paralleled a sharp increase in church influence in the UPA, which overcame the lingering residue of anti-clericalism among nationalist youth. Catholic services on Easter and other holy days became regular features of guerrilla life in Galicia. A German translation of Ukrainian material notes that a theologian, "Ihor," had replaced a previous political propaganda director, "Miron," in the "Prokop" staff. Such changes appear to reflect the desires of a large number of Galician peasants. XXIV. Panzer Korps, Ic, June 5, 1944 (T 314, Reel 212—*Litopys*, Vol. VI, p. 159).

[26]The son of Mstyslav (Skrypnyk), the vicarial bishop of Kiev, joined the division; see Report by an unidentified official of the Ostministerium to Rosenberg, June 30, 1944, CXLV a 66, in Centre de Documentation Juive Contemporaine (hereafter referred to as CXLVa 66).

[27]CXLVa 60. This document was submitted as a secret report, under the pseudonym "Dr. Frédéric," to the German foreign office by a fairly well-known French student of East Europe, who had become an active collaborator with the Germans. On a visit to L'vov in the late summer

creation of the Galician Division, and sent one of his clergy, Dr. Laba, to act as chief chaplain.[28] Bishop Joseph Slipyi conducted a service in St. George's Cathedral in L'vov, celebrating the inauguration of the division.[29]

German permission to provide chaplains and the absence of Nazi indoctrination among the soldiers helped make the unit acceptable to the church. The chief reason which induced the Metropolitan to sanction the project, however, was similar to that which motivated other nationalist leaders. He felt that German defeat was only a matter of time and that the small military support which the division could provide for the faltering Wehrmacht could not be decisive. At the same time, he thought the existence of a nationalist military force of some strength would be invaluable in the chaos which would succeed a German collapse and might even be necessary to preserve the lives of a considerable portion of the Ukrainian population of Galicia. Sheptyts'kyi's chief concern in this connection was aroused by extremist elements among the Poles who were killing their opponents among the Ukrainians, just as the OUN-B was slaughtering Poles in Volhynia and Galicia.[30]

More than twelve months were spent in recruiting and organizing the division. The response of young men to the call for enlistment was so great that the quota set for the unit was overfilled many times, and tens of thousands had to be rejected.[31] Nevertheless, the SS officers in control appear to have been

---

of 1943 this man talked with a number of Ukrainians, including the Metropolitan. The report appears to reflect the Metropolitan's attitudes accurately, and in large measure substantiates accounts such as those of Stepan (Stephen) Baran, *Metropolyt Andrei Sheptyts'kyi* (Metropolitan Andrew Sheptyts'kyi) (Munich: Vernyhora Ukraïns'ke Vydavnyche Tovarystvo, 1947), pp. 114-15, and Father Myhailo Sopuliak, "Pam'iati velykoho Mytropolyta" (Memories of the Great Metropolitan), *Chas*, December 14, 1947, p. 3. This, and the following paragraph, is also based on Il'ko (Elie) Borshchak, *Un Prélat Ukrainien: Le Metropolite Cheptyskyj (1865-1944)* (Paris: Editions Franco-Ukrainiennes, 1946), pp. 55-56; and on Interview 63.

[28]SS Obergruppenführer Berger to Himmler, July 26, 1943, HH 263, in Hoover Library. The same file contains a sermon delivered by Father Laba in which he calls upon the Galicians to help "Hitler and the German people" destroy Bolshevism. An accompanying letter from Berger to another SS official, Brandt (July 22, 1943), notes that Laba's sermons contain "dangerous expressions," but that "we will soon pull this tooth." Himmler's own attitude is indicated by Brandt's statement that his chief was willing to use the influence of the clergy in the division, but that if they began to agitate they would be thrown out, and the Metropolitan himself would have to bear part of the consequences. A lengthy but highly polemical work by a Soviet Ukrainian, Sergei T. Danilenko, *Dorohoiu Han'by i Zrady* (On the Road of Shame and Treachery) (Kiev: "Naukovo Dumka," 1970) presents (pp. 250-56) several alleged German documents for the period March 24-April 20, 1944, purporting to show that Father Hryn'okh, under the alias "Herasymov" was acting as Sheptyts'kyi's agent in coordinating UPA and German activities against Soviet forces.

[29]*Nastup*, May 16, 1943, p. 2.

[30]See Chapter VI for a brief sketch of Ukrainian-Polish violence. A voluminous literature on Ukrainian-Polish wartime relations has appeared in Poland since 1945. The subject is too peripheral to the theme of this book to permit an extended examination. Moreover, neither my grasp of the Polish language nor of the intricacies of changing political restrictions on Polish historiography permits me to treat the Polish sources in detail. The best reference tool is the detailed subject index of the Centre de Documentation Internationale Contemporaine, now housed in the University of Paris-Nanterre library. Some thirty items there deal with Ukrainian-Polish relations; for the most part they are short military memoirs on encounters with the UPA.

[31]Interview 44. As early as May 1943 Berger reported to Himmler (T 175, Reel 74) that 50,000 of 80,000 volunteers had been accepted provisionally, but that only 25,000 were expected ultimately to be found qualified, mainly because of the minimum height of 1.65 meters. If that were slightly reduced, manpower for a second division would be available.

suspicious of the loyalty of their command and hesitant to use it. Meanwhile the Nazis' vast conquests in the Ukraine were falling into the hands of the Soviet army. In March, 1943, the Soviet forces took Kharkov, only to lose it in May. They captured Kharkov once again, and September, 1943, brought them from Kharkov to the gates of Kiev. There they halted a month, but the remaining fall and winter of 1943-44 ended with the reconquest of practically all of the pre-1939 Soviet Ukraine, plus most of Volhynia.

It was not until the summer of 1944 that the real battle for Galicia was joined. At this point, the SS command finally decided to commit the new Ukrainian division to battle. The front ran from just east of Kovel to a point in the Carpathians south of Ternopol'; a key point was the little town of Brody, on the main highway from Rovno to L'vov. Here, in late June, the SS division was put into the line to assist in covering the Galician capital. For three weeks it maintained its position, in the face of fierce Soviet attacks and encircling operations, but by July 20 was no longer effective as a fighting unit. Twenty-seven percent of its complement fell back with the German armies toward the Carpathians, and many of the remainder escaped to join the UPA or to filter back to the German lines.[32]

After the victory of Brody, the Soviet army rapidly conquered east Galicia, Bukovina, and the Carpatho-Ukraine. By fall, substantially all of the Ukrainian lands were again under the dominion of Moscow. This time the repression exercised by the Communist rulers was harsher and less disguised than it had been five years before. The Ukrainian Catholic Church was attacked ruthlessly. Bishop Slipyi, who had succeeded Metropolitan Sheptyts'kyi after the latter's death in late 1944, was arrested and deported to the interior of the Soviet Union. Most of the hierarchy of the Ukrainian Catholic Church, as well as hundreds of its clergy, were likewise banished. Orthodox priests subservient to the Patriarch of Moscow enlisted the aid of a minority of the Catholic clergy, who renounced their allegiance to Rome and joined in constructing a new hierarchy of the Russian Orthodox Church in Galicia. The same tactics were pursued in the Carpatho-Ukraine.[33]

According to reports of refugees from the area, very severe measures were taken against the population at large. Men from the ages of eighteen to fifty are said to have been drafted into the Red Army in a mass, without regard for their state of health.[34] Once enlisted, they were said to be watched over by special *politruks*, given inferior arms, and sent into battle after eight days' training.[35] In addition, there was a renewed collectivization of agriculture and Sovietization of all phases of life.

---

[32]See Heike's memoir; numerous contributions to *Brody*; and *Visti Bratstva kol. Voiakiv 1. UD UNA*, for detailed descriptions of military operations of this battle and of the other Ukrainian forces serving with the Wehrmacht. Cf. Wehrmacht Frontaufklärungstrupp 324 with Hungarian First Army, "Hirsch" Report, September 1, 1944 (T 78, Reel 565 — *Litopys*, Vol. VII, p. 18).

[33]Cf. Baran, *Mytropolyt*, pp. 137 ff.; Mykola D. Chubatyi, "Russian Church Policy in the Ukraine," *Ukrainian Quarterly*, I (Autumn, 1945), pp. 51-53. See also Chapter XIII below, and John A. Armstrong, *The Soviet Bureaucratic Elite: A Case Study of the Ukrainian Apparatus* (New York: Frederick A. Praeger, 1959), Chapters 8 and 9.

[34]SS war reporter Oleh Lysiak in *Krakivs'ki Visti*, December 2, 1944, p. 3; Chief of the SP and the SD Einsatzgruppe H (Slovakia), Tagebuch No. 101/44, November 29, 1944 (T 175, Reel 640).

[35]Oleh Lysiak in *Krakauer Zeitung*, November 30, 1944, p. 6.

A strong effort appears also to have been made to overcome the nationalism of the West Ukrainians, which the Communists recognized as a danger to their regime. Several months before the Soviet army reconquered Galicia, Khrushchev, the First Secretary of the Communist Party of the Ukraine, addressing the sixth session of the Supreme Soviet of the Ukrainian SSR, denounced the nationalists in vitriolic terms. He concentrated his attack upon the nationalist partisans:

> If one asks the Ukrainian-German nationalists how many of the German occupiers they destroyed, how many German formations they wiped out, how many bridges they blew up, in order to prevent the aggressors from transporting arms for subjugating and annihilating the Ukrainian people, they can make no reply.[36]

His remarks served to set the theme for Soviet propagandists, who condemned the adherence of Bandera, Mel'nyk, and "Bul'ba" as agents of the Germans, in contrast to the "true patriots of the Soviet fatherland."[37] An obvious effort to split the peasantry and the laboring class from the intellectuals was made. The former were declared deceived, while the latter were said to be the chief propagators of the dangerous doctrine.[38] Soviet propagandists promised that "special attention" would be given to the West Ukrainian intelligentsia, who did not have the "advantage" of having been brought up in Soviet schools, but had been, rather, in "bourgeois" schools, which inculcated "bourgeois ideology," and who, as a result, had aided the "Ukrainian-German nationalist bandits."[39] In view of the usual fate of social elements so violently denounced by the Soviet rulers, it is likely that a large part of the intelligentsia was "liquidated as a class."

At the same time, a certain outlet was offered to nationalist feeling, with a class-conscious twist, by emphasizing the heroic feats of certain Ukrainian leaders of Red partisan units in the L'vov area.[40] This theme was relatively subdued, however, probably because there were not enough Ukrainian subjects for glorification. Far more significant, in the long run, was tacit Soviet acceptance of the policy of driving the Polish minority out of eastern Galicia. A compulsory "exchange of populations" arranged with the Communist-led government of Poland accomplished this aim by early 1945. Since the move

---

[36]Dmytro Manuïls'kyi, *Ukraïns'ko-nimets'ki natsionalisty na sluzhbi u fashysts'koï Nimechchyny: Dopovid' 6-ho sichnia 1945 roku na naradi uchyteliv zakhadnykh oblastei Ukraïny* (The Ukrainian-German Nationalists in the Service of Fascist Germany: Report of January 6, 1945, to the Conference of Teachers of the Western *Oblasts* of the Ukraine) (Kiev: Ukraïns'ke Derzhavne Vydavnytsvo, 1945), p. 21.

[37]01. Kasimenko, "Ukraïns'ko-nimets'ki natsionalisty—liutshi vorohy ukraïns'koho narodu" (The Ukrainian-German Nationalists—The Fiercest Enemies of the Ukrainian People), *Radians'ka Ukraïna*, December 10, 1944, p. 2.

[38]*Ibid.*

[39]"Ideino-politychne vykhovannia inteligentsii" (Idea-Political Education of the Intelligentsia), *Radians'ka Ukraïna*, December 12, 1944, p. 1.

[40]*Pravda Ukrainy*, July 26, 1945, p. 3.

was unconcealed, it was apparently designed to meet Ukrainian desires for an "ethnically pure" eastern Galicia.[41]

In the Carpatho-Ukraine, where the Red partisans had evidently attracted genuine support as liberators from the de-nationalizing Hungarian regime, the appeal to Ukrainian sentiment was employed much more extensively. Whole lists of partisan leaders, including at least one priest, were published. Moreover, one partisan was explicitly declared to speak "pure Ukrainian," and apparently all bore Ukrainian names.[42] This propaganda was followed up by the customary practice of forming a People's Committee which requested union of the province with the Soviet Union.[43] Even after the war was ended and the new acquisition securely incorporated into the Soviet Ukraine, however, an article was published which, had it been written by a non-Communist, would have been denounced as "racist." It was stated that some villages in the Carpatho-Ukraine spoke only Magyar, but that their "purely Ukrainian" character was shown by the family names of the inhabitants and their "Slavic appearance."[44]

Fortunately for them, the majority of the West Ukrainian nationalist intelligentsia did not stay behind to enjoy the benefits of Soviet "re-education." It is one of the strange paradoxes of German-Ukrainian relations during the war, however, that at the very period when Germany was most in need of securing Ukrainian support, and when a minimal amount of such assistance was being developed in the form of the Galician Division, a new wave of repression fell upon the nationalist leaders. This occurred in the fall of 1943; its immediate causes cannot be determined, but it appears that it was basically a result of that tendency to strive for large results by employing force and trickery which marred so much of German relations with the eastern peoples. One of the first Ukrainian leaders to fall a victim to these methods was Borovets'. About a month before he started on his forlorn trip to Warsaw to obtain help in rebuilding his guerrilla force, German officials interested in the matter had decided that it was necessary to negotiate with the partisan leaders, so that they might discover who they were and arrest them during the course of the negotiations if this appeared to be desirable.[45] Whether there was any direct connection between this plan and the fate which overtook Borovets' is unknown; the procedure used toward him, however, closely paralleled that outlined. After the Wehrmacht had started conversations with "Bul'ba," the police suddenly intervened, arrested him and his assistant Oleh Shtul', and incarcerated them in Sachsenhausen concentration camp along with Bandera and his deputies.[46]

---

[41]This was the motive ascribed to the Soviet move by the German Embassy in Slovakia. Report of February 14, 1945, to Auswärtiges Amt (T 78, Reel 565, and T 175, Reel 640—*Litopys*, Vol. VII, pp. 168-70).

[42]*Radians'ka Ukraïna*, December 14, 1944, p. 2.

[43]*Radians'ka Ukraïna*, December 23, 1944, p. 2.

[44]*Pravda Ukrainy*, July 28, 1945, p. 3.

[45]Memorandum by Taubert, Occ E-4 (1).

[46]Interviews 12, 29, 72; Taras Borovets', *Zboroina borot'ba Ukraïny* (1917-50) (The Armed Struggle of the Ukraine [1917-50], 1951), p. 12; Taras Borovets', *Armiia bez Derzhavy: Spohady* (An Army without a State: Reminiscences) (Winnipeg: "Volyn'," 1981), p. 281.

The group was soon joined by the most prominent members of the OUN-M. After Mussolini's overthrow, Eugene Onats'kyi, spokesman of the Ukrainian nationalists in Italy, had written an article criticizing Fascism as a form of government, stating that it sheltered a privileged class. This essay was indiscreetly printed by *Ukraïns'kyi Visnyk* and thus came to the attention of the German police, which arrested Onats'kyi on September 29, 1943, but did not transfer him to Sachsenhausen from Regina Coeli prison in Rome until December 12.[47] Throughout his period of confinement, he was closely questioned concerning connections of Mel'nyk and Konovalets' with Ukrainians in Allied countries.[48] Apparently these connections, at least in the forms of inspiring anti-German material in the Allied press and contacts with Ukrainian organizations outside the German orbit, were one reason for the arrest on January 26, 1944, of Mel'nyk himself, together with the Provid foreign affairs specialist, Dmytro Andriievs'kyi.[49] Apparently the chief ground for the arrest of the OUN-M leaders was the discovery of anti-German clandestine publications of the OUN-M in the East Ukraine and in Kandyba's quarters in L'vov.[50] Kandyba and numerous other members were arrested about the same time, and *Nastup* was suppressed. Three members of the Provid had been killed within the preceding fourteen months, so that of the directorate only the aged generals Kapustians'kyi and Kurmanovych were left at large.[51]

Most of the OUN leaders were kept in close confinement throughout the crucial months when the West Ukraine was slipping under Communist domination. By October, when they were released,[52] virtually all of the Ukrainian lands had passed out of German control. There remained, however, some two million persons of Ukrainian origin in the hands of the Germans—thousands of refugees, over a million *Ostarbeiter*, several hundred thousand prisoners of

---

[47]Ievhen (Eugene) Onats'kyi, *U babylons'komu poloni (spomyny)* (In Babylonian Captivity [Memoirs]) (Buenos Aires, 1948), p. 15.

[48]*Ibid.*, p. 59.

[49]Interviews 52, 67; *OUN u Viini* (The OUN in the War), Information Section of the OUN (UNR), April, 1946, p. 101.

[50]*OUN u Viini*, p. 103.

[51]Kandyba and Chermeryns'kyi had replaced the murdered Senyk and Stsibors'kyi, but Chermeryns'kyi was killed by the Germans in the execution of the *Ukrains'ke Slovo* group in Kiev. Baranovs'kyi had been killed by the OUN-B in Galicia in May, 1943. A few months later, Sushko, too, was assassinated. A Fremde Heere Ost report of November 1, 1944, Anlage 2, "Führende Personlichkeiten der ukrainischen Freiheitsbewegung," blames the OUN-B, and puts Sushko's death at the "end of 1943" (T 78, Reel 562). Other evidence also points to the Banderists, but it is possible Sushko was killed by Communists or German police agents dissatisfied with his conduct.

[52]Bandera, Mel'nyk, Borovets', and all of their principal adherents were set free, except Kandyba and Gavrusevych, who had died in prison.

war, and about a quarter of a million auxiliary troops.[53] Most of the latter were scattered throughout various small units of *Osttruppen*, totaling about 700,000.[54]

The Nazi leaders wished to use this considerable reserve of manpower to bolster their collapsing defenses. The major part of their efforts centered around Vlasov, who at last was given a comparatively free hand to organize an anti-Soviet political center and military units of division size. Vlasov was backed by Himmler and a number of other high officials of the SS, who were by now ready to seize any possibility of staving off defeat. At the same time, other Nazi circles, including SS officers as well as the Ostministerium officials, endeavored to form a central Ukrainian political body.

A major German motive, after the evacuation of the West Ukraine in the summer of 1944, was to establish liaison with the nationalist partisans there.[55] Early in 1944, German military officers—if only because they had faced a comparable problem with Red partisans before their evacuation of the East Ukraine—keenly appreciated the significance of guerrillas operating behind the Soviet lines. Consequently, the German command not only envisaged a general agreement for cooperation with the Ukrainian nationalist guerrillas, but also authorized local commanders to make tactical alliances, so long as they avoided political questions.[56] The Germans recognized the guerrillas' limitations more than they did themselves: lacking officers experienced in tactical command of large formations, UPA dreams of "holding the front" against the advancing Soviet army were chimerical. Even the typically large formation employed in Volhynia and during the UPA campaign against Kovpak in 1943 in Galicia had to be replaced by the company-strength unit

---

[53]Rosenberg wrote Bormann on September 7, 1944 (NO 2997), that there were then one million "legionnaires and volunteers," one million prisoners of war, and two million *Ostarbeiter* drawn from the Eastern peoples. It is safe to assume that at least one-third of the prisoners of war were Ukrainian (see note 75, below). The figure of two million *Ostarbeiter* appears to be rather low, in view of the total of one and one-half million given for the Ukraine alone (see Chapter V). *Ukrainskaia S.S.R. v Velikoi Otechestvennoi Voine Sovetskogo Soiuza* (Kiev: Izdatel'stvo Politicheskoi Literatury Ukrainy, 1975), Vol. III, p. 153, gives a figure of 2,244,000 "driven into German slavery," but this number probably includes a large proportion who never departed from Ukrainian territory. It is certain that a considerable majority of the workers from the Soviet Union were drawn from the Ukraine, for it had the bulk of the population which was under German control for a long period, and was, moreover, more completely exploited in this regard than were the army areas and the Reichskommissariat Ostland. Taubert, in a memorandum printed in B. Dvinov, *Vlasovs'koe dvizhenie v svete dokumentov* (The Vlasov Movement in the Light of Documents) (New York, 1950), p. 110, estimated the proportion of Ukrainian *Ostarbeiter* as 60 percent. The figure for military personnel appears a bit high, but it is fairly clear that the Ukrainians totaled at least one quarter of this group (Interview 22 referred to a total of 220,000 Ukrainians in the German forces). Refugees not enrolled in any of these categories were not numerous. Cf. Dallin, *German Rule in Russia*, p. 452.

[54]NO 1068.

[55]The intentions of Arlt and the Ostministerium are outlined by Berger in the memorandum in Dvinov, *Vlasovs'koe dvizhenie*, pp. 109-11. Although Dvinov's work is highly tendentious, this document appears to be authentic.

[56]German documents in UHVR archives, *Litopys*, Vol. VI, pp. 152-55; XIII Army Corps, February 12, 1944 (T 314, Reel 523—*Litopys*, Vol. VI, p. 114); Abwehrkommando 105, Tagebuch No. 86/44, June 5, 1944 (T 78, Reel 565—*Litopys*, Vol. VI, pp. 155-58); Armee Oberkommando XIII Ic, January 21, 1944 (T 314, Reel 523).

(*sotnia*). The basic UPA plan became withdrawal to the more rugged portions of the Carpathians, along the border between Galicia and Hungarian-ruled Transcarpathia.[57]

The UPA command had a corresponding need to seek German assistance. As early as April, 1944, "Okhrim" (Dmytro Kliachkiv'skyi, at that time commander of the UPA in Galicia) sent a letter offering to provide information on Soviet military dispositions to the Germans. To be sure, the offer was contingent upon receipt of munitions (which the Germans were prepared to send by air) and liberation of Bandera (which was under consideration in Berlin).[58] As cautious field commanders, the German recipients nevertheless sought independent corroboration of nationalist guerrilla capacities and intentions. Several scouting expeditions were dispatched. Apparently the most important was the force commanded by a Captain Kirn, who stayed a month behind Soviet lines. Reports were favorable, both in regard to UPA cooperation and capacities, despite continued German warnings against "Ukrainian exaggeration." The central army intelligence staff, Fremde Heere Ost, estimated that 95 percent of all UPA units were behind the Soviet lines by September, 1944, holding down two or three Soviet cavalry divisions and fifteen to twenty NKVD regiments. Some men escaping from shattered German auxiliary units had constituted guerrilla bands asserting allegiance to Vlasov; but Kirn discovered that the UPA had a far stronger organization in eastern Galicia, for many of its accomplishments had been attributed erroneously to the Vlasovites.[59]

Initial moves by Soviet reoccupying forces probably enhanced UPA strength. Soviet efforts to seize all persons suspected of collaborating with the UPA eroded the long-run resistance capacity of the nationalist underground; but in the short run these Soviet tactics drove suspects, whether they sympathized with the UPA initially or not, to join it in its forest refuges. Sporadic reintroduction of collective farms and a military draft which threatened all able-bodied Ukrainian men produced additional recruits for the nationalist guerrillas. Gradually the Soviet authorities introduced more effective, but extremely ruthless measures. Villages which sheltered nationalists were burned. In one instance, ten peasant women and their children were shut in a burning house to compel their menfolk to return from the woods. In another case Soviet agents posing as Germans tricked peasants in three villages into

---

[57]Commander of the SP and the SD in Slovakia, "Nachrichten aus dem Raum hinter den sowjetischen Front," March 1, 1945 (T 175, Reel 640); Superior SS and Police Leader in the Generalgouvernement, Ic, May 17, 1944 (*Litopys*, Vol. VI, pp. 137-39).

[58]"An das Oberkommando der deutschen Armee in Galizien," (translation transmitted by Heeresgruppe Nordukraine, Abteilung Ic, April 18, 1944) (T 78, Reel 565 – *Litopys*, Vol. VI, pp. 124-26).

[59]Frontaufklärungskommando 202, Heeresgruppe A (signed "Kirn"), November 27, 1944 (T 78, Reel 565 – *Litopys*, Vol. VII, pp. 106-11); Fremde Heere Ost (B/P), September 9, 1944 (T 78, Reel 565 – *Litopys*, Vol. VII, pp. 28-33).

providing information, whereupon Soviet forces exiled the entire population.[60] As 1944 drew to a close, the policy of evacuating villages to create a "dead" zone devoid of shelter, supplies, and information in the neighborhood of nationalist forest bases became more widespread.

As elsewhere, the brutal policy of uprooting peasants—the water in which the guerrilla fish swim, to use the Maoist metaphor—proved effective. At first the UPA fought Soviet units carrying out the evacuation, while ordering the peasants to refuse to deliver goods to the authorities. Increasingly, though, the UPA had to avoid armed confrontations, employing instead small detachments for killing Soviet officers and civil officials. An eyewitness informed German intelligence of a Soviet general killed in a nationalist ambush in L'vov in autumn 1944.[61] In fact, as their ability to confront the Soviet forces declined, nationalist activity centered for a time on the outskirts of large towns like L'vov and along transportation lines, as well as along the eastern edge of the Carpathian Mountains. The German report, apparently the last referring to the UPA, of April 1, 1945, emphasized its great decline in strength due to village evacuation.[62] Yet the nationalist guerrillas remained potentially useful to the Germans right up to their final defeat because of the specialized diversionary and intelligence operations just described. Hence German expectations for continued UPA cooperation remained a significant incentive—second only to the hope of deploying major regular formations recruited among Ukrainians—for German deference to nationalist wishes during the final stages of World War II.

Dr. Fritz Arlt, the Waffen SS officer who had played a prominent part in dealing with Ukrainians in the Generalgouvernement in 1939-41, was a central figure in the efforts to form a Ukrainian national committee. Apparently both Mel'nyk and Bandera refused to discuss such proposals while they were in prison.[63] Soon after his release on September 27, 1944, however, Bandera suggested to Arlt that he approach Dr. Horbovyi, an OUN-B member who had played a leading role in organizing the Ukrainian National Committee in Cracow in June, 1941. Arlt could reach no agreement with Horbovyi,

---

[60]Fremde Heere Ost (IIIf), translation of Soviet Lieutenant Colonel Shevelov's interrogation, "Die Partisanenbewegung in der Ukraine," November 5, 1944 (T 78, Reel 566—*Litopys*, Vol. VII, pp. 84-86); AOK 17, Ic, "Lage- und Stimmungsbericht," November 25, 1944 (T 78, Reel 566, excerpts from field reports concerning UPA—*Litopys*, Vol. VII, p. 135); Commander of the SP and the SD in Slovakia, January 24, 1945, transmitting UPA leaflet "Visti s Kraiu" (News from the Homeland) (T 175, Reel 640—*Litopys*, Vol. VII, pp. 156-58); Frontaufklärungskommando 202, Heeresgruppe Mitte, March 1, 1945 (UHVR archive, *Litopys*, Vol. VII, p. 192); Frontaufklärungstrupp 324 with Hungarian First Army, "Hirsch" report, September 1, 1944 (T 76, Reel 565—*Litopys*, Vol. VII, pp. 16-20); Leitstelle 1 Ost für Frontaufklärung (Rü/T), Tagebuch No. 1062/45, January 19, 1945 (T 78, Reel 566—*Litopys*, Vol. VII, pp. 147-48); Fremde Luftwaffen Ost, No. 1332-45, January 22, 1945, "Ukrainische Bewegung," January 22, 1945 (T 78, Reel 565—*Litopys*, Vol. VII, pp. 149-53).

[61]Frontaufklärungskommando 202, Heeresgruppe Mitte, March 1, 1945 (*Litopys*, Vol. VII, pp. 188-90); Reichssicherheit Hauptamt Militär, No. 23576/3.45, "Die Tätigkeit der UPA in January, 1945," March 7, 1945 (T 78, Reel 566—*Litopys*, Vol. VII, pp. 198-99).

[62]*Ibid.*; Frontaufklärungskommando 202, Heeresgruppe Mitte (signed "Kirn"), April 1, 1945 (T 78, Reel 566—*Litopys*, Vol. VII, pp. 202-3).

[63]*OUN u Viini*, p. 106; Interview 51. The Mel'nyk and Bandera accounts agree—except that each side says that it persuaded the other not to form a committee to cooperate with the Germans.

however, and turned to Mel'nyk, who had been released on October 17, Mel'nyk was apparently able to secure an agreement among all important nationalist leaders, including Bandera, Livyts'kyi, and Skoropads'kyi, on the stand to be taken in relation to the German proposals, but Arlt and his collaborators could not accept the demands the nationalists made.[64]

Unable to induce the major Ukrainian nationalist leaders to take the lead in forming a national committee under conditions acceptable to the Nazi rulers, Arlt turned to elements which had so far been less active in politics during the war. The first two Ukrainian leaders offered the post of chairman of a national committee, General Petriv and Professor Mazepa, declined, in view of the risks which, with German defeat almost certain, such a position involved. Finally, however, General Paul Shandruk, a UNR officer and a close associate of Andrew Livyts'kyi, accepted, with the blessing of the latter, Bandera, and Mel'nyk.[65] As Shandruk and his associates saw the matter, it was absolutely necessary to have a Ukrainian committee recognized by the Germans, not only to avoid subordination of all Ukrainians in Germany to Vlasov, which would prevent their seizing an opportunity for independent negotiations with the Allies, but because the sheer existence of the *Ostarbeiter* and prisoners required that their compatriots be in a position to exercise influence on their behalf. To Shandruk and his associates, the loss of prestige involved in collaboration with an infamous and moribund power was not sufficient to outweigh these considerations.[66]

At the same time, Vlasov and his followers were busily endeavoring to secure a Ukrainian representation which would accept their claim to leadership and would agree to postpone any decision on independence for the Ukraine until after the Soviet rulers had been overthrown. Most Ukrainians whom they approached refused to cooperate, being convinced that if a predominantly Russian group such as Vlasov's ever succeeded in replacing the Communists in the Kremlin, it would create conditions which would make impossible a free expression of the wishes of the Ukrainian people on the question of union with Russia. Nevertheless, Vlasov succeeded in securing the support of a certain number of prominent Ukrainians for a Committee for the Liberation of the Peoples of Russia (Komitet Osvobodzheniia Narodov Rossii — KONR), which met in Prague on November 14, 1944. It is remarkable that practically all of

---

[64] Arlt to Rosenberg, November 21, 1944, NO 3039 (hereafter referred to as NO 3039); apparently the demands correspond to those contained in the petition quoted below on p. 141. For more details on this affair see Dallin, *German Rule in Russia*, pp. 620-25. See also Berger to Himmler and Rosenberg, October 6, 1944, on Berger's conversation with Bandera — "an able, ardent" "fanatic Slav" "useful but dangerous" (T 175, Reel 125), who adamantly refused to cooperate with Vlasov.

[65] Interviews 9, 22. One informant (Interview 24) states that while Bandera followers would not give their approval officially, they felt that Shandruk performed a highly useful and patriotic function. According to Shandruk, *Arms of Valor* (New York: Robert Speller & Sons, 1959), pp. 200, 231, Mel'nyk later withdrew his approval. Cf. Chief of Einsatzgruppe A of the SP and the SD, Slovakia, Tagebuch 95/44g., November 29, 1944 (T 175, Reel 640), which asserts that, although Bandera will not cooperate with Vlasov personally, he will permit Iaroslav Stets'ko to join the National Committee.

[66] Interview 22.

these were from the single city of Kiev.[67] In part this appears to be due to the fact that certain highly respected Kiev leaders, like Professor Theodore Bohatyrchuk, were convinced of the need of continued union with Russia and through their influence secured the adherence of their friends to the new body.[68] Unquestionably, however, the reaction in Kiev to the mistakes of the Nationalists and the somewhat unusual social and cultural background of the capital played their part.

The Ukrainian nationalist groups immediately reacted violently against the KONR proclamation, which claimed to express the aspirations of all the peoples of the Soviet Union. Four days after the Manifesto was issued, ten of the non-Russian national groups addressed a vigorous appeal to Rosenberg for help against this undermining of their position. Perhaps because as yet there was no officially recognized committee for the Ukraine, Mel'nyk signed the petition "for the Ukrainian national political groups."[69] After reciting the history of the struggles of their nations for independence from Moscow, and asserting that the Russians alone had not shown any zeal in combatting Bolshevism, the nationalist leaders stressed their claim to German gratitude:

> It is therefore not astounding that these (non-Russian) peoples greeted the outbreak of the German-Russian war with the greatest joy. They placed themselves at the side of the German army from the first day on, helped where they could, welcomed the troops with open arms, and with cordial friendship. Standing shoulder to shoulder with the German soldiers in battle, they proved their loyalty to the national idea.[70]

At the same time, the signers of the protest did not hesitate to criticize German policy. They asserted that the failure to recognize the striving of the peoples of the Soviet Union for independence had presented Stalin with an opportunity which he had utilized by granting independent diplomatic representation to the "so-called Soviet republics" the previous spring, thus pretending to offer more scope to national aspirations than did the Germans. Rejecting all claims of Vlasov to speak for their nations, they demanded in categorical terms, backed up by the threat that otherwise they could not "accept responsibility for the consequences which may result among our compatriots from the Vlasov action," that the Germans make the following concessions:

---

[67]These included Theodore Bohatyrchuk and George Muzichenko, who signed the Manifesto of Prague; Constantine Shtepa and Eugene Arkypenko, chief editor of the peasants' paper, *Uraïns'kyi Khliborob*; and the four officials of the Kiev administration whom Kinkelin had proposed in 1943 as members of a Ukrainian National Committee. Apparently Forostivs'kyi, the mayor, collaborated with the group for a time at least.

[68]Interview 19.

[69]The text of the protest is contained in NO 2998.

[70]*Ibid.*

1. Forbid any claim of General Vlasov to the leadership of our peoples;

2. Recognize the right, to take effect immediately, of our peoples to independent states and to pronounce a definite recognition of our national representative bodies;

3. Organize our national military formations under unified command of their own leaders, subject to the German Wehrmacht in operative matters, for the fight against Bolshevism, and turn over the political leadership within these formations to our national representatve bodies.[71]

Whether Rosenberg turned over this document to Hitler is questionable, in view of its uncompromising terms, but it is certain that on the same day it was presented he himself sent a very strong protest to his Führer against Vlasov's committee.[72]

Either because neither faction among the German leadership could secure Hitler's unequivocal approval, or because the most powerful Nazi leaders still desired, at the eleventh hour, to pursue their customary tactic of *divide et impera*, no definite choice was ever made between Vlasov and the Ukrainian leaders. The latter were allowed to continue with their efforts to organize their compatriots. At the same time, Vlasov was free to attract those Ukrainians whom he could prevail upon to join his movement.

The Ukrainian-language press was left under nationalist control. The principal paper for the *Ostarbeiter* and other workers in Germany, *Holos*, remained under the editorship of Bohdan Kravtsiv, a determined nationalist, while a leading East Ukrainian journalist, George Muzichenko, left its staff shortly after he joined the Vlasov information bureau.[73] Two other papers, *Ukraïns'kyi Dobrovolets'* (the journal of the military units) and *Za Ukraïn-*, were kept in the hands of nationalist editors, who were able to direct oblique attacks on Vlasov.[74]

Nevertheless, it is certain that Vlasov was given some advantages, and secured considerable success, in his efforts to recruit prisoners of war of all Soviet nationalities for his Russian Liberation Army (Rossiskaia Osvoboditelnaia Armiia—ROA). Even according to Ukrainian nationalist sources, only half of the prisoners of Ukrainian origin were fully "nationally

---

[71]*Ibid.*

[72]NO 1815.

[73]*Krakivs'ki Visti*, December 8, 1944, p. 3. A few weeks earlier the Vlasov group had made a strong effort to secure control of these and other Ukrainian papers in Germany. Cf. NO 3039.

[74]For example, the latter newspaper published the translation of an article from *Das Schwartze Korps* (an SS organ) harshly criticizing Russian émigrés, on January 18, 1945, p. 2.

conscious," and many could not even speak the Ukrainian language.[75] Moreover, Vlasov was able to secure a number of high-ranking ex-Soviet officers of Ukrainian origin for his staff, including the commander of the first ROA division, General Buniachenko. Altogether, units, in various stages of integration in the ROA, totaled 300,000 by January, 1945, and of this number perhaps 35 to 40 percent were of Ukrainian ethnic stock.[76]

Apparently no direct threats or compulsion were used to secure adherence of civilians to the KONR.[77] On the other hand, Ukrainian nationalist sources maintain that the apparent German favor enjoyed by Vlasov was a powerful inducement to the demoralized and physically worn-out prisoners to accept his invitation as a way out of confinement. They assert that a number of the units formed from prisoners or from the auxiliary units brought back by the Wehrmacht in its retreat abandoned the ROA, even without German permission, to join nationalist Ukrainian forces.[78] To a certain degree, this assertion is supported by one of the German officers most closely associated with the eastern military units, who states that difficulties were experienced in subordinating Ukrainians or mixed Ukrainian-Russian units which had been under German commanders, to Russian officers from the ROA, although there was generally no objection to attachment to Vlasov's overall command.[79]

In addition to this struggle for influence within groups which were subordinated to General Vlasov, there was an entirely separate military organization for the Ukrainians. Not only was the Galician Division reformed as the First Ukrainian Division; organization of a second division, to be composed of East Ukrainians, was begun. These and a number of other units, totaling some 75,000 men, were eventually classified as the Ukrainian Liberation Army (Ukraïns'ke Vyzvol'ne Voisko—UVV). The nominal commander-in-chief was

---

[75]M. Les', "Chomu ia buv 'Vlasovtsem'?" (Why was I a "Vlasovite?"), *Visti Bratstva kol. Voiakiv 1. UD UNA* (October-November, 1952), 3, states that 50 percent of the Ukrainian prisoners were "nationally conscious," 40 percent somewhat so, and 10 percent not at all. A contemporary account (*Krakivs'ki Visti*, October 23, 1941, p. 2) states that many of the letters addressed by Ukrainian prisoners to the newspaper which the Germans had established for them (*Nova Doba*) were in Russian, but notes that they were sent to the Ukrainian rather than the Russian paper, *Klich*. The latter also carried material evidently intended for a Ukrainian audience. Other contemporary accounts of the prisoners differ as to whether they could speak the Ukrainian language. One insists that 80 percent were "nationally conscious," and that the Russian prisoners accepted the fact that the Ukrainians were "separatists" without anger, for while the latter wanted an independent state they had always lived peacefully with the Russians and other minorities in the Ukraine (*Krakivs'ki Visti*, December 5, 1941, p. 2).

[76]Unsigned list of units from the eastern peoples, January, 1945, NO 5800 (hereafter referred to as NO 5800). For the percentage of Ukrainians see Les', "Chomu ia buv 'Vlasovtsem'?" p. 3, and MS H, which states that Vlasov told Shandruk that 70 percent of the first ROA division were Ukrainians. If so, this figure must have been reached by including persons with very little Ukrainian nationalist feeling whom the Russian National Socialist leader, Bronislav Kaminskii, recruited in the Lokot' area on the border of the Ukrainian and Russian Soviet Republics, since (according to Thorwald, *Wen sie verderben wollen*, p. 44) Kaminskii's brigade alone formed more than a third of the division.

[77]Interview 45.

[78]A. Kovach, *Ukraïns'ka vyzvol'na borot'ba i "Vlasovshchyna"* (The Ukrainian Liberation Struggle and the "Vlasov Affair") ("Germany," 1948), p. 51, states that 65 percent of the trainees in the Dabensdorf officers' school of the ROA were of Ukrainian origin.

[79]Interview 15; MS C.

General Shandruk, but German officers actually commanded each unit. At the very end of the war, however, the commander of the First Ukrainian Division relinquished his command to Shandruk. In the meantime, this division, scarcely retrained following its decimation at Brody, was dispatched by the SS higher command to suppress an uprising of Slovak military units. Apparently both German and Ukrainian divisional cadres believed—incorrectly—that the uprising was Soviet-sponsored, hence a suitable target for suppression. Three months later, in January, 1945, the division was transferred to southeast Austria and northern Slovenia to fight Tito's partisans and advancing Soviet forces. There it remained until its surrender to British troops moving up from Italy.[80]

The final months of the war brought no substantial change in the overall situation of the Ukrainian nationalists vis-à-vis Vlasov and the Germans. Borovets' was released from prison after a few months and commissioned to form a parachute detachment to land behind the Soviet lines to aid the nationalist guerrilla struggle.[81] Ukrainian (UVV) units were permitted symbolic distinctions such as the *trizub* (trident, instead of the ROA St. Andrew's cross, the traditional Russian symbol). But a majority of auxiliary units with Ukrainian ethnic majorities could not be brought under UVV control. Efforts to find a *modus vivendi* between the groups headed nominally by Shandruk and by Vlasov were unsuccessful, in spite of a personal meeting between the two generals. On the contrary, the Ukrainians went ahead with the setting up of their own national committee. Shandruk became president and the vice-presidents were Volodymyr Kubiiovych and Alexander Semenenko, mayor of Kharkov under the occupation. Thus the "old emigration" (Shandruk was born in Lubny), the West Ukraine, and the Soviet Ukraine were represented.[82] Aside from a certain moderation in German treatment of the Ukrainian *Ostarbeiter*, however, the group was able to accomplish little. In the last weeks of Germany's hopeless struggle the organization was officially recognized and allowed to issue a proclamation in Weimar on March 17, 1945, as the Ukrainian National Committee. The deterioration of German power enabled the Committee to take a strong stand for an independent Ukrainian state, without giving even lip service to alliance with the Germans. However, the document made it clear that the main practical objective was care for the interests of the Ukrainian refugees, workers, and soldiers in Germany.[83]

The proclamation also announced that the Ukrainian soldiers were henceforth to be united in the Ukrainian National Army. Under the circumstances, this could mean little, apart from General Shandruk's ultimate command of the First Division.[84] Of more practical importance was the fact that Shandruk

---

[80]For a detailed account see Heike, *The Ukrainian Division*, pp. 84-135, and Shandruk's book. General Shandruk had in his possession a mimeographed copy of the order from the German general, Freitag, turning over command of the First Ukrainian Division to him, but only on April 27, 1945. See also Oleh Lysiak, "Volyns'kyi Batalion" (The Volhynian Battalion), *Visti Bratstva kol. Voiakiv 1. UD UNA* (March, 1951), p. 2. This unit, formed from pro-Mel'nyk guerrillas, was eventually incorporated in the First Ukrainian Division.

[81]Borovets', *Zborona borot'ba*, p. 15; Interview 37.

[82]Interviews 9, 22.

[83]From a printed copy furnished me by General Shandruk.

[84]Interview 22, and order by General Freitag already cited.

and other Ukrainian leaders had been able to get in touch with Allied military quarters even before the surrender of the First Ukrainian Division. While its personnel were of course treated as prisoners of war, their commanders were able to convince the Western authorities that the unit was composed wholly of Galicians. As West Ukrainians, they had thus never been *de jure* citizens of the Soviet Union in the eyes of the Western powers. Consequently, they were spared the disastrous fate, which overtook so many who had resisted the Soviet regime, of being turned over to the Soviet repatriation authorities.[85]

It is difficult to appraise the value to the Ukrainian nationalist movements of their military collaboration with the Germans. As in the case of the nationalist partisan activity, the ends sought were not attained, for the calculations of the Ukrainians in regard to the international situation were not fulfilled. Instead of a balance of power in the East which would have enabled even feeble military forces to assume importance, there ensued complete Soviet victory. The Ukrainian contingents were unable to prevent the conquest of Ukrainian ethnographic territory by the Soviet Union. They were, however, of some value in enabling a number of young men to escape to the West. More significant, perhaps, for the future of the nationalist movement, the military units and their political committee offered a rallying point for Ukrainians who might otherwise have attached themselves to the Vlasov movement as the only available anti-Soviet organization.

---

[85]Heike memoir; Interview 22; Julius Epstein, *"Operation Keelhaul": The Story of Forced Repatriation from 1944 to the Present* (Old Greenwich: Devin Adair Co., 1973). See also Chapter XIII below.

VIII
Nationalism and the Church

The principal propagators of Ukrainian nationalism in the occupied Ukraine were political groups. They were, however, not the only bearers of the concept of Ukrainian distinctiveness. Religious organizations also played an important role. The relation of the Greek Catholic Church to the nationalist parties has already been discussed. Unlike the political parties, most of which at least claimed to represent the entire Ukrainian nation, however, the Greek Catholic Church was almost wholly confined to Galicia, since the great mass of the East Ukrainian Christians were members of the Orthodox faith.

In the Orthodox lands, religion and national affiliation have always been closely related. Most of the East and South Slavic peoples identify their church with their national existence. Some of the same characteristics which have enhanced the distinctiveness of these peoples have also formed the basis of divisions among the Orthodox Slavs. One such feature is the lack of a supreme authority within the Orthodox Church. Each body of the church, existing in a given territory in a given period, has a well-defined hierarchy, usually governed by a council of bishops and frequently headed by a patriarch or metropolitan. There is, however, no pope at the head of all Orthodoxy. It is true that the Orthodox Church, like the Roman Catholic Church, recognizes the authority of an ecumenical council, but such a council has not been held in the East for a millennium.

A difficult question arises at this point: how is the "body of the faithful" or "territory" of each group to be defined? This problem has, in fact, been an extremely troublesome one in the history of the Orthodox Church, for in the absence of a central ecclesiastical authority there can be no final solution. In practice an answer has been provided by another characteristic feature of the Orthodox Church—its close dependence on the secular authority. Historically, the Orthodox Church has been the official church par excellence; union of church and state is not only a legal expression but a vital reality in the history of Eastern Europe. Consequently, the actual extent of authority of each body of the church has usually coincided with the boundaries of the state in which it exists. A corollary of this coincidence of state and ecclesiastical authority has been the establishment of, or the endeavor to establish, a new hierarchical authority whenever a major change in state sovereignty has taken place.

Moreover, as nationalist movements became powerful in the Orthodox lands in the nineteenth century, they often demanded a separate church organization as a consequence of their growing sense of national distinctiveness, and as a preparation for their separate statehood.

Until 1917, almost all Orthodox East Slavs were united in a single state, the Russian Empire, with a single church, the Russian Orthodox Church. Since the seventeenth century this church had lacked the customary patriarch or primate, and was connected to the secular power, and to a considerable degree controlled by it through an imperial official, the Procurator of the Holy Synod. The October Revolution destroyed the formal links between these historically intertwined institutions. At this point, the growing strength of Ukrainian national consciousness gave rise to a demand for state independence. It was in accord with the history of Orthodoxy that this demand should have been accompanied by a parallel movement for the establishment of a church organization independent of Moscow, for that seat of ecclesiastical authority had lost its preeminent prestige through the disestablishment of the Russian Orthodox Church, while its role as a symbol of East Slav unity was necessarily repudiated by those who saw the Ukrainian future as distinct from that of Russia.

Had the group desiring continuation of the Russian state (whether as an empire or a constitutional democracy) won out, it is probable that ecclesiastical unity would have been restored, since the Russian church, while it lost many of its privileges after the February Revolution, stood to gain in prestige through the reconstitution of the office of Patriarch of Moscow. Had, on the contrary, an independent Ukrainian state been able to maintain itself for a few years, very likely a separate Ukrainian hierarchy would have been generally recognized. In the situation which followed from the Bolshevik triumph, neither clear-cut solution was achieved. Instead, a large body of the lower clergy and the faithful split off from the Russian hierarchy in the Ukraine. When no member of the episcopacy could be found to consecrate a new bishop for the dissident group, the Ukrainian church body resorted to the "laying on of hands" by priests as a method for consecrating Father Lypkivs'kyi as prelate of their organization. Thus a new Orthodox Church was formed, which rapidly came to embrace the great majority of organized Orthodox believers in the Ukraine; by 1923 it had no less than 3,000 parishes and thirty-five bishops, headed by Lypkivs'kyi, then known as Metropolitan Basil.[1] In spite of this apparent prosperity, the Ukrainian Autocephalous Church, as it was called, lay under the shadow of two great weaknesses. In the first place, it was not recognized by any other body of the Orthodox Church, for the method of consecration of the new bishops was regarded throughout the Orthodox world as

---

[1] John S. Reshetar, "Ukrainian Nationalism and the Orthodox Church." *American Slavic and East European Review*, X (February, 1951), pp. 43-45. The basic work on the Ukrainian religious background is Friedrich Heyer, *Die Orthodoxe Kirche in der Ukraine von 1917 bix 1945* (Köln-Braunsfeld: Verlagsgesellschaft Rudolf Müller, 1953). While in the Wehrmacht during World War II, Heyer had numerous personal contacts with church leaders, and apparently acquired notes or documents dealing with ecclesiastical affairs. His account is similar to that given below, but he ascribes somewhat greater importance to the Autonomous Church. While Heyer devotes much attention to purely ecclesiastical affairs which I do not attempt to cover in detail, his abundant details on the extent of reorganization of religious life and the response of the population are very valuable.

uncanonical, a violation of the essential principle of apostolic succession. From the point of view of the traditional believer, the bishops of the new church were illegitimate; consequently, priests ordained by them (but not those who had joined the Autocephalous Church after ordination by a validly consecrated bishop) were not truly endowed with sacerdotal functions. Secondly, and of more immediate significance, the phenomenal growth of the new church was possible only because of the comparatively indulgent attitude shown by the Communist authorities who, at that time, were more antagonistic to the Russian church than to dissident bodies. When the Soviet power turned to restriction of Ukrainian national activity, as a potential threat to the unity of the USSR, the Autocephalous Church also came under attack. Its entire hierarchy and the great bulk of its clergy were executed or banished in 1929-30.[2]

In view of the close connection between church and state in the Orthodox world, it was only natural that, when the Russian Empire collapsed and a considerable body of Orthodox believers came under Polish dominion, an effort was made to establish a separate hierarchy in Poland. The leader in this effort was Dionysius, a Russian bishop who, with recognition from the Patriarch of Constantinople, became Metropolitan of Warsaw and head of the Autocephalous Orthodox Church in Poland.[3] In addition to the Belorussian archbishop of Pinsk, there were four bishops in Volhynia: Archbishop Alexius, with his residence in the famous Pochaïvs'ka Lavra (monastery), and his vicars Polykarp, bishop of Lutsk; Anthony (Martsenko), bishop of Kamen Kashirsk (Kamin Koshyrs'k); and Simon, bishop of Ostriz. These bishops were Ukrainian but subject to Dionysius.[4]

When the Soviet Union acquired Volhynia in September, 1939, its efforts to convert the Russian Orthodox Church into an auxiliary of the Soviet government were already well under way. A special deputy of Patriarch Sergius of Moscow, Nicholas, Exarch of the West Ukraine, was sent to coordinate the church of the newly occupied area with the government-approved ecclesiastical organization. The existing bishops were not deposed, with the exception of Alexander of Pinsk. The latter was not molested physically, but his ecclesiastical jurisdiction, now in the Belorussian Soviet Republic, was divided between a bishop of Brest and a bishop of Pinsk sent from Moscow.[5]

While it is not likely that Alexius or his adherents (including Polykarp) were pleased with the subjugation of their province by Moscow, they appear to

---

[2]*Ibid.*, p. 46.

[3]*Ibid.*, p. 48; Stepan Baran in *Krakivs'ki Visti*, October 28, 1941, p. 1.

[4]*UAPTs* (*Ukrainskaia Avtokefalnaia Pravoslavnaia Tserkov'*) (UAPTs [Ukrainian Autocephalous Orthodox Church]), by "A. V." (Pravoslavnyi Beloruss, 1951; mimeographed), p. 2; cf. Baran in *Krakivs'ki Visti*, October 28, 1941, p. 1. There was also a Bishop Timothy (Shreter) in a monastery in the Generalgouvernement, but he played no role in the controversies which followed (Occ E-4 [1]).

[5]OCC E-4 (1); *Krakivs'ki Visti*, December 27, 1941, p. 3. The Bishop of Brest (Benjamin) had been a monk of the Pochaïvs'ka Lavra (Heyer, *Die Orthodoxe Kirche*, p. 168). Alexander had pleaded retirement as a reason for not going to Moscow to see Sergius; Anthony was also apparently in retirement. For more details on the complicated controversies concerning the relations of the various ecclesiastics with Moscow church authorities see especially Heyer.

have conformed to the Orthodox tradition of submission to the secular power, even when the latter is not basically sympathetic to the Orthodox religion. Although it did not suppress the Orthodox Church, the Soviet government imposed severe restrictions and onerous financial obligations upon it, as well as upon the Greek Catholic Church in Galicia. As a result, many of the priests fled, or took up secular occupations. In order to satisfy the resulting need for clergymen, Alexius is said to have consecrated a large number of new priests, many of them persons unfitted by background or training for the performance of clerical duties.[6] Thus the fabric of the church was to some extent weakened and demoralized. At the same time, however, the Soviet-allied church in Moscow endeavored to extend its influence into an area which had had few Orthodox communicants since the seventeenth century, by consecrating as bishop of L'vov, under the name of Panteleimon, a priest, Rudyk, who was a native Galician but had always favored a union of the province with Russia.[7]

That there was nothing inherently agreeable in their enforced submission to Soviet control is indicated by the fact that the Orthodox bishops in the West Ukraine, both those who had exercised episcopal functions in Volhynia prior to 1939 and those who owed their status to the Moscow-inspired endeavors to reorganize the Ukrainian church, failed to evacuate with the Red army when the Germans invaded the region. The sole exception was the Exarch Nicholas, who soon assumed an active role in appealing to the patriotic and religious sentiments of the peoples of the USSR to secure support of the Soviet regime. Under the title of Metropolitan of Kiev and Galicia, he issued numerous statements against the Germans and the Ukrainian nationalists.[8]

As the German armies drove on beyond the pre-1939 Polish border into areas which had been under Soviet control for twenty years, they discovered that there remained considerable numbers of Orthodox clergymen. For example, there were one hundred in the Zhitomir area alone, and two small churches had remained open in Kiev under Soviet rule.[9] There were also Archbishops Anthony (Abashidze) in Kiev, who was, however, too old and crippled to exercise any considerable degree of influence; Anatole in Odessa; Theophilus in Kharkov; and Bishop Damaskin in Kamenets-Podols'k.[10]

As soon as conditions had become somewhat stablized in the West Ukrainian lands, Alexius and his associates proceeded to call a meeting of all Ukrainian bishops in areas liberated from the Soviet regime. This gathering, known

---

[6]*Krakivs'ki Visti*, August 12, 1941, p. 2; Baran in *Krakivs'ki Visti*, October 28, 1941, p. 1.

[7]*UAPTs*, p. 2; *Krakivs'ki Visti*, August 12, 1941, p. 2.

[8]Nicholas happened to be in Moscow when war began (Heyer, *Die Orthodoxe Kirche*, p. 169). For a report on clandestine propaganda against the Germans in the Ukraine issued over Nicholas's signature, see PS 051. There are a number of reports of Orthodox priests, especially in Kiev, who acted as Soviet agents (cf. Occ E-4 [1]). One of Nicholas's wartime writings was even distributed abroad by the Soviet Union—i.e., Nikolai (Nicholas), Metropolitan of Kiev and Galicia (ed.), *The Russian Orthodox Church and the War against Fascism* (Moscow: The Patriarchate of Moscow, 1943). At a later period, Nikolai frequently employed the title Mitropolit Krutitskii, pertaining to the Moscow monastery of which he was titular head. Nicholas ostensibly retired in 1961, but it was rumored that even he was insufficiently pliable for the Soviet regime. He died in 1961.

[9]PS 053.

[10]*Ukraïns'ka Diisnist'*, October 15, 1941, p. 4. Erich Koch evidently rejected a suggestion that Anthony head the Ukrainian church (Heyer, *Die Orthodoxe Kirche*, p. 172).

as the Sobor of Volhynian Bishops, met in the Pochaïvs'ka Lavra in mid-August, 1941, and on August 18 proclaimed the reorganization of the Autonomous Orthodox Church in the Ukraine.[11] Subordination to the Patriarch of Moscow was declared to be in abeyance so long as the Communists maintained control over him, but a nominal canonical adherence of the Ukrainian church to the Patriarch was recognized. At the same time, two new bishops were consecrated to carry out the task of reorganizing church life.[12]

This task was already under way, at least in the Zhitomir area. All surviving priests were registered and their status examined by two archimandrites (monastic archpriests), one sent by Alexius and one from the famous Monastery of the Caves in Kiev.[13] The great majority of the surviving clergy had been consecrated in the old canonically recognized Russian church, since Soviet persecution had greatly reduced the Autocephalous ranks. Some of the latter remained, however, and had to accept reconsecration at the hands of the bishops of the Volhynian Sobor before receiving appointments to parishes. Understandably, this demand for repudiation of the position on the validity of the Autocephalous consecration taken by their deceased leader, Lypkivs'kyi, was deeply resented, especially since many of the priests previously consecrated by Alexius were not, as has been pointed out, models of devotion to the sacerdotal vocation.[14]

Whether the greatly weakened "Lypkivites," as the Autocephalous adherents were known, could have made any effective objections by themselves is doubtful. There was, however, a powerful ally at hand. During the time when the Soviet authorities were bringing the Volhynian church under their control, Ukrainian influence in Orthodox ecclesiastical life in the Generalgouvernement was greatly increasing, particularly in the Chelm area. As part of the restoration of the Orthodox Church to a position of strength, Dionysius, in October, 1940, consecrated Professor John Ohiienko, who had long been active in religious affairs as a church historian and philologist, as Hilarion, Archbishop of Chelm.[15] Two months later he consecrated a bishop, Palladius, for the small Orthodox population in the Lemko region.[16] Both of these men were strong nationalists. Hilarion in particular had long desired to see the separation of the Ukrainian church from Moscow.[17]

---

[11] *Ukraïns'ka Diisnist'*, November 15, 1941, p. 3.

[12] *UAPTs*, p. 3, names eight appointed at this time. Contemporary sources refer to two only, and it appears likely that the others were consecrated somewhat later, probably for the most part at the *sobor* in December. Cf. *Krakivs'ki Visti*, December 27, 1941, p. 3, and *Ukraïns'ka Diisnist'*, January 20, 1941, p. 1. Heyer, *Die Orthodoxe Kirche*, p. 176, names only three new bishops chosen in this period. Evidently there were sixteen Autonomous bishops (*ibid.*, p. 182).

[13] Fedir S. Iefremenko in *Krakivs'ki Visti*, October 24, 1941, p. 4; the archimandrite from Kiev, Leontius Fillippovych, was consecrated bishop (as Leontius) at the August *sobor*.

[14] *Ibid.*

[15] *Krakivs'ki Visti*, November 24, 1940, p. 1.

[16] *Krakivs'ki Visti*, February 12, 1941, p. 3. Palladius became bishop of Cracow; this move was viewed by some as an unwarranted invasion by the Orthodox Church of a predominantly Greek Catholic section of the Ukrainian territory. Cf. Mykola Andrusiak in *Nastup*, October 12, 1940, p. 4. But it is possible that Greek Catholic circles influenced by Metropolitan Sheptits'kyi favored the move (see Heyer, *Die Orthodoxe Kirche*, pp. 163-64, who gives Palladius's consecration date as February 9, 1941).

[17] Stepan Baran in *Krakivs'ki Visti*, January 17, 1942, p. 3.

When the Volhynian Sobor was called, Alexander, the archbishop of Pinsk, was not invited, for, it was explained, he was a Belorussian.[18] Nevertheless, his Moscow-appointed successor, Benjamin, was not only present but acted as secretary of the conference. In view of the fact that Alexander's opposition to the Communists had been the cause for Benjamin's appointment, it is understandable that this arrangement excited discontent. Moreover, the position of Dionysius, who had been the superior of all the Volhynian bishops before the Soviet occupation, was unclear.[19] If Soviet occupation of Volhynia had been illegitimate, presumably his authority had only been suspended by physical barrier of the frontier which had separated German-controlled Warsaw from Soviet-occupied territory. Nevertheless, after Soviet evacuation, Alexius had proceeded to reorganize the whole Ukrainian church on the assumption that a reunion with Moscow had been legally constituted, although publicly holding the position that this union was inoperative because of continued Soviet control of the church in Moscow. Doubtless influenced by these considerations, Polykarp, the bishop of Lutsk, declined to attend the *sobor*, presenting the excuse of "difficult conditions of communication," although his episcopal see was less than fifty miles from the Pochaïvs'ka Lavra.[20] Shortly afterwards Dionysius appointed Polykarp "vicar" of the Vladimir Volynsk and adjacent Gorukhov (Horukhiv) areas; at the time, apparently neither explicitly rejected Alexius as head of the Orthodox hierarchy in Volhynia.[21]

During the fall of 1941, opposition to Alexius's predominance gradually mounted. In addition to the friction over the investiture of the Lypkivite priests, great resentment arose from the fact that the bishops of Alexius's group were either predominantly of Russian origin or were known for past adherence to the church of Moscow. The acceptance of continued subordination to Moscow, however theoretical the tie might be under the prevailing conditions, was of course resented by the Ukrainian nationalist elements. Moreover, many among the latter, especially the intelligentsia, strongly desired the replacement of the Old Slavonic liturgy by services in the living Ukrainian language, while the Volhynian *sobor* had merely provided for certain prayers in the latter speech.[22] As these points of friction accumulated, prominent Orthodox laymen like Stephen Skrypnyk, the publisher of the newspaper *Volyn'* in Rovno, rallied to the side of the Autocephalous group.[23] On November 28, Polykarp definitely broke with Alexius, declaring the Archbishop's group

---

[18]*UAPTs*, p. 3; *Ukraïns'ka Diisnist'*, November 15, 1941, p. 3.

[19]*Krakivs'ki Visti*, December 27, 1941, p. 3, expresses the indignation felt at the exclusion of the Autocephalous bishops in the Generalgouvernement. It is not clear whether Alexander had actually opposed the Communists, or had merely evaded collaboration with them (Heyer, *Die Orthodoxe Kirche*, p. 168).

[20]*UAPTs*, p. 3; *Ukraïns'ka Diisnist'*, November 15, 1941, p. 3.

[21]*Ukraïns'ka Diisnist*, November 15, 1941, p. 3. In a move evidently designed to conciliate Polykarp, the *sobor* had named him bishop of Kamenets-Podolsk (*ibid.*).

[22]*Ukraïns'ka Diisnist'*, November 15, 1941, p. 3.

[23]Cf. Skrypnyk's article in *Volyn'*, reproduced in *L'vivs'ki Visti*, January 11-12, 1942, p. 5, and an article from the Kremenets *Kremianets'kyi Visnyk*, cited in *Ukraïns'ka Diisnist'*, October 15, 1941, p. 4.

"anarchical," and repudiated him as ecclesiastical superior.[24] Shortly afterwards, Alexius replied by proclaiming himself Metropolitan of the Ukraine, in accordance with a decision of a second *sobor* of Volhynian bishops.[25]

While the Orthodox Church in the Ukraine was splitting into two antagonistic factions, the leader of the Greek Catholic Church was endeavoring to effect an ecclesiastical union of all Ukrainians. The separate development of the Greek Catholic Church has been sketched already. It may be pointed out, however, that what had originally been regarded as an instrument of the Poles for consolidating their dominion in the western Ukrainian lands had long since developed into a truly national church, in the sense of being independent of any foreign secular power, although it was largely confined to one province of the Ukraine. Since the Greek Catholic Church of the Ukraine possessed a rite and a body of ecclesiastical regulations quite different from that of the churches of the neighboring Catholic nations, which were of the Latin rite, the mere fact of adherence to it tended to set the Galicians apart as a national entity. As was pointed out, Metropolitan Andrew Sheptyts'kyi had long been a vigorous supporter of the Ukrainian nationalist movements, although he had tried to turn them away from an extreme nationalism incompatible with Christianity. His influence was naturally greatest among his own coreligionists, but extended also to Ukrainians of the Orthodox faith. Hence Metropolitan Sheptyts'kyi felt that the Soviet retreat offered an opportunity for bringing about the union of all Ukrainians in a single national church within the framework of the universal church in which he believed. The immediate opportunity for advancing this desire was a letter, October 21, 1941, to Archbishop Hilarion, congratulating him on his elevation to the episcopacy; Sheptyts'kyi explained that he could not do so before because of the severance of communications between the Soviet- and the German-dominated areas. Together with cordial felicitations, the Metropolitan expressed his hope that Hilarion would play a leading role in cleansing the Ukrainian church of "uncanonical" "Muscovite" influences introduced by Peter the Great, and hoped that this process would prepare the way for union of all the Ukrainian churches.[26] Two months later he addressed a letter of similar import to all "Orthodox archpriests in the Ukraine and in the Ukrainian lands."[27]

The replies were courteous, but not encouraging. Hilarion answered in a cordial, even humble fashion, but he did not fail to point out that, while the liturgy of the Ukrainian Orthodox Church had indeed suffered from Russian infiltration, that of the Greek Catholic Church had been permeated with Latin elements, and he suggested that the latter body also needed purification from foreign influences.[28] Alexius likewise replied to the second letter in a friendly fashion, but said that unification could come about only through a change in human nature, perhaps at the end of the world, and expressed the view that,

---

[24]*L'vivs'ki Visti*, January 11-12, 1942, p. 5 (Skrypnyk's article cited).

[25]*Krakivs'ki Visti*, December 27, 1941, p. 3. There had been additional synods under Alexius's direction (Heyer, *Die Orthodoxe Kirche*, pp. 176-77).

[26]The text of the letter is printed in Stepan (Stephen) Baran, *Mytropolyt Andrei Sheptyts'kyi* (Metropolitan Andrew Sheptyts'kyi) (Munich: Vernyhora Ukraïns'ke Vydavnyche Tovarystvo, 1947), pp. 123-24.

[27]*Ibid.*, pp. 127-28.

[28]*Ibid.*, pp. 124-27.

after all, diversity had its advantages in promoting the search for the good.[29] Still not giving up hope, Sheptyts'kyi appealed in an open letter of March 3, 1942, for the support of the Ukrainian Orthodox intelligentsia, who, he said, exerted great influence in their church.[30] This effort was also fruitless. Probably its only result was to play a part in inducing the Autocephalous Church in the Generalgouvernement to present a final reply to his overtures by an uncompromising resolution of the *sobor* of bishops in Warsaw, in May, 1942, to the effect that his wishes could easily be fulfilled, if only all Greek Catholics would join the Autocephalous Church.[31]

The failure of the Metropolitan's efforts was doubtless due fundamentally to the deep cleavage which separates Orthodox from Catholic, the former viewing submission to the authority of the Pope as a renunciation of the valid tradition of the Christian church, which they believe that their body has maintained. An additional compelling reason for the rejection of Sheptyts'kyi's overtures in the winter and spring of 1942 was the incontestible fact that gestures of reconciliation with Rome would have been regarded by many of the Orthodox laity as treason, and would therefore very probably have weakened the church which participated in such measures. This was a vital consideration, for by midwinter the conflict between the two tendencies in the Orthodox Church represented by Alexius and Polykarp had turned into an active struggle for supremacy.

On December 24, 1941, after the second *sobor* of Volhynian bishops had endowed Alexius with the title of metropolitan, Dionysius appointed Polykarp administrator of all Volhynia. Six weeks later, Archibishop Alexander who, it will be recalled, had been left out of the Autonomous Church conference, joined with the Autocephalous Church in Poland in calling a new *sobor* in Pinsk.[32] While Alexander was not a Ukrainian by origin, he now had a fairly clear title according to Orthodox usage to participate in Ukrainian church affairs, since his archepiscopal see had been included in the territorial limits of the Ukraine, as defined by the boundaries of the Reichskommissariat. He was a welcome support to the group opposed to Alexius, and they made no difficulty about recognizing his authority to call the *sobor*. Since, however, the other authority for calling the conference was Dionysius, the constitutive assembly of the new Ukrainian church was established by non-Ukrainian prelates. The moving spirits, however, were the strongly nationalist Ukrainians, Polykarp and Hilarion. With them went Palladius, the third Ukrainian bishop of the Autocephalous Orthodox Church in Poland. Together they decided to form a new ecclesiastical body to be known as the Ukrainian Autocephalous Orthodox Church (Ukrains'ka Avtokefal'na Pravoslavna Tserkva — UAPTs), which was to unite as quickly as possible with the remnants of the church of the same name founded by Lypkivs'kyi.[33] Somewhat

---

[29]*Ibid.*, pp. 128-30; *Krakivs'ki Visti*, February 15, 1942, p. 3.

[30]*Krakivs'ki Visti*, April 5, 1942, p. 3; Baran, *Mytropolyt*, pp. 130-31.

[31]Baran, *Mytropolyt*, p. 132.

[32]*Krakivs'ki Visti*, March 22, 1942, p. 4. Heyer's account (*Die Orthodoxe Kirche*, p. 174 ff.), based to a greater extent on sources sympathetic to the Autonomous position, appears to attribute greater responsibility for the initial break to the Autocephalous group.

[33]*Ibid.*

later Damaskin of Kamenets-Podolsk rejected Alexius and adhered to the new group.[34] Their ranks were also augmented by the consecration as bishops in February of two Volhynian priests, Abramovych and Huba, who became members of the hierarchy as Nikanor and Ihor.[35]

While the basic reason for the foundation of a new church, and its rapid growth at the expense of the body under Alexius, was the nationalist feeling of the Ukrainians, which demanded a fully national church divorced from any connection, however theoretical, with Russia, German policy had also played a role in division of the Orthodox communion. Fundamentally, Nazi policy was permeated with violent hatred of all religion. The guiding principle for selection of German officials for the east ensured that this basic theme would persist in the application of policy: "The whole Christian outlook makes one incapable of carrying on work in the east, for the community of the hymnbook is put ahead of the needs of the Reich."[36] Within this blanket opposition to the church, however, even the fanatical anti-clericalism of Rosenberg and his staff permitted compromises to secure tactical advantages. In their eyes, Catholic Christianity was the chief religious danger in the east. The leaders of the Catholic Church had long hoped for an opportunity to bring their doctrines to the peoples of the Soviet Union. On the outbreak of war, they attempted to send a number of priests, including several trained in the Ukrainian College in Rome, as missionaries. The Ostministerium rigorously opposed this endeavor, and with the exception of a few clergymen who were able to penetrate the Ukraine as chaplains in the Italian army, the Vatican's efforts were thwarted.[37] Similarly, the efforts of Polish Catholics to conduct activities in the East Ukraine, even among the considerable body of communicants of the Latin rite in Volhynia, were quickly suppressed.[38]

In contrast to the Catholic Church, the Orthodox Church was not to be opposed openly, provided it was not Russian dominated but Ukrainian in character. Moreover, any other purely Ukrainian sects were to be permitted. It was hoped that by allowing a multitude of religious bodies, the Orthodox Church as such would be weakened, for "the corruption and cultural backwardness of the clergy prepared the ground for Bolshevism."[39] When, however, the Ukrainian Autocephalous Orthodox Church was founded as a distinctively national church, it appeared to the Ostministerium to be a useful means of furthering its aim of strengthening Ukrainian nationalism and driving a wedge between the Ukrainian and the Russian elements. Consequently, it felt that the Autocephalous Church under the leadership of Polykarp should

---

[34]*Krakivs'ki Visti*, March 22, 1942, p. 4. Apparently Damaskin later returned to the Autonomous Church. Cf. Heyer, *Die Orthodoxe Kirche*, p. 188.

[35]*Ibid.*; and *Krakivs'ki Visti*, February 28, 1942, p. 1.

[36]Memorandum on personnel for the east, from the Rosenberg files, July 9, 1941, PS 1040 (hereafter referred to as PS 1040).

[37]Directive by Alfred Meyer, "Die Frage der konfessionellen Verbände," July 29, 1941, PS 1047 (hereafter referred to as PS 1047). On the training of missionaries of the Greek Catholic rite for missionary work in the USSR after the conquest, see also Aldo Valori, *La Campagna di Russia* (Rome: Grafica Nazionale Editrice, 1951), Vol. I, p. 244.

[38]PS 053.

[39]PS 1047.

be recognized and accorded a position of distinct superiority in comparison to the Autonomous Church headed by Alexius.[40]

As was frequently the case, the policy formulated in Rosenberg's ministry failed of all practical results in the Ukraine. The Reichskommissariat decided to pursue a diametrically opposed course. Thus it proclaimed confessional freedom in June, 1942, but ordered all ecclesiastical organization limited to individual *Generalbezirke*.[41] In particular, it decided a little later to order the dissolution of the governing bodies of both the Autonomous and the Autocephalous Churches, the *sobors* headed by Alexius and Polykarp respectively.[42]

One reason for this decision to restrict religious organization was undoubtedly the fact that the Autocephalous Church had shown great vigor in organizing a new hierarchy. In May a second *sobor* of Autocephalous bishops had gathered in Kiev and consecrated no less than seven new bishops. The majority had been Volhynian priests, but two were laymen who had played prominent roles in the development of the new church body: Stephen Skrypnyk, who became bishop of Pereiaslav as Mstyslav, and a Kiev professor, Haievs'kyi, who became Bishop Sylvester.[43] Strong efforts were made to secure the support of all the surviving Lypkyvites, with great success, apparently because there was no demand for reconsecration, although at first there was friction between the new and the old Autocephalous bodies.[44] The new consecrations raised the total number of the higher clergy to fourteen: two archbishops (Polykarp and Alexander, Hilarion being still a member of the hierarchy of the Polish church, i.e., that in the Generalgouvernement) and twelve bishops, with five hundred parishes and a still greater number of priests under their authority.[45] The vigor and unity of the church alone was sufficient to make it repugnant to those Germans who feared any independent center of Ukrainian life. For example, the Generalkommissar in Nikolaev wrote Erich Koch expressing his fear that the Autocephalous Church, which was strong in the northern part of his area, was becoming a "national church," and said that

---

[40] Draft of a directive of Rosenberg to the Reichskommissare Ostland and Ukraine, May 13, 1942, CXLVa 15, in Centre de Documentation Juive Contemporaine (hereafter referred to as CXLVa 15). I do not know whether the directive was ever actually sent, but it certainly expresses the opinion of the predominant group in the Ostministerium, as opposed to that of Koch's officials.

[41] Report by an unidentified official of the Ostministerium to Rosenberg, June 30, 1944, CXLVa 66, in Centre de Documentation Juive Contemporaine (hereafter referred to as CXLVa 66).

[42] Directive of Reichskommissar Ukraine (signed by Dargel, head of the political section) to the Generalkommissare, October 1, 1942, CXLVa 20, in Centre de Documentation Juive Contemporaine (hereafter referred to as CXLVa 20).

[43] *Krakivs'ki Visti*, May 28, 1942, p. 2; *Nastup*, July 12, 1942, p. 2.

[44] *Krakivs'ki Visti*, February 8, 1942, p. 3; Dmytro Doroshenko in *Ukraïns'ka Diisnist'*, November 10, 1942, p. 1.

[45] Tarkovych in *Krakivs'ki Visti*, July 1, 1942, p. 4, based on information from Bishop Mstyslav. Apparently in addition to the bishops I have referred to as adhering to the Autocephalous Church, a new member of the hierarchy, Korenistov, was consecrated as bishop of Brest and auxiliary of Alexander of Pinsk. Doroshenko in *Ukraïns'ka Diisnist'*, November 10, 1942, p. 1, also refers to fourteen members of the UAP hierarchy. Cf. Heyer, *Die Orthodoxe Kirche*, p. 181, who lists fifteen, including George (Korenistov) of Brest.

all priests were being closely watched.[46] Koch himself conceived a violent antipathy for Mstyslav, whom he described as "Skrypnyk, a prominent Ukrainian politician in Kiev," asserting that the bishop was trying to turn the Wehrmacht against the Reichskommissariat officials.[47]

As a result of these feelings of distrust, the Reichskommissariat refused to follow the policy of favoring the Autocephalous Church as against the Autonomous Church. With the desertion of the nationalist Ukrainians, the latter was coming more and more to be the confession of Russophile elements in the Ukraine, or at least of those elements which favored equality between Russians and Ukrainians in cultural and political life. In an effort to build up a counterweight to the nationalist forces, the Reichskommissariat officials began to favor the Autonomous Church. First the Reichskommissar decided that a balance should be maintained between the two churches.[48] Later his henchmen used the Autonomous Church as a means of weakening the Autocephalous Church when the latter threatened to become powerful. The reverse tactic was also used occasionally, but the general tendency appears to be that taken by the Stadtkommissar of Kiev, who openly indicated the preference of the German officials for the Russian-oriented church by transferring to it in a public ceremony the principal cathedral of the city, St. Vladimir's (St. Volodymyr's).[49]

The general policy of the Reichskommissariat toward union of the two Orthodox bodies was governed by the same principle of doing everything which would weaken forces which might slip beyond its control. In May, when it appeared that the nascent strength of the Autocephalous group might be curbed by securing its subordination to Alexius, this line of action was favored, though in a tentative way, because the specter of a single united church, whatever its stand on the national question, was also abhorrent to the autocratic Nazi group.[50] By October, when the Autocephalous Church had become so strong that Alexius was obliged to seek unification on terms favorable to it, the Germans intervened to render abortive all attempts at conciliation.[51] Actually, the negotiations between Alexius on the one side and Polykarp, Mstyslav, and Nikanor on the other, proceeded so far that on October 8, 1942, an act of union was signed. A new synod of bishops, consisting of Polykarp and Alexius as metropolitans, with Alexander, Simon (an Autonomous bishop) and Nikanor as members, and Mstyslav as secretary, was to be formed. Thus the Autocephalous group would have obtained a clear majority in the directing body. The episcopal sees were to be so rearranged as

---

[46]April, 1942, CXLVa 474, in Centre de Documentation Juive Contemporaine (hereafter referred to as CXLVa 474).

[47]PS 192.

[48]CXLVa 20.

[49]*Volyn'*, May 2, 1943, p. 4.

[50]On May 4, 1942, at a conference in Rovno, an official of the Reichskommissariat expressed the wishes of the German authorities that the two churches unite, but declared that the Germans would maintain neutrality and not intervene at that time to secure union (*Krakivs'ki Visti*, June 14, 1942, p. 3).

[51]The directive of the Reichskommissar Ukraine to the Generalkommissare previously cited (CXLVa 20) provided that all efforts at union should be opposed. Heyer, *Die Orthodoxe Kirche*, p. 184, lists Polykarp and Simon as archbishops, Alexander as metropolitan.

to allow places for all or most of the bishops hitherto consecrated by both groups.[52] The strong German intervention, however, combined with the opposition of a number of Autonomous bishops, headed by Panteleimon, forced Alexius to retract his signature.[53]

From what has just been said, one would assume that there would be a close connection between the Autocephalous Church, which within a few months had come to be the church of most believing Ukrainian nationalists, and the nationalist parties. To a certain extent this is true, for many members of the latter, who were prevented by the danger of violent death from pursuing any national political activities, turned to the cultivation of the church as a means for expressing and propagating their feelings. A number of the leading members of the Autocephalous Church were affiliated with the UNR, and the Het'man group also displayed great interest in religious development, in line with its conservative and traditionalist principles. More particularly, Mstyslav, the member of the UAP hierarchy who was most intimately acquainted with and interested in political affairs, was an old adherent of the UNR.[54]

As has been previously indicated, however, the really active parties in the East Ukraine were the two factions of the OUN. Hence the fact that the church leaders tended to associate with other groupings acted as a certain impediment to close collaboration. Moreover, a strong element in both wings of the OUN was opposed to religion in principle. This ideological bias against utilizing the church as a major instrument of national expression was undoubtedly given greatly increased weight by the experience of the nationalists in the East Ukraine. The churches — both Autonomous and Autocephalous — had no difficulty in attracting communicants, for there were many millions who had longed for the remembered solace of religion throughout the years of Communist oppression. These adherents of the church were, however, drawn very largely from the lower classes, the less educated elements of the population, especially the peasantry.[55] Since the OUN groups — as will be shown — concentrated their efforts on the intelligentsia, they placed comparatively little emphasis on aspects of nationalist feeling which were prevalent only in the village. More important, the younger generation everywhere, even in the rural areas, was hostile or at least indifferent to religion. Both OUN groups were intent upon winning the allegiance of youth; they soon came to see that any close connection with the church would be interpreted by a large segment of the latter as "reactionary." Hence they abandoned or played down their contacts with the clergy, rather than jeopardize their success with the youth.[56]

While the factors just described prevented any wholehearted collaboration between the church and the nationalist political movements, there were numerous cases in which the two nationalist tendencies moved in parallel

---

[52]*Nastup*, November 15, 1942, p. 2; *Ukraïns'ka Diisnist'*, December 10, 1942, p. 2.

[53]*Ukraïns'ka Diisnist'*, December 10, 1942, p. 2. Chief of the SP and the SD, Reports from the Occupied Eastern Territories, No. 34, December 18, 1942 (T 175, Reel 236).

[54]Interview 69.

[55]See Chapter IX for details and sources on the attitude of the social classes and age groups toward religion.

[56]Interviews 18, 65, 76. As indicated in Chapter VI and Chapter VII above, by 1944 the OUN guerrillas (UPA) and associated groups were expressing more religious devotion, but that was largely a Galician phenomenon.

paths. This was especially the case in Kiev, where Panteleimon, the most outspokenly pro-Russian of Autonomous bishops, and hence the most obstinate foe of Ukrainian national independence, was opposed to Mstyslav, the most active nationalist among the Autocephalous bishops. Nationalist Ukrainians abstained from any contact with the Autonomous Church there; they had the support of a number of prominent figures in the city administration, including the mayor, Forostivs'kyi, who had himself been a priest under Lypkyvs'kyi. The anti-Nationalist element around Shtepa and Bohatyrchuk was perhaps not so enthusiastic about Panteleimon's church, and appears to have maintained a modicum of good relations with the Autocephalous clergy, but in general the alignment of political groups closely corresponded to confessional differences.[57]

This was even more the case in Dniepropetrovsk, where a strong proponent of a revived Russian Empire, Dimitrius, was installed as Autonomous bishop. The nationalist elements were violently opposed to his policies, and apparently considerable popular opposition was awakened by his efforts to revive the pomp of the old Russian Orthodox Church.[58] On the other hand, strong Russian nationalist elements, encouraged in all likelihood by the strongly Russophile city administration and press, vigorously supported Dimitrius. This support resulted in several cases of actual vandalism directed against rival churches. The leader of the Autocephalous Church, Genadius, enjoyed good relations with both Mel'nyk and Bandera groups in the Dnieper city. Genadius aided the Bandera underground workers to escape from the German authorities, while one of his principal assistants was affiliated with the OUN-M, and the university faculty, which was strongly influenced by the Mel'nyk group, taught courses to prepare aspirants for his clergy.[59]

It is necessary to stress the extent — and the limits — of collaboration between the nationalists and the Autocephalous Church because of two incidents which have been widely taken as proof that the latter institution was involved, to an extent that could hardly be compatible with Christian principles, with some of the more violent elements of the OUN. The first incident concerned the head of the Autonomous Church, Archbishop Alexius. Early in the morning of May 7, 1943, the prelate started on a trip from his monastery near Kremenets.[60] He was in a German vehicle, part of a small convoy; why he chose this means of transportation is unclear, but it seems likely that the Germans would have urged a man of his prestige to accept such an accommodation, for as will be remembered the Volhynian roads at this time were in danger of attack from Red partisan bands or from nationalist bands disguised as such. At eight o'clock, as the little convoy was passing through a wood, it was suddenly attacked by a section of "Khrin's" partisan group; in the volley of shots,

---

[57]Interview 19. See Chief of the SP and of the SD, Reports of *Einsatzgruppen* and *Kommandos*, No. 191, May 10, 1942 (T 175, Reel 235), p. 41, concerning December, 1941, attempts by OUN-M leaders in Kiev to influence newly consecrated Bishop Panteleimon.

[58]Interview 18 supported the statement in *Nastup*, August 22, 1942, that about thirty churches in the Dniepropetrovsk area joined the UAP church when a bishop was named by it for Dniepropetrovsk.

[59]*Krakivs'ki Visti*, May 19, 1942, p. 2; Interview 18.

[60]*UAPTs*, p. 5.

the occupants of the archbishop's automobile were all killed, and the wrecked vehicle was seized by the partisans. They were shocked to discover the prominent clergyman in a group which they thought included only German officials. Afterwards, however, they asserted that their remorse was dissipated by the finding of papers indicating close collaboration between the archbishop and the German police.[61]

If the above account, which appears to be highly probable, is true, it is certain that the killing was unintentional and unpremeditated and consequently does not indicate any plan of the nationalists to aid the Autocephalous Church by destroying the chief prelate of the opposing group. That such a plan is even more unlikely is shown by the fact, attested by a source not involved in the dispute, that Alexius was the chief moderating influence in the Autonomous Church.[62] As has been shown, he tried to bring about union, and was on terms of friendship with at least one of the chief Autocephalous churchmen. These circumstances also go far to refute the charge that Alexius was in the service of the German police or, as has also been alleged by nationalist writers, in the service of the NKVD.[63] His personal character, as evidenced by his writings,[64] and the respect in which he was held even by opponents militate against such an accusation, even had not his conciliatory tendency refuted the main burden of the charge that he had fostered the disruption of the church to further the ends of the Germans and the Soviets. The whole incident was in all probability a tragic accident, utilized afterwards as propaganda for the rival groups.

So clear-cut a judgment cannot be offered concerning the second incident involving the slaying of an Autonomous bishop. In the late summer of 1943, Emmanuel, then Autonomous bishop of Vladimir Volynsk, was seized by a band of the UPA (controlled at that time by the OUN-B), taken to one of their forest headquarters, and there, after a "trial," executed as a traitor and a spy. Charges similar to those made against Alexius were the basis for the accusation against his colleague, and, in addition, Emmanuel is supposed to have confessed to having acted as an agent for the German police in betraying underground members.[65] Whether this is true cannot be determined, but certain factors cast considerable doubt upon it. The fact that the same charges were made against Alexius, who was very likely innocent, renders suspicious the accusations made against Emmanuel. The latter was regarded, for another reason, as a traitor, for he had originally been consecrated as bishop of Belaia Tserkov' by the Autocephalous Church, and his subsequent defection to the Autonomous Church, on grounds of the dubious canonical validity of the nationalist religious body, must have been a sore blow to Ukrainian nationalist

---

[61]*Ukraïns'ka Diisnist'*, June 1, 1943, p. 2; Baran, *Mytropolyt*, p. 122; Interview 12. Cf. Sergei T. Danilenko, *Dorohoiu Han'by i Zrady* (On the Road of Shame and Treachery) (Kiev: "Naukovo Dumka," 1970), p. 277, who alleges a Gestapo-Autocephalous-Banderist plot, and even suggests another version including Uniate participation.

[62]CXLVa 66.

[63]Mykola Selez', "Iak diiut stalins'ki agentury?" (How Do the Stalinist Agent Systems Operate?), *Vpered*, May, 1949, p. 11.

[64]See his letter to Sheptyts'kyi in Baran, *Mytropolyt*, pp. 128-30.

[65]Selez', "Iak diiut stalins'ki agentury?" p. 11; Interview 63.

feeling.⁶⁶ He had also issued public statements calling for all the faithful to avoid aiding the nationalist partisans; while nearly everyone in a public position in Volhynia (including an OUN member like the editor of *Volyn'*) was forced to make such statements, it appears likely that Emmanuel may have been rather more vigorous and sincere than others in his circumstances.⁶⁷ On the other hand, there is no really trustworthy evidence that he engaged in spying, or other indisputably dishonorable activity, and those who knew him best tend to doubt the charge.⁶⁸ Consequently, it appears that his death was due to the fanatic and ruthless spirit which dominated the OUN-B in Volhynia at the time.

On the other hand, there is no evidence to implicate the Autocephalous Church in his killing, and all appearances point to its having been decided upon independently by the partisan forces. It is true that Emmanuel's position was especially distasteful to the UPA because of the contrast it offered to the stand of the most active Autocephalous prelate in Volhynia, Bishop Platonius of Rovno, who actively aided the underground, and is said even to have gone to the UPA camp in Derman to offer his support.⁶⁹ It should be pointed out, however, that Platonius was comparatively uninfluential in Autocephalous Church councils. The more typical attitude was that of Polykarp—also resident in Volhynia—who offered vigorous protests against German attacks on the clergy and against the brutal treatment of his people,⁷⁰ yet never gave open support or encouragement to the rebels. In this policy of submission to the secular power, even to an evil one, Polykarp was, according to his own statement, following the tradition of Orthodoxy.⁷¹

A few months after the tragid episodes just described, nearly all of the East Ukraine was reconquered by the Red army. The great majority of the Orthodox bishops, of both the Autocephalous and the Autonomous groups, did not await the vengeance which could be expected to follow their opposition to the Soviet plan for using Orthodoxy as a propaganda weapon but fled to the Generalgouvernement. Here they were given considerably more courteous treatment than had been their lot in the Reichskommissariat.⁷² Moreover, the Ostministerium felt able at last to push forward its plans for formation of a national church. The project envisaged by Rosenberg's ministry called for union of the two rival branches. Ostensibly this union would have been a compromise, but, like the abortive agreement signed by Alexius, it would have favored the Autocephalous group. The Ostministerium officials in charge of the negotiations were obviously sympathetic to Mstyslav and Hilarion, though

---

⁶⁶Selez', "Iak diiut stalins'ki agentury?" p. 11; *UAPTs*, p. 5.

⁶⁷Cf. his address to the Ukrainian population, in *Volyn'*, August 8, 1943, p. 3.

⁶⁸Interview 38.

⁶⁹*UAPTs*, p. 10; Interview 18.

⁷⁰CXLVa 66. See also the sharp but respectful protest of Hilarion against the shooting of Autocephalous priests in the Generalgouvernement for contacts with escaped prisoners of war in the spring of 1942—long before there was any widespread nationalist partisan activity (Occ E-2 [2]).

⁷¹CXLVa 66.

⁷²*Ibid.* See also Chief of the SP and the SD *Einsatzgruppen*, IIIc, "Conveyance of Orthodox Bishops into the Reich," September 20, 1944 (T 175, Reel 640).

somewhat cooler toward Polykarp.[73] On the other hand, they viewed Panteleimon, the real leader of the Autonomous group, as a "Russian" and obstinate; they proposed to induce him to leave the Ukraine altogether by offering him the vacant Orthodox see of Riga.[74] The Autocephalous desire for a union in which there would be for a time "Russian bishops for the Russian minority," who would later be absorbed into the "Ukrainian church," obviously envisaged a relegation of the Autonomous bishops, or at least of those who persisted in favoring Russian cultural and ethnic elements, to an inferior position, yet it was apparently not opposed by the Ostministerium.[75]

The plans for a nationalist church were frustrated, however, by the refusal of the Autonomous bishops to accept the role assigned them by the Ostministerium and by the impotency of the latter agency to enforce its wishes. Instead of uniting with the other bishops from the Ukraine, the surviving Autonomous hierarchs adhered to the émigré Russian Orthodox Church represented by the Karlovtsi Synod. At least two of them had done so by the beginning of October, 1944, and the remainder soon followed.[76] The coincidence of these steps with the adherence of certain prominent Ukrainians to the Committee for the Liberation of the Peoples of Russia suggests that the same German forces which encouraged the Vlasov movement may also have supported the decision of the church group. The fact that such a step was taken, however, confirms the appraisal of the Autonomous Church as an organization closely linked to those elements which desired the continuance and the prevalence of Russian culture in the Ukraine and the maintenance of political ties with Russia.

The organization, tactics, and specific objectives of the Autocephalous Church were distinct from those of the nationalist parties during the war period. The very concept of an independent Ukrainian church served to promote a feeling of Ukrainian national distinctiveness, however, and since the Autocephalous clergy were usually propagators of nationalism, no consideration of the nationalist movements in the Orthodox East Ukraine under

---

[73]*Ibid.*

[74]*Ibid.* The nominal leader of the Autonomous Church, elected to succeed Alexius, was Damaskin of Kamenets-Podolsk, who appears by this time to have returned to the Autonomous fold (cf. *Volyn'*, July 1, 1943, p. 3).

[75]CXLVa 66. Although this project could not be carried out, the Ostministerium continued to favor to the limit of its capacities the Ukrainian national group in religious as well as political affairs. Cf. Memorandum of Rosenfelder (specialist in the Ostministerium) to Chef des Führungsstabes Politik, December 14, 1944, concerning plans for increasing the influence of the Autocephalous Church among the *Ostarbeiter* at the expense of the Russian Orthodox Church, CXLVa 76, in Centre de Documentation Juive Contemporaine (hereafter referred to as CXLVa 76).

[76]Rosenfelder to Chef des Führungsstabes Politik, October 4, 1944, CXLVa 74, in Centre de Documentation Juive Contemporaine (hereafter referred to as CXLVa 74); *UAPTs*, p. 6. At least one Autocephalous and three Autonomous bishops remained behind when the Soviet Army reoccupied the East Ukraine. Two of the former Autonomous bishops, Anthony (Martsenko) and Hiob (Kresovych), were apparently permitted to exercise episcopal functions under Soviet rule. Cf. Wassilij Alexeev, *Russian Orthodox Bishops in the Soviet Union, 1941-1953: Materials for the History of the Russian Orthodox Church in the USSR* (New York: Research Program on the USSR, 1954), p. 134 ff. (mimeographed, with Russian language text).

NATIONALISM AND THE CHURCH / 161

German occupation which failed to take into account the role of the Autocephalous Church would be complete. Since the rival Autonomous Church sought to maintain ties with Moscow, it is especially illuminating to compare its influence with that of the nationalist church. Consequently, the activities of the two rival churches will be noted frequently in the following chapters on the East Ukraine.

IX
Channels of Nationalist Activity

Though the church did in some measure provide an institutional framework through which nationalist sentiment could be expressed, its usefulness for the propagation of a political doctrine was necessarily limited. Such organizational channels were essential to the nationalist movements if they were to achieve large-scale results in the occupied East Ukraine. To be sure, the underground parties themselves provided a network of contacts and a minimum of central direction. In comparison with the vast area to be covered—populated in 1941-43, even after wartime dislocations, by thirty millions—resources under their direct control were microscopic. Clandestine publications could be issued by mimeograph machines or small hand presses and circulated from one trusted individual to another. Such propaganda could, however, reach only a few thousand. As underground groups, the nationalist parties necessarily had extremely small memberships. For example, a group of twelve members of the OUN-B in Kramatorskaia (Kremators'ka) in the Donbas is referred to by one of the leaders of the party in that area as a "big" cell.[1] Again, the entire number of active OUN-M workers in Kiev in late 1942 never exceeded thirty.[2] It is certain that the members of each of the OUN organizations in the chief cities after early 1942 could be counted in dozens and that the total number of active workers in the East Ukraine numbered only a few hundred.

For a conspiratorial organization, however, the number of members is not necessarily a criterion of effectiveness. By infiltrating key positions in public institutions, the nationalist parties might obtain influence out of all proportion to the number of their adherents. Moreover, even when centrally organized parties like the two factions of the OUN were unable to penetrate institutional channels, it was sometimes possible for nationalist groups limited to specific localities to do so. No appraisal of the strength of nationalism in the East Ukraine during 1941-43 would be complete without an examination of this penetration of the institutional framework by nationalists. In such an examination it is essential to proceed with great caution, for it is all too easy

---

[1] Interview 66.

[2] Interview 65.

for adherents of Ukrainian nationalist groups to ascribe in retrospect an exaggerated importance to their influence during the years of occupation. It would be tedious to describe the complicated and frequently unsatisfying ways in which the element of fact in inflated postwar accounts has been sought. Suffice it to say at this point that the basic approach has been the testing of the details of proper names, place names, and dates contained in each narration (whether in the form of printed memoir or oral testimony) against the abundant but superficial material contained in the Ukrainian press during the war years. In addition, the available wartime underground publications and German reports have been utilized. In this fashion, at least the extent of the real acquaintaince of the narrator with the area he describes can be estimated, and frequently the validity of his assessment of the role of persons and events can be surmised by reading between the lines of descriptions published legally — but with a trace of "Aesopian" language — during the war.

Primary targets for the efforts of nationalist elements in their campaign to win access to the East Ukrainian masses were the administrative apparatuses existing at the local level throughout the area of German occupation. The general outline of the machinery of government established by the Nazi regime in the occupied eastern territories has been described, and the policy of the officials in charge traced. The ruthless policy pursued made open activity of the OUN groups impossible, and their failure to understand this fact in time resulted in the slaughter of many of their adherents. The extent to which nationalist administrative officials could survive in the capital has already been indicated, however, and what was true of Kiev was true to a more marked degree of many of the smaller centers of the Ukraine. In spite of the determined efforts of Erich Koch and his cohorts to bring every aspect of life under their control, the sheer extent of the Ukraine and the size of its population prevented complete success. For example, in the *Generalbezirk* Nikolaev, there were only five hundred Germans on the administrative staff, charged with governing a population of 1,920,000, in an area of nearly 17,000 square miles.[3]

The limitations on control arising from the small number of German personnel available were made yet narrower by the language barrier. The extent to which the Wehrmacht was dependent on nationalists as interpreters has already been described. Since few Reichskommissariat officials knew the Slavic languages and yet in general rejected the use of émigrés or West Ukrainians as aides, they were thrown back on local interpreters and assistants as intermediaries between themselves and the masses. Supposedly reliable persons, often ethnic Germans, were employed. These physical limitations, however, compelled the German officials to concentrate on keeping the "commanding heights" of the administration — economic controls, armed force, and means of communication — in their hands, while turning over most other aspects of public affairs to administrators drawn from the native population. In these fields they could lay down policy and occasionally intervene brutally to punish real or fancied violations of their directives. They could play one group against another and thereby secure a check on the development of movements threatening to pass from German control. They could place all aspects of life under a crushing weight of fear and material deprivation.

---

[3] *Deutsche Bug-Zeitung*, December 2, 1942, p. 1; *Volyn'*, February 25, 1943, p. 4.

Lacking a body of supporters extending down to the smallest units of society, however, they could not enforce a positive program of indoctrination and—except in an intermittent and incomplete fashion—they could not prevent those who were in contact with the masses of the population from imparting their own ideological tinge to their activities.

The physical limitations of German power meant that the local administrative machinery in the East Ukraine was to a large extent left to the inhabitants. Local men were of course especially predominant in the administration of rural areas, but for reasons which will be discussed in the next chapter, little is known about their activities in connection with nationalism. The city administrations were more closely supervised by the Germans, but their size prevented them from being completely controlled. In spite of the fact that the populace soon realized that only the shadow of power was permitted the local administrations, the concept of the omnipotence of state control was so well established that even the outer signs of authority behind the nationalist cause were of some importance in winning support for it. Throughout the occupied Ukraine, except for the Donbas, which was very mixed ethnically, the languages of administration were German and Ukrainian only. Although it is said that the officials who carried on the governmental work in the prescribed language frequently spoke Russian as soon as they had left their desks, and sometimes even wrote their reports and orders in that language,[4] having them translated into Ukrainian, the prestige value of the change was considerable. The same was true of the widespread use of national symbols, which had been forbidden under Soviet rule, such as the trident and the blue and yellow colors; they appeared on the uniforms of the police, as banners decorating the administrative buildings, even on the streetcars. On the other hand, the removal of these symbols, when Russophile elements were introduced into the administration to replace the nationalists, was equally important as a negative token of loss of prestige; the official language, however, always remained Ukrainian.[5]

Some indication of the influence exerted upon the overt attitudes of the inhabitants of the East Ukraine by the apparent ascendancy of Ukrainian nationalism is furnished by nationalities statistics obtained from censuses taken by various city administrations in late 1941 and early 1942,[6] since each citizen was usually permitted to determine his own nationality. There was an enormous increase in the proportion of persons claiming Ukrainian nationality as compared to the Soviet census of 1926, which had been conducted in a similar fashion. That many factors were involved in the shift is indicated by the extreme variations from city to city, which will be touched upon in a later chapter. There is, moreover, little doubt that pressures, ranging from fear of the nationalist-dominated police (which, in Zhitomir at least, took the census)

---

[4]*Krakivs'ki Visti*, May 14, 1942, p. 3.

[5]When the *Ukraïns'ke Slovo* group was arrested, the cultural department of the Kiev city administration was ordered to remove all tridents and Ukrainian flags; see Iurko Stepovyi, *Syn Zakarpattia: Ukraïns'ke revoliutsiine pidpillia v Kyïevi 1941-1942 r.* (A Son of Transcarpathia: The Ukrainian Revolutionary Underground in Kiev 1941-42) (Munich, 1947), p. 11. In Dniepropetrovsk, the Germans followed up the destruction of the Ukrainian *oblast* administration by removing the trident from the masthead of *Vil'na Ukraïna* (The Free Ukraine), the city's newspaper, and changing its name to *Dnipropetrovs'ka Hazeta* (Interview 77).

[6]See Appendix.

to desire to obtain material benefits reserved for Ukrainians only, were significant. There is no question, however, that a large number of those who claimed Ukrainian nationality in 1941-42 were influenced by a desire to "climb upon the band wagon" by obtaining affiliation with the national group which they thought would be in favor in the future. The nationalist mayor of Kiev, Leontii Forostivs'kyi, during whose administration the census in the capital was taken, freely admits the importance of this factor.[7]

From a material standpoint, too, the municipal administration played a considerable role in the provision of support for nationalist activity. The funds at its disposal were not inconsiderable, the Kharkov city budget amounting to the equivalent of some eight million dollars annually.[8] The number of municipal employees was also sizable. In Kiev the total under Bahazii's direction, evidently largely dependent on the central municipal authority for their positions, was 20,000.[9] This figure was regarded as so excessive by the Germans that it figured in the charges made against him, but several months after his arrest the number employed by the city—apparently the purely administrative branches only, exclusive of education and manufacturing and commercial enterprises—was still 1,138, and 1,065 more were working for the *raions*.[10] Even the smaller figures are quite significant in a city whose total population had by that time sunk to 350,000, an extremely small percentage of which consisted of employable men. From the point of view of political sentiment, as will be shown, the composition of the administrative force made it even more significant, for over one-fourth were of the upper levels of the intelligentsia — those having a higher education — while another 35 percent were probably of the Soviet "intelligentsia," since they possessed secondary educations.[11] The city administrations, with their appurtenances of schools and publications, thus served as refuges for the intellectual class in general, which was shorn of its customary economic role by the terrible dislocations of war. Consequently the orientation of the structure in which they found a place could play a vital role in determining the direction this group's sentiments would take.

At least two East Ukrainian mayors,[12] in addition to Bahazii, lost their lives for too ardent devotion to the nationalist cause. Even when they were not in conflict with the occupying power, the mayors knew that their positions singled them out for Communist vengeance, from either secret agents or the returning Red army. That a considerable group of officials was found to remain true to the nationalist cause—even if a bit timidly at times—is an indication that a considerable reservoir of leadership for nationalism existed in the East Ukraine.

---

[7]Leontii Forostivs'kyi, *Kyïv pid vorozhymy okupatsiiamy* (Kiev under Enemy Occupations) (Buenos Aires: Mykola Denysiuk, 1952), p. 50.

[8]*L'vivs'ki Visti*, May 23-24, 1943, p. 2, quotes Mayor Semenenko as saying the budget for the last quarter of 1942 totaled 50,000,000 *karbovontsi* (10 *k.* = 1 RM = $0.40).

[9]PS 192.

[10]*Ukraïns'ka Diisnist'*, May 10, 1942, p. 1.

[11]*Ibid.*

[12]In Kamenets-Podolsk and Poltava.

While the city administration as a whole was both a symbol of Ukrainian nationalist ascendancy and an instrument for advancing the nationalist cause, the individual departments were frequently of equal or greater significance. Their importance derived in large measure from the fact that administrative divisions entrusted with very important functions were frequently operated in considerable independence of the central municipal administration.

In practice the amount of authority exercised by any major official depended more on his own character and his relations with the German authorities than upon any formal apportionment of power. This was especially the case in the large cities, where in addition to the *Stadtkommissar* who stood above the native mayor, there were German officials in charge of each of the departments of administration. In such cases the department heads who were on good terms with their German superiors seem to have been able to pursue courses substantially independent of the mayor, and this was also to an extent true of the firmer or more clever of those who wished to exert their own authority even without special German support. Consequently, it sometimes happened that one or more sections of a municipal administration were strongholds of nationalist activity, while the city as a whole was administered by elements opposed to Ukrainian independence.

Under the Soviet system, the municipal administrations had included departments of finance, communal economy, internal trade, health, popular education, social security, and cadres, as well as a general department, a planning commission, and sometimes departments of local manufacturing and agriculture. In the city administrations under German occupation, there was evidently some consolidation of departments, but in general the Soviet division was little changed, except for the elimination of the planning commission. On the other hand, several new departments were added for functions which had been performed by higher Soviet administrative levels but which the Germans wished to allocate, under their own control, to the cities. One was the propaganda department, which will be discussed somewhat later. Another was the juridical department, which operated a system of lower courts.[13] It was, however, of little or no importance as a channel of nationalist activity. Much more significant in this respect were the police departments. Some indications of their activity in nationalist affairs have already been given. The Germans, of course, exerted great efforts to keep this element of authority, the only branch of the local administration which could have offered armed resistance to their rule, under firm control. Since the police power was regularly in the hands of German SP officials, who frequently maintained only a nominal subordination to the *Stadtkommissar*, the Ukrainian chief of this department was correspondingly independent of the mayor. Moreover, since there were several German police authorities—ordinary security police, secret police, railway police—operating in the same area, unified at the top but having different Ukrainian subchiefs operating under them, the possibility of several competing or antagonistic influences existed. In spite of the special concern of the Reichskommissariat to root out all OUN members in the police, the latter were able for many months to maintain their positions in several cities. For example, while the city administrations of Vinnitsa and Dniepropetrovsk were in

---

[13]On the legal system in the Reichskommissariat, see Nicholas Laskovs'kyi, "Practicing Law in the Occupied Ukraine," *American Slavic and East European Review*, XI (April, 1952), p. 124 ff.

the hands of Russophile elements opposed to Ukrainian nationalism, the police chief in the former city[14] and the Ukrainian in charge of the secret police in the latter[15] were supporters of the OUN. Close as was the supervision of the German police authorities, it was obviously impossible for them to watch every action of their subordinates, so that possession of such support within the police force was of great value to the nationalist groups.

In the wave of repression in Kiev in December, 1941, the fact that his sympathizers controlled the police in the *raion* in which he was arrested allowed the chief of the OUN-M in the East Ukraine, Dr. Kandyba, to secure his release, thus enabling him to prolong his activities for more than two years.[16] Moreover, the presence of nationalist elements in the police force served to prevent the control of these groups by secret Communist agents, who were successful in penetrating the police in a number of places in the southern Ukraine, and for a while in Kiev itself, through the German practice of retaining the Soviet *militsiia* as a matter of convenience.[17] Whatever value the nationalist penetration of the police force may have had in this connection was largely offset by the odium which attached to the nationalist groups when it became known to the population that they were collaborating with the Germans in this fashion. Moreover, the ill repute of the police was sometimes increased by the actions of the nationalists themselves who used the police as an instrument for terrorizing non-Ukrainians.[18]

Of less obvious importance than the police sections, but nevertheless of great significance were the agencies concerned with health, social security, and welfare. The extreme limitations placed upon the efforts of the local administrations to maintain their starving citizens have already been described. Nevertheless, the fact that they could carry on activity was of some importance, both from the practical standpoint and from that of providing the population with token participation in administration. The Germans were undoubtedly content to leave this arduous and thankless task to the local leaders. Welfare activities were in part the responsibility of municipal departments, in part the function of volunteer organizations. This duplication gave rise to the possibility of conflicting political trends in the same field of operation. In Kiev the head of the welfare department, until his consecration as an Autocephalous bishop, was Professor Haievs'kyi,[19] and even after his resignation the department seems to have been in the hands of nationalist elements. The paucity of the resources available to this section has been indicated in a preceding chapter; nevertheless, it was able to arrange for the provision of buildings for care of the

---

[14]Interview 1.

[15]Interviews 1, 18.

[16]L. Dniprova, article in *Ukraïns'ke Slovo* (Paris), June 18, 1950, p. 3.

[17]Interview 59.

[18]It is said that the Ukrainian police in Kiev, when ordered to secure hostages after explosions set off by Communist agents in Kiev in the autumn of 1941, arrested only Russians, scores of whom were then shot (Interviews 19, 59). However, a German order provided that Ukrainians were not to be taken as hostages while Russians were to be arrested for this purpose (Order of Befehlshaber des Ruckwärtigen Heeresgebiets Süd, August 16, 1941, NOKW 1691; hereafter referred to as NOKW 1691).

[19]*Ukraïns'ka Diisnist'*, May 10, 1942, p. 1.

distressed.[20] At the same time, the Ukrainian Red Cross, which had been formed as an organ of the city government and which had carried on extensive operations in relieving the horrible conditions in the prisoner-of-war camps, had been dissolved by the Germans. Apparently this action was due in part to its use by Nationalist elements as a screen for their activities, but more particularly to its humane exertions. Its leader, Professor Theodore Bohatyrchuk, who, after having welcomed collaboration with the OUN-M group, had become disgusted with its excesses in Kiev, now turned to support of the Russophile element.[21] His organization, which was reformed as the All-Ukrainian Aid Committee (Vseukraïns'kyi Komitet Dopomohy), was able, even on the eve of German evacuation, to provide meals for 36,000 persons (children and others unable to work),[22] one-sixth of the city's population; its great popularity[23] was of tremendous importance in enabling Bohatyrchuk to secure support for his stand in favor of coalition with anti-Soviet Russians. On the other hand, in Dniepropetrovsk, where the city administration was largely in the hands of pro-Russian elements, the Ukrainians, inspired by an OUN-M organizer, formed a Red Cross organization which acted as a center for nationalist forces.

The nationalist element was more successful in the field of cooperative organization. While each city administration contained a department of trade, the cooperatives, as quasi-public bodies, appear to have been considerably more important as channels of local initiative. Far from being a product of the Communist regime, the cooperative movement was indigenous to both East and West Ukraine, having played an important role before the First World War, when it was already imbued with nationalist overtones.[24] In the NEP period of Soviet rule, and until the late twenties, the cooperatives had been able to maintain a considerable degree of independence and had, at least in the Kharkov region, served as a center for nationalist elements which worked with the Republican government.[25] In the Five Year Plan periods, the urban cooperatives had become adjuncts of the state trading systems, and other cooperatives had been closely integrated into state commercial operations.[26]

---

[20]Ibid.

[21]Interviews 19, 71.

[22]*Nove Ukraïns'ke Slovo*, September 19, 1943, pp. 4-5; see also *Volyn'*, January 28, 1943, p. 3.

[23]Tarkovych in *Krakivs'ki Visti*, February 8, 1942, p. 4.

[24]For abundant details on the complex system of cooperatives developed in the Ukraine prior to 1917, see Eugene M. Kayden and Alexis N. Antsiferov, *The Cooperative Movement in Russia During the War* (New Haven: Yale University Press, 1929), a volume in the *Economic and Social History of the World War*, ed. James T. Shotwell, Russian Series, compiled for the Carnegie Endowment for International Peace, Division of Economics and History. Cooperatives were far more developed in the Ukraine than in most other heavily populated areas of the Russian Empire (*ibid.*, pp. 40, 41, 266-69, 357), and served educational as well as economic development. Kharkov was the chief cooperative center in the Ukraine and was largely independent of the Russian centers.

[25]Interview 73.

[26]Alexander Baikov, *The Development of the Soviet Economic System* (New York: Cambridge University Press, 1946), p. 253; Arthur C. Arnold, *Banks, Credit, and Money in Soviet Russia* (New York: Columbia University Press, 1937), p. 477.

When the Germans arrived, surviving leaders of the former independent cooperatives were again able to assert themselves. As early as the winter of 1941-42, there was a total of 643 cooperative organizations in the Kiev region, including forty-eight *raion* food societies which bought agricultural produce and carried on economic organization;[27] in the city of Kharkov there were 150 cooperatives, which maintained close contacts with their sources of food stocks in the countryside.[28] There were, in addition to numerous distributing cooperatives, twenty-eight producing cooperatives in Kiev, in such diverse fields as transport, printing, and haberdashery.[29] The Ukraïnbank (All-Ukrainian Cooperative Bank), which had been formed in 1922 for financing all types of cooperatives, but incorporated in the Soviet central Torgbank in 1936, was revived.[30]

Moreover, there were more direct links to the nationalist movements. An effort was made, with German approval, to organize a general center for the food cooperatives, known as the All-Ukrainian Cooperative Society (Vseukraïns'ka Kooperatyvna Spilka), which coordinated local organizations, published a bulletin, and restored the museum of the history of cooperative development, an institution of considerable significance for nationalist sentiment.[31] Under an old officer of the Ukrainian army, Professor Perevertun, a close collaborator of the OUN-M, it carried out activities on a large scale in the Kiev area, especially training replacements for the diminished ranks of cooperative workers.[32] In addition to more indirect fostering of nationalist sentiment, its aid to the nationalist cause included employing persons whom the Germans had dismissed from the municipal administration.[33] In early 1943, however, such activities resulted in the execution of the director.[34]

Like the cooperative movement, popular education had long been a cornerstone of Ukrainian nationalism, more important in many respects than direct political action. In the conflict between the national Communists in the Ukraine and the Stalinist centralists, it was especially the commissars of education, such as Shums'kyi and Skrypnyk, who had led the fight for Ukrainization of cultural life. Consequently it was natural that nationalist Ukrainians were determined to control the municipal departments of education under German occupation.

A major aim of the Reichskommissar and his henchmen, however, was to prevent the development of a cultured Ukrainian class, to convert the people

---

[27]*Krakivs'ki Visti*, February 4, 1942, p. 3.

[28]*Krakivs'ki Visti*, February 24, 1942, p. 2.

[29]*Krakivs'ki Visti*, February 5, 1942, p. 2.

[30]*Krakivs'ki Visti*, February 10, 1942, p. 4. Cf. Baikov, *Development of Soviet Economic System*, p. 86, and Arnold, *Banks ... in Soviet Russia*, p. 477, for the background of this bank.

[31]*Krakivs'ki Visti*, February 4, 1942, p. 3. See also Otto Bräutigam, *Überblick über die besetzten Ostgebiete während des 2. Weltkrieges* (Tübingen: Studien des Instituts für Besatzungsfragen, No. 3, January 1954, mimeographed).

[32]*Deutsche Ukraine Zeitung*, July 11, 1942, p. 3.

[33]*OUN u Viini* (The OUN in the War), Information Section of the OUN (UNR), April, 1946, p. 75.

[34]*Ibid.*; *Entsyklopediia Ukraïnoznavstva* (Encyclopedia of Things Ukrainian), eds. Volodymyr Kubiiovych and Zenon Kuzelia (Munich: Naukove Tovarystvo im. Shevchenka, 1949), p. 585.

into a race of submissive peasants. Rosenberg's vision of a university in Kiev went by the board, and the standard schooling for every Ukrainian child was set at four years.[35] Few material injuries were as deeply resented as this drastic curb on the opportunities for education. Since there were real shortages of materials, books, and teachers, the Ukrainians held to the hope that the restriction did not represent a permanent policy, even in the face of the closing of *gimnaziias* which had been reopened under the army administration through the efforts of the local population itself.[36]

To a limited extent the ban on secondary and higher education was evaded by the extensive use made of a loophole in the German regulations which allowed the reopening of technical schools. The enormous loss of artisans and professionally trained persons incurred by the annihilation of the Jewish inhabitants compelled even the power-mad Nazis to recognize the need for training Ukrainians in such occupations. A large number of technical secondary schools, agricultural schools, and even institutes of higher education like medical faculties, were permitted. The extent to which these facilities were utilized by the Ukrainian population is indicated by the fact that the enrollment of the Kiev medical institute reached 2,000 in 1943 when the total population of the city was only 300,000, while Kherson, with a fifth that number of inhabitants, had 541 students in its medical school.[37] Medical institutes were also reopened in Stalino, Dniepropetrovsk, and Vinnitsa, and perhaps in other cities, although it is doubtful if any of these were the centers of nationalist youth organization which the faculty in Kiev became under the leadership of the OUN-M.[38]

The educational structure described in the preceding paragraph was designed for adolescents or young adults, and thus could be used for direct propagation of nationalist concepts. It was, of course, partly for this reason that the Germans confined advanced training within such narrow limits. Even these restrictions were not the end of the difficulties faced in inculcating a nationalist type of education in those about to assume the role of citizens, for the technical schools were frequently emptied of their students and faculty to meet the demands of the *Ostarbeiter* recruiters. The elementary schools were also drained of teachers by the *Ostarbeiter* program, and the pupils, though too young for forced labor, were decimated by famine and plague. If the task of building national consciousness had to be viewed as a long-term one, then the four-year elementary school offered a considerable field for cultivation.[39]

The problem confronting the nationalist leaders in education was twofold: they had to ensure a basis for the development of an independent Ukraine by making certain that all instruction was in the Ukrainian language, so that the rising generation would be fully at home in this speech; and they

---

[35] Report of Rosenberg to Hitler, August 11, 1942, PS 42 (hereafter referred to as PS 42); PS 1198.

[36] E.g., in Berdichev (*Nastup*, September 20, 1941, p. 3, quoting *Nova Doba* [Berdichev] for September 1), Zhitomir (Iefremenko in *Krakivs'ki Visti*, November 1, 1941), and Belaia Tserkov' (*Natsionalist*, December 20, 1941, p. 2).

[37] Occ E-4 (1); *Ukraïns'ka Diisnist'*, October 10, 1942, p. 1.

[38] See Chapter V.

[39] In Kiev alone there were fifty elementary schools with 17,000 students (*Krakivs'ki Visti*, April 11, 1942, p. 2).

had to replace the Communist ideology by a positive nationalist concept. The first task was relatively uncomplicated, though far from easy in practice. In line with their policy of encouraging the purely nonpolitical aspects of Ukrainian nationality, the Germans ordered all instruction to be in Ukrainian. The nationalist directors enthusiastically supported this rule, but it was sometimes difficult to enforce it, since even teachers who were themselves nationalist in sentiment were not always able to conduct classes in Ukrainian.[40]

It was much more difficult to secure a predominant place for the nationalist ideology in the schools. As is usually the case in nationalist indoctrination in the schools, the efforts were concentrated upon the teaching of history.[41] This was especially important, since the justification of the Ukrainian independence movement is largely based upon the conception of a proud history distinct from that of the people of Moscow. Naturally enough, no Soviet textbooks were acceptable for the teaching of history from this point of view or from the general standpoint of eradicating Communist indoctrination. To some extent the gap was filled by books published in the year preceding the Soviet war by the educational press of the Ukrainian Central Committee in Cracow.[42] Some texts were printed by the cultural department of the Kiev city administration. An amateurish effort was made also by certain OUN-B organizers to print locally a new version of Ukrainian history with an introduction of their own composition.[43] In view of the great material shortages and the brief time available, however, the lack of printed materials could not be made good. Consequently, a great deal depended on securing the proper teachers. To what extent the many thousands employed in the schools adhered to the nationalist doctrine is of course impossible to determine, but a number of purely indigenous formulations of nationalist concepts to be inculcated in the schools attest to the strength of nationalist feeling. The head of the Mariupol' school system proposed to stress the native language, love of the fatherland, and respect for elders; the educational ideology advocated by the group of young men who reorganized life in Krivoi Rog was instillation of Cossack ideals, the code of the Zaporozhian Sich, which was to lead to a spiritual, moral, and physical regeneration.[44]

Since the formal school program was largely confined to young children, great efforts were also concentrated on developing a voluntary system of adult education. The Prosvita societies had been founded by the nationalist intelligentsia of the East Ukraine many years before the Revolution. They were now revived, after long suppression by the Communist regime, to carry on the work of developing national culture and inculcating a feeling of national identity. The two aims could be combined because all nationalist Ukrainians felt it

---

[40]Tarkovych in *Krakivs'ki Visti*, July 12, 1942, p. 4; M. Prykhod'ko in *Krakivs'ki Visti*, June 5, 1942, pp. 3-4; *Krakivs'ki Visti*, January 27, 1943, p. 4, quoting D. Nitsenko in *Nova Ukraïna* (Kharkov).

[41]Prykhod'ko in *Krakivs'ki Visti*, June 5, 1942, pp. 3-4.

[42]Druzhynnyk in *Krakivs'ki Visti*, October 10, 1941, p. 2.

[43]Zynovii Matla, *Pivdenna pokhidna hrupa* (The Southern Task Force) (Munich: Tsitsero, 1952), p. 28.

[44]*Krakivs'ki Visti*, September 29, 1942, p. 2; November 15, 1941, p. 2; and November 18, 1941, p. 3 (referring to an article in *Dzvin* [Krivoi Rog], September, 1941).

essential to instill a love of the indigenous popular arts and customs, emphasizing their distinctive nature. That this effort had a political as well as a cultural significance is indicated by the fact that not only the Soviet regime (both before 1941 and upon reconquest, as in Kharkov)[45] but the German police as well attacked the Prosvita societies, and in the Reichskommissariat they were able, for varying periods, to lead only a clandestine life. The desire for national expression was shared by so many, however, that the Germans felt it was impossible to dam up all outlets; therefore the Prosvita was generally permitted, though under close observation.[46] Together with the church (and a few local societies not using the Prosvita name but having the same function), it was one of the few organizations of a nationalist character which was not under direct German control.

The work of the Prosvita groups, although arranged in various ways in different localities, may be classified under four general headings. Playing a major role everywhere were musical activities, particularly choral groups, in which the Ukrainians had always excelled, and which served as a powerful intellectual and emotional stimulus to nationalist feeling, since most of the songs were distinctively Ukrainian. In addition, groups of *bandura* players (the *bandura* is a small lute-like stringed instrument indigenous to the Ukraine) were sponsored, and orchestras were trained. In the larger centers, Prosvita collaborated with regular professional musical organizations, such as conservatories and operas, to produce nationalist-inspired performances. For example, operas were reopened in Kiev and Kharkov, and offered a considerable repertoire of native Ukrainian pieces (*Taras Bul'ba, Natalka Poltavka*, etc.) as well as traditional Western operas such as *Madame Butterfly* and *Les Cloches de Corneville*. Like other forms of national expression, however, operatic performances ran afoul of the Nazi hatred of independent activity. At first, the desirable places in the Kiev opera were reserved for Germans, and then, in December, 1942, the performances were suspended altogether, an action which aroused the indignation of all elements of the population.[47]

Within a matter of days after the Red army was driven out, active theatrical groups likewise sprang up, usually with Prosvita sponsorship, even in the smaller cities of the East Ukraine. For example, a theater had been started in Zhitomir before the first month of German occupation was past.[48] Even in cities like Chernigov and Simferopol' (in the Crimea), where evidences of nationalist activity were scanty, the theater was soon in full career.[49] Since the players were generally amateurs interested in using this medium of expression of their nationalist feeling, the performances were nationalist in content as well as language (evidently to a greater extent than the opera which, being

---

[45]Cf. *Nastup*, September 26, 1943, p. 3 (based on *Vinnyts'ki Visti*, August 29, 1943), on the destruction of Prosvita and its personnel in Kharkov during the Soviet interlude in February-March, 1943.

[46]MS E; PS 3943, May 22, 1942.

[47]Interrogation of Shtepa, CXLVa 78; PS 1198.

[48]*Ukraïns'ka Diisnist'*, September 15, 1941, p. 1 (from *Ukraïns'ke Slovo* [Zhitomir], August 3, 1941).

[49]*Krakivs'ki Visti*, December 6, 1941, p. 4 (based on an interview with Theodore Pipa, the Chernigov editor).

composed largely of professional performers, was imbued with an "all-Union," i.e., Russian, character, at least behind the scenes).[50] Some presentations were so strongly imbued with nationalist ideology that they were censored by the Germans; the author of one of the most popular, Constantine Hupalo, was arrested for nationalist activity.[51]

Prosvita and related groups sponsored a wide variety of more directly educational activities. These included lectures, valued as a means of propagating knowledge of the language as well as for their content; libraries and reading rooms, vital to the spread of the printed word in view of the extreme scarcity of even periodical literature; nationalist cultural work in the schools; and research and discussion on themes of national history and ethnography. In the more vigorous and less restricted societies, like the Prosvita in Kharkov, these activities were greatly extended. The latter group operated a House of Popular Culture which served as a center for most nationalist organizations in the city, and came close to developing into an unofficial government.[52] Moreover, under the leadership of the energetic Professor V. V. Dubrovs'kyi, it undertook economic as well as purely cultural activities, such as book publishing and the provision of material aid for needy teachers and students.[53] Some indication of the scope of Prosvita's activities in Kharkov is provided by the fact that membership reached one thousand, while 4,000 persons attended one of its concert series.[54]

In most places *Prosvita* and other cultural activities appear to have developed quite independently of the Nationalist party organizers from the west. To a certain extent the ideology of the Nationalists, especially that of the OUN-B, made them contemptuous of such gradual and unspectacular methods of developing nationalist strength.[55] To be sure, in centers such as Kiev and

---

[50]Cf. Tarkovych in *Krakivs'ki Visti*, July 15, 1942, p. 3.

[51]His play, entitled *The Triumph of Procurator Dal'shii*, was a drama of the Ukrainian nationalist movement under Soviet rule (*OUN u Viini*, p. 74).

[52]Cf. Serednopolets'kyi in *Krakivs'ki Visti*, February 24, 1942, p. 2, on organizations operating in the House of National Culture. Erich Koch, in his letter to Rosenberg of March 16, 1943 (PS 192), complained that the Wehrmacht permitted the Kharkov Prosvita to become a sort of national government, and its role as a political as well as a cultural force is confirmed by Interview 73.

[53]*Nastup*, September 26, 1943, p. 3, based on an interview with a leading member of the Kharkov Prosvita, Professor P. Petrenko, in *Vinnyts'ki Visti*, August 29, 1943.

[54]*Krakivs'ki Visti*, February 10, 1943, p. 2.

[55]For example, Ievhen (Eugene) Stakhiv ("E. Pavliuk"), "Borot'ba ukraïns'koho narodu na skhidno-ukraïns'kykh zemliakh, 1941-1944: Spomyny ochevydtsia i uchasnyka" (The Struggle of the Ukrainian People in the Eastern Ukrainian Lands, 1941-44: Memories of an Eyewitness and Participant), in *Kalendar Provydinnia na 1947 rik. Stovaryshennia Ukraïns'kikh Katolykiv v Amerytsi* (Calendar for 1947 of the Providence Society of Ukrainian Catholics in America) (Philadelphia: Ameryka, n.d.), p. 40, writes that it was necessary for OUN-B members to withdraw from Prosvita, amateur groups, etc., as these (after the introduction of the Reichskommissariat) were only tools of the Germans, and nationalist participation in them gave color to the Communist propaganda which represented the OUN as an agency of the Germans. On the other hand, the clandestine *Biuleten'* (No. 4, previously cited), in calling for an extension of OUN-B activity to all fields of life, criticizes those who condemn activity which is not of a strictly terroristic, revolutionary nature as "Prosvitanstvo." Cf. Lev Shankovs'kyi, *Pokhidni hrupy OUN* (March Groups of the OUN) (Munich: Vydavnytstvo "Ukraïns'kyi Samostiinyk," 1958), p. 135, who writes that OUN-B members avoided Prosvita only because they feared work in it would jeopardize their clandestine position.

Zhitomir, which were strongly permeated by the OUN-M forces, cooperative relations existed between the latter and the local founders of Prosvita, but the Nationalist party did not have the personnel to carry on cultural work itself and apparently did not find the Prosvita organization well adapted to its tactic of underground work after German suppression.[56] On the other hand, the extremely important Kharkov Prosvita was organized almost entirely by local residents who had in many cases been associated with the Prosvita of pre-Soviet days, and who were unassociated with, or even to some extent hostile to, the OUN-M.[57] Here again, there is strong indication of the survival in the East Ukraine of leadership able to take direction of important aspects of national life. That this leadership was directed to such a considerable extent to the less aggressive aspects of national development, however, indicates that a certain gap existed during the war years between nationalism in the East and the West Ukraine.

The means employed in the educational systems and in the cultural societies for propagating the national ideology can be classed for the most part under the heading of oral propaganda. The face-to-face type of communication has a long history of effective use in the East Slavic countries and, under the name "oral agitation," has been widely cultivated as a means of strengthening the Communist regime. Hence the population was used to this type of propaganda. Moreover, it was especially suited to the work of the nationalist groups, which were seeking to spread ideas frowned upon by the German authorities. The latter could suppress a performance or dissolve a society, arrest or execute a leader, but with their small number of personnel, their ignorance of the language, and their lack of sufficiently numerous and reliable local agents, they could not overhear everything and thus prevent the clever teacher or cultural worker from communicating political concepts to his audience. Since nationalist propagandists were so few and ill-equipped by organization and training to cope with the gigantic task of indoctrinating a population of thirty million, however, the problem of securing access to mass communication media under control of the propaganda departments of the municipal administrations was vitally important. Through such media nationalism might reach thousands where oral methods by the same number of agitators reached scores and live theatrical performances reached hundreds.

The principal activity of the propaganda department of a Ukrainian municipal administration under German occupation centered around the local newspaper, for other media such as the radio and motion pictures were under complete German control. It is worth devoting considerable attention to journalistic activity throughout the East Ukraine because of the value such study can have in elucidating the whole problem of the extent of nationalist activity in that area. Newspapers not only reached large numbers, but represented a symbol of authoritative pronouncement to a people accustomed to viewing

---

[56] Interview 61.

[57] Interviews 57, 73.

the statements of the Soviet press as announcements of policy not subject to question.[58]

However much the German authorities may have feared the existence of a Ukrainian press, it was absolutely essential for them to authorize and support it for their own purposes. Under the Wehrmacht administration, especially in the early days, a very nonrestrictive policy was pursued, as was indicated by the ideologically independent nature of *Ukraïns'ke Slovo* in Zhitomir and Kiev. General ground rules laid down included prohibition of the term "Ukraine" in the sense of a state, rather than as a territorial expression; insistence on reference to Germany as the "protector" of the Ukraine, rather than as an "ally"; and designation of the Wehrmacht as "saviors" rather than "occupiers."[59] Under army control newspapers sprang up in scores of towns, including all of the important cities of the East Ukraine, although in at least one (Poltava) the establishment of a paper was considerably delayed by the unwillingness of any officer to accept the responsibility of censoring it.[60] One reason for the Wehrmacht's liberality was a desire to carry propaganda to the numerous deserters who, if they were afraid to submit to German authority, might join the Red partisans. Consequently, papers were fostered in the swamp and wooded regions, even in small towns such as Ovruch, Olevsk, and Shchors. Indeed, the propaganda section of the army itself played a major role in founding newspapers, and even provided for the journalistic staffs in Zhitomir, Kiev, Poltava, and Kharkov the services of a competent and comparatively neutral Galician journalist, Peter Sahaidachnyi.

However, as was previously noted, the OUN-M took a leading role in establishing the papers in Zhitomir and Kiev. Its importance was also considerable in a number of the smaller cities. In Kharkov, Dniepropetrovsk, and Krivoi Rog, on the other hand, the initiative was taken by persons who had been journalists under the Soviet regime. In Krivoi Rog, Michael Pronchenko, a writer and poet who had been imprisoned by the Soviet regime, but later worked for the local Communist paper, upon Red army evacuation took over the Communist press and, with the aid of other young men, began publishing a paper called *Dzvin* (The Bell).[61] In Kharkov, it was a former member of the staff of the defunct *Sotsialistychna Kharkivshchyna* who proposed immediately after the German arrival to start a newspaper under the name of *Novyi Chas*

---

[58]There is considerably more information available on newspaper activity than on other politically significant aspects of the East Ukraine. Since many of the observers who have written accounts of the war period were themselves journalists, they naturally paid considerable attention to this field of activity. Moreover, the West Ukrainian newspapers published during the same period, which furnish the principal source of material on the East Ukraine, were also especially interested in journalistic enterprises. Consequently, one must guard against the assumption that the real importance of these newspapers was as great as the attention devoted to them indicates. Nevertheless, they were unquestionably very significant as means of transmitting nationalism and reflecting national feeling.

[59]PS 053.

[60]USSR Exhibit 278; Chief of the SP and of the SD, Reports of *Einsatzgruppen* and *Kommandos*, February 4, 1942, p. 8 (T 175, Reel 234) stresses that pro-Mel'nyk elements predominated in provincial newspapers, even using them to print illegal brochures.

[61]*Krakivs'ki Visti*, November 15, 1941, p. 3; Interview 7.

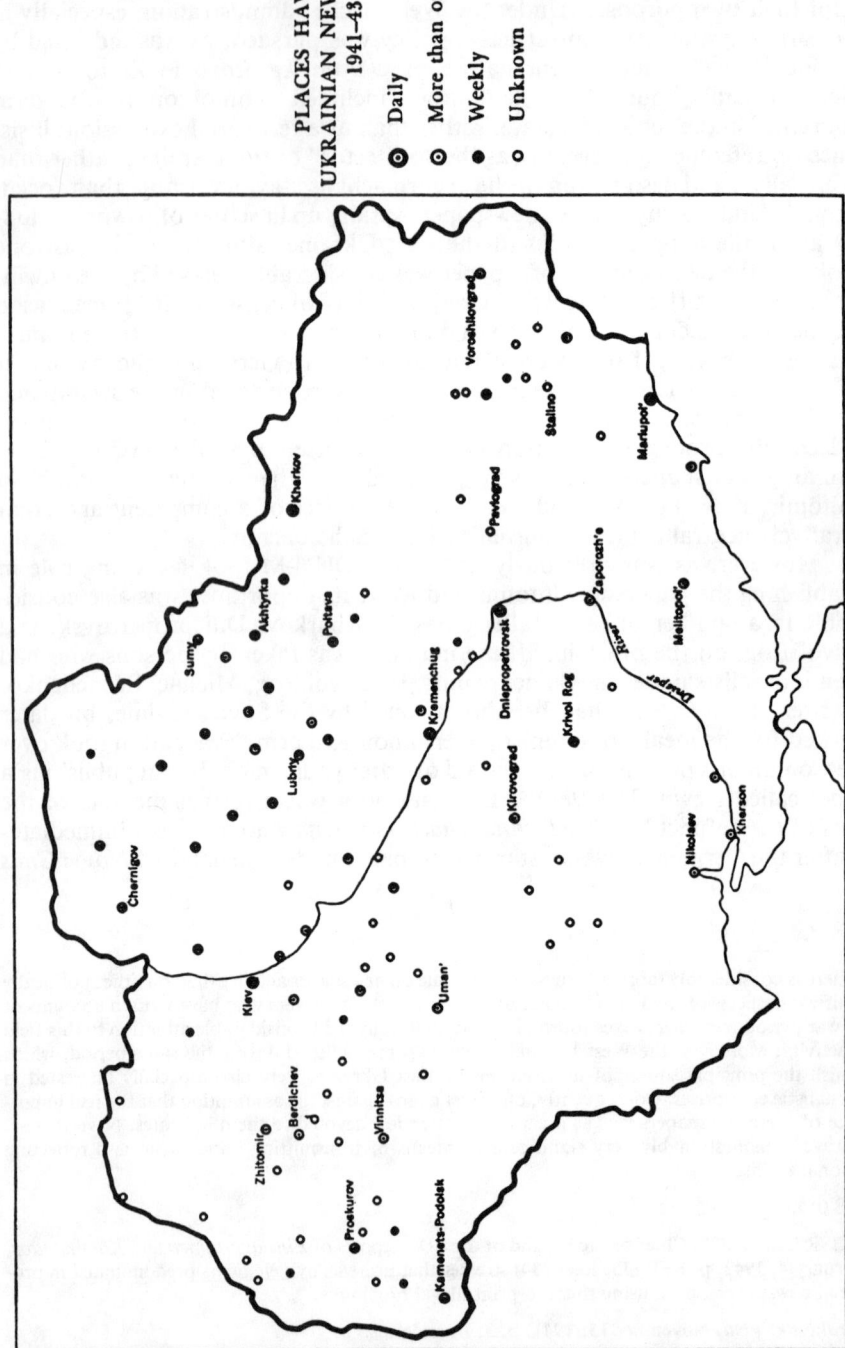

(The New Times).⁶² It was some weeks before the paper could actually be started; the name then became *Nova Ukraïna*, and a large number of Mel'nyk adherents were on the staff. The chief editor and a majority of his subordinates, however, were local persons unaffiliated with the OUN. In a number of places Bandera organizers, too, assisted local men to establish papers.

When the Reichskommissariat took over the bulk of the East Ukraine, a quite different policy was pursued; the outspokenly nationalist organs were suppressed, their staffs executed. Even the official policy of the Reichskommissariat, presumably approved by the Ostministerium, provided that all matters concerning newspapers in the native language should be submitted to the Press and Enlightenment Division of the Reichskommissariat. Newspapers were to be held to the minimum necessary to satisfy the Ukrainian desire for news, and they were to be founded only where "politically unobjectionable" journalists and adequate censorship machinery were available.⁶³ Nevertheless, as even this directive indicates, the need for a Ukrainian press could not be questioned. It was absolutely essential to have some means of reaching the population with directives, of quieting rumors, and of playing up the few positive features of the German administration. Since there were very few German personnel who could write Ukrainian, local men had to be turned to, although strong requests for newspapers were frequently refused when the Germans felt the burden of providing censors outweighed possible gains in propaganda or administrative convenience.

While important as a symbol of Ukrainian nationalist ascendancy, the newspaper had certain severe limitations as a vehicle for nationalist ideology. Its frequency and size limited its utility. There were a few dailies, but the vast majority of newspapers appeared much less frequently, as the following figures on East Ukrainian newspapers show:⁶⁴

Papers issued	
daily	5
three times a week	18
twice a week	25
weekly	9
unknown	41
TOTAL	98

Moreover, none exceeded four pages, and a large number could print only one page (being printed on the back of Soviet posters, etc.). This sharp curtailment was due primarily to the extremely severe paper shortage, especially in the south. *Nova Ukraïna* in Kharkov was forced to reduce its printing from 50,000 to 25,000 daily;⁶⁵ the daily *Mariiupil's'ka Hazeta* had to limit publication to three times a week; one paper in the Taurida *Generalbezirk* had to issue

---

⁶²Arkadii Liubchenko, *Shchodennyk* (Diary), Vol. I, ed. M. Dmytrenko (Toronto: Novi Dni, 1951), pp. 7-9.

⁶³PS 702.

⁶⁴Figures compiled from numerous sources. It is very probable that the papers marked "unknown" appeared infrequently.

⁶⁵*Krakivs'ki Visti*, August 21, 1942, p. 3.

one copy of each number to each commune in the area, rather than to individuals.[66]

If all the limited space available had been at the editor's disposal, it would have sufficed for the expression of a wide range of political comments. Actually, a large part, usually the front page, was taken up with "news," mostly military or concerning the allegedly superior attributes of the Germans.[67] Another large body of material consisted of notices and orders of the German administration. Furthermore, the editors were frequently compelled to write, or to print over their signatures, editorials prepared by the German propaganda officers stressing some point (usually fictitious), such as the joys of the *Ostarbeiter* program or the rapid progress of land distribution, which the authorities desired to have propagandized. There was also a considerable number of articles of a factual nature, designed to "educate" the Ukrainians on some topic such as agricultural techniques, in which the Germans thought them to be deficient; these were frequently translated from the German press. A certain number of notices of the activity of Ukrainian agencies — the local administrations, the church, cultural activity — was permitted under close surveillance against political propaganda. A very small number of articles on history, literature, and other cultural topics was allowed.

These limitations came close to placing the Ukrainian editor in a strait jacket. It is almost universally recognized by persons who were active in journalism at this time, however, that there were a few points at which the jacket might be stretched enough to justify the effort to use the newspaper as an outlet for nationalist expression. The few literary articles permitted, while deprived of overt political content, could be used to a certain extent to stress themes which were basic to the formation of national pride, themes such as the nobility of Ukrainian literature, the separate development of Ukrainian and Russian history, and the value of Ukrainian folkways. Articles ostensibly directed against Communists or Jews could contain oblique thrusts at Moscow and the Russians as well; sometimes such articles did indeed represent extremes of xenophobia. Even the articles giving purely factual accounts of Ukrainian activity were prized by the nationalists, since they brought to the public's attention phases of national life which had been prohibited by the Soviets. The fact that a considerable number of such items could be found for reprinting in the relatively free West Ukrainian and émigré presses (although of course the articles so treated were far from representative) indicates that the censorship barrier was not insuperable, and simple a priori consideration of the difficulty of

---

[66]PS 1693.

[67]With the exception of a few issues of *Ukraïns'ke Slovo* and *Nove Ukraïns'ke Slovo* from Kiev, the actual copies of these East Ukrainian papers have uniformly disappeared, so that it is impossible to make an investigation based on direct inspection. Their disappearance is readily explained by the hasty evacuation of the Ukraine by the German forces, the danger of having German organs on one's person in a flight to the West when one might fall into Soviet hands, and above all by the desperate need for paper of any kind for ordinary household uses. As a matter of fact, extensive, but by no means complete sets were gathered by the Institute for the Study of the Ukrainian Liberation Movement in Prague, as well as by certain émigré newspapers. The former collection, however, remained in the Czechoslovak capital after the end of the war and eventually fell into Soviet hands after the Communist coup (Interview 30). As a result, the presentation followed here must be based almost entirely on postwar information, and especially upon the numerous descriptions of East Ukrainian newspapers and reprints of their articles contained in the West Ukrainian and émigré press.

securing alert and reliable censors for such a large body of publications substantiates this assertion.

While it was therefore true that the newspapers could be used, to a limited extent, for nationalist propaganda, the fact that they were edited by writers known to be nationalists had a certain negative effect on the regard in which the nationalist cause was held by the population, since the newspapers were obviously tools of the Germans. Communist propaganda—and Bandera propaganda after the OUN-B workers were forced from editorial posts—made a great deal of this fact. The most courageous nationalist editors tried to overcome this accusation of serving German interests by occasional sly attacks on the Germans, using the "Aesopian" language which the subjects of the Soviet empire had been forced to learn. Thus one editor, when ordered to write an article glorifying the *Ostarbeiter* program, described in glowing terms the luxurious dining cars on the trains to Germany; few Ukrainians observing the miserable cattle cars actually provided could miss the irony.[68] Not a few editors were willing to pursue such dangerous tactics.

As far as can be detected, the only papers which were controlled by pro-Russian elements (aside from the Russian-language papers) were *Nove Ukraïns'ke Slovo, Dnipropetrovs'ka Hazeta*, and possibly one or two of the Ukrainian-language papers in the Donbas. A number of papers in the latter area and a few in the southwest Ukraine were influenced by Bandera agents, although edited by local people, and maintained a semblance of independence from German control. The important papers in Vinnitsa and Proskurov remained under OUN-M editors, who, however, had to exert the utmost care to avoid arrest. Some papers, like a group in the area northwest of Poltava, which were led by a young resident of Mirgorod (Myrhorod), Michael Voskobiinyk, who was the editor of the paper there, did what they could to propagate nationalist sentiment, while others in the same district were completely subservient to the Germans.[69]

It is probably safe to say that the majority of editors would have liked to insert nationalist themes in their papers, and did so in the early days before the repression. The terrible danger to which they were exposed, however, seems to have induced most to go even further than was necessary for safety's sake in eliminating every vestige of independent writing and in slavishly following the German line. This was, as some of them were ready to admit, largely a heritage from the spirit-crushing Soviet regime, for West Ukrainians in similar positions were willing to display more initiative even though exposed to greater risks.[70] It was also very probably due to the fact that the editors lacked any experience in journalism, for many had been teachers or had followed other professions which left them ill-prepared for their new tasks. The suspicion which attached to any who had worked for the Soviet press, and had thus been compelled to write anti-German material, forced journalists with Soviet

---

[68]Interview 3.

[69]Interview 47.

[70]This was admitted by an East Ukrainian in *Ukraïns'kyi Visnyk* in a sharp criticism of the editorial staffs who continued the Soviet tradition of complete subservience to authority in journalism, so that in some cases the Germans themselves had to urge them to be more enterprising (March 22, 1945, p. 1).

experience to be especially cautious.[71] Whatever the reasons, on the whole the East Ukrainians, when deprived of Nationalist support, made a rather poor showing as journalists. With some notable exceptions,[72] they did not measure up to the standards of the West Ukrainians or of old veterans of the Republican period like Nicholas Stasiuk, the editor of *Mariiupil's'ka Hazeta*. As will be shown, the administrative officials were also generally drawn from the intelligentsia, especially those of the academic or teaching profession, and had not been trained for the roles they assumed. That they nevertheless made a better showing of independence and devotion to national aims may possibly be explained by the fact that the Soviet regime had encouraged an attitude of limited self-assertion in local administrative bodies, so long as no questions of policy were at stake, while newspaper staffs were much more rigidly confined to transmission of Communist Party-inspired material and even more minutely controlled. Many persons of initiative must have felt it was better to take posts in which real service of a non-political nature could be rendered, rather than assume the unattractive function of mouthpiece for a repressive regime. The question of the characteristics of the East Ukrainian intellectual can be considered in a larger context in the next chapter.

---

[71]One of the causes for the dismissal of Pronchenko from directorship of *Dzvin* was the accusation by his enemies that he had written an article against Hitler in a Soviet paper (Iuryi Semenko, "Pam'iati Mykhaila Pronchenka" [Memories of Michael Pronchenko], *Novi Dni*, April, 1953, pp. 10-13); Liubchenko feared that a similar charge would be made against him, and wrote that Shtepa told him outright that persons active in the Soviet press could not be employed on *Nove Ukrains'ke Slovo*, although this may simply have been an excuse to avoid hiring the nationalist writer (Liubchenko, *Shchodennyk*, pp. 26, 64).

[72]Among these were Voskobiinyk, Hrynenko (Zhitomir), and a number of editorial writers in Kharkov, as well as those mentioned earlier as founding newspapers, although their careers were generally limited to a few weeks.

X
Nationalism and the East Ukrainian Social Structure

The study of the role of Ukrainian nationalist groups in administration and educational life has shown that urban-centered activities played a preponderant role in the development of the nationalist movements in the East Ukraine under German occupation. The more highly developed urban educational systems were primary targets for nationalist organizers, while the cities served as centers from which the nationalists sought to secure popular support by controlling cultural activities and the press. This emphasis on urban activity has a long history in the development of nationalism in both the East and the West Ukraine. Since the rural districts in both areas were strongly Ukrainian in all linguistic and cultural attributes, many felt that it was not immediately necessary to cultivate nationalist sentiment there; they felt these attributes would maintain the national distinctiveness of the villagers. Whether this was a wise view can be more adequately discussed a little later.

During the Second World War, however, this tradition did result in the nationalist groups' devoting a great portion of their limited resources to the East Ukrainian cities, where it was necessary to start almost from the bottom in building national life. An impressive number of accounts by nationalist Ukrainians testify to the predominance of Russian speech and manners in the cities of the East Ukraine throughout the war period.[1] The explanation is, of

---

[1] In addition to numerous remarks of this nature already cited in relation to particular situations, see *Krakivs'ki Visti*, May 14, 1942, p. 3; November 27, 1942, p. 4; March 2, 1943, p. 2; T. Liakovych in *Krakivs'ki Visti*, May 17, 1942, p. 3; Iu. Tarkovych in *Krakivs'ki Visti*, July 12, 1942, p. 3. It may appear surprising that so many convinced adherents of the nationalist movement should have admitted and even stressed the non-Ukrainian cultural character of the cities, since usually nationalist movements endeavor to claim as large a proportion as possible of the inhabitants of a disputed area as members of their national group in origin and attitude. It must be remembered, however, that the OUN, and some other Ukrainian nationalist groups, were not democratic in ideology; hence the wishes of a majority at a particular time were of little importance in their eyes. Rather, this failure to possess the adherence of the inhabitants of an area which they regarded as theirs through the "rights" of history and blood served as an additional proof of the iniquities of the Soviet regime and of Russians in general and as a stimulus to more strenuous efforts to "correct" the situation.

course, that a vast number of city dwellers were Russified Ukrainians. Naturally enough, the nationalist leaders felt that no secure basis for their program could exist as long as the municipalities of the country were islands of foreign culture.

Within the urban group, nationalist efforts and nationalist sentiment were largely concentrated in one social stratum. Nationalist movements throughout the world have usually been the work of the middle class. Since there had been no East Ukrainian capitalist middle class of any significance before 1920, and since there was no possibility that one could arise under Soviet conditions, except for a few traders carrying on a precarious business under the NEP, a commercial class continued to be lacking. The counterpart to private commercial enterprise which existed under the Soviet regime, the state trading system, was apparently largely operated by Jews and other non-Ukrainian elements.[2] Unfavorable appraisals of the activity of this system, plus distasteful memories of the "profit-and-run" techniques of the nepmen had produced an unattractive image of the private businessman in the minds of most East Ukrainians.[3] Although, under German occupation, a few gestures were made by some city administrations toward encouraging individual enterprise, the chief factors in production and distribution, insofar as the appalling economic conditions made such activities possible at all, were public and cooperative enterprises. Hence the development of a middle class on the traditional Western model did not take place.

Actually, in the Ukraine, as in many other countries in which nationalist movements have developed, it was other components of the middle class which played the leading role. These were the intellectuals, the professionals, and the bureaucrats, together with the student body from which they were recruited. All four of these categories, together with a vast number of persons who would in Western usage be classified simply as clerks, technicians, or even custodial personnel, are lumped together in Soviet classifications as "intelligentsia" — i.e., all whose work does not involve a large measure of manual labor.[4] The leaders of the nationalist movements came from a narrower stratum however. The majority of this leadership consisted of intellectuals par excellence; that is, it was drawn from the academic or literary profession.

This crucial statement requires some proof, which is difficult to present in the absence of statistics or the possibility of sampling, both of which are unavailable for obvious reasons. However, the preponderance of intellectuals is indicated indirectly by figures previously cited on the extremely high proportion of persons with higher or secondary education employed in the Kiev city

---

[2]Some Ukrainians today (Interview 35) state that many wartime ascriptions of all the evils of the Soviet system to the Jews were highly exaggerated, in most cases a forced concession to Nazi racism, but insist that there was a good deal of anti-Semitism in the Ukraine because Jews predominated in retail distribution, and in the conditions of extreme shortage used their positions for selfish purposes. In view of the occupations of most Jews before the Revolution, their numerical predominance in the state distributive system is probably a fact, and it is fairly obvious that any recognizably alien group in such a position would be resented when they could not satisfy the consumers' wants, whether or not peculation played a role in their activities.

[3]Interview 65.

[4]For a discussion of the concept in Soviet usage, see Julian Towster, *Political Power in the USSR* (New York: Oxford University Press, 1948), p. 324 ff.

and *raion* administrations in 1942,[5] and by the statements from well-informed participants that these and other administrations, as well as editorial staffs, served as refuges for intellectuals displaced from their normal occupations.[6] Furthermore, the efforts of nationalist groups, whether OUN or local, were directed very largely toward assisting and encouraging the teachers and writers, a factor which suggests that they were closely tied to these segments of the population. For example, Mel'nyk organizers in Kiev in the winter of 1941-42 made special efforts to secure work in the cooperatives for teachers in order to enable them to avoid forced labor for the rebuilding of bridges.[7] Similarly, the strong East Ukrainian nationalist group in Kharkov took the unusual step of utilizing Prosvita as a relief organization for educators.[8] In addition, the very ability of nationalist elements to maintain themselves in the educational systems when other departments of administration had passed from their hands indicates that the staffs of these branches of administration were especially imbued with nationalism. The comparatively small number of cases and lack of availability of any sampling technique precludes generalization solely on the basis of cases known to the writer of this study. It may be noted, however, that of some sixty East Ukrainians prominent in the nationalist movement whose occupational background is known, about three-fifths were either instructors in higher schools, teachers, journalists, or writers. As examples, some of the most prominent may be mentioned. All three mayors of German-occupied Kiev were educators. The chief of the *oblast* administration in Dniepropetrovsk, organized with OUN-B help, was the dean of the electro-technical faculty of the university; later, a member of its medical faculty played the leading role in organizing a "national council" for the OUN-M.[9] The great majority of the Kharkov group, including all of the major organizers of Prosvita, as well as at least two of the OUN-M Ekzekutyva, were university professors; so were the editors of the nationalist-oriented papers in Stalino and Voroshilovgrad (Luhans'k).[10] Among the new Autocephalous bishops, the single East Ukrainian who did not have a clerical background, Professor Haievs'kyi, was also an educator. Writers, while much less prominent, were important. Arkadii Liubchenko, perhaps the best known of all who joined the OUN, has already been described. Most of the nationalist editors were drawn from trained writers, although as in the case of the poet Pronchenko in Krivoi Rog, they appear to have been more often men whose careers were in belles-lettres than professional reporters or editorial workers.

That such a high proportion of available leadership for the nationalist movement came from educators and writers is probably due in part to the leading role played by "national Communist" educational commissars like

---

[5]See Chapter IX.

[6]See Chapter V.

[7]Iurko Stepovyi, *Syn Zakarpattia: Ukraïns'ke revoliutsiine pidpilla v Kyïevi 1941-1942 r.* (A Son of Transcarpathia: The Ukrainian Revolutionary Underground in Kiev 1941-42) (Munich, 1947), p. 16. According to one account, the Red Cross in Kiev also aided the intelligentsia (along with prisoners of war) to a special degree (*Krakivs'ki Visti*, December 4, 1942, p. 2).

[8]*Nastup*, September 26, 1943, p. 3, referring to *Vinnyts'ki Visti*, August 29, 1943.

[9]Interviews 1, 48.

[10]Interview 66.

Shums'kyi and Skrypnyk more than a decade earlier in fostering national culture. Evidently even the repeated Communist purges could not wholly eradicate the permeation of the educational system by nationalist ideas. Indeed, Skrypnyk and other Communists of that period were praised openly by writers in the war years as defenders of the Ukrainian "national idea,"[11] and Skrypnyk's plan for an orthographical commission to set standards for Ukrainian publications was formally revived. It should be noticed, however, that direct links between nationalist leaders of the war period and the Skrypnyk group were very few. Moreover, the Russophile leaders were also predominantly intellectuals.[12] The general conclusion appears to be that the intellectuals (using the term in the Western sense) as a group were the most disaffected stratum in Soviet society capable of assuming a leadership role. Of great significance is the fact that a very high proportion of all those who were active in nationalist life under the German occupation had direct reasons for resentment against the Soviet regime, either because they had been barred from intellectual work or because they had been imprisoned for anti-Soviet activity. Also they had a wider historical perspective and hence were quicker to react to the new situation.

The second most important group was composed of engineers and other technical specialists like agronomy experts and chemists. Several of these were closely associated with academic life. Others seem to have been drawn from the operating staffs of Soviet industrial establishments, as in the great metallurgical center of Krivoi Rog, where a group of young men composed predominantly of engineers took over the rebuilding of city life soon after the Soviet troops withdrew.[13] One of their number became mayor, was active in nationalist work, probably in connection with the OUN-B, and as a result was executed by the Germans.[14] The most active local recruit of the OUN-M in Kiev, who led the organization after the West Ukrainian and émigré leaders had been forced to withdraw, was an engineer. On the whole, however, it may be said that engineers were more concerned with material reconstruction than politics, and did not play proportionately as significant a role as did engineers in the nationalist movements abroad and in Galicia.

The predominance of intellectuals and technical specialists in the nationalist movement imparted a certain specific color to the activities. In the first place, from the purely administrative point of view, the lack of trained men was a serious handicap. While the purely material aspects of city life were carried on about as well as might have been hoped in view of the destruction, shortages, and German obstruction, the conduct of public administration was

---

[11] Victor Prykhod'ko in *Krakivs'ki Visti*, January 18-19, 1942, p. 2.

[12] Although two of their most prominent leaders (Bohatyrchuk and the mayor of Vinnitsa) were physicians, they were also occupants of academic chairs.

[13] *Krakivs'ki Visti*, November 22, 1941, p. 3.

[14] Iuri Semenko, "Pam'iati Mykhaila Pronchenka" (Memories of Michael Pronchenko), *Novi Dni*, April, 1953, pp. 10-13; Ievhen (Eugene) Stakhiv ("E. Pavliuk"), "Borot'ba ukraïns'koho narodu na skhidno-ukraïns'kyhkh zemliakh, 1941-1944: spomyny ochevydtsia i uchasnyka" (The Struggle of the Ukrainian People in the Eastern Ukrainian Lands, 1941-44: Memories of an Eyewitness and Participant), in *Kalendar Provydinnia na 1947 rik. Stovaryshennia Ukraïns'kikh Katolykiv v Amerytsi* (Calendar for 1947 of the Providence Society of Ukrainian Catholics in America) (Philadelphia: Ameryka, n.d.), p. 39.

far from adequate. This was, indeed, one of the major causes of the downfall of the OUN-M regime in Kiev, whether the worst defects consisted of favoritism and speculation by officials, or simply poor organizational and human relations. Nationalist fervor, enthusiasm, facility in the use of literary Ukrainian, were no substitutes for managerial skills and personnel psychology. Yet it was precisely these abilities which intellectuals who were excluded from public life, as were Soviet Ukrainian educators suspected of adherence to the Skrypnyk group, could not acquire. At the same time, so much of their energy had been turned in upon their academic and cultural cultivation of things Ukrainian, such as language and history, that the intellectuals failed to place the emotional and abstract aspects of the nationalist cause in a balanced framework when the opportunity for action arose. It cannot be said that the intellectuals were less courageous than others might have been in striving for national ends in the face of German terrorism; many lost their lives, although, as has been pointed out in the case of some of the small-city editors, others were sometimes found to act as pliant tools for the occupiers. It does, however, appear that persons more inclined to take a functional instead of an emotional approach to administration might have been more successful in evading German demands.

Very striking is the almost total lack of legal expression among almost all participants in administrative work. Probably the basic reason for this omission was that lawyers were few and far between among non-Communist elements in the Ukraine. A confidential Wehrmacht report ascribes to this lack the difficulty experienced in getting the court system started,[15] and one Ukrainian account states that of 250 lawyers in the Kharkov *oblast* under Soviet rule only thirty-five were not Jews.[16] While an anti-Semitic bias in this statement may need to be discounted, it does appear likely that the vast majority of a professional group which was already very small (there are few Western cities where there is only one lawyer per 4,000 population!) was largely non-Ukrainian.

Of the few prominent legally trained Ukrainians, none had been able to practice his profession for many years. Alexander Semenenko, the mayor of Kharkov, had been educated as a lawyer under the tsarist regime and had practiced for a time in the early years of Communist rule. In the thirties, however, he was imprisoned for a number of years, and was a fugitive from the NKVD when the German army occupied the city.[17] Volodymyr Dolenko, who with Professor Dubrovs'kyi was the principal organizer of the strong nationalist group in Kharkov, had also been trained as a lawyer under the old regime, and he too had been prevented by the Communists from practicing.[18] Alexander Iatseniuk, head of the Zhitomir *oblast* administration, a judge under Nicholas II, had been relegated to the position of lecturer in a higher school by the Soviets.[19] His administration included a number of other jurists.

---

[15] PS 1693.

[16] *Krakivs'ki Visti*, March 1, 1942, p. 4.

[17] *Krakauer Zeitung*, May 14, 1944, p. 4.

[18] Interview 73.

[19] Iefremenko in *Krakivs'ki Visti*, November 1, 1941, p. 2; the reporter states that the directives of the city administration were "precise and factual," not full of "romantic phrases."

The want of training in the law was particularly striking in the Ukrainian nationalist movements. The failure to attempt to form a codified set of principles of either a legal or an administrative nature, the frequent arbitrary action in allotting positions on a basis of partisan enthusiasm rather than objectively determinable qualifications, the frequent tendency to accept an extreme nationalist position and then to push it even further, might all have been curbed by a stronger legal tradition. Perhaps by coincidence the administrations in Zhitomir and Kharkov were comparatively tolerant of minority groups, and awakened no such violent opposition from Russophile elements as in Kiev. Indeed, as has already been pointed out, the Zhitomir administration in 1941 included a Pole and a Russian in prominent posts, apparently working in harmony with other officials, while the nationalist group in Kharkov during the occupation attracted the lasting support of at least one academician of Russian origin. These groups were also able to avoid destruction by the Germans, in spite of considerable harassment, perhaps because their activities were not so violent as to arouse the public outcry which served as an excuse for the attack on the Kiev group.

The severe shortage of lawyers was paralleled by an even greater lack of administrators with experience in posts of great responsibility. This deficiency doubtless arose primarily from the fact that persons holding high administrative posts were almost universally strong adherents of the Communist regime. In a number of cases, leading Soviet officials such as chairmen of city soviets organized underground sabotage against German installations or led partisan groups for the Communist cause, and the large majority no doubt evacuated with the Red army. It would have been difficult in any case for such a highly placed member of the Soviet regime to join the nationalist cause, as he would probably have been executed in short order by the *Einsatzgruppen*, whose tasks included the killing of all "kommissars." Nevertheless, it is worth remarking that no Soviet military, party, or state official of any importance, as far as is known to the present writer, ever joined the Ukrainian nationalist cause, either through the local groups in the East Ukraine or through the prisoner-of-war camps, although several from these groups did join the Vlasov movement.

What the East Ukraine lacked in trained legal and administrative personnel, the West Ukrainian organizers failed to supply. Indeed, they appear not to have seen the need. They recognized the desirability of sending in journalists (the West Ukrainians were more effective as editors, although the extremely propagandistic nature of much of their work exacerbated the defects already existing in the intellectual nationalist tendencies in the east).[20] They also recognized the need for trained military officers to lead the police units, as well as for organizers of cooperatives, merchants, and other personnel to reorganize economic life.[21] Since the Galicians, unlike their East Ukrainian fellows, had been brought up under the influence of the Roman law tradition transmitted by the Austrian administration and the Catholic Church, one might have thought that they would provide a balancing element of legal thought. Actually, although there were numerous lawyers in the legal parties in Galicia,

---

[20]Iu. Tarkovych in *Krakivs'ki Visti*, November 6, 1941, p. 2.

[21]*Ibid.*

lawyers were even rarer among OUN leaders than among prominent East Ukrainians. Moreover, the whole current of revolutionary romanticism and the glorication of "illegalism" necessarily militated against the development of legalistic elements in the thinking of the nationalist factions. At the same time, of course, underground oppositional work had afforded the western group no experience in the responsibilities of public administration; the older émigrés who might have provided a modicum of such experience were kept out of the East Ukraine by the Germans. As the following statistics on the émigré group in Bohemia-Moravia indicate, however, the possible supply was not great, even if one accepts the figures which were obtained by listing, presumably at their own valuation, persons available to return to the East Ukraine in 1941.[22]

Workers of various skills	1,788
Students	560
Liberal professions (journalists, writers, merchants, artists, etc.)	313
Teachers	252
Engineers	343
Administrators	178
Jurists	11

Compared to the occupational differences in nationalist activity, differences of age and sex played a minor role. There is little information on the activity of women. Evidently they carried on most of the welfare work; one German report states that a major reason for permitting the functioning of the Ukrainian Red Cross was a desire to absorb the energies of the women intellectuals, who had been highly "politicized" by the Soviet regime.[23] There are a few cases of prominent nationalist work by women, for example, by the poet Olena Teliha who headed the OUN-M literary circle in Kiev until its suppression by the Germans. In general, nationalist observers agree that the women were less active politically than the men. While there is too little evidence to warrant a firm conclusion on this score, it is just possible that the nationalist

---

[22]From a registration by a Ukrainian community organization in Prague, September 28, 1941 (*Krakivs'ki Visti*, October 4, 1941, p. 3). For comparison, the occupations of the postwar emigration (largely West rather than East Ukrainian, in contrast to the interwar émigré group) may be given:

ÉMIGRÉS IN GERMANY

	U.S. Zone (total 85,646)	British Zone (total 44,987)
Peasants	30 percent	44 percent
Workers	16	21
Artisans	18	14
Intellectuals	23	8
Miscellaneous	13	13

(Michael Pap, *Die Probleme der ukrainischen Staatlichkeit und der Emigration*, Inaugural Dissertation zur Erlangung der Doktorwürde vorgelegt der Hohen Philosophischen Fakultät der Ruperts-Carola Universität zu Heidelberg, 1948 [Typescript available in the Library of Congress]).

[23]USSR Exhibit 278.

movements neglected a useful source of support, which was certainly tapped by the Communist underground.[24]

Youth, on the other hand, played a prominent part in nationalist work. While a large number of Mel'nyk supporters were drawn from the older generation, and the OUN-B made special efforts to capture the younger group, there was here no "conflict of generations" in respect to adherence to the two factions. Since only physically active persons were useful in the east, even the Mel'nyk organizers were predominantly youthful, and thus could approach their contemporaries more readily. The strength of the youth organizations dominated by the OUN-M in Kiev and Zhitomir has already been described. Other young men, of course, rejected both nationalist groups as too extreme, and formed centers of their own, while still others appear to have arisen in complete independence of outside stimulation. Thus the whole administration and cultural life of Pavlograd, a small town east of Dniepropetrovsk on the way to the Donbas, was organized by a group of graduates from the local *gimnaziia*.[25] They owed their nationalism, according to reports by visitors, entirely to the work of an inspiring teacher (who had in turn received his nationalist indoctrination in Kharkov University) who had taught there until caught by the NKVD some years previously.[26]

The division of nationalist youth among both factions of the OUN, and locally formed groups, parallels closely the division of their elders in the East Ukraine. In one respect, however, the younger generation was different; there was a considerable number of youths who had been active adherents of Communist organizations but who now joined the nationalist movements.[27] The most prominent ex-Komsomol was the son of Alexander Iatseniuk who, after an extremely active career in OUN-M organization in the Zhitomir area, fled to the Volhynian woods where as "Volynets'" he became an important nationalist partisan leader. On the other hand, large numbers of young people were daring enough to praise the Soviet openly, or took part in underground activity, while condemning the Ukrainian language and customs.[28]

On the whole, in their reaction to nationalist political activity, there does not seem to have been any marked difference between the younger and the older generations, at least not nearly so sharp a difference as in Galicia. It is fairly certain that a large percentage of the youth who joined nationalist activities were influenced by their parents. Others—sons of kulaks, priests, and intellectuals who had been persecuted by the Soviet regime—resented the Soviet order because of their parents' misfortune.

Apparently whatever advantage the nationalist movement may have enjoyed among the older generation because of the latter's memory of Petliura and the nationalist activity of the twenties was at least partly offset by the greater appeal of a romantic, activist movement like the OUN to youth, or by the latter's desire in other cases to rearrange life to suit themselves. There is a

---

[24]PS 3876.

[25]*Krakivs'ki Visti*, December 12, 1942, p. 3; *Nova Doba* (Berlin), July 5, 1942, p. 3; *Krakivs'ki Visti*, July 3, 1942, p. 2.

[26]*Krakivs'ki Visti*, July 3, 1942, p. 2.

[27]*Krakivs'ki Visti*, September 23, 1941, p. 2, based on an article from *L'vivs'ki Visti*.

[28]R. Sutor in *Krakivs'ki Visti*, August 12, 1942, p. 3.

faint suggestion that the Soviet regime may already have become the "old order" against which revolutionary youth is wont to rebel. On the other hand, these very qualities which made the nationalist *political* movement attractive to the younger generation had the effect of keeping it antagonistic to religion. As has already been pointed out, there is almost universal agreement that youth in the East Ukraine was cool, even hostile, to the churches.[29] In the south, the Protestants and dissident Orthodox groups seem to have been somewhat more successful, but they had no direct relation to the nationalist movement.[30]

The OUN-B, it will be recalled, placed special emphasis on securing the allegiance of youth, since its young agitators were unable to attract the support of the intelligentsia.[31] There is a small amount of evidence to indicate that the nationalist movements attracted a broader occupational group from the youth than from among its elders. So little is known concerning the role of the laboring classes, however, that no conclusions can be offered. Historically, the working class in the East Ukraine had been predominantly Russian or Russified. The working class was also generally more loyal to the Soviet system than most of the other social groups. Even if the Ukrainian claim that a large influx of dispossessed peasants and their children during the thirties had resulted in a Ukrainization of the urban laboring class be accepted, there is no evidence that such persons became interested in politics or had any important part in nationalist activity. Probably those who were mature when they left the village continued to be peasants in outlook, while a few rose into the intelligentsia, acquiring its coloration.

As frequently observed in this study, the disproportion of material available is no sure indication of a corresponding difference in the importance of factors involved. Since in many instances only fragmentary evidence is at hand, what is presented may be drawn too heavily from particular sources or may too greatly concern special aspects. In the case of urban-rural differences in nationalist activity, it is certain that such a bias exists in the character and extent of the evidence. For one thing, any single activity in a city of some size, such as the development of a Prosvita society, or the control of an administration, is sufficiently important to merit a place in contemporary reports, while a similar rural activity, conducted on a much smaller scale but equally important in its limited area, would probably pass unrecorded. Since the main channels of communication—newspapers and personal contacts of West Ukrainian and émigrés with local figures—were predominantly urban, they would naturally leave behind many more reports on city developments. Perhaps most important is the fact that the higher degree of articulateness of urban dwellers, in the Ukraine as elsewhere, tends to give them a disproportionate share in the written expression which later becomes the historical record.

In the cities, there was no positive goal to compete with the nationalist movements for the hopes and enthusiasms of the populace. The terrible deprivations, the German executions, the *Ostarbeiter* program, the fear of

---

[29]Cf. articles in *Krakivs'ki Visti*, October 12, 1941, p. 3; October 3, 1942, p. 2.

[30]*Krakivs'ki Visti*, October 3, 1942, p. 2; PS 1693.

[31]See the clandestine leaflet from the Odessa area previously referred to for sharp OUN-B criticism of the intelligentsia as tools of the Germans. Lev Shankovs'kyi, *Podhidni hrupy OUN* (March Groups of the OUN) (Munich: Vydavnytstvo "Ukraïns'kyi Samostiinyk," 1958), pp. 94-101, claims that the OUN-B was able to recruit a considerable number of working-class youths.

Communist agents, were factors which had a far greater significance for the average urban person than did the efforts of the nationalist movements; but a general effect was to promote passivity and resignation. On the land, however, a positive goal was before all eyes, which for a large segment of the peasantry far outweighted any prospect of national independence, however desirable that might be in itself.[32] This transcendent goal was the destruction of the collectivized system of agriculture and its replacement by a system in which individual initiative and the demands of the peasants would play a greater part. The nature of the agrarian question and the Germans' fumbling efforts to use the peasants' desire to gain support, while retaining the old restrictive kolkhoz system to make exploitation of the peasant easier, has already been described in general terms; it would exceed the scope of this study to treat the subject itself in greater detail. It is absolutely essential to stress the key nature of this problem, however, for it is almost beyond doubt that any movement which had offered a fully satisfactory solution to the agrarian problem would have won the adherence of the mass of the peasantry, regardless of its stand on the national question.

Superficially, the situation in the countryside was satisfactory from the nationalist standpoint. It is true that certain peasant traits of a distinctively national character had been subjected to erosion by the developments of the Soviet period. The handicrafts, including making of the national costume, had almost vanished under the joint impact of material shortages and growing availability of factory products.[33] The physical appearance of the villages had been altered too and much of their distinctiveness lost through the Soviet destruction of the cemeteries.[34]

In the more basic matter of language, the changes had not been so great, although in some areas at least many "town words" in the "all-Soviet" (i.e., Russian) tongue had been introduced.[35] From the point of view of developing replenishments for the intellectual elite from peasant stock, the situation was worse, however, for the Ukrainian tongue was frequently scorned as the speech of "Ivany i Maryny z kolhospu" — "Johns and Marys off the farm."[36] Even more significant, the mere fact that the peasants spoke Ukrainian, and even had a certain affection for the language as their mother tongue, did not necessarily prove that they possessed any consciousness of nationality. A Ukrainian visitor to one of the villages in the Taganrog district of the lower Don, just beyond the border of the Ukrainian SSR, reported that all the inhabitants spoke pure Ukrainian and retained Ukrainian customs. When addressed as Ukrainians, however, they denied the appellation, insisting that the "Ukrainians" lived over to the west, across the border. The nationalist reporter pointed out the identity of speech and manners with the population to the

---

[32]This is implied even by nationalist writers; for example, Iu. Tarkovych notes that the first question of peasants in the area between Kiev and Chernigov was, "When will the land be divided?" (*Krakivs'ki Visti*, January 18-19, 1942, p. 3).

[33]R. Sutor in *Krakivs'ki Visti*, June 26, 1942, p. 3.

[34]*Krakivs'ki Visti*, February 15, 1942, p. 4.

[35]R. Sutor in *Krakivs'ki Visti*, August 12, 1942, p. 3.

[36]Iu. Tarkovych in *Krakivs'ki Visti*, July 12, 1942, p. 3.

west, but they replied, "Yes, they are our brothers," yet persisted in denying that they were themselves Ukrainian.[37]

The means at hand to stimulate a sense of nationality among the peasants were rather meager. Most important, undoubtedly, was the church. Within a few months after the Communists were driven out, many hundreds of parishes had been reestablished.[38] Undoubtedly the older people who had received some religious training welcomed the reappearance of the clergy. Baptisms and marriages took place in large numbers, and the churches were well attended. Since the Germans forbade the use of public funds for payment of the salaries of the clergy, the latter had to depend on the generosity of their flocks or the produce of their own land. Apparently the parishioners responded by furnishing their pastors with sufficient income in kind.[39] In most areas, there developed a conflict between the Autocephalous and the Autonomous clergy. At first, the latter (or, in the "Left Bank" region, simply the clergy consecrated in the orthodox fasion who used the Slavonic liturgy) predominated in the villages, but as more Autocephalous priests were consecrated, and more of the older priests came to accept the Ukrainian language service, they evidently won the support of the peasantry. Strange as it may seem in view of reputed village conservatism, the living language was apparently more popular as a religious vehicle in the country than in the town,[40] and cases are recorded in which the peasants actually drove out the priest who persisted in the use of Slavonic.[41]

Religion as a stimulus to nationalist feeling was, however, subject to severe limitations. One was the inadequate background of the clergy. Many were simple peasants up to the time of their consecration, although an effort was made to train them in short courses. Where such a man was of sound character and good common sense, as was the case in one Podolian village, he could accomplish a good deal. There, according to the report, the priest, one of the local peasants until his recent consecration, was highly respected for his good example. His sermons stressed brotherly love, the importance of industriousness, mutual assistance, proper education of children, and self-control.[42] Generally, however, the clergy was unable to reach many of the Soviet-trained youth; in several villages the latter even objected to returning the church buildings to religious use, preferring that they should be used for Prosvita clubs.[43]

One of the chief agencies by which secular national concepts penetrated the village was indeed the Prosvita organization. How effective it was in general is impossible to say in the absence of more detailed evidence, but in

---

[37]*Krakivs'ki Visti*, January 22, 1942, p. 2.

[38]See Chapter XI.

[39]PS 1693.

[40]Report from a *gimnaziia* teacher in Poltava (*Krakivs'ki Visti*, April 12, 1942, p. 3); *Nastup*, April 26, 1942, p. 2; Iu. Tarkovych in *Krakivs'ki Visti*, June 25, 1942, p. 2.

[41]Iu. Tarkovych in *Krakivs'ki Visti*, June 25, 1942, p. 2. For a differing interpretation of the relative success of the Autocephalous group (in the Poltava area), see Friedrich Heyer, *Die Orthodoxe Kirche in der Ukraine von 1917 bis 1945* (Köln-Braunsfeld: Verlagsgesellschaft Rudolf Müller, 1953), p. 209.

[42]*Ukraïns'kyi Visnyk*, April 4, 1943, pp. 6-7.

[43]Iu. Tarkovych in *Krakivs'ki Visti*, January 18-19, 1942, p. 3.

some cases it evidently did at least provide reading material and some cultural contacts of a nationalist character. In this respect the rural teachers were especially important. There is considerable difference of opinion as to their effectiveness as propagators of nationalism, some observers feeling that they did an excellent job under difficult circumstances, others asserting that they lacked national consciousness and were imbued with Communist ideas.[44]

The great difficulty was in finding persons who were sufficiently educated and receptive to nationalist concepts to act as transmitters of propaganda. In the Podolian village referred to above, for example, the physician, who had been a UNR officer, played the chief role in stimulating nationalist feeling. He was greatly assisted in his task by his wife, the village *feldsher* (a sort of trained nurse or secondary category of medical worker); the priest described above; four teachers; and a lawyer. These constituted the "real intelligentsia" as compared with the "half-intelligentsia," consisting of the village elder, the village secretary, two cooperative workers, three kolkhoz directors, three agronomists, four bookkeepers, and three account-keepers, who were described as having "no unified outlook," being still "under the influence of Bolshevik ideology."[45] This criticism of the lower strata of clerical workers in the Soviet intelligentsia, which formed such a key segment of the rural population, is not uncommon in nationalist writers.[46] To a certain extent it may be due to resentment against the clerical workers' unresponsiveness to nationalist propaganda, or even to simple snobbery toward those aspiring to the title of "intelligentsia" without a formal education. In part it appears, however, to correspond to a real lack of breadth of mind among this lowest group of the Soviet intelligentsia, a deficiency which would have made it difficult to use them for any political or social movement not tied immediately to their customary frame of thinking.

On the other hand, there were often elements in the villages which were available for some sort of political activity. The memory of Petliura was still present; some refused to believe that he was dead, thinking the story to be Communist propaganda.[47] In another area, both the president of the village soviet and the head of one of the collective farms remained behind and organized life in cooperation with nationalist elements.[48] Yet, in another case, a man of some education in one of the villages, who was related to an émigré minister of the UNR, after expressing fervently nationalist sentiments, recoiled with horror at the idea that his auditor might recommend him to the Germans for an official post, fearing the vengeance of Communist agents.[49] The presence of the latter was, indeed, a great handicap to nationalist organization in the rural areas, where the protection of the police force was not so great (especially in partisan-infested areas) as in the towns, and where the naturally

---

[44]Cf. *Ukraïns'kyi Visnyk*, April 4, 1943, pp. 6-7; *Krakivs'ki Visti*, November 18, 1941, for favorable reports; and Zynovii Matla, *Pivdenna pokhidna hrupa* (The Southern Task Force) (Munich: Tsitsero, 1952), pp. 28-29, for some criticisms of the rural teachers.

[45]*Ukraïns'kyi Visnyk*, April 4, 1943, pp. 6-7.

[46]*Krakivs'ki Visti*, September 23, 1941, p. 2, reprinting an article from *L'vivs'ki Visti*.

[47]R. Sutor in *Krakivs'ki Visti*, June 13, 1942, p. 4.

[48]R. Sutor in *Krakivs'ki Visti*, July 31, 1942, p. 3.

[49]R. Sutor in *Krakivs'ki Visti*, June 13, 1942, p. 4.

cautious peasant hesitated to commit himself until assured the Soviet administration would never return.[50]

Since the organized nationalist forces were so few in members, they could not undertake any direct or continuous indoctrination of the rural population, unless they abandoned their efforts to win the cities. They had to rely primarily on the Prosvita branches, the country schools, and the village administrations. Printed material was also used whenever it could be controlled by nationalist Ukrainians. As a matter of fact, a large proportion of the newspapers in the smaller towns were directed principally at rural readers; the extreme shortage of papers[51] in many areas prevented their being of great influence even when they had some nationalist content. Moreover, the central periodical for farmers, *Ukraïns'kyi Khliborob*, with a weekly printing of 70,000, was edited by Eugene Arkypenko, who later joined the Vlasov movement.[52] While this publication was not used against the nationalist cause, it was devoid of positive nationalist material, being confined entirely to technical agricultural articles.

The less-than-lukewarm supporters of the nationalist movements who constituted the bulk of the personnel in positions which provided access to the rural population apparently did not do a great deal to convert the dormant cultural nationality of the peasants into active nationalism. There is no question that the cities inevitably constituted a prime target for nationalist efforts. Probably, in view of the severe limitations imposed by lack of time and nationalist personnel, by Red partisans and German restrictions, the enormous task of overcoming village inertia toward a purely political movement could not have been carried out in any case. Nevertheless, the initial failure of the nationalist groups (at least the OUN and others coming from the west) to grasp the overriding importance of the land question, and the necessity of making this a prime means by which the rural population could be won to the nationalist cause, must certainly be ranked as one of the great lost opportunities of this period. If the nationalists had from the beginning used all their energies to present a positive program of agrarian reform as the heart of their message, they might not have left any tangible organization to withstand renewed Soviet occupation, but they might have left behind a concept of the Ukrainian nationalist movement as a defender of the interests of the peasantry. This, along with the vaguer memories of the Republican era, might have left an enduring imprint on the peasantry.

---

[50]R. Sutor in *Krakivs'ki Visti*, July 31, 1942, p. 3.

[51]D. Myronovych in *Krakivs'ki Visti*, July 9, 1942, p. 4.

[52]*Volyn'*, June 17, 1942, p. 4; Interview 45.

XI
Geographical Variations of Nationalism

In comparison with the contrasts in nationalist feeling and nationalist activity disclosed by an examination of city and countryside in the occupied East Ukraine, variations by geographical areas are minor. Nevertheless, even when not highly pronounced, these variations help to identify some of the features of Ukrainian nationalism in the recent past which illuminate its role in the complex history of the country. Since, to a certain degree, class structure varies from district to district, examination of differences in nationalist feeling in relation to these variations is useful. By indicating the complexity of the factors involved in nationalism, it helps avoid leaving an impression of the East Ukraine as a uniform entity.

The northernmost region, Polessia, is the forest belt described in connection with the discussion of partisan warfare. In the section east of the Dnieper nationalist activity was scanty, for the rapid growth of the Red partisans made the rural areas which comprise the great bulk of the region unsafe for anti-Soviet elements. That there was some nationalist penetration, apparently by Mel'nyk supporters working in close collaboration with the Germans, is attested both by Soviet sources, which denounce "West Ukrainian nationalists" in the rural administration, and by OUN-M sources, which claim contacts with the editors in Konotop and Chernigov, the largest cities of the area.[1]

West of the Dnieper, nationalism was somewhat more evident. The short-lived "Olevsk Republic" established in 1941 by Borovets' introduced a local administration composed for the most part of West Volhynian nationalists.[2] The Bazar section farther east was temporarily controlled by Mel'nyk sympathizers, as was previously described.[3] Under the conditions of German repression the nationalist parties could not afford to devote their limited strength to maintaining the initial advantage gained in these comparatively unimportant areas. By 1943, under the impact of rapidly growing Soviet partisan operations, nationalist activity seems to have ceased in Polessia west of the Dnieper.

---

[1] Interview 50.
[2] Interview 54; see Chapter IV.
[3] See Chapter V.

South of Polessia runs a broad band of territory which falls into the natural vegetation region of the wooded steppe, i.e., a region of mixed prairie and woods. In contrast to the rather poor gray soil of most of Polessia, it is a land well suited for intensive agriculture, and as a result has supported for centuries the densest agricultural population of the East Ukraine.

As in the case of Polessia, the principal dividing line within the wooded steppe region is the Dnieper River. The area west of the river forms the heart of what have been known in Ukrainian history as the "Right Bank" lands. Kiev and the surrounding district had been acquired by the Russian tsar in the eighteenth century, but most of the area west of the Dnieper remained under Polish rule until 1792. The section closest to the river had had a considerable share in the Cossack tradition, but the more westerly sections, which were included in the historic provinces of Volhynia and Podolia, were deeply affected by the independent Cossack movement only during the height of Bohdan Khmel'nyts'kyi's career. This meant that serfdom had a longer and more oppressive history there than in the regions to the south and the east. While the peasants were thoroughly Ukrainian in language and customs, the cities included many Poles and Russians and an especially high percentage of Jews, who comprised from one-third to one-half of the urban population. This concentration of Jews, too, was a result of the historical background of the region; Poland had tolerated them, while the tsars had forbidden them to leave the Pale formed by the lands acquired in 1793 and later.[4]

Since the "Right Bank" was immediately contiguous to the nationalist bases in the West Ukraine, it was natural that the nationalists made a strong effort to extend their influence to the region. A large part of these efforts were concentrated on Kiev and Zhitomir. In Vinnitsa, the largest city of Podolia, on the other hand, the situation developed unfavorably for the nationalists soon after the German arrival. When the Germans captured the city, they were impressed by the activity of the director of the medical institute and his ability to speak German, learned while a student in Germany. Consequently, they appointed him mayor. Of mixed Russian and Ukrainian descent, the new mayor considered himself Ukrainian, but favored the continuance of ties with Russia. His administration contained other pro-Russian elements, while the Vinnitsa *oblast* administration was headed by an ethnic German said to have had Russophile tendencies. The police, on the other hand, and the newspaper were controlled by OUN-M adherents, although both were men of exceeding caution.[5] Vinnitsa played only an indirect role in stimulating Ukrainian nationalism; the unearthing in June, 1943, of enormous mass graves of victims of NKVD executions in 1937-38 and during the retreat of 1941, including, it is said, a number imprisoned for nationalist activities, served to increase the dread felt of the rapidly materializing prospect of Soviet reconquest.

If Vinnitsa was the chief anti-nationalist stronghold, Proskurov, a smaller city to the northwest, was the headquarters for the OUN-M in Podolia. There the Mel'nyk group counted the mayor and the police chief (a Carpatho-Ukrainian trained in the Czechoslovak army) among its members.[6] It also

---

[4]Actually, the Pale included all the Ukraine in the nineteenth century, but Jews were less numerous on the "Left Bank."

[5]Interview 1.

[6]Interviews 1, 50.

controlled the newspaper, *Ukraïns'kyi Holos*, which had a circulation of 13,000, said to have been more than double that of the Soviet paper which had been published in Proskurov.[7] Farther east, the districts west and southwest of Kiev were under strong nationalist influence. While the OUN-M was establishing its headquarters in Kiev, newspapers and local administrations were being formed in a number of small cities such as Vasilkov, Belaia Tserkov', Tarashcha, Korsun', Smela (Smila), Cherkasy, and Uman'. The formation of the National Rada by the Mel'nyk group made a great impression on the intellectuals of the smaller towns. OUN-M writers and propagandists appear to have maintained regular contact with them for several months in 1941, and it is apparent that the Kiev *Ukraïns'ke Slovo* served as a model for many of the new editors.[8] Schools were opened under the direction of nationalist educators, Prosvita and theatrical groups were formed, cooperatives linked with *Vukospilka* were active. Apparently, too, the town administrations were largely in Ukrainian hands; the municipal authorities in Uman' issued a sweeping order forbidding the use of the Russian language in any office, school, or enterprise under their jurisdiction.[9]

The influence of the nationalists in the towns penetrated to some degree to the countryside in the area west of the Dnieper. For example, nationalist papers like *Nova Doba*, published in Berdichev, seem to have had a moderately large circulation in the villages. There also seem to have been nationalist influences of a purely local character in some places, aside from those brought in by the nationalist parties. Zvenigorodka, a small town about a hundred miles due south of Kiev had been the home of the Free Cossacks, a nationalist organization of the wealthier peasants during the revolutionary period. The group was revived by some of the villagers under the German occupation, and, together with a mimeographed newspaper, served as a focal point for local nationalism.[10]

The influence of the church, especially in the rural areas, was not entirely on the side of Ukrainian nationalism. The Autonomous clergy under Alexius made an early start in reorganizing religious life in this region. They established a diocese of Vinnitsa and Zhitomir, and during most of the period of occupation were supported by the influential Bishop Damaskin (Maliuti) of Kamenets-Podolsk. Damaskin's diocese included nearly five hundred churches, with a 160 priests.[11] Apparently most of this large organization, which was overwhelmingly concentrated in the rural districts, had no objection to Damaskin's allegiance to the Russophile church. The Autocephalous Church established its own organization, installing a bishop in Zhitomir, as well as the energetic Ihor in Belaia Tserkov'. Ihor was replaced for a time by Emmanuel, but when the latter passed over to the Autonomous Church, he took a new post in western Volhynia, perhaps because he found the rather strong nationalist atmosphere in Belaia Tserkov' unpleasant. The fact that the Autonomous Church was able to maintain such a strong organization indicates that

---

[7]*Nastup*, December 25, 1941, p. 4, citing *Ukraïns'kyi Holos*.

[8]Interview 30.

[9]*Nastup*, May 3, 1942, p. 2.

[10]R. Sutor in *Krakivs'ki Visti*, July 31, 1942, p. 3.

[11]*Krakivs'ki Visti*, October 13, 1942, p. 2.

sentiment in the rural areas was not always ardently nationalist, even in the most "pure" of Ukrainian lands.

The wooded steppe region east of the Dnieper, the "Left Bank," constituted the second half of the traditional Ukrainian heartland. The western part had been for centuries under Polish and Lithuanian rule, coming under Moscow in the late seventeenth century, together with Kiev. The eastern part, roughly equivalent to the Kharkov *oblast*, had never been under Polish rule, but had owed allegiance to the tsars. It served as a refuge for serfs escaping from their Polono-Lithuanian masters, and hence was known as the "Slobozhanshchyna" or "Free Land." Since even the western part of the "Left Bank" had been annexed by the Russian Empire long before the partitions of Poland, however, its history diverged considerably from that of the "Right Bank."

The most interesting nationalist developments in this region during 1941-43 took place in Kharkov. While Kharkov was always claimed as the second city of the Ukraine, it never occupied the place in nationalist thinking which Kiev held, and the fact that the Russian ethnic and linguistic element there was strong aroused less indignation. Some account of the differences in the nationalist movements in Kiev and Kharkov has already been given. The essential divergence arose from the fact that the OUN-M organizers reached the latter city only in November, when their period of grace was already running out. Enthusiasm was great enough for them to secure powerful support from local people. A strong *ekzekutyva* was formed with a mayor of one of the city *raions*, an ardently nationalist professor, George Boiko, and several other local people, in addition to Kononenko, the chief West Ukrainian organizer, as members.[12] The adherence of Arkadii Liubchenko (really a citizen of Kiev, but known throughout the Ukraine) to the OUN-M added considerable prestige. The *raion* mayor, Semenenko, who was later to become city mayor, was also sympathetic to the Mel'nyk group, as were a number of journalists, including the brother of the editor of *Nova Ukraïna*, the daily newspaper.[13] At the same time, or even before the Mel'nyk group's arrival, however, a local organization, comprised primarily of old adherents of the Republic who had managed to survive the Soviet regime, was formed under the leadership of V. V. Dubrovs'kyi and Volodymyr Dolenko.[14] The background of these men and their group and the instrumentalities through which they exerted influence have been described. It should be stressed here that the group was formed independently; although there were certain sympathies for the old UNR, there were no contacts with Andrew Livyts'kyi's émigré regime.[15] While the movement was never able to attain power at all comparable with that exercised by the Mel'nyk group in Kiev during its period of predominance, it was able to exert steady influence of a moderate nature.

---

[12]*OUN u Viini* (The OUN in the War), Information Section of the OUN (UNR), April, 1946, p. 75; Interview 57.

[13]Interviews 47, 73.

[14]*Entsyklopediia Ukraïnoznavstva* (Encyclopedia of Things Ukrainian), eds. Volodymyr Kubiiovych and Zenon Kuzelia (Munich: Naukove Tovarystvo im. Shevchenka, 1949), p. 584.

[15]Interview 73. Chief of the SP and of the SD, Report of *Einsatzgruppen* and *Kommandos*, April 10, 1942, No. 191, p. 33 (T 175, Reel 235) alleged that Kharkov opposition was mainly from Russian nationalists.

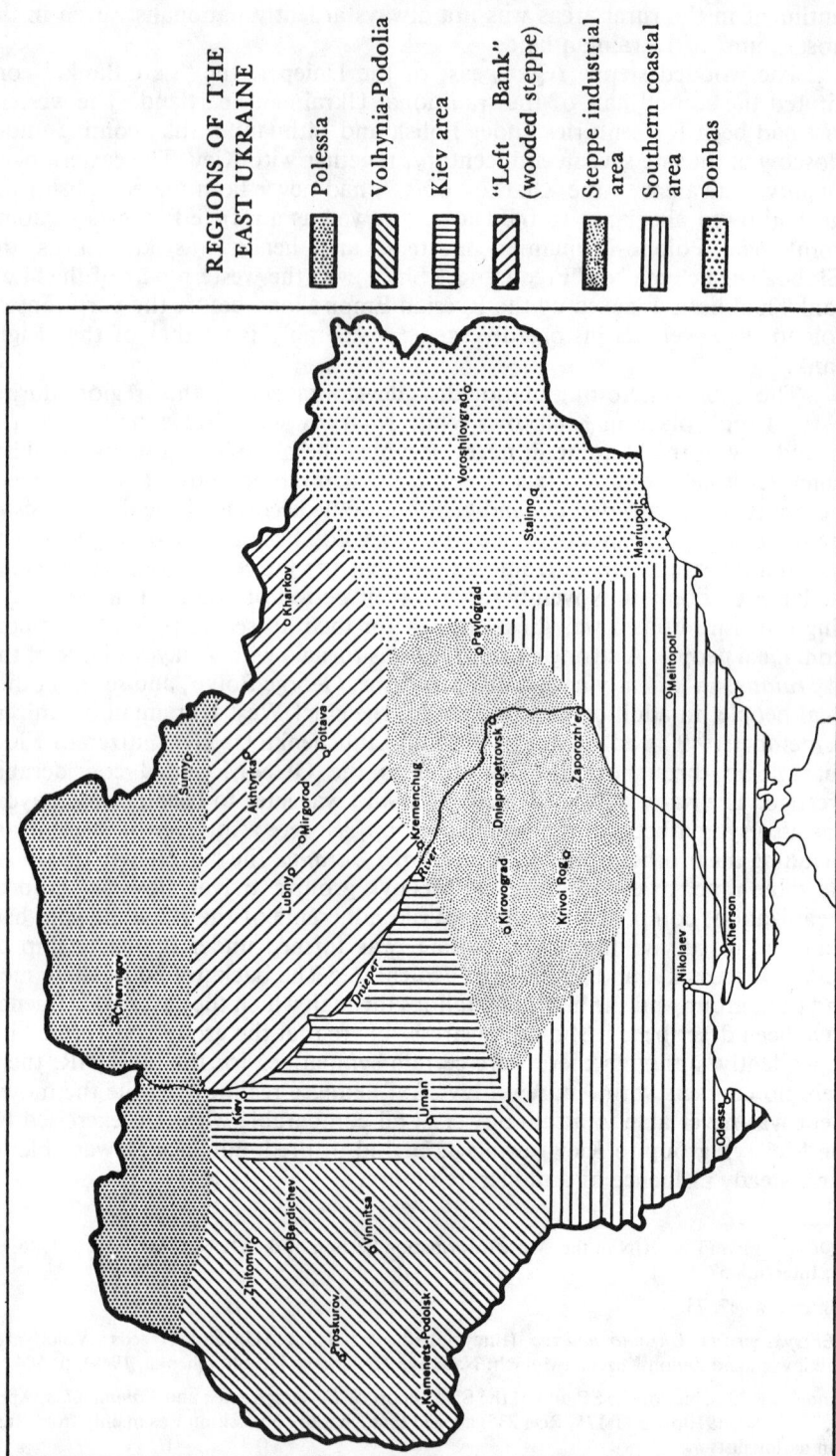

Affected perhaps by the fact that Kharkov was less Ukrainian than Kiev, as well as by the different background and tactics of the nationalist movements there (its late start and quick loss of prestige after the Kiev debacle forced the Mel'nyk group also to use restrained tactics, although some of its adherents were every bit as extreme as those in Kiev), a quite different situation developed in the eastern center. There was no sudden reversal of fortune; no prominent Ukrainian aligned himself then or later with Russophile movements. Perhaps, too, the famine, which was probably worse there than in any other Ukrainian city in the winter of 1941-42, and the comparatively tolerant regime of the army combined to conciliate the ethnic groups or at least to divert their energies from open conflict.

The nature of the nationalist movement in Kharkov was important, not so much because the city was representative of the surrounding areas, as because it exerted influence upon them. The chief channels by which it did so were the Prosvita organizations, the newspaper, and the church. A leader of the independent nationalist group estimates that its influence, exercised primarily through the Prosvita, reached as far west as Lubny and Poltava,[16] and there is evidence that it also played a part in organization as far south as the northern Donbas.[17] *Nova Ukraïna* was also widely known, serving as a model for nationalist editors in the "Left Bank" region who wanted to pursue as independent a line as possible and hence rejected the guidance of *Nove Ukraïns'ke Slovo*.

The special role played by the church of Kharkov merits more than passing mention. When the Germans arrived, they found that an elderly prelate, Archbishop Theophilus, had survived the Soviet period. Seventy-six years old, a native of a village of the Khoral (Khorol) region in the heart of the "Left Bank" Ukraine, he had become a priest in 1885.[18] With the aid of local clergymen, he reassumed control of ecclesiastical life in Kharkov in late 1941 and claimed to be in charge of the entire "Left Bank" as Metropolitan of the Ukraine.[19] Many—especially in the Autocephalous Church—criticized him because he was consecrated bishop in the Russian Orthodox Church (in 1923) and because he continued to use Old Slavonic in the liturgy.[20] Others, however, saw him as a Ukrainian patriot, since he was Ukrainian by birth, spoke pure Ukrainian, celebrated a service in commemoration of Kruty, and praised the Ukrainian newspaper.[21] At any rate the dissidents were able to make little

---

[16] *Ibid.*

[17] Interview 68.

[18] *Krakivs'ki Visti*, May 15, 1943, p. 3. Sergei T. Danilenko, *Dorohoiu Han'by i Zrady* (On the Road of Shame and Treachery) (Kiev: "Naukovo Dumka," 1970), pp. 270-73, alleges a discussion between Theophilus and Soviet officers on February 16, 1943, in temporarily reoccupied Kharkov, in which the archbishop reported severe pressures to join the UAP as well as incentives from the pro-German Slovak government to convert to Catholicism.

[19] *Krakivs'ki Visti*, March 5, 1943, p. 2; March 6, 1942, p. 3.

[20] Interview 69. *Ukraïns'ka Diisnist'*, February 10, 1942, p. 4, presents a letter to Archbishop Hilarion from a former pupil in the Kharkov area which, by asking advice on church reorganization, suggests dissatisfaction with Theophilus. The OUN-B underground (*Visnyk*, No. 11 [1943], p. 13) denounced him as an "old regimist" and an "indivisibilist" (i.e., a proponent of "indivisible" Russia).

[21] *Krakivs'ki Visti*, May 5, 1942, p. 4; January 24, 1943, p. 2; May 15, 1943, p. 3.

progress against him; only two Lypkivite priests had survived, while Theophilus's clergy numbered more than one hundred.[22] However, the latter appear to have been subjected to very loose control by the archbishop and to have employed Ukrainian or Slavonic in the services according to their own inclination. Consequently, the divergences of the clergy can be used as a gauge of popular feeling on the "Left" as well as the "Right Bank," but the actual conflicts were muted, as were the strictly political rivalries, by the presence of a respected, moderate central authority.

It is true, however, that conflict was sharper in the area west of Kharkov than in its immediate vicinity. Poltava, the second city of the region under consideration, was one of the most purely Ukrainian of cities of considerable size. Too far east to have been the center for a large Jewish population, the removal of this group and the drastic reduction of the Russian element made it more than 90 percent Ukrainian, according to the city census. The nationalist groups were quick to organize there; largely with the help of OUN-M workers, the paper came under their control in November, 1941, and an East Ukrainian member of the Mel'nyk group, a former officer of the Republic army, became mayor.[23] Cultural life was rapidly renewed, two Ukrainian theaters being opened.[24] On the other hand, church organization was disrupted by quarrels between the priests preferring to introduce Ukrainian into the services and those wishing to retain Slavonic; the latter predominated in the city.[25] The former group, however, with sixty parishes in the countryside, joined the Autocephalous Church, and Ihor of Belaia Tserkov' was appointed their bishop.[26] Theophilus continued, however, to claim their alligiance.

Sometime in 1942, the Ukrainian editorial staff and the mayor were shot by German police; the city passed under the control of a Russian mayor, while the new Ukrainian editor could not assert himself against the tight German control.[27] Even earlier, several other nationalist editors in the area had been shot for evading German restrictions.[28] Some of the newspapers came under the control of nonentities who were fully subservient to the German authorities; in a few other places, including the important towns of Lubny and Akhtyrka (Okhtyrka), editors continued their endeavors to stimulate national feeling.[29] Remarkably, the editor in the former town was a Russian who, after his pro-Ukrainian work brought him to the verge of arrest, was able to secure a new post as editor of a Russian-language paper in the Kursk *oblast*.[30] Most

---

[22]*Ukraïns'ka Diisnist'*, February 10, 1942, p. 4; *Krakivs'ki Visti*, March 5, 1943, p. 2. Eventually Theophilus adhered to the UAPTs. Friedrich Heyer, *Die Orthodoxe Kirche in der Ukraine von 1917 bis 1945*. (Köln-Braunsfeld: Verlagsgesellschaft Rudolf Müller, 1953), p. 178.

[23]*OUN u Viini*, p. 76; Interview 42.

[24]D. Myronovych in *Krakivs'ki Visti*, July 9, 1942, p. 4.

[25]*Nastup*, April 26, 1942, p. 2; *Krakivs'ki Visti*, April 12, 1942, p. 3.

[26]*Lvivs'ki Visti*, September 6-7, 1942, p. 2. Possibly he never resided in Poltava, for he is later reported as bishop of Belaia Tserkov' again, and ultimately as bishop of Uman'. Chief of the *Einsatzgruppen* of the SP and the SD, IIIc, September 20, 1944 (T 175, Reel 640).

[27]Interviews 1, 42; *OUN u Viini*, p. 76.

[28]Interview 47.

[29]Interviews 47, 50.

[30]Interview 47.

active of all this group, however, was the young editor of the Mirgorod paper, Michael Voskobiinyk, who pursued a line independent of the Nationalists yet modeled on the work of the *Nova Ukraïna* group.[31]

In general, nationalism in the "Left Bank" region under German occupation can be said to have been characterized by more influence of locally led and organized ecclesiastical and political bodies than the area to the west of the Dnieper. Moreover, it was marked by somewhat less friction between the Ukrainian and Russian elements and a willingness of some of the latter group to cooperate with the effort for Ukrainian nationalist revival. Probably the basic reason for this difference is the fact that both OUN groups were suppressed in this area before they could become very influential, and the nationalist structure which was built up afterwards was formed of persons who feared the extremist program of the integral nationalists. It may be also that the history of the region, with its lack of comparatively recent memories of oppression by Polish lords and the relative independence with which nationalist life could develop, created an atmosphere of self-confidence which militated against the more violent aspects of nationalist egoism.

To the south of the wooded steppe belt just discussed lies a broad region of more open steppe; in general the agricultural population of the area is considerably less dense than that of the region just described. The open plain with its very rich black soil and somewhat lesser rainfall lends itself to the cultivation of cereal crops which require smaller amounts of manpower, in contrast to the mixed sugar beet, dairy, potato, and grain agriculture of the more northern region. The reasons for the smaller farm population are historical rather than purely economic, however. Most of the area was fully settled many generations later than the more northern regions, for it was the principal area of conflict of the Slavic settlers moving down from the north and the Tatar warriors based on the Crimea. The major instrument of colonization was the Cossack fortress settlement or *sich*. In the mid-seventeenth century the Cossacks accepted the suzerainty of the Orthodox tsar, but it was only in the late eighteenth century, after the Russian conquest of the Crimean Tatars, that the steppe was fully opened to peaceful development. These new lands, frequently called "Southern Russia," came to include considerable bodies of non-Ukrainian settlers, mostly Russians, but also large numbers of Germans and Serbs. In 1917 the Provisional Government in Petrograd strongly rejected demands of the Ukrainian Rada for the extension of its authority to the *guberniias* of Kharkov, Ekaterinoslav, Kherson, and Taurida, the last three corresponding roughly to the southern steppe region, since it felt they were not Ukrainian in character.[32]

The northern section of the steppe region, comprising the northern halves of the *Generalbezirke* Nikolaev and Dniepropetrovsk, did contain a preponderantly Ukrainian peasantry. The presence of two very important natural resources—the iron mines of Krivoi Rog and the water power of the Dnieper rapids—had led to rapid industrialization of this area during the period of the

---

[31] *Ibid.*

[32] John S. Reshetar, *The Ukrainian Revolution, 1917-1920: A Study in Nationalism* (Princeton: Princeton University Press, 1952), pp. 72-73.

Soviet Five Year Plans, with a consequent large increase in the urban population. According to the census of 1939 five of the fifteen Ukrainian cities of over 100,000 population lay in this region.[33] At the start of the period of industrialization, in 1926, the city population was very largely non-Ukrainian. For example, Ukrainians formed less than half the total in Kirovograd (then Zinovevsk), Jews being the next largest ethnic group, closely followed by Russians.[34] In Dniepropetrovsk and Zaporozh'e the proportion of Jews was somewhat lower, but the Ukrainians were even fewer, being scarcely more than one-third of the population.[35]

The figures for Kirovograd in 1942 are hardly enough upon which to base generalizations.[36] Apparently, however, a great shift to Ukrainian national affiliation, much larger than that which took place in the average northern city, had occurred. As in the case of the other figures, it is not certain that this represents a real change, although it is probable that a large part of the interwar growth was composed of Ukrainian peasants. A number of circumstances suggest, however, that part of the difference arose from a real shift in allegiance of numerous elements of Russian origin, i.e., a shift induced not so much by expectation that persons classing themselves as Ukrainians would have a favored position in a new Ukrainian state, as by a sincere feeling of belonging to a "Ukraine" defined on a geographic rather than an ethnic basis. The readiness of technical specialists, who took the lead in Krivoi Rog, to adopt with enthusiasm Ukrainian symbols, while devoting their major attention to economic reconstruction, suggests that this acceptance of a territorial basis of national identity may have played a role, while the support of Russian cultural and political tendencies by a similar group in Dniepropetrovsk indicates the instability of this choice. Apparently the situation was something like this: as long as the Ukrainian state which the Germans seemed to favor appeared to be an instrument for the overthrow of Communism and the rebuilding of new life, it was readily acceptable; when it became a romantic creed of ethnocentrism it was repugnant as an obstacle to the satisfaction of down-to-earth needs and the development of smooth human relations.

---

[33]Frank Lorimer, *The Population of the Soviet Union: History and Prospects* (Geneva: League of Nations, 1946), pp. 250-53.

[34]Union of Soviet Socialist Republics, Tsentralnoe Statisticheskoe Upravlenie, *Recensement de la Population de l'URSS*, XIII (Moscow, 1929), 13-14.

[35]*Ibid.*

[36]See Appendix. The necessity for caution in interpreting the extremely great shift in Kirovograd is indicated by the fact that the only other large city in the area for which data are available, Dniepropetrovsk, showed a comparatively small shift. It will be recalled, however, that the latter city was under a Russophile administration. Unfortunately, there is no information available concerning the tendencies of the city administration in Kirovograd for the time the census was taken. It is mathematically demonstrable, however, that the decline of the Russian group can be accounted for in Kirovograd only on the basis of a shift of persons formerly classed as Russians to the Ukrainian group, unless one of two rather unlikely assumptions is made, namely that (1) the Russian population actually declined between 1926 and 1941, or (2) numerous Jews later massacred listed themselves as Russians in 1926. Some information on conditions in Kirovograd is presented by Stepan Hlid, an OUN-B underground worker, in *Fragmenty zhyttia i muk* (*Spohadi z chasiv nimets'koi okupatsii Ukrainy*) (Fragments from Life and Struggle [Remembrances of the Period of German Occupation of the Ukraine]) (London: Vydavnytstvo Soiuza Ukraïntsev v Velykii Britanii, 1955).

There were, however, many variations on this theme. Both the initial stimulation and the ensuing withdrawal from nationalist ideology on the part of many persons in the area was due, according to numerous and consistent reports of eyewitnesses, to the activities of Bandera organizers. The great predominance of Mel'nyk adherents in the northern Ukraine was matched by the ascendancy of the younger faction in the south. In part this circumstance was accidental. Both OUN parties had planned to send organizing groups into all areas of the Ukraine. The Mel'nyk group destined for the south, however, was evidently weakened intentionally to permit a concentration on the northern area, where historical tradition and experience in the revolutionary period led the older men to expect greater success.[37] For the most part, the Bandera groups in the north were wiped out by the SP, while their emissaries in the south got off to an early start and were well entrenched by the time the slower acting Mel'nyk group arrived there.[38] Although a certain amount of rivalry persisted in the largest city in each of the two main areas—Kiev and Dniepropetrovsk—after the Mel'nyk group was also proscribed by the Germans, there was for the most part a tacit acceptance of the territorial division of activity which had developed in the early months.[39]

This circumstance renders the investigation of the southern region more difficult. While the Bandera followers have been active since the war in describing their exploits, the fact that at no time, even in the early months, could they engage in large-scale open activities makes it difficult to check their accounts with contemporary journalistic reports. For example, German police reports state that in early October, 1941, a group of fifteen West Ukrainians, all or most of whom were Bandera adherents, tried to secure control of the administration and newspaper in Zaporozh'e.[40] Apparently these men were executed by the Germans; no further reports on nationalist activity in Zaporozh'e are available. This obscurity surrounding OUN-B activities makes itself felt especially in any effort to trace the relationships between OUN-B organizers and locally active groups. In Krivoi Rog, the mayor, Sherstiuk, the editors, Pronchenko and Potapenko, and a number of other local figures were strongly nationalist in sentiment, but whether they were ever adherents of the Bandera movement, or were brought into its organization, is a matter of dispute between the survivors of the Krivoi Rog group and OUN-B members

---

[37]Interview 61.

[38]The headquarters of the Bandera group remained in Kiev, where Myron, the director of its work in the entire East Ukraine, resided until he was killed (evidently by a German police agent) in 1942; after that OUN-B headquarters was in Dniepropetrovsk. Cf. Chief of the SP and of the SD, Reports from the Occupied Eastern Territories, No. 18, August 28, 1942 (T 175, Reel 235) (*Litopys*, Vol. VI, pp. 63-65).

[39]Interview 1.

[40]Chief of the SP and the SD, Report of *Einsatzgruppen* and *Kommandos*, No. 143, December 8, 1941, p. 5, NO 2827 (hereafter referred to as NO 2827). Lev Shankovs'kyi, *Pohidni hrupy OUN* (March Groups of the OUN) (Munich: Vydavnytstvo "Ukraïns'kyi Samostiinyk," 1958), pp. 162-63, gives details on later OUN-B activities in the Zaporozh'e area.

familiar with the area.⁴¹ What appears most likely is that an initial "honeymoon" of cooperation was succeeded by strife arising from the uncompromising demands of the OUN-B for adherence to the integral nationlist line.⁴²

In the case of Dniepropetrovsk, some corroboration of postwar accounts is furnished by a German police report. An OUN-B group arrived soon after the German army entered the city. Under the Galician organizer Rehei, who was helped by the Wehrmacht commander, a new *oblast* administration was established to offset the locally formed city administration.⁴³ Apparently the local group was at first neutral on the Russo-Ukrainian question, but the fanatic demands of the OUN-B and its efforts at counterorganization drove the local group completely into the Russian alignment, which was tolerated by the German police authorities after they dispersed the Bandera group. At least one prominent member actually joined the Natsional'no-Trudovoi Soiuz (NTS – National Workers' Union), the Russian counterpart to the OUN. When the OUN parties, including a relatively important Mel'nyk group which was especially active in educational circles, continued their work underground, they gained or regained some support, partly as a reaction to the lengths to which the Russophile element, especially the Autonomous Church, went, and partly because of an increasing moderation in their own ideology.⁴⁴

No simple conclusion can be drawn from an analysis of these complex situations. The picture is further complicated by a tendency, illustrated in a number of instances, for Russians living in the Ukraine to accept a moderate Ukrainian nationalist position when not exposed to the pressure of an extreme Nationalist and strongly anti-Russian ideology. One strong adherent of the Ukrainian ethnic nationalist position was much impressed on finding in Novomirgorod (Novomyrhorod), near Kirovograd, a young teacher and his wife who both felt themselves to be Ukrainian, although born in Russia, and who "hated the Bolsheviks just as much as we do."⁴⁵ In another small town in the area (Novo Ukrainka) a nationalist organizer found most of the teachers to be "still under the influence of Communist ideology," which probably meant among other things that they did not consider the "purity" of Ukrainian

---

⁴¹Zynovii Matla, *Pivdenna pokhidna hrupa* (The Southern Task Force) (Munich: Tsitsero, 1952), pp. 29-31; Ievhen (Eugene) Stakhiv ("E. Pavliuk"), "Borot'ba ukraïns'koho narodu na skhidnoukraïns'kykh zemliakh, 1941-1944: Spomyny ochevydtsia i uchasnyka" (The Struggle of the Ukrainian People in the Eastern Ukrainian Lands, 1941-44: Memories of an Eyewitness and Participant), in *Kalendar Provydinnia na 1947 rik. Stovaryshennia Ukraïns'kikh Katolykiv v Amerytsi* (Calendar for 1947 of the Providence Society of Ukrainian Catholics in America) (Philadelphia: Ameryka, n.d.), pp. 39, 41, 45, 53; Iuryi Semenko, "Pam'iati Mykhaila Pronchenka" (Memories of Michael Pronchenko), *Novi Dni*, April, 1953, pp. 10-13; Interviews 7, 66.

⁴²That this was the case is indicated by an article in *Krakivs'ki Visti*, November 15, 1941, p. 2, evidently based on discussions with Pronchenko and Potapenko. It contained the complaint that the newspaper *Dzvin* would have little space left for the news of the day if it was necessary to print "catechisms on the *trizub* or the national name," essays on the development of National Socialism, the New Europe, etc. Cf. Semenko, "Pam'iati Mykhaila Pronchenka," and Shankovs'kyi, *Pohidni hrupy OUN*, p. 145 ff.

⁴³Chief of the SP and the SD, Report of *Einsatzgruppen* and *Kommandos*, No. 132, November 12, 1941, pp. 10-11, NO 3830 (hereafter referred to as NO 3830). Cf. Shankovs'kyi, *Pohidni hrupy OUN*, pp. 32-33, 150-51, who describes continued underground activity of the OUN-B group.

⁴⁴Interview 1.

⁴⁵R. Sutor in *Krakivs'ki Visti*, August 2, 1942, p. 3.

culture of the greatest importance.⁴⁶ There seems to have been a fairly widespread tendency on the part of many Ukrainians and of many Russians living in the Ukraine, to reject any ethnic national creed in favor of some ideology based on territorial identity. It would not do to overemphasize this factor, however, for there was considerable support, especially in the northwestern area around the see of Kirovograd, for the Autocephalous Church,⁴⁷ which stressed the Ukrainian language, and isolated smaller places like Pavlograd were real centers of devotion to all things Ukrainian. Even such a large center as Dnieprodzerzhinsk had a nationalist mayor and a nationalist editor.⁴⁸

The extreme south, the coastal strip along the Black Sea and the Sea of Azov, from Odessa to Osipenko (Berdianka), had had a still shorter history of settlement than the area immediately to the north. Best suited of all Ukrainian lands to large-scale wheat farming with a small agricultural working force, it had a relatively sparse rural population, very mixed ethnically, with many German villages and some districts of Russian majority. The cities were still more heterogeneous, with Ukrainians forming a small minority in the larger ones, according to the census of 1926.

The study of conditions in this area is seriously hampered by the fact that the western third fell to Rumanian-occupied Transnistria. To prepare the way for the annexation of Transnistria, and, in addition, to gratify the desire of high officials for loot and profiteering, the Rumanians sent in a large number of their own administrators.⁴⁹ Since the rather backward Moldavians comprised only a small proportion of the total population, one of the Slavic elements had to be tolerated. Believing that German victory would lead eventually to the creation of an independent Ukraine, which would inevitably demand the land west of the Dniester as an irredenta, the Rumanians favored the Russians; the position of Russian nationalist elements in Odessa resembled that of the Mel'nyk group in Kiev and Zhitomir before their suppression by the Germans. Russian was an official language, along with Rumanian and German; a Russian theater was opened; several Russian publications were started.⁵⁰ The guiding organization of the Russians was a group called the Union of Russian Officers, which had the St. George cross as its emblem and evidently was strongly tsarist in its ideology.⁵¹ It is said to have maintained contacts with émigré groups in Serbia and elsewhere and to have refused cooperation with the Vlasov movement.⁵² At any rate, with Rumanian encouragement, it was bitterly anti-Ukrainian, adopting the slogan, "The Ukraine never was, is not, and never will be."⁵³

---

⁴⁶Matla, *Pivdenna pokhidna hrupa*, p. 28.

⁴⁷On the question of language to be used in church service, cf. Chapter VIII.

⁴⁸Interview 10; *Ukraïns'kyi Visnyk*, June 14, 1942, p. 7.

⁴⁹*Ukraïns'kyi Visnyk*, February 7, 1943, p. 1, based on a Zentraleuropa agency report.

⁵⁰*Krakivs'ki Visti*, April 17, 1943, p. 3; Interview 18; Arkadii Liubchenko, *Shchodennyk* (Diary), Vol. I, ed. M. Dmytrenko (Toronto: Novi Dni, 1951), p. 122.

⁵¹Clandestine publication from Odessa region previously cited.

⁵²*Ibid.*; Interview 18.

⁵³Interview 18.

Since this group and its Rumanian backers controlled all aspects of cultural and public life, any open Ukrainian nationalist activity even of a cultural nature was suppressed. A clandestine publication and a considerable amount of postwar testimony indicate that the OUN-B maintained a strong underground organization, started by a division of the southern task force even before Rumanian occupation began and later reinforced from the headquarters in Dniepropetrovsk.[54] They are said to have been able to operate an illegal printing press in Odessa and to have kept a nucleus group there.[55] A great deal of their attention was directed to the Rumanian-occupied rural areas to the north, and especially to southern Podolia, where they conducted a propaganda effort to induce the Ukrainian villagers to resist colonization by Moldavians.[56]

To the east, the southern part of the *Generalbezirk* Nikolaev was more open to Ukrainian activity. The mayor of Nikolaev was a Mel'nyk adherent.[57] In the second-largest city of the area, Kherson, the Bandera group built a considerable organization, including the assistant mayor and the police chief, but was apparently liquidated by the SP by the end of 1941.[58] Nevertheless, the mayor, apparently an ethnic German, assisted the Ukrainian intellectuals in organizing cultural activity many months after the OUN-B had been suppressed.[59] The newspaper, too, is said to have been edited by a nationalist journalist.[60] In this city and the *Bezirk* capital, the Autonomous Church was active, having formed an archdiocese of Kherson at an early date.[61] As was related previously, the *Generalkommissar* was suspicious of the Autocephalous Church and urged that steps be taken against it when it grew strong in the north of his area. Later, Michael (Khoroshyi), bishop of Kirovograd, was to come to Nikolaev as archbishop, and was recognized by the *Generalkommissar*,[62] but the pro-Russian ecclesiastical group seems to have maintained a strong position. On the other hand, the extremely large shift in national affiliation in Kherson indicated by the city census suggests that the same factor of adoption of loyalty to the Ukraine as a territorial entity may have been at work

---

[54]Ie. Stakhiv, "Borot'ba," p. 45; Mstyslav Z. Chubai, *Reid organizatoriv OUN vid Popradu do Chorne More* (The Raid of the Organizers of the OUN from Poprad to the Black Sea) (Munich: Tsitsero, 1952), p. 48 ff.; Interview 18; clandestine publication from Odessa area previously cited.

[55]Ie. Stakhiv, "Borot'ba," p. 45. See also Shankovs'kyi, *Pohidni hrupy OUN*, pp. 215-92, and the clandestine *Visnyk*, No. 10 (Spring, 1943).

[56]Clandestine publication from Odessa area previously cited.

[57]Chief of the SP and the SD, Report on Events in the USSR, October 2, 1941, pp. 3-4, NO 3137 (hereafter referred to as NO 3137).

[58]Chief of the SP and the SD, Report of *Einsatzgruppen* and *Kommandos*, January 14, 1942, p. 30, NO 3279 (hereafter referred to as NO 3279). For later OUN-B activities (apparently rather obscure), see Shankovs'kyi, *Pohidni hrupy OUN*, pp. 141-43.

[59]*Ukraïns'kyi Visnyk*, September 5, 1943, p. 6.

[60]Interview 42.

[61]*Ukraïns'ka Diisnist'*, January 20, 1942, p. 1. The archbishop was Anthony (Martsenko), who received his appointment in 1941 from the Sobor of Volhynian Bishops. Up to the time of the definite split between the Autonomous and the Autocephalous churches he was apparently still sympathetic to the Ukrainian nationalists as his secretary is reported to have been an OUN member (NO 3279).

[62]*Deutsche Bug-Zeitung*, March 6, 1943, p. 5.

here as well as farther north.[63] Farther east along the coast, in the *Generalbezirk* Taurien (Taurida), with its capital in Melitopol' (Melitopil'), there appears to have been little effort at nationalist organization; the newspapers, police, and other agencies were Ukrainians, but seem to have been completely subject to German control.[64]

Beyond the coastal strip just discussed lies the most easterly section of the Ukrainian SSR, the Donbas. This area, in which agriculture takes the form of large-scale wheat farming, as in the far south, is known as the "Ruhr"—or better, one of the "Ruhrs"—of the Soviet Union. Its industry, which grew at a tremendous pace in the interwar period, is based primarily upon rich coal deposits. Its five cities of more than 100,000 population in 1939 had nearly tripled their total number of inhabitants since the previous census. It is probable that this increase resulted in a substantial gain for the Ukrainian ethnic component, which previously had been very small, as the surrounding peasantry is largely, though not overwhelmingly, Ukrainian. As far as the technical staffs, which composed the bulk of the educated classs, are concerned, however, Ukrainian nationalist observers themselves admit that the great majority was drawn from "all over the Union." Consequently, the area could be expected to be very lukewarm in its reaction to the nationalist movements. This tendency was reinforced by the great distance of the region from the stimulation center in the West Ukraine—Stalino is nearly 1,000 miles from L'vov—and by the lack of strong historical ties with the Ukraine. Two special factors also played a role: the suppression of the Kiev OUN-M group came before a nationalist revival could get under way in the area, and the news frightened the few nationalist Ukrainians away from public life; and the German army authorities who were in charge were reluctant to permit even the formal and linguistic ascendancy permitted Ukrainians elsewhere.[65] Finally, even according to an OUN organizer active in the area, the Ukrainians were inclined from long habit to allow the Russians priority.[66]

As a result, in a large number of cities in the Donbas, including Slaviansk, Artemovsk (Bakhmut), Debal'tsevo, and Snezhnoe, the Russians succeeded in establishing a cultural ascendancy without, however, its taking on much political significance. This ascendancy included, in particular, the publication of Russian-language newspapers, which as a rule were not allowed in the former Ukrainian Soviet Republic.[67] A number of Ukrainian-language papers were also founded, some expressly designed for the rural population. In Stalino, with the help of OUN-B organizers, a nationalist editor was able to transform an originally Russian paper into a Ukrainian organ, while for a time Ukrainian-language papers with nationalist tendencies were published in Voroshilovgrad and Kramatorskaia (Kramators'ka).[68] In Enakievo an administration of Ukrainians was installed with the aid of Italian troops which occupied the town, while Ukrainian officials were also found in other city

---

[63]See Appendix.

[64]PS 1693.

[65]PS 051.

[66]Interview 66.

[67]*Krakivs'ki Visti*, July 23, 1942, p. 3.

[68]Interview 66.

administrations.⁶⁹ All efforts at nationalist organization were hampered by the fact that the area was not conquered until late 1941, and, except for a brief period in 1942, it lay within a short distance of the front. A few OUN-M organizers were active in the area, and a considerable Bandera network directed by Eugene Stakhiv did what it could to encourage national tendencies among the local Ukrainians.⁷⁰

The city of Mariupol' was an outstanding exception to the conditions prevailing throughout most of the area. While Mariupol' was administratively part of the Donbas, lying in the Stalino *oblast*, it is over fifty miles from the Donets basin itself, on the shore of the Sea of Azov. Like the other cities of the Donbas, however, it had grown enormously, more than tripling in size between the two Soviet censuses. Even after the losses of war, its population numbered 178,358, placing it not far below the largest Ukrainian metropolises.⁷¹ What is remarkable for a city in the Donbas, or indeed in the whole southern area, is that it was under full Ukrainian control. Its well-developed Prosvita society and Ukrainian educational system have already been mentioned. The Orthodox Church is said to have been active and oriented toward Ukrainian nationalism, although here as elsewhere in the far south Protestants and dissident Orthodox sects played an important role.⁷² In addition, the mayor was outspokenly nationalist, encouraging the formation of a Ukrainian military force.⁷³ Probably the guiding spirit in the nationalist development in the city, however, was Nicholas Stasiuk, minister of supply under the Rada in 1918, who had managed to survive the Soviet period by working as a park attendant.⁷⁴ He took over the editorship of *Mariiupil's'ka Hazeta* which, although restricted by the paper shortage especially acute in the treeless south, was the second most influential Ukrainian paper on the "Left Bank" (next to *Nova Ukraïna*). While necessarily cautious, its tone was strongly nationalist. Moreover, in addition to Stasiuk, there were a number of nationalist journalists to aid in carrying on the newspaper's work. Stasiuk himself is said not only to have carried on this legal pronationalist activity, but to have assisted the OUN-B underground which made its area base in the city.⁷⁵

It is uncertain just why Mariupol' was so different from the Donbas as a whole in the extent of nationalist activity. Very likely, as was so frequently the case, the presence of a few strongly nationalist and yet temperate and resourceful men was sufficient to turn the balance in a situation in which the vast majority was neither able nor willing to engage in political activity. Of

---

⁶⁹*Krakivs'ki Visti*, March 12, 1942, p. 3.

⁷⁰Ie. Stakhiv, "Borot'ba," p. 50; Interview 66; Ie. Stakhiv, "Geneza evoliutsii OUN" (Genesis of the Evolution of the OUN), *Ukraïns'kyi Prometei*, Nos. 44, 45, 46, 1955; Tamara Saidak, "Donets'kyi kriazh" (Donets Mountain), *Ukraïns'ki Visti*, August 19, 1954; Ie. Stakhiv, "Ukraïns'ke revoliutsiine pidpillia v Donbasi v rr. 1941-43" (The Ukrainian Revolutionary Underground in the Donbas in 1941-43), *Ukraïns'ki Visti*, October 3, 1954.

⁷¹*L'vivs'ki Visti*, August 27, 1942, p. 2; *Krakivs'ki Visti*, July 24, 1942, p. 2.

⁷²*Krakivs'ki Visti*, October 3, 1942, p. 2.

⁷³Cf. Chapter VII.

⁷⁴Interview 66; *Krakivs'ki Visti*, August 7, 1942, p. 2.

⁷⁵Ie. Stakhiv, "Borot'ba," pp. 52-54; Interview 66. The nationalist tone of *Mariiupil's'ka Hazeta* is apparent from the considerable number of its articles reprinted in the West Ukrainian and émigré press.

course, the city was also under the comparatively lenient German army regime; it may well be that the army deliberately fostered a center of Ukrainian nationalist activity at this point, so close to the front, especially to the hard-fought Kerch Peninsula battlefield, in order that it might serve as a rallying point for Ukrainian feeling and a possible base for the development of a Ukrainian fighting force.

The Ukrainian nationalists have always claimed as Ukrainian ethnic territory large areas beyond the eastern frontiers of the Ukrainian SSR, principally the southern part of Kursk *oblast*, the area around Rostov on the lower Don, the Crimea, and the Kuban' river valley. As far as the Kursk area is concerned, the war period yields no evidence, for the district was almost constantly a battlefield between the Red army and the Germans. One clear indication concerning the Rostov district is the report cited in the preceding chapter of the Ukrainian speech but lack of nationalist feeling among the peasantry.[76] Another report by a nationalist Ukrainian confirms this, saying that 90 percent of the children spoke Ukrainian, but most of the older people spoke Russian habitually, and there was very little national feeling.[77]

In 1941 Ukrainians comprised only a small proportion of the population of the Crimea. The Ukrainian nationalist claim to the peninsula was based primarily on geographical proximity and the lack of any clear majority for another ethnic group, since the prewar Crimea also had large numbers of Russians and Tatars, as well as smaller settlements of Italians, Greeks, and Germans. Hence it is not surprising that in 1942 the capital, Simferopol', should have had a Russian rather than a Ukrainian newspaper and that the only Ukrainian activities were cultural and educational.[78]

The Kuban', the large and fertile region to the northwest of the Caucasus, undoubtedly has a larger Ukrainian ethnic component, but its distinct historical development—the area was settled by groups of the Cossack type recruited by the tsars to further expansion against the Moslem tribes—had apparently led to a different ethnic affiliation. During the war period the area was occupied only a short time by the Germans. In this period, five newspapers were founded in the principal cities, all in Russian.[79] That this may not be an indication of Russian predominance is suggested by a German official concerned with the area during the war who says that the army censorship authority was

---

[76] See Chapter X.

[77] *Krakivs'ki Visti*, September 18, 1942, p. 2.

[78] For a description of Ukrainian cultural, educational, and religious activity in Simferopol' see Iaroslav Savka in *Krakivs'ki Visti*, February 18, 1942, p. 4. For the vigorous, but only marginally successful OUN-B effort to establish an underground in the Crimea and the Kuban', see Shankovs'kyi, *Pohidni hrupy OUN*, pp. 181-92.

[79] They are listed in *Nastup*, January 10, 1943, p. 2; *Krakivs'ki Visti*, January 14, 1943, p. 2, also lists the paper in Krasnodar', the capital, as Russian, and says the Russian language also predominated in the theater.

in the hands of an extremely pro-Russian Balt.[80] At any rate, there is practically no evidence of Ukrainian activity.[81]

Ethnic nationalist feeling—which included support of the OUN-M, large-scale development of Prosvita, Ukrainian cultural activities, Ukrainian newspapers, emphasizing national history, and above all a tendency to condemn and discriminate against all non-Ukrainian elements—was most prevalent in the old northern centers of Ukrainian life, especially in the northwest. In these areas the historic struggle against Polish overlords, the difficult position of the rising Ukrainian intelligentsia because of the predominance of Jews, Russians and Poles in the towns, the contrasting strength of Ukrainian popular culture in the village, appear to have led to bitterness or at least to a strong feeling of ethnocentrism among the nationalist intellectuals.

The south, on the other hand, had long been recognized as less Ukrainian by all who were familiar with the country. Yet, while the manifestations of Ukrainian cultural activity were sparser and the influence of the OUN groups much less, there seems to have been a fairly strong tendency for a large portion of the inhabitants, of whatever ethnic origin, to accept the Ukraine as their motherland because they lived in it and were attached to it. Moreover, if earlier experiences of the nationalist movements are a trustworthy guide, this feeling represented a change from the conditions of the "South Russia" and "New Russia" of imperial days. Hence there is strong ground for suggesting that territorial patriotism has grown under the Soviet regime. The significance of this observation, and other evidence which supports it, must be treated in a larger context in the next chapter.

---

[80]Interview 33.

[81]The Krasnodar' paper (*Kuban'*) published an article by "A. Kuban'skii" on December 20, 1942, telling of the Ukrainian cultural revival in the early days of the Soviet regime (*Nastup*, February 20, 1943, p. 4). There were also a few OUN organizers in the area, probably with German units. I have seen one OUN-B leaflet designed for the Kuban' population: *Kubantsi potomki zaporozhs'kykh kozakiv!* (Kubaners, Descendants of the Zaporozhian Cossacks!).

XII
Perspectives of Wartime Nationalism

Ukrainian nationalism is but one thread in the immense tapestry of the Second World War. In following the intricate pattern of this thread it is easy unconsciously to magnify its importance. One must constantly remind oneself that the active participants in the nationalist struggle were pitifully few and weak in comparison with the powerful forces which fought for control of Eastern Europe. In the six years covered by this study numerous events took place in the Ukraine which were of far greater immediate significance for the course of history than those described here. In order to follow the single thread of nationalism, many others which frequently formed the dominant pattern were given only brief mention, or neglected altogether. The vast military campaigns, the fantasies of German policy, the network of Communist espionage and terror, the complex agricultural problem, are but a few of these other aspects of the wartime Ukraine.

The question of national identification, however, is more basic, because less transitory, than problems imposed by foreign forces. Nationalism strikes deep into the psychological substance of a people, and is capable of stimulating an enthusiasm not easily aroused by most other influences. The goals set by nationalism may not attract the pure rationalist, but they often have a profound emotional appeal. In the past century the world has seen numerous political programs, which for many years attracted only a small, fanatical following, suddenly become powerful when circumstances permitted them to capture the emotions of the "common man." If a movement appears to possess such potentiality, it is not wise to disregard it, even though its present manifestations be limited.

A major purpose of this study has been to inquire whether Ukrainian nationalism possessed the potentiality of arousing such emotions, and to determine the circumstances under which such potentiality, if it existed, could become reality. From this point of view, the examination of developments in the West Ukraine is of restricted significance. There is little doubt but that a large majority of the Ukrainian population of Galicia opposed both German and Soviet occupation, and would have preferred its own government to a return to Polish rule. During the first years of German occupation, when conditions were comparatively bearable, the Ukrainian Central Committee, working as an auxiliary administration, was undoubtedly supported by most of the inhabitants. The constructive and orderly operation of this body is an indication, if a limited one, of the possibilities for the existence of a stable Ukrainian administrative organization under more favorable circumstances. Even the radical OUN elements, which publicly demanded complete independence, were reluctant to disturb the operation of the Galician administration, for they knew that they would not secure popular support in that fashion and would only destroy their own secure base of operations.

While less evidence concerning the Carpatho-Ukraine and Bukovina could be presented, it seems evident that the Ukrainian populations of those areas would have preferred a nationalist administration to that of Hungary, Rumania, or the Soviet Union. The situation in Volhynia was less clear, for it was possible for Communist partisans to recruit substantial numbers of followers, especially in the northern region. The widespread support given the various groups of nationalist partisans indicates, however, that nationalist feeling was strong in Volhynia. Evidently the moderate, though somewhat indecisive tactics of the "Bul'ba" partisans were at first preferred by the peasants, who desired a leadership composed of their own countrymen, yet not highly doctrinaire or radical in its demands. Later, the depredations of the German administration and the general unrest prevailing in Volhynia appear to have led large numbers of the younger peasants to support the more extreme course taken by the Bandera followers.

This tendency of sizable elements of the population to support radical nationalism is a very important feature of the nationalist movements in the West Ukraine. According to Western democratic standards, there was a marked deterioration in the quality of Ukrainian nationalist political thought between the two wars. The generation of 1918 had thought in terms of a state based on parliamentary institutions and concerned primarily with the civil rights and social welfare of its citizens. To a limited extent this tradition survived in the UNR, although even there it was obscured by personal and factional ambitions. It was revived in a rather primitive form by the group around Borovets', and might have achieved a new synthesis of democracy and socialism had the Mitrynga faction been able to develop its theories. The older generation which had controlled the legal parties in Galicia was basically democratic. The really dynamic force in Ukrainian politics during this period, however, was the OUN.

The theory and teachings of the Nationalists were very close to Fascism, and in some respects, such as the insistence on "racial purity," even went beyond the original Fascist doctrines. In order to understand Ukrainian integral nationalism, however, it is necessary to examine the environment in which it developed. Probably it is safe to say that there was a general deterioration in the quality of political groups in Eastern Europe during the period between the two world wars. The victory of Communism in the Russian Empire led some elements to resort to extreme measures to prevent its further spread and to ape its tactics in combatting it. The post-1918 peace settlement was an attempt to satisfy the national aspirations of certain groups, but seemed only to exacerbate the nationalism already growing among the peoples of the area. The West Ukrainians—and the East Ukrainian émigrés who were associated with them—suffered from both these developments. The denial of moderate demands for Ukrainian national expression by the ultranationalist governments of Poland,

Rumania, and later Hungary produced an extreme reaction. For a few years Communism appeared to present a vehicle for the expression of national resentment; consequently it was able to attract the temporary support of many Ukrainians.

Even those who were never directly moved by the Communist appeal were frequently impressed by the success of Communist tactics, Again and again in the course of this study, features of the OUN have been mentioned which recall the organization of the Communist Party. To some extent these features are, of course, older than Communism, having been part of the tradition of revolutionary movements like the Narodnaia Volia in Russia and of various nationalist organizations in Eastern and Southern Europe. The triumph of Communism gave these tactics a new vogue, especially among those who declared themselves to be the most vigorous opponents of Bolshevism—the Fascists. Basic to the new fashion of party conflict was the assertion that the end justifies the means; this tenet was not only tacitly followed but deliberately exalted. The same step was taken by integral nationalists like the followers of the OUN. It soon proved impossible to limit the application of the priniciple to non-Ukrainians, however. First Polish officials and Soviet representatives were assassinated; then the Nationalists turned on one another; finally even nominally non-political figures like the clergy fell victims to the new fashion of ruthlessness. To some extent, of course, this resort to violence was due to the fearful circumstances of the time, when in the midst of the mass executions carried out by Nazis and Communists alike the sacrifice of a few more lives to attain important results seemed of little consequence. Yet the general blunting of moral sensibility, the willingness, even eagerness, of men to undertake such actions could hardly have progressed so rapidly had they not been indoctrinated beforehand by an ideology which purported to furnish an idealistic justification for their violence.

Conspiracy, too, had its models in both Communism and Fascism. The underground system contained obvious imitations of Communist and Fascist practices, such as the elite secret police, the Sluzhba Bezpeky, which served as the control agent in the OUN-B. Moreover, the split in the OUN had its parallels in the Nazi and the Bolshevik parties. Unlike these movements, however, the OUN did not control a state apparatus; hence neither faction could forcibly restore monolithic control. Instead, a deadly internecine struggle sapped the strength of the Nationalist movement and discredited it in the eyes of the people. In other ways, too, the lack of opportunity for experience in responsible political activity was harmful to the underground party. "Voluntarism," the emphasis on action as opposed to thought, will as opposed to reason, was given an extreme interpretation; in practice it was frequently confounded with sheer egoism. Where authority, nominally exalted, was not backed by force, it was readily flouted by ambition. Those who were least inhibited by doubts of their own capacity to rule, and who were ready for the most extreme action, triumphed in the struggle for support of the younger members of the party. This circumstance placed a premium upon ruthlessness.

It also led to a dangerous lack of caution. Probably the reckless challenge to German authority in June, 1941, had little long-range effect, since the Nazi rulers would not in any case have sanctioned Ukrainian autonomy. The "deconspiration" of the partisan movement in the face of imminent Soviet occupation was much more serious; it almost surely resulted in the uncompensated loss of many of the most vigorous nationalist fighters, who might have been saved had the movement adhered to its previous tactic of operating in small bands, which could disappear among the peasantry in the face of approaching danger. If the younger element in the OUN-B was responsible for these actions, the Mel'nyk group—or at least its advance units—must bear the major portion of the responsibility for extremist activities in the East Ukraine. The lack of a positive program of social and political reform during the early stages of penetration of the east was intimately connected with the excessive emphasis on the "purity" of national culture and the subordination of rational planning to romantic phrasemaking. At this stage the Nationalists called themselves revolutionists, but, lacking a coherent concept of a new social and political order, they were at best only rebels.

The failure of the OUN to present a constructive program adapted to the needs of the East Ukraine makes it difficult to approach the major question posed in this study: How strong was nationalism in the East Ukraine? To a considerable extent, the initial experience of the East Ukrainians with propagators of nationalist doctrines was negative. In addition to its lack of concern for civil rights, economic progress, and social reform, the OUN and its more extreme adherents recruited locally repelled many East Ukrainians by their insistence on the elimination of non-Ukrainian cultural elements and on the removal of the non-Ukrainian members of society themselves. Naturally enough, many East Ukrainians confused nationalism itself with the extreme brand offered by the OUN.

In addition to the confusion arising from the activity of the OUN, several other factors make it difficult to judge the extent of nationalist feeling in the East Ukraine. The scarcity of information, the impossibility of direct observation or measurement, are great handicaps. The constant pressure of German occupation and the furtive but equally constant threat presented by Communist agents militated against the open expression of nationalist sentiments. Moreover, the extreme hardships of the war period drove the national question into the background just as, according to many accounts, the terror of Soviet rule had induced a feeling of solidarity among oppressed persons of all nationalities. It is hazardous to attempt to estimate the relative importance of the preoccupations of the population during the war, but probably the following order is fairly correct:

1. Physical survival—avoidance of starvation or death at the hands of the Germans or the Red partisans

2. Economic welfare—elimination of exploitation by the government or by individuals, especially in agriculture

3. Stable and orderly government, including a measure of freedom for the individual

4. Equality of persons, with some form of popular participation in government

5. National expression in culture and perhaps in government

Many will argue that the attainment of the first three aims listed is dependent upon the securing of the last two, but to the average East Ukrainian any party which was excessively concerned with the last alone appeared remote and unrealistic.

The preceding paragraphs have stressed the numerous defects of the wartime nationalist movement. They are, however, only one side of the picture. On the other side are the energy and bravery of the members of the Nationalist parties, exhibited both in the underground and partisan activities in the West Ukraine and in the propagation of OUN doctrines in the east. If ever a group was prepared to fight against seemingly hopeless odds, it was the OUN. A few thousand inexperienced and ill-equipped young men not only set out to supersede the gigantic Communist apparatus, but dared to challenge the apparently indomitable German war machine as well. In a world in which timidity in the face of advancing tyranny is often the rule, such courage offsets many shortcomings.

The OUN—both its factions—was youthful not only in its willingness to face great odds, but in its flexibility. While many of the old elements of autocratic control, scorn of rational planning, and ruthlessness persisted in the Nationalist groups, the evolution of their thinking on social and economic questions is striking. Even under the extreme pressure of the struggle for survival in the underground or in guerrilla warfare, many members of the OUN were able to profit from their contact with East Ukrainians to revise their program. The demand for national independence continued to occupy a central position, but it was supplemented by provisions for an agricultural order to be based on the wishes of the peasants, an organization of industry preserving public ownership while eliminating centralized direction, guarantees of civil liberties, and many other features which appealed to the East Ukrainians. Unquestionably the diminished opportunity for propaganda in the later stages of the war prevented the new program of the OUN from reaching a majority of the population, but small groups, at least, became aware that a program based on nationalism could also serve as a foundation for a new social order.

The West Ukrainian and émigré parties were not the only propagators of nationalism in the East Ukraine. The role of the churches, especially that of the Autocephalous Church, was important. Like the OUN, the Autocephalous Church had its base in the West Ukraine; the church, however, was much closer in many respects to the mentality of the east, which had been formed by centuries of Orthodoxy, than was the predominantly Galician political movement. Religion in general, however, was a doubtful ally of nationalism in the East Ukraine. Undoubtedly the church's appeal to the older elements of the population, especially in the village, was considerable; to the extent to which it awakened their feeling of national identity, it was valued by the nationalists. For very many of the younger generation who had grown up under the Soviet system, religion was a matter of indifference, or even of hostility; hence any identification of nationalism with religion tended to deprive the former of numerous potentially useful recruits.

Religion reached down to the less-educated strata of the population, but the predominant support for nationalism in the East Ukraine was found among the intellectuals. At the same time, this group, together with technical specialists, played the leading role in reorganization of life under German occupation. While in practice the Germans retained many of the lower Soviet administrative officials because they were apparently tractable, although often really in sympathy with the Communists, in principle all those prominently associated with the Soviet regime were eliminated from the administration. The gap was filled by teachers, engineers, university professors, and professional men. The limitations of these elements as organizers of a new administration were considerable; to what extent they could have successfully established order and maintained essential services without the framework of German control is hard to say. Certainly the difficulties encountered in establishing security forces, combatting Communist infiltration, and utilizing the press indicate that the East Ukrainians alone would have found completely unassisted operation of the administrative framework to be an almost impossible task. Under the circumstances which actually existed, however, with valuable assistance from West Ukrainian organizers in key tasks such as the development of police units, the East Ukrainian administrations were able to perform such essential functions as the Germans permitted.

After discouraging experiences with the OUN many of the intellectuals become hostile to Ukrainian nationalism as a political movement; still more were indifferent. In most areas, however, a sufficient number were attracted to nationalism to give a stimulus to the movement, and in several cities nationalist elements were dominant. The reasons for this attraction are complex. In the East Ukraine nationalism had always secured most of its active adherents from among intellectuals; many of the older generation remembered with nostalgia the brief and turbulent period of national independence during the Revolution, or were sons of men who had been active at that time. Under the Soviet regime, intellectuals had been influenced by the "national Communism" of the Skrypnyk period, and the encouragement given Ukrainian culture had stimulated the nationalist feeling of many persons educated during that period. Intellectuals had suffered especially during the succeeding period of Stalinist repression, and many were ready to embrace any anti-Soviet movement.

The nationalist movement gained incalculable advantage by the fact that the Germans permitted its propaganda in the crucial months immediately following Soviet evacuation. Moreover, even after they had suppressed the OUN, they continued to favor the Ukrainian language and culture. To the very end of the occupation many East Ukrainians assumed that the Germans would eventually support some form of Ukrainian state, and were consequently eager to be classified as Ukrainians. Although elements which indirectly furthered continued union with Russia were sometimes favored by the Germans as an offset to the Ukrainian nationalists, explicit propagation of such an alternative to independence was not permitted until almost the end of the occupation. Since intellectuals under the Soviet system had been habituated to conformance not only to the existing official policy, but also to that which they anticipated would be pursued in the future, even the limited support given Ukrainian nationalism by the Germans was highly significant. That such a large contingent of Ukrainian intellectuals who had occupied administrative positions in Kiev and elsewhere joined the Vlasov movement when it was finally authorized indicates that, during the occupation, many had given merely surface allegiance to the concept of Ukrainian independence. On the other hand, it is noteworthy that numerous intellectuals continued to be strongly nationalist even after they were disillusioned by the excesses of the OUN and by the discovery that it lacked the German backing which it had claimed. Sometimes, as in Kharkov, they formed vigorous and successful local nationalist organizations independent of, and even hostile to, the OUN. A considerable number of the members of these organizations, as well as East Ukrainian adherents of the OUN, proved their devotion to the nationalist cause by running grave risks to further it, in spite of the extreme penalties imposed by the Germans upon all suspected of unauthorized political activity. A withdrawal from political life, a reluctance to take the initiative, seem to have been inculcated by life under the Soviet regime, but once the East Ukrainian intellectual had become really convinced of the values of the nationalist movement, he was frequently as devoted a follower as the West Ukrainian, although much more cautious.

Reluctance to take part in public affairs was much more prevalent among the less educated elements of the population, especially the peasantry. What action such groups took was generally limited to matters of direct concern to the individual or the intimate group, such as the division of kolkhoz land. In spite of this passivity, numerous observers reported that there was a widespread desire for positive programs, a demand for a clear-cut solution to the vacuum left by the removal of Communist direction. The people rejected the Communist regime as such, yet they were accustomed by years of propaganda and planning from above to the existence of a fully formulated program which offered a long-range goal, an explanation of the course of events, and a series of immediate instructions. Unexplained orders, vague slogans, were insufficient substitutes. Above all, a program which offered satisfaction of the basic interests listed earlier in this chapter was desired.

The German authorities were unable to present such a program because of the ill-concealed determination of the Nazi leadership to convert the Ukraine into an exploited colony. Russian anti-Communist organizations were hampered by the initial advantages secured by the Ukrainian Nationalists, and in any event appear to have had neither the vigor nor the organizing personnel necessary to achieve any significant penetration of the Ukraine. Ukrainian nationalism was, therefore, in the most favorable position to act as a galvanizing force and to overcome the passivity of the population liberated from Soviet rule. By securing the support of a large portion of the East Ukrainian intelligentsia, its chances were considerably enhanced. This was the only elite group which was overwhelmingly opposed to a return of Communism and was the only medium by which nationalist ideas could be brought to the bulk of the population.

Nationalism, however, as propagated by the West Ukrainian and the émigré organizers, and as understood by most of the East Ukrainian intelligentsia, was based primarily on ethnic and cultural factors. To be sure, the East Ukrainians were generally much milder in their interpretation, recognizing the value and rights of other cultures, and seeking to secure a dominant, not an exclusive place for the Ukrainian cultural pattern. To both groups, however, the Ukrainian was born, not made. To most of the people, even to those with some degree of education, on the other hand, the question of the predominance of the Ukrainian language and culture was of minor significance, although, as the spread of the Autocephalous Church shows, there was a certain feeling of satisfaction, at least in rural areas, in having their mentors use the native language. There does seem, however, to have been a real though undefined attachment to the Ukraine as a territorial entity within the boundaries established by the Ukrainian SSR. This feeling in some cases led even persons of known Russian origin to consider themselves Ukrainian. Moreover, an equally vague preference for local administration seems to have been aroused by the decades of overcentralized oppression directed from Moscow.

That the mass of the population was attracted by the concept of territorially decentralized government, while the intellectual elite was concerned primarily with independence based on cultural distinctiveness suggests that a considerable gap separated the two elements. Where the nationalist concept, even when containing a moderate emphasis on cultivation of the Ukrainian language and arts, was combined with a vigorous program of social and economic reform, and was promoted by realistic men well acquainted with the local situation, however, it secured considerable support. The success of the Prosvita group in Kharkov is a good example of such popularity, but it should be remembered that this group directed the economically beneficial cooperative organization as well as purely cultural activities.

Ukrainian nationalism was the only dynamic anti-Communist movement which was able to carry on extensive propaganda in the East Ukraine under German occupation. It possessed a body of devoted followers to serve as its organizers; it was capable of arousing enthusiasm and exacting sacrifices. Lack of experience and judgment cost its adherents dearly. The movement proved, however, to be flexible enough to adapt its program to the demands for social measures which the Soviet experience had instilled in the East Ukrainian population. It attracted a large proportion of the intellectuals and technicians who comprised the only group capable of reorganizing life after the Soviet evacuation, but it was unable to penetrate the mass of the population to any great extent. The galvanizing force was present; the cadres which might have transmitted it were half-formed; but the essential mass remained uncommitted.

XIII
After the War

In 1954, when this book first went to press, scarcely nine years had elapsed from the close of the Second World War in Europe. Those nine years had been extremely eventful in the Ukraine. Taken together, circumstantial assertions by émigré sources, one-sided but detailed charges by Stalinist organs, and a wide variety of rumors produced a hazy picture of tragic upheavals. Without documentary evidence or reliable secondary studies, even for the closing months of the war, however, it was impossible to present a detailed, coherent account of the preceding decade of Ukrainian nationalism within the Soviet Union.

For the third edition of *Ukrainian Nationalism*, the author confronts almost the opposite problem. After forty-four years, for the overwhelming majority of readers the Second World War is a historical episode rather than a contemporary memory. Connecting the analysis of wartime nationalism with more recent developments is imperative. Although still fragmentary, evidence for these developments is far more diverse and substantial than that available during the early 1950s. Indeed, available materials are so voluminous that another monographic examination, at least as extensive as that reported in the preceding pages, would be required to treat postwar nationalism in detail. Fortunately, this task need not be undertaken, for admirable secondary analyses provide guides to the postwar evidence. The present chapter, therefore, is a summary of postwar evolution of Ukrainian nationalism, rather than an attempt at definitive treatment. The primary aim is to show the relevance of the wartime experience for subsequent developments.

An element of this experience which reverberates throughout the postwar period is the armed struggle of the Ukrainian Insurrectionary Army. One way to understand this reverberation is to consider the UPA as *myth*. In this instance, the term "myth" carries no implication of fiction; on the contrary, as detailed in Chapter VI, the UPA myth is firmly grounded in historical fact. For two postwar generations of Ukrainians, especially in the West Ukraine and in emigration, the Ukrainian Insurrectionary Army is not merely part of the historical record; it is a major constituent of beliefs, transcending history, which form their identity. As recounted in Chapter I, the Cossack heritage remains the basis of the constitutive myth of all Ukrainians. In the West Ukraine, however, the intense wartime experience of resistance and suffering has tended to supersede (without replacing) other twentieth-century episodes such as the First World War struggle for independence.

As an epic experience, the story of UPA not only competes with, but parallels, mythic themes in the Soviet system. Nominally, the constitutive myth of the Soviet system is the triumph of the heroic proletariat through the Bolshevik Revolution. For legitimizing the postwar elite, however, that remote (and ambiguous) episode was submerged by the story of the "Great Patriotic War," which the elite claimed as its own "heroic age." Such emphasis facilitated an amalgam of the Soviet myth with centuries-old elements of the Russian myth, notably the ultimate "in-gathering" of East Slavs, including Ukrainians, through victory in the Great Patriotic War. In this way, the revised Soviet myth clashed irreconcilably with the postwar Ukrainian nationalist myth. The antipathy was highlighted by the fact that both myths emphasized guerrilla struggle: on the nationalist side, the UPA; on the Soviet side, the Red partisans. During the Khrushchev period (to a lesser degree under Stalin and Brezhnev) the Red partisan story provided a major indoctrination theme for Komsomol (Communist Youth) literature. Tales of underground and guerrilla heroism are inherently dramatic. For the elite, moreover, the partisan epic could be manipulated to demonstrate Party heroism, whereas straight military history redounded to the prestige of the professional soldiers. Conversely, for the Ukrainian emigration, UPA resistance to totalitarian enemies on two fronts was a more attractive theme than the comparably significant, but politically ambiguous, accomplishments of regular nationalist military forces recounted in Chapter VII.

The following pages contain examples of the reverberation of these opposed myths, particularly in Soviet propaganda. An evident Soviet objective was to isolate East Ukrainians from the intense wartime experience of the West Ukrainians which had reshaped their national identity. As will be shown, this Soviet effort has produced some successes. But the mere fact that Soviet propaganda devotes so much attention to the UPA suggests that, as myth, it is especially threatening to the official myth.

The situation of the UPA during the final months of the Second World War, when it operated entirely behind Soviet lines, foreshadows the declining curve of nationalist guerrilla strength in the postwar years. As noted in Chapter VII, the UPA held down an impressive force of Soviet army formations as well as NKVD regiments. With the cessation of regular hostilities, however, available repressive forces multiplied. From this fact alone, one could infer the impossibility of UPA confrontation with Soviet troops in the field. German reports had noted much earlier a tendency to break up the large formations characteristic of guerrilla combat in Volhynia and against Kovpak in Galicia. Instead—despite propaganda references to "divisions" and "armies"—the principal nationalist combat formation became the company-sized detachment, the *sotnia*. Additional considerations led to this reduction in size of the partisan unit. Because they relied primarily on non-Ukrainian informants such as *Volksdeutsche* and Poles, German occupying forces were often deprived of direct sources of information on nationalist movements. The Soviet regime, despite its general unpopularity, never completely lost its attraction for a small minority of Galician Ukrainians, some affiliated earlier with the defunct "Communist Party of the West Ukraine," others attracted after 1939 by sheer opportunism. Nearly all such persons no longer had roots in the Galician villages; but in favorable circumstances they could act as channels to informants there. Thus the *potential* for a far-flung but spotty informant network—the bane of any resistance movement not relying on strict conspiratorial methods—was present. Nevertheless, Soviet concentration on uprooting villages sympathetic to nationalist partisans demonstrates that informers were inadequate. As noted in Chapter VII, the process of depriving the UPA of the sympathetic peasant "sea" in which guerrilla "fish" could swim was well under way by the end of 1944, a few months after Soviet reoccupation. Intensification of this process in succeeding years constitutes a major aspect of regime reaction to Ukrainian nationalism.

A third factor militating against large-scale UPA operations was lack of a secure base or outside support. Rather quickly, no region of the Soviet Ukraine—not even the deep forests or high mountains of the Carpathians—remained a safe "rear area." Without such areas for regrouping and recuperation, major military operations were practically impossible. Even if outside resupply had been available, lack of a secure base would have hampered delivery. This circumstance had hindered German efforts to support the nationalist partisans; after April, 1945, no alternative support was forthcoming. Soviet sources have indeed maintained that British and American intelligence services established contacts with the guerrillas, apparently many months after the war had ended. Even if this allegation is true, the Anglo-American intelligence agents could have provided no significant material aid to harried underground fighters lacking even temporarily secure bases. By 1946 at the latest, the UPA consisted of hard-pressed men (and their women allies, indispensable as scouts and messengers) relying on stealth to visit villages for provisions and information. Between operations, guerrillas often tried to pose as simple peasants. To avoid reprisals, their families endeavored to conceal their links with the insurrection. The winter of 1945-46 was very hard for these loyal UPA members. The leafless trees provided little shelter from MGB troops equipped with planes, while the snow cover made tracking easy.[1] Many nationalist partisans were forced to spend most of the winter in underground dugouts or "bunkers." Soviet penetration of the countryside, accompanied by large-scale collectivization, was inexorable. UPA groups operating in the small Ukrainian settlements in territory which remained Polish (under Communist rule) after 1945 were in an especially exposed position. At the end of 1947 the UPA command ordered them to endeavor to escape, either by posing as workers being resettled in the Donbas or by fighting their way to the American occupation zones in Germany and Austria. Apparently a considerable number of the Galician insurgents also took the latter desperate road.[2] During 1947 several hundred UPA partisans succeeded in finding asylum after traversing the length of Czechoslovakia.

By that time the remainder of the UPA had gone underground. During the winter months, at least, this frequently meant literal self-entombment in

---

[1] In early 1946 the People's Commissariat of State Security (NKGB), then in charge of Soviet police troops, was renamed the Ministry of State Security (MGB).

[2] See New York *Herald Tribune*, September 22, 1947, p. 6, which mentions the influx into the Western zones, but (in a thoroughly garbled account of the background of the nationalist movement) says that "Allied sources" suspected the UPA of collaboration with the Soviet regime. In fact, Soviet police terror extended to all Ukrainians, mainly women, in rural areas. See, for example, "Teror Enkavedivs'kykh Garnizoniv na ukraïns'kykh zemliakh" (Terror of NKVD garrisons in the Ukrainian lands), *Litopys*, Vol. IX, pp. 271-306.

bunkers. The hardships experienced in these damp, poorly lighted, ill-ventilated holes (according to survivors) were almost indescribable. After the MGB began using police dogs on a large scale, even the smell of a burning candle could betray the location of a bunker. Aside from the physical suffering, inactivity and lack of information tended to induce severe psychological depression. Still, the hardier members of the nationalist forces persisted in preparing propaganda materials for distribution after the winter had passed, and in planning small-scale attacks on police agents, "renegade" intellectuals, and collective farm officials. Determination to pursue these activities — which amounted to replying to Stalinist terror with sporadic small-group terrorism — was strengthened by two developments. Intensification of persecution of the Ukrainian Catholic Church, beginning with the arrest of Archbishop Joseph Slipyi and other members of the hierarchy (April, 1945), was a major factor. Then Soviet police, in an intensive effort to compel the Ukrainian Catholic priests and their congregations to adhere to Orthodoxy, seized church property and arrested many of the priests.[3] As noted in Chapter VII, the tinge of anti-clericalism which had marked the early OUN had faded during the war. By 1946 it was apparent that Soviet persecution of the church meant suppression of Ukrainian national traditions, particularly since Orthodox priests, imported, largely, from Russia, replaced recalcitrant Ukrainian Catholic clergy. Consequently, the UPA assumed the role of champion of religious as well as national freedom. UPA countermeasures were directed especially against Galicians who assisted the Soviet drive against the Ukrainian Catholic Church. Father Gabriel Kostelnyk, a Catholic priest who played a prominent role in securing further conversions after he had accepted Orthodoxy, was assassinated in September, 1948.

Nationalist sources did not admit UPA responsibility for this assassination, but they have freely accepted responsibility for killing Iaroslav Halan, a fairly prominent Galician writer who had long been sympathetic to Communism. After the Soviet reoccupation, Halan specialized in anti-clerical propaganda, including such publications as *With the Cross or with the Knife* and *The Twilight of the Strange Gods*, which assailed the Ukrainian Catholic Church, including the revered Metropolitan Sheptyts'kyi, and the nationalist organizations.[4] While Halan himself was an atheist (and eventually a Communist) he evidently collaborated with defectors to Orthodoxy like Kostelnyk.[5] His death was the signal for a still more intensive effort to link the nationalist underground and the Catholic Church.[6] According to a Soviet

---

[3] Pantelei D. Indichenko, "Proval agrarnoï polityky nimets'kykh fashystiv na tymchasovo okupovanoï Radians'kii Ukraïni, 1941-1944"(The Collapse of the Agrarian Policy of the German Fascists in the Temporarily Occupied Soviet Ukraine, 1941-1944) (unpublished dissertation, Kiev University, 1949), pp. 242-43; cf. especially Bohdan R. Bociurkiw, "The Uniate Church in the Soviet Ukraine," *Canadian Slavonic Papers*, V (1965), pp. 99-107.

[4] *Istoriia ukraïns'koï literatury* (History of Ukrainian Literature), Vol. II (Kiev: Vydavnytstvo Akademiï Nauk Ukraïns'koï RSR, 1957), p. 804.

[5] *Ibid.*

[6] *Ibid.*, p. 794. Cf. *Istoriia Ukraïns'koho Viis'ka* (History of the Ukrainian Army) (2nd ed.; Winnipeg: Vydavets' Ivan Tyktor, 1953), p. 813, which gives the date of Halan's assassination as October 23, 1949; Bociurkiw, "The Uniate Church," pp. 107-9.

informant, a motion picture based on this theme was shown in the East Ukraine.[7]

The increasingly drastic measures carried out by Soviet police in the countryside probably constituted an equally potent reason for bitter resistance, for a large majority of the remaining UPA fighters were of Galician peasant background. At first the principal repressive measure was quartering of police units in villages. Later, entire village populations were deported.[8] To replace the natives, settlers arrived from distant parts of the USSR. In this way, the solid support upon which the partisans depended was broken. Even where a West Ukrainian peasantry remained, the introduction of the Soviet administrative apparatus facilitated gathering information on nationalist activities. The widespread introduction of the kohkhoz (collective farm) system was intended to intensify such administrative penetration. But collectivization was a slow process, impeded by peasant passive resistance and fierce UPA attacks on imported collective farm chairmen. As late as October, 1949, Nikita Khrushchev reported that 61 percent of the peasants in the West Ukraine were in kolkhozes.[9] From this figure, even if it was not exaggerated, one can infer that even at that late date most peasants in the principal Galician mountain areas of UPA operations had not been collectivized, since collectivization was approaching completion in the large regions of the West Ukraine less suited to underground resistance.

It was not long, though, before the Soviet police apparatus brought the principal UPA leaders to bay. On March 5, 1950, the supreme commander, Shukhevych, was killed in a village near L'vov.[10] His death did not mean the end of UPA activities; but by late 1950 the remaining members of the organization were so few and harried that little reliable news concerning their activities could reach the outside world.

If one takes into account duration, geographical extent, and intensity of activity, the UPA very probably is the most important example of forceful resistance to an established Communist regime prior to the decade of fierce Afghan resistance beginning in 1979. By the mid-twenties, the Soviet regime had established an effective monopoly of force throughout nearly all of the territory then in the USSR. In the extreme reaches of Central Asia the Turkic Basmachi groups offered sporadic resistance until about 1930. In the European USSR, however, serious forceful resistance to the Soviet regime was not revived even by the extreme popular antipathy aroused by collectivization.

---

[7]Cf. *Istoriia ukraïns'koï literatury*, p. 794, and Sergei T. Danilenko, *Dorohoiu Han'by i Zrady* (On the Road of Shame and Treachery) (Kiev: "Naukovo Dumka," 1970), p. 337, on the efforts of R. A. Rudenko, chief prosecutor of the Ukrainian S.S.R., to link Uniates to the assassination during investigatory interrogations. In 1970 another "documentary film" on the Ukrainian Catholic Church was produced. See A. Leonenko, "Since the Times History Remembers...," *Liudyna i Svit*, July 1970 (excerpted in *Digest of the Soviet Ukrainian Press*, XIV (November, 1970), p. 21.

[8]Marko Boeslav, "Vlasni Syly—Dinamit i Tsement Natsiï," (One's Own Forces—Dynamite and Cement of the Nation), *Litopys*, Vol. IV, p. 134.

[9]*Pravda Ukrainy*, October 30, 1949, p. 2. See especially, David R. Marples, "The Soviet Collectivization of Western Ukraine, 1948-1949," *Nationalities Papers*, XIII (Spring, 1985), pp. 24-44.

[10]See article by P. Symonenko in *Komunist Ukraïny*, No. 2, February, 1961, pp. 82-88, excerpted in *Digest of the Soviet Ukrainian Press*, V, No. 4 (April, 1961), p. 8.

Desperate peasants driven to banditry lurked in the forests of Belorussia and western Russia. Mass uprisings occurred in the Ukraine and elsewhere, but they were suppressed before they could become organized rebellions. Somewhat more sustained opposition to Soviet rule occurred in the early stages of the Second World War. Aside from the fighting against Red partisans which the Ukrainian groups and a few Russian groups like that of Bronislav Kaminskii carried on, there was the independent and widespread rebellion of the Moslem mountaineers in the North Caucasus in the autumn of 1941. Though relatively little is known about this rebellion, its careful clandestine organization, synchronized outbreak, and effective character appear to place it among the most important anti-Soviet uprisings. The size of the populations involved—a few hundred thousand—limited the importance of the North Caucasus uprisings, however. To go farther afield, the same limitation of size has applied to other instances of vigorous and sustained rebellion against Communist regimes, such as the Tibetan and Turkestani rebellions against the Peking Chinese government or the riots in East Germany (1953) and Poland (1956). The Hungarian revolution of 1956 was, of course, far more important, involving to some degree a population of nine million, and rapidly developing a complex organization. The Hungarian revolution, however, lasted only a few weeks. In contrast, the more or less effective anti-Communist activity of the Ukrainian resistance forces lasted from mid-1944 until 1950.

It is impossible to provide a complete analysis of the factors which made protracted resistance by the UPA possible. In summary, however, they appear to have been the following: (1) favorable terrain—relatively impenetrable to large bodies of regular troops, yet close to sources of food; (2) nearly unanimous support of the rural population; (3) a fairly large nationality group (about 3,500,000, considering the Ukrainian Catholics alone) as a supporting base; (4) a very powerful—indeed fanatic—nationalist ideology; (5) a highly integrated, authoritarian organizational structure; (6) a considerable period of preparation under favorable conditions; and (7) a moderate degree of outside arms supply at the outset. Quite possibly one or more of these factors could have been absent without lessening the effectiveness of the resistance movement, but it would appear that the majority of the factors, taken together, were necessary conditions.

Granting the effectiveness of the UPA in terms of extent of resistance, what did it really accomplish? Undoubtedly the UPA was a drain on Soviet resources for a few years, but it is equally clear that this drain did not endanger the Soviet system or seriously impede its material progress. The accomplishments of the UPA must, then, be measured in political and psychological terms. Even in this regard, the record is somewhat mixed. It can be argued that UPA activities, especially the large-scale partisan warfare between 1944 and 1947, indirectly weakened Galician ability to withstand the pressure of the Soviet system. Many thousands of the most vigorous Galician youths were killed (though the UPA saved some prospective Soviet army draftees from death at the front) and a considerable portion of the Galician population was exiled. The chaotic conditions caused by the partisan movement disrupted the social fabric, thereby helping to break down institutional and family patterns which elsewhere have been impediments to complete Soviet control. On the other hand, it can be argued that the Soviet regime would in any case have imposed absolute control upon the Galician population, as evidenced by the rigor of the collectivization drive and the harsh persecution of the Church. That being the case, the UPA, perhaps at the cost of somewhat greater human suffering, provided an intangible but nonetheless extremely important psychological support for the oppressed population. It showed that there was an alternative, however desperate, to submission to totalitarian control. In the end the West Ukrainian population saw this alternative fail; but many must realize that in altered international circumstances the outcome would have been different. One can safely predict that the memory of sustained armed resistance will not die out among the West Ukrainians for many years. This memory has become a major component of the constitutive myth of national identity in this region. As a result, West Ukrainians are in a sense a people apart from most of those under Communist rule. Since this is the case, no outsider can render a final judgment as to whether UPA resistance was worth its terrible cost.

According to a principal nationalist source on the later history of the UPA, less than 10 percent of its operations took place in the Volhynian *oblasts* (Volyn' and Rovno) between mid-1946 and mid-1949.[11] While the authenticity and significance of these figures are subject to considerable doubt, other evidence also indicates that the importance for nationalist guerrillas of the Volhynian swamp and forest lands was much reduced after German withdrawal. No doubt the terrain was less suitable than the rugged Carpathians. A similar explanation may apply to the low level of nationalist partisan activity in Bukovina (Chernovtsy *oblast*). It is rather more difficult to explain why nationalist partisan activities were slight in Carpatho-Ukraine (Transcarpathia *oblast*). The rugged forested terrain of the province and its proximity to Hungary, Slovakia, and Rumania, where Communist control was not yet fully established in the 1940s would seem to have made the Carpatho-Ukraine an ideal site for extensive guerrilla operations. Some Ukrainian informants do maintain that UPA operations there were considerable, but the data cited earlier in this paragraph indicate that less than 1 percent of UPA operations during 1946-49 took place in the Carpatho-Ukraine. The considerable number of Soviet works on this oblast also provide no clue to the existence of extensive armed opposition to Soviet occupation.[12] While one cannot rely on Soviet sources as a guide to nationalist activity, their virtually complete silence in this

---

[11] *Istoriia Ukraïns'koho Viis'ka*, pp. 806-10; cf. the English version of Lev Shankovs'ky's account in *The Ukrainian Insurgent Army in Fight for Freedom* (New York: United Committee of the Ukrainian-American Organizations of New York, 1954), p. 44.

[12] The most important Soviet book on the Carpatho-Ukraine during and since the war is I. F. Evseev, *Narodnye Komitety Zakarpatskoi Ukrainy: Organy gosudarstvennoi vlasti (1944-1945)* (The People's Committees of Transcarpathian Ukraine: Organs of State Power [1944-1945]) (Moscow: Gosudarstvennoe Izdatel'stvo Iuridicheskoi Literatury, 1955). V. A. Anuchin, *Geografia Sovetskogo Zakarpat'ia* (Geography of Soviet Transcarpathia) (Moscow: Gosudarstvennoe Izdatel'stvo Geograficheskoi Literatury, 1956) is of some value (especially pp. 120-25). The Czechoslovak officials František Nemeć and Vladimir Moudry, in *The Soviet Seizure of Subcarpathian Ruthenia* (Toronto: William B. Anderson, 1955), provide an outside report on the last months of the war period, while Vasyl Markus, in *L'Incorporation de l'Ukraine Subcarpathique à l'Ukraine Soviétique, 1944-1945* (Louvain: Centre Ukrainien d'Etudes en Belgique, 1956), represents a Ukrainian nationalist viewpoint. None of these accounts indicates extensive UPA activity in the Carpatho-Ukraine, although Evseev does write of efforts to form nationalist partisan groups in the area.

instance is in marked contrast to their elliptical but revealing comments on nationalist activity north of the Carpathian range.

One circumstance which apparently made Soviet control easier in the Transcarpathian province was the division of the population during the war between "Magyarophiles" who collaborated with the Hungarian regime and the Ukrainian nationalists. To a considerable extent this division coincided with that between those who were ardent adherents of Ukrainian culture and those who looked upon themselves as "Russians." The latter group in turn largely coincided with the Orthodox, as contrasted to the Ukrainian Catholic population. These divisions implied a loss of solidarity among the rural population which, as noted above, was a prime requisite for successful nationalist guerrilla activity. It may also be—though there is scarcely any evidence on this point—that the OUN-M, entrenched in the Carpatho-Ukraine as in Bukovina, was reluctant to cooperate with the UPA, dominated as it was by the OUN-B.[13]

Probably a more significant factor was the comparatively well-established position of the Communist Party in the Carpatho-Ukraine. Under Czechoslovak administration the poverty of the region made the people receptive to Communist propaganda, which continued illegally under Hungarian rule. As noted in Chapter VII, Communists were able to develop a considerable partisan movement in the Carpatho-Ukraine during the latter period. The network of local Communists provided a foundation for the construction of a Soviet administrative apparatus with some genuinely indigenous roots, and no doubt also facilitated the formation of a network of informers in the villages. The Red partisan cadres were used in the formation of security units.[14] As a result, extensive nationalist guerrilla activity would have confronted very great obstacles; quite probably the UPA leadership, recognizing this situation, wisely refrained from devoting much of its limited resources to the Carpatho-Ukraine. Similar considerations curtailed UPA operations in the East Ukraine. For a short time during the Second World War, as a postwar Soviet work admits, some nationalist partisans operated in Kirovograd and Chernigov *oblasts*; but, apart from some raids into Zhitomir, Kiev, and Kamenets-Podolsk (now Khmel'nits'kii) oblasts, nationalist partisans do not appear to have penetrated deeply into the East Ukraine after the war.[15]

The real impact of nationalist wartime activities, mostly underground propaganda, on the East Ukraine can be better appraised in the discussion, later in this chapter, of dissidence during the 1960s and 1970s. Under the extremely harsh repression maintained by Stalin until his death in March, 1953, manifestations of such nationalist influence were scarcely to be expected. Again and again Stalinist publications emphasized that "bourgeois nationalism" was the principal enemy of the Soviet system. In the Ukraine, not only were such characterizations sharper and more frequent than elsewhere,

---

[13] An OUN-M account, *Organizatsiia Ukraïns'kykh Natsionalistiv, 1929-1954* (Organization of Ukrainian Nationalists, 1929-1954) (n.p., 1955), p. 222, does attribute the failure of nationalist partisans in the adjoining Bukovinian Carpathians in part to frictions between OUN-M and OUN-B.

[14] See John A. Armstrong, *The Soviet Bureaucratic Elite: A Case Study of the Ukrainian Apparatus* (New York: Frederick A. Praeger, 1959), pp. 108-10.

[15] *Istoriia Ukraïns'koï RSR* (History of the Ukrainian SSR), Vol. II (Kiev: Vydavnytstvo Akademiï Nauk RSR, 1958), p. 553.

they were accompanied by terrifying evidence of Stalin's animus in the suppression of churches (the Ukrainian Autocephalous Orthodox as well as the Ukrainian Catholic), compulsory collectivization of agriculture, and suppression of the intelligentsia. Three years after Stalin's death, Khrushchev admitted Stalin's hatred of the Ukrainians—whom he would have deported save for the fact that "there were too many of them and there was no place to which to deport them."[16] In the atmosphere of complete terror created by such attitudes and actions, overt nationalism could hardly be expected.

Such being the case, open nationalist expression down to the mid-1950s could occur (apart from the dwindling UPA underground) only in emigration. But even this milieu was drastically affected by the terror in the USSR. During the interwar period Ukrainian nationalist political life, even in exile, had remained anchored to reality through its close contact with large centuries-old Ukrainian populations in Poland, Czechoslovakia, and Rumania. Especially during the first postwar decade, impermeability of the Iron Curtain prevented such invigorating contact. Instead, émigré politics was carried out at first mainly among the enormous number of Ukrainians (probably exceeding one million) in the Western zones of occupation in Germany and Austria. But "normal" political reactions in this emigration were drastically affected by forced repatriation. Even today the origins of this Anglo-American policy are unclear. It admitted, however, one loophole: persons who had been resident in the areas annexed by the Soviet Union in 1939 or later were allowed to remain in the Western zones. In other words, only Ukrainians who could pass themselves off as West Ukrainians could avoid return to Soviet control, for

> Under terms of Yalta agreement US policy is to repatriate to Soviet Union all claimants of Soviet citizenship whose claims are accepted by Soviet authorities. In practice this means ... that Soviet citizens originating from within 1939 boundaries of Soviet Union are repatriated irrespective of individual wishes.... It is contrary to US policy to facilitate the involuntary repatriation of Baltic nationals ... Poles, Croats, and Slovenes ... and Slovaks.[17]

---

[16]Nikita S. Khrushchev, *The Crimes of the Stalin Era: Special Report to the 20th Congress of the Communist Party of the Soviet Union* (annotated by Boris I. Nicolaevsky) (New York: New Leader, 1956), p. 44.

[17]Acting Secretary of State Joseph Grew to the Assistant to the President's Personal Representative at Vatican City, Harold H. Tittman, Jr., July 11, 1945, in United States, Department of State, *Foreign Relations of the United States, Conference of Berlin (Potsdam), 1945*, Vol. I (Washington: Government Printing Office, 1960), p. 801. See also the *Congressional Record*, 84th Congress, 2nd Session, Vol. 102, Part 11B (Washington: Government Printing Office, 1956), p. H1884. Cf. especially Julius Epstein, *"Operation Keelhaul": The Story of Forced Repatriation* (Old Greenwich: Devin-Adair, 1973). Some additional information on this question is given in George Fischer, *The Soviet Opposition to Stalin* (Cambridge, Mass.: Harvard University Press, 1952); Alexander Dallin, *German Rule in Russia, 1941-1945: A Study of Occupation Policies* (London: Macmillan & Co., Ltd., 1957), p. 659; and Jürgen Thorwald, *Wen sie verderben wollen: Bericht des grossen Verrats* (Stuttgart: Steingruben Verlag, 1952), p. 570 ff. Interesting details from the Soviet side appear in *Pravda Ukrainy*, September 9, 1945, p. 2, and in A. Briukhanov, *Vot kak eto bylo: O rabote missii po repatriatsii sovetskikh grazhdan, vospominaniia sovetskoi ofitsera* (That's How It Was: On the Work of the Mission for Repatriation of Soviet Citizens, the Memoirs of a Soviet Officer) (Moscow: Gosudarstvennoe Izdatel'stvo Politicheskoi Literatury, 1958), pp. 62-63, 83. For a poignant Ukrainian nationalist account see V. Koval", *My Ukraïntsi!* (We Are Ukrainians!) ("Germany," 1948), pp. 70, 88-89.

Apart from the personal tragedies arising from repatriation, it had farreaching effects on the future of the nationalist emigration. Since the vast majority of the East Ukrainians were returned to the USSR, West Ukrainians became the numerically dominant element in the displaced persons (DP) camps where most émigrés lived for three or four years after the close of the war.[18] Moreover, East Ukrainians in the camps had remained only because they had told the camp authorities that they were from the West Ukraine. Even when the repatriations ceased, the fugitives understandably lacked confidence in the Allied authorities' intentions. As a result, the East Ukrainians felt themselves to be at the mercy of their West Ukrainian compatriots, who could easily report their true status. According to widespread and circumstantial rumors, West Ukrainian nationalists used the threat of such revelations to compel East Ukrainians to adhere to the nationalist cause. In some cases, it is said, nationalists also resorted to violence to control the camp administrations and maintain a monopoly of propaganda.[19]

In this competition, Stephen Bandera's followers, known after the war as the OUN-r (revolutionary), were successful in attracting most young Galician nationalist émigrés. It far outmatched the Mel'nyk followers (known by then as the OUN-s, solidarist). But the latter had important centers of support, especially in France, where Oleh Shtul' (one-time adviser to the Borovets' partisans) was the main OUN-s press spokesman.

After 1946, two forces worked to moderate the internal struggle. A major factor was the large North American population of Ukrainians. Statistics for groups like Ukrainians, not usually classed as such on immigrating into foreign countries, are notoriously inaccurate. It appears, however, that there were one-half to one million persons of Ukrainian descent in the United States at the close of the Second World War. The Canadian-Ukrainians, at that time rather more than half as many as Ukrainians in the United States, grew much more rapidly as émigrés sought permanent homes. So did the relatively small Ukrainian settlements in Australia and South America. Politically and socially Canadian-Ukrainians early took the lead, not only because of their growing numbers, but because their concentrated settlements (especially in Ontario, Sasketchewan, and Alberta) enabled them to attain strong political influence in the multiethnic Dominion.

Most of the pre-First World War immigrants in all overseas countries were peasants seeking to escape poverty and conscription in Austria-Hungary and the Russian Empire. Many of their descendants retained only vestigial

---

[18]There were over 100,000 Ukrainians in Germany and Austria two years after the war ended. Cf. Stanislaw Paprocki (a former director of the Polish Research Institute for Problems of Nationalities who was none too sympathetic to Ukrainian nationalism), "Political Organization of the Ukrainian Exiles after the Second World War" in *The Eastern Quarterly*, V (January-April, 1952), pp. 41-50; Ivan Rudnyts'kyi ("Kedryn"), a Ukrainian, published "Ukrainian Political Scene Today" in *Ukrainian Quarterly*, V, No. 4 (Autumn, 1949), pp. 300-309, and Michael Pap, "Die Probleme der ukrainischen Staatlichkeit und der Emigration," Inaugural Dissertation zur Erlangung der Doktorwürde vorgelegt der Hohen Philosophischen Fakultät der Ruperts-Carola Universität zu Heidelberg, 1948, p. 141, is valuable.

[19]See especially Stephen Baran, "TsPUE i UNDO" (The Central Representation of the Ukrainian Emigration and the Ukrainian National Democratic Union), *Ukraïns'ki Visti*, May 15, 1949, p. 2, and the attack on Baran (for his earlier criticism of the Bandera group) by Roman Il'nits'kyi in *Chas*, October 19, 1947.

links with Ukrainian fraternal associations. A small proportion, especially in Canada, was attracted by Communist organizations, but after the Second World War these faded rapidly.[20] Concomitantly, nationalist organizations increased in influence, partly because of the prestige of Dmytro Dontsov, the nationalist ideologist who apparently leaned toward the OUN-r.

A second force working to moderate émigré divisions consisted of the churches. Immediately after the war ended the Ukrainian Catholic Church and the remnants of its close ally, the Ukrainian National Democratic Union (UNDO), was an active moderating force. As the situation of East Ukrainians became more secure, the Ukrainian Autocephalous Orthodox Church in emigration played a similar role.

In June, 1948, nearly all parties, including the two branches of the OUN, acknowledged a "Ukrainian National Rada" headed by Andrew Livyts'kyi as the legitimate successor state of the Ukrainian National Republic constituted in 1917. Quickly, however, it became apparent that OUN-r participation was unstable. Surprisingly, it was the more moderate wing of the Bandera faction, headed by Nicholas Lebed' and Father John Hryn'okh, which broke with both the émigré state grouping and Bandera himself. Lebed' and Hryn'okh, claiming to be in close contact with the UPA and its political arm, the UHVR, presented the UHVR "representation in Western Europe" as an alternative supra-party body. This attracted some members of the URDP (Ukrainian Revolutionary Democratic Party), a successor to the UNDP formed by OUN-B dissidents (mainly East Ukrainians) among Borovets' partisans in 1942.

After the split in the OUN-r, those remaining with Bandera and Iaroslav Stets'ko also broke off from the National Rada; they adhered to a new "supranational" as well as "supra-state" organization, the Anti-Bolshevik Bloc of Nations (ABN). Its Ukrainian organizers traced this body to wartime Volhynia, when guerrillas from various nationalities met to form a political union. Various Eastern European and even Asian representatives, mostly representing extreme right wing positions or minority ethnic groups like the Slovaks, were constituent members. In practice, Iaroslav Stets'ko, the chairman of the ABN Central Committee, was dominant.

Such dissension, splintering, and re-combination have been characteristic of nearly all émigré politics for centuries. As the immediate hopes and concerns of the wartime period receded, such fragmentation became especially injurious for the Ukrainian national cause, however. A demonstrable need for a united Ukrainian position arose in 1950, when the American Committee for Liberation of the Peoples of Russia began planning the organization, in Munich, of émigrés from the USSR. Within a short time this organization, whose very name recalled Vlasov's "Committee for the Liberation of the

---

[20]Luka Palamarchuk, "Ukraïntsi v Kanadi" (Ukrainians in Canada), *Ukraïna* (a Soviet journal published in Moscow during the German occupation of the Ukraine) (April-May, 1943), pp. 49-51. On more recent Soviet attention to Communist-led Ukrainians in Canada, see A. M. Kolchuk, "The Past and Present of Ukrainians in Canada as Presented by a Canadian Encyclopedia," *Ukraïns'kyi Istorychnyi Zhurnal*, No. 4 (July-August, 1959), pp. 38-140 (partially translated in *Digest of the Soviet Ukrainian Press*, III, No. 10 [October, 1959], pp. 24-26); Ivan Vir, "Wide Field for Work of Slavicists," *Literaturna Hazeta*, May 5, 1959, p. 4 (partially translated in *Digest of the Soviet Ukrainian Press*, III, No. 6 [June, 1959], pp. 23-24); "8th Convention of the Society of United Ukrainians of Canada," *Pravda Ukrainy*, January 28, 1958, p. 4 (translated in *Digest of the Soviet Ukrainian Press*, II, No. 5 [March, 1958], pp. 22-23).

Peoples of Russia," established a moderately well-financed research organization, the Institute for the Study of the USSR, and an increasingly effective radio broadcasting system to penetrate the Soviet Union. Although nominally a private organization, it was clear that the Committee had generous financing to support these extensive activities; nearly two decades later, it was officially recognized that the United States Central Intelligence Agency had played a major role.

Both the connotations of the Committee's name and the strongly pro-Russian position of several of its key emissaries alienated all major Ukrainian political groups. They refused to cooperate even after the name was changed, successively, to "American Committee for Liberation from Bolshevism" and "American Committee for Liberation." Thus they left the field clear for two new parties, the "Ukrainian Liberation Movement" and the "Union of Ukrainian Federalist Democrats," to enjoy the benefits of the American-backed Munich center. Since several leaders of these two parties had collaborated with Vlasov, many Ukrainian nationalists condemned them as mere fronts for Russian émigrés. A major result was the recognition by all elements of the Ukrainian nationalist leadership that they needed stronger political influence in the North American capitals. In particular, the reinvigorated Ukrainian Congress Committee (initially organized in 1940) was supported, with varying degrees of consistency and enthusiasm, by virtually the entire range of Ukrainian factions in the United States. Apart from considerable success in attaining symbolic recognition in the form of U.S. congressional resolutions, reports, and authorizations for monuments, the Ukrainian Congress Committee may have influenced the shift of Radio Liberation (later Radio Liberty) policies, providing greater scope for non-Russian elements.

A second period in the impact of Ukrainian nationalism on the postwar Soviet Ukraine was initiated by two dramatic events in 1953: Stalin's death and, not coincidentally, an armistice in Korea. For the émigré nationalist parties, the latter event effectively terminated the expectation that a United States-USSR clash would loosen the Soviet grip on the Ukraine. Exaggerated hopes, aroused during the 1952 presidential campaign, of a "roll-back of the Iron Curtain" had already been dashed by the Eisenhower administration's complete rejection of forcible support for Berlin rioters protesting harsh Soviet measures in June, 1953. At the same time, Stalin's departure seemed to be opening up new vistas for nationality expression in the USSR. Throughout the spring a campaign against unfair treatment of non-Russians, centering on the Ukrainian Party apparatus, was orchestrated. Many aspects of this campaign are still mysterious. It is virtually certain that the immediate instigator was the dreaded police supervisor, L. P. Beria; but in the Ukraine the campaign put A. I. Kirichenko, the first native Ukrainian to hold that post, in the office of Party first secretary.[21]

Kirichenko was an obvious ally of Nikita Khrushchev, indeed the first example of a long line of Ukrainian apparatus officials whom Khrushchev used to consolidate his control of the Communist Party of the Soviet Union. But Beria was soon executed, and hints of nationality oppression by Russians as quickly vanished. Evidently Khrushchev realized that the later decades of Stalin's rule had so entrenched Russian values in the nominally Leninist regime

---

[21]Armstrong, *The Soviet Bureaucratic Elite*, pp. 145-46.

that anyone hoping to lead it had to adhere to them. Khrushchev's most successful years had been spent directing the Party in the Ukraine. Yet he denied that he even spoke Ukrainian well—thereby implicitly rejecting any Ukrainian antecedents in his ethnically mixed native region of Kursk. Soon it became apparent that Khrushchev's aim was to consolidate the Soviet Union around a solid core of East Slavs, with Belorussians and Ukrainians regarded as junior partners of the Russians.[22]

Khrushchev's policy measures were so erratic that at times they afforded leeway for very circumscribed nationalist expression; at other times he countenanced fierce suppression of core elements of nationalist identity. As noted above, his secret speech to the 1956 Party Congress explicitly denounced Stalin for his hatred of Ukrainians. Yet, as nominal supervisor of the Partisan Staff of the Ukraine, Khrushchev had a tremendous stake in promoting the myth of wartime Red partisan heroism, and correspondingly in eradicating the nationalist guerrilla myth. Moreover, Khrushchev did not appear to have had Stalin's inclination (in his later years) to use the Russian Orthodox Church to suppress other religious bodies in the Ukraine. In the late 1950s, Khrushchev apparently was a sincere but bitter atheist. Thus visitors—Ukrainian Christians and Russian Orthodox alike—were denied access to the prime symbol of Ukrainian Christianity, the Pecherska Lavra (Monastery of the Caves) in Kiev. Khrushchev was evidently also sincere in trying to eradicate the image of Stalin as a benevolent leader. Against a powerful coalition of Party ideologues and oligarchs (evidently headed by M. A. Suslov, who feared that Stalin was an essential component of the new Soviet myth), Khrushchev, during his later years of power, sporadically sheltered literary figures intent on denouncing the evils of the Stalin era. The most famous, Alexander Solzhenitsyn, was a strong Russian nationalist; but the range of Stalin's crimes made it possible for cautious proponents of almost any ethnic element to find a fulcrum for efforts to pry concessions by attacking the dead dictator.

Such leverage was not immediately available to Ukrainians, probably because the Hungarian Revolution, following quickly on Khrushchev's secret speech, led the apparatus to tighten its scrutiny in areas bordering on Hungary. Nevertheless, efforts to rehabilitate dissident writers of the Stalin era, notably Nicholas Khvylovyi, who in the 1920s had openly advanced the slogan "away from Moscow," began at the session of the Ukrainian Writers Union of January, 1957.[23] This was unsuccessful, but the film director Alexander Dovzhenko, who more positively emphasized Ukrainian culture, was rehabilitated. Obviously, any effort to incorporate the wartime nationalist

---

[22]*Ibid.*, pp. 146-50; John A. Armstrong, "The Ethnic Scene in the Soviet Union," in Erich Goldhagen (ed.), *Ethnic Minorities in the Soviet Union* (New York: Praeger, 1968), pp. 14-21.

[23]Much of the following discussion is based on Kenneth C. Farmer, *Ukrainian Nationalism in the post-Stalin Era: Myth, Symbols, and Ideology in Soviet Nationalities Policy* (The Hague: Martinus Nijhoff, 1980), see especially p. 83. Cf. Michael Browne (ed.), *Ferment in the Ukraine: Documents by V. Chornovil, I. Kandyba, L. Lukyanenko, V. Moroz and Others* (New York: Praeger, 1971); *Dissent in the Ukraine: The Ukrainian Herald, Issue 6*, Introduction by Yaroslav Bilinsky (Baltimore: Smoloskyp Publishers, 1977); and Yaroslav Bilinsky, *The Second Soviet Republic: The Ukraine after World War II* (New Brunswick: Rutgers University Press, 1964, and subsequent editions); Orest Subtelny, *Ukraine: A History* (Toronto: University of Toronto Press and Canadian Institute of Ukrainian Studies, 1988) is very good for all periods, but (p. 512 ff) is especially useful for developments after the Second World War.

resistance theme would have been harshly rejected—and there is no evidence that the writers of the late 1950s and early 1960s admired this theme or even understood it. Instead, cultural promoters of Ukrainian themes in the Soviet Ukraine before Stalin's terror became the heroes of the new literary generation. By exercising sufficient caution, the writers could turn also to core elements of the constitutive myth of Ukrainian identity, especially the Zaporozhian Sich.[24] Even cultivation of the Ukrainian language—the central accomplishment of those working within the Soviet system during the mid-1920s—could be defended cautiously. Whereas low-level Russian officials in the Ukraine under Khrushchev continued efforts to reduce instruction in the native language as "overburdening" students, at the top of the Ukrainian Party there was once again evidence of sympathy for its expansion as a medium for textbook publication.[25]

The possible connection between high-level official protection and efforts to reduce Russification is most intriguing in the case of Ivan Dziuba. A thirty-four-year-old writer already well-known in Ukrainian circles, Dziuba produced a remarkable book-length critique of Russification. Essentially it was an idealized but detailed interpretation of Lenin's nationalities policy. Dziuba contended this policy had been implemented in the Ukraine during the 1920s, but completely distorted by Lenin's successors. By December, 1965, when Dziuba openly addressed copies to the Ukrainian Party Central Committee, these successors included Khrushchev, who had been ousted in Moscow fourteen months previously.[26] In the meantime, for reasons never specified, Kirichenko had disappeared from the ruling circles, and in 1963 his successor as Party chief in Kiev, Nicholas V. Podgorny, had been promoted to the Moscow Secretariat where he became a key figure in ousting Khrushchev. His replacement as Ukrainian Party chief in 1965, like Podgorny a man of Ukrainian origin who had risen through the Kharkov apparatus, was Peter E. Shelest. Apparently Shelest did not condemn Dziuba's critique outright, for he is said to have sent copies to the provincial Party secretaries.[27]

A few months earlier, Dziuba had already become embroiled with Ukrainian Party ideological authorities, headed by Central Committee Secretary A. D. Skaba, who had held the corresponding position in Kharkov oblast under Podgorny. The occasion, in the spring of 1965, was the first major series of arrests of Ukrainian literary figures since Stalin's death. Apparently the repressive action was part of a broader campaign by Khrushchev's successors. At their head was another Ukrainian apparatus alumnus, Leonid I. Brezhnev. Although born in the Ukraine, Brezhnev was of Russian origin; he had risen through the Dniepropetrovsk apparatus, relatively remote from national literary circles in Kiev and Kharkov. As a loudly proclaimed hero of Soviet military resistance to the German conquest of the Ukraine, Brezhnev had at least as great a stake as Khrushchev in denigrating the nationalist struggle for

---

[24]Farmer, *Ukrainian Nationalism*, pp. 90-93.

[25]Bohdan Krawchenko, *Social Change and National Consciousness in Twentieth-Century Ukraine* (New York: St. Martin's Press, 1985), pp. 231 ff., 238; cf. Farmer, *Ukrainian Nationalism*, p. 122.

[26]Ivan Dziuba, *Internationalism or Russification? A Study in the Soviet Nationalities Problem* (3rd ed., New York: Monad Press, 1974), see especially the preface by M. I. Holubenko, pp. xvi-xvii.

[27]*Ibid.*, cf. Farmer, *Ukrainian Nationalism*, pp. 170-71.

independence, and less concern for attacking Stalin's record.[28] Brezhnev continued Khrushchev's policy of introducing Ukrainian apparatus figures to All-Union posts, but relied on a narrower circle associated mainly with the Dnepropetrovsk apparatus.[29]

In ideological control, the major change in Moscow, in any case, had been enhanced power for Suslov, who apparently had engineered Khrushchev's replacement by Brezhnev. Although Suslov obviously had little sympathy for Ukrainian national expression, the decisions to crack down on Ukrainian figures so soon after Khrushchev's ouster were, it seems, part of a broader strategy to resume control of literary expression which Khrushchev had tolerated in the interest of intensifying criticism of Stalin. The key victims were Andrew Siniavskii and Julius Daniel, during the early 1960s writers of major Russian-language works sharply criticizing Stalin. After lengthy interrogations, they were brought to trial in February, 1966; the main charge (which they admitted) was sending manuscripts for publication abroad as early as 1963.[30] Thenceforward, official charges against all types of dissent tended to center on the charge of association with foreign powers.

This trend was particularly dangerous for Ukrainian national writers, because Soviet propaganda had concentrated for so many years on the evils of "bourgeois nationalism," including by definition all nationalist émigrés. Yet, although Dziuba had defended the arrested Ukrainian writers, at first he was not subjected to the most insidious accusation of trafficking with émigrés. He regained an editorial position and continued (as did Solzhenitsyn in Moscow) to refute openly his official detractors. In July, 1968, however, his protest to the Central Committee was published in book form as *Internatsionalizm chy Russifikatsiia?* (Internationalism or Russification?) by the Ukrainian nationalist publishing house "Suchastnist'" in Munich, and appeared in English in London the same year. Dziuba (like Solzhenitsyn) disavowed such use of his manuscript, and was temporarily allowed to remain at liberty.[31]

In the meantime, developments were by no means entirely discouraging to Ukrainian culture. A politically inconspicuous but incrementally massive element was publication of the twenty-six volumes of *Istoriia Mist i Sil Ukraïns'koï RSR* (History of the Towns and Villages of the Ukrainian SSR). Volumes began to appear in 1964, but clearly the immense work of lining up collaborators, examining local archives, and coordinating draft submissions began years earlier. The net result was the most comprehensive collection of local history of any Soviet republic, perhaps of any country. Despite strict adherence to Soviet myths, the sheer accumulation of information in the collection on all periods of Ukrainian history could not fail to impress its readers (i.e., those competent in Ukrainian) of the grandeur of their history. Moreover, it was a sign of the change from Stalin's era (when major publication projects were halted in mid-course) that shifts in policy could not interrupt the

---

[28]K. S. Hrushevoi, *Togda, v Sorok Pervoi...* (Then, in '41...), (2nd ed., Moscow: Voennoe Izdatel'stvo, 1974).

[29]Joel C. Moses, "Regional Cohorts and Political Mobility in the USSR: The Case of Dnepropetrovsk," *Soviet Union*, V (1976), pp. 63-89.

[30]"The Trial of Sinyavsky and Daniel," *New York Times Magazine*, April 17, 1966, based on notes surreptitiously taken at the trial.

[31]Farmer, *Ukrainian Nationalism*, p. 195.

series. Although one-third of the volumes were still incomplete in 1972, all appeared during the following two years. At that point, a member of the Ukrainian Academy of Sciences, under the title "A Chronicle of Our Native Land," pointed out that "inspiration for this publication (some 2,500 signatures) came from workers of our republic. The Central Committee of the Communist Party of the Ukraine supported their initiative."[32]

Possibly Skaba's replacement by F. D. Ovcharenko in March, 1968, had something to do with successful completion of this monumental tribute to the Ukraine. His first prominent posts were as secretary of the Party committee of the Ukrainian Academy of Sciences and director of the cultural and scientific section of the Ukrainian Central Committee. Many observers saw Shelest's hand in the cadres change. But it is also possible that Shelest was the direct patron of the *Istoriia Mist i Sil*, as of other Ukrainian cultural projects. Certainly by the late 1960s he—and his close collaborators—were at work on *Ukraïno nasha Radians'ka* (O Ukraine, Our Soviet Land), which appeared in Kiev in 1970. Like the *Istoriia*, but on a brief, popularized level, this book denounced "bourgeois nationalists" and praised the Soviet system; but it focused on the Ukraine, past and present, in a manner bound to excite national pride.

With Moscow increasingly alarmed by the first wave of Polish strikes, following just two years after massive Soviet military suppression of Czechoslovak liberalization, such encouragement of national feeling in the largest non-Russian nation of the Bloc was unacceptable. Shelest's little book could not be allowed to remain the "ultimate criterion of correctness for some of our scholars, propagandists and artists in interpreting certain past and present events."[33] In May, 1972, Shelest was summarily removed from the First Secretary post. The move had been prepared a year and a half earlier by replacing Shelest's protégé heading the Ukrainian KGB with a figure pliant to Moscow.[34] In the interval two sinister developments foreshadowed the First Secretary's fall: the arrest of a Belgian subject of Ukrainian ancestry, whose forced "confession" implicated several important dissident intellectuals as spies for the OUN; and in early 1972, quickly following on this KGB concoction, a broad purge of cultural figures, especially heads of Party and state educational institutions and editors—i.e., peripheral apparatus figures who, under Shelest, had sheltered Ukrainian culture. Pressure was so intense that several prominent dissidents recanted, among them Dziuba, who publicly "thanked" his jailors for "benefitting" him by pointing out the errors in *Internationalism or Russification*?[35] Given his poor health and the deadly threat of

---

[32]M. Suprenenko, "Chronicle of Our Native Land," *Literaturna Ukraïna*, April 26, 1974, p. 3, excerpted in *Digest of the Soviet Ukrainian Press*, XVIII (June, 1974), pp. 19-20; successive volumes were reviewed by John A. Armstrong in *American Historical Review*, LXVI (1971), pp. 1570-73; LXVII (1972), pp. 546-47; LXVII (1973), p. 716; and LXIX (1974), pp. 193-94. A Russian edition of *Istoriia Mist i Sil* appeared in the USSR several years later.

[33]"Concerning the Faults and Errors of One Book Editor," *Komunist Ukraïny*, No. 4 (April, 1973), pp. 77-82, full text in *Digest of the Soviet Ukrainian Press*, XVII (May, 1973), pp. 1-6.

[34]Farmer, *Ukrainian Nationalism*, p. 189.

[35]Holubenko, Preface to Dziuba, p. xxii; Dziuba letter to editor, *Literaturna Ukraïna*, November 9, 1973, p. 4, full text in *Digest of the Soviet Ukrainian Press*, XVII (December, 1973), pp. 22-23.

implication in conspiracy with émigré nationalists, this abject end of a decade of literary struggle for Ukrainian assertion is humanly understandable.

What was the real significance of that decade for the constitutive myth of Ukrainian identity? Clearly, apart from marginal incidents in the West Ukraine, support, even covert, for the kind of nationalism which had characerized the wartime movement was absent. At one level, the regime's devious efforts to condemn Ukrainian writers and officials for foreign contacts indicates a calculation that memories of the predominantly Galician nationalists of 1941-42 were a liability for anyone trying to revive national sentiment. As Kenneth A. Farmer has aptly put it, the regime still finds "bourgeois nationalism" to be a "very potent 'condensation symbol'" for condemning all its enemies at once — "fascists," "imperialists," "Zionists," and even "Maoists."[36] At another level, however, the frantic effort to associate "away from Moscow" ideas with all the bugbears of the Soviet past and present demonstrates that, in the long run, "younger brother" Slavs will be denied any meaningful national expression. It is highly significant that even the Ukrainian branch of the Society for the Preservation of Historical and Cultural Monuments declined in prestige after Shelest. Its "idealization of the past" was officially attacked during the late 1970s, the very years when the Russian counterpart of this society was achieving unprecedented influence.[37]

Entirely apart from real contacts, there was a certain natural convergence between the evolution of intellectual nationalists in the 1960s and the wartime movement. One resemblance was their turning to underground activity. For the writers, this consisted mainly of *samvydav* (clandestine circulation of materials denied official outlets — equivalent to Russian *samizdat*). Another similarity was the cult of heroism, up to the point of martyrdom. For example, Valentyn Moroz — perhaps the most talented literary dissident — wrote that it was immoral to begin dissenting at all if one (like Dziuba) was ultimately unwilling to sacrifice every value, including life itself, to deny the regime the symbolic satisfaction of one's recantation.[38] A third resemblance was stress on the Ukrainian language, particularly preservation of its purity from corruption by Russian forms. A more essential similarity, going to the heart of Ukrainian identity, was the way in which the 1960s dissidents ultimately came to stress the Cossack component of Ukrainian history, as 1930s nationalists like Taras Borovets' had done from the beginning.

Nevertheless, differences between 1960s dissidents and their West Ukrainian predecessors remained significant. On the whole, the 1960s group welcomed cooperation with all residents of the Ukraine, regardless of their language. Dziuba called for Jewish-Ukrainian cooperation; Viacheslav Chornovil and General Peter Hryhorenko worked closely with civil-rights dissidents

---

[36]Farmer, *Ukrainian Nationalism*, pp. 195-97.

[37]Roman Solchanyk, "Politics and the National Question in the Post-Shelest Period," in Bohdan Krawchenko (ed.), *Ukraine after Shelest* (Edmonton: Canadian Institute of Ukrainian Studies, 1983), p. 14; see also K. Stetsiuk, "To Preserve for Our Descendants," *Radians'ka Ukraïna*, August 10, 1976, p. 4, excerpted in *Digest of the Soviet Ukrainian Press*, XX (October, 1976), pp. 26-27.

[38]Farmer, *Ukrainian Nationalism*, pp. 173-75.

in Russia.³⁹ Despite the strong strain of romanticism, the flight from reason implied by "thinking with the blood" was totally alien to the 1960s dissidents. Perhaps the obvious futility of violence goes a long way to explain the writers' passive resistance; but, in any case, they completely rejected the cult of violence. Very similar differences shaped the OUN underground's "learning experience" when its activists encountered the East Ukrainian milieu during the Second World War; on their own ground, East Ukrainian dissidents of the 1960s had less to unlearn.

It is not surprising that developments in the East Ukraine paralleled a certain decline of the OUN in emigration. The closure of opportunities in 1953-56, when the United States and other Western countries rejected armed assistance to Soviet Bloc rebels was one cause. Yet, although deprived of significant opportunities to influence events within the East Ukraine, the Nationalists were not immune from covert attacks by the KGB. The most serious of these struck the OUN-r. On October 15, 1959, Bandera died suddenly in his home near Munich. Two years later, a Ukrainian was arrested for poisoning him; ultimately a German Federal Republic court found the accused guilty on the basis of his confession.⁴⁰ Direction of both the OUN-r and the ABN passed to Stets'ko until his own death in 1987. Yet the Soviet regime continued to regard the emigration as a significant threat. In the late 1960s several Ukrainian scholars, such as Dr. R. H. Symonenko, specialized in studying "bourgeois nationalism" in the historical section of the Ukrainian Academy of Sciences—under the direction of A. D. Skaba in his new post.⁴¹

The most dynamic, and potentially the most significant changes among Ukrainians in North America corresponded to the maturation of a generation completely educated in English-speaking countries. Most of this generational change became evident after the Shelest era, as young Ukrainian-Americans and Ukrainian-Canadians (reinforced by a small but growing number of Ukrainian specialists of non-Ukrainian origin) became a major component of the corps of East European specialists. A veritable flood of substantial scholarly publications supplemented the scanty literature hitherto available in English (though the classics of Ukrainian historiography remained, for the most part, untranslated). This important scholarly advance was assisted and articulated by new institutions: the Harvard Ukrainian Research Institute; the University of Alberta Canadian Institute of Ukrainian Studies; and significant smaller centers in Ontario. These developments brought Ukrainian studies into the mainstream of North American scholarship, thereby enhancing both their academic utility and the prestige of Ukrainian culture.

The continued work of the Ukrainian Academy of Sciences in America (UVAN) and the Shevchenko Scientific Society linked these advances to an older generation. But some of the older controversies were also perpetuated. As the 1980s drew to a close, vigorous UHVR activities—which earlier had, to

---

³⁹*Ibid.*, p. 165.

⁴⁰*New York Times*, October 17, 1959, p. 5; November 18, 1961; *ABN Correspondence* (November-December, 1961), pp. 1-3.

⁴¹Personal observations of the author at the XIII International Congress of Historical Sciences, Moscow, August, 1970; "The General Meeting of the Divisions of the Academy of Sciences of the Ukrainian SSR," *Visnyk Akademii Nauk Ukrains'koï RSR*, No. 6 (June, 1972), pp. 59-60, excerpts in *Digest of the Soviet Ukrainian Press*, XVII, No. 2 (February, 1973), pp. 24-25.

be sure, played a significant part in reconciling OUN ideology to East Ukrainian tendencies — disturbed many outside of neo-Nationalist circles. A relative decline of the Ukrainian Congress Committee (its influential leader, Lev Dobriansky, had departed as United States Ambassador to the Bahamas) may have diminished the ability of Ukrainians to speak with a single voice in Washington, particularly in regard to Radio Liberty. Procedures against Ukrainian immigrants alleged to have been war criminals, and, more important, sweeping and undemonstrable allegations by certain publications and former prosecutors, produced excessive defensiveness among some articulate elements of the Ukrainian émigré communities. Such hypersensitivity tended, in turn, to exacerbate the problem of influencing agencies and opinion outside the Ukrainian communities.[42]

Such incompatible trends in emigration life curiously correlated, chronologically, with a period of confusion in Soviet politics in the Ukraine. Between 1972 and 1982, V. V. Shcherbitskii supervised a period of relative stability, characterized, as noted earlier, by suppression of intellectual activity. In 1982, M. A. Suslov's death, along with Brezhnev's increasing infirmities, may have begun a new period. In view, however, of the short terms of Iurii V. Andropov and K. U. Chernenko as General Secretaries, it is hard to draw firm conclusions about their policy directions. But it is clear that, from 1985 on, General Secretary M. S. Gorbachev has downgraded the "Dniepropetrovsk" coterie and Shcherbitskii in particular, ultimately ousted in September 1989.[43]

Gorbachev began loosening central controls as a by-product of his effort to stimulate the economy. His policy of *glasnost'* ("openness"), like Khrushchev's disclosure of Stalin's misdeeds, provided opportunities for submerged national dissent. In several regions, this ferment produced drastic upheavals. Demonstrations, unprecedented in scope, proved the pent-up strength of Estonian and Latvian insistence on preserving their national distinctiveness against Russian immigration and linguistic encroachment. Throughout 1987, Kazakh protests (occasionally violent) demanded retention of preferential quotas for the indigenous population. More serious disturbances occurred in Armenia and Azerbaidzhan during 1988. Hitherto accounted the strongest supporters of Moscow among major Soviet nationalities, Armenians vociferously demanded revision of unfair Transcaucasian boundaries. Retaliatory pogroms by Azerbaidzhani Moslems unleashed a spiral of violence and disorder. Although between two historically antagonistic ethnic groups, this shocking conflict inevitably impaired the credit of the Moscow regime. A brutal Soviet army suppression of Georgian protestors, followed later in the spring of 1989 by intra-Moslem riots in Uzbekistan, demonstrated the

---

[42]See chapters in Yury Boshyk (ed.), *Ukraine during World War II: History and Its Aftermath, A Symposium* (Edmonton: Canadian Institute of Ukrainian Studies, 1986); and review of this book by John A. Armstrong, *American Historical Review*, XCII (1987), 713-14.

[43]See especially Yaroslav Bilinsky, "Shcherbytskyi, Ukraine, and Kremlin Politics," *Problems of Communism*, XXXII (July-August, 1983), 1-20, who points to evidence that Shcherbitskii's position was weakening in Brezhnev's later years. Cf. Mark Beissinger, "Ethnicity, the Personnel Weapon, and Neoimperial Integration: Ukrainian and RSFSR Party Officials Compared," *Studies in Comparative Communism*, XXI (1988), 76, 85, who points out that, although pre-Gorbachev appointments had already decreased the proportion of Ukrainian *oblast* secretaries in the Ukraine, Gorbachev's efforts to break up local patronage coteries further diminish the Ukrainian proportion.

insecurity of Soviet order. Nor could the increasingly shrill Russian nationalism of *Pamiat'* be curbed even by repeated denunciations in official organs.

Amid such turmoil, Ukrainian voices, although not entirely absent, were unusually restrained. A major reason, perhaps, was the extent to which active dissidents had been persecuted in the preceding decade. A few who had made their peace with the regime, like Vitalyi Korotych, editor of the Moscow magazine *Ogonek*, had attained influential posts offering scope for advocating change, as long as it remained moderate. Both motivations fit in with the regime's determination—possibly even stronger under Gorbachev than his predecessors—to maintain solidarity in the core of the Soviet system, the East Slav nations.

In this atmosphere, the most persistent manifestation of Ukrainian national traditions has apparently been religious. Even in the mid-1970s an official publication complained that urbanization—expected to enhance secularization—was not making atheistic propaganda any easier. Rapid statistical urbanization was accompanied by more "sectarian" (i.e., non-Orthodox) religious activity, because rural migrants resided in suburbs where they maintained or even deepened their religious attachments.[44] In the West Ukraine, persistence of Ukrainian Catholic (Uniate) attachments was equally evident. Concerned with establishing foreign contacts, even with the Vatican, the Gorbachev regime relaxed the harshest measures against Uniates. The response was a pious manifestation which presented an embarrassing problem for regime propagandists. On the anniversary of the Chernobyl atomic power plant disaster (which Gorbachev's *glasnost'* policy tried to discuss frankly), peasants in Hrushiv (L'vov *oblast*) reported an apparition of the Virgin on the balcony of the village chapel. Within weeks immense crowds gathered—in a region of hills and swamps which had been a stronghold of guerrilla resistance during the 1940s.[45] Instead of merely condemning the "improbable" report, a Moscow correspondent cautioned against violating the freedom of conscience of the pious crowd.[46]

The religious trends just noted are important because they constitute some of the few positive indicators of mass adherence to national traditions, as contrasted to the large body of evidence on intellectuals' concern for the Ukrainian way of life. At the close of the summary of wartime experience (Chapter XII), it was concluded that, in the East Ukraine, the "essential mass remained uncommitted." Given the paucity of evidence, especially for the East Ukraine, one cannot be sure whether this conclusion still holds. In view of the intense pressure on Ukrainians to adopt a junior partnership relation in the "family"

---

[44] B. Perevezev, "Specific Features of Urban Conditions," *Liudyna i Svit*, No. 10 (October, 1975), pp. 28-30, excerpts in *Digest of the Soviet Ukrainian Press*, XX, No. 4 (April, 1976), pp. 26-27.

[45] According to *Istoriia Mist i Sil Ukraïns'koï RSR: L'vivs'ka Oblast'* (Kiev: Holovna Redaktsiia Ukraïns'koï Radians'koï Entsiklopediï, 1968), p. 317, "bourgeois nationalists" killed the collective farm chairman in Hrushiv during the war period. Incidentally, this kind of local information — for whatever reasons it was published—could make the *Istoriia Mist i Sil* a treasurehouse for scholars correlating nationalist claims and Soviet admissions of losses.

[46] "'Miracle' in Grushevo," *Literaturnaia Gazeta*, August 19, 1987, excerpts in *Current Digest of the Soviet Press*, XXXIX, No. 36 (1987), p. 19; "The Inertia of Simplification," *Moskovskie Novosti*, September 13, 1987, condensed in *Current Digest of the Soviet Press*, XXXIX, No. 39, p. 24.

of East Slav "brothers," considerable Russification might be expected, however. A recent critic suggests that young Ukrainians refer to the Soviet Union as "Russia," and asks if that indicates the direction one is obliged to take along the road to "Soviet peoplehood."[47] Certainly urbanization will facilitate Russification by eroding village strongholds of national customs. Linguistic statistics and other quantitative behavioral indicators, while inconclusive for the long term, do indicate small changes in this direction. The emergence during the 1960s of a vocal, self-sacrificing literary dissidence, partially supported by high officials of Ukrainian origin, certainly demonstrates that Russification policies may backfire. As an elite manifestation of adherence to Ukrainian traditions, however, the dissidence of the 1960s and 1970s resembles the nationalist movement of the Second World War, apart from the West Ukraine. The small bits of evidence of religious revival, on the other hand, suggest the persistence of mass phenomena which may perpetuate the tradition of the peasant mass as the unconquerable custodian of national identity. During the late summer of 1989, traditional rural adherence to national identity was heavily reinforced by mass demonstrations in L'vov for restoration of the Ukrainian Catholic Church. Reports from visitors indicated a surprising revival of openly expressed national sentiments, not only in the West Ukraine, but in Kiev. Evidently the Ukrainian nationalist movement stands on the threshold of a new era.

---

[47]Solchanyk in Krawchenko, *Ukraine after Shelest*, p. 19.

Appendix
Populations of
Ukrainian Cities

APPENDIX: POPULATIONS OF UKRAINIAN CITIES / 243

POPULATIONS OF UKRAINIAN CITIES
(in thousands)

	1926[a]			1939[a]		1941–42			1926 Ratio of Ukrainians to Russians	1941–42 Ratio of Ukrainians to Russians	Ratio of increase of proportion of Ukrainians to Russians (Column 8: Column 7)
	Total	Ukrainians	Russians	Total	Total	Ukrainians	Russians				
Kiev[b]	513.8	216.6	125.5	846.3	352.0	282.0	50.2		1.73	5.6	3.2
Kharkov[e]	417.3	160.2	154.4	833.4	450.0	290.0	150.0		1.04	1.9	1.8
Dniepropetrovsk[d]	232.9	83.8	73.4	500.7	234.2	164.1	52.0		1.14	3.16	2.8
Poltava[e]	92.0	62.8	8.1	130.3	68.7	64.0	4.7		7.75	13.6	1.8
Kirovograd[f]	66.5	29.6	16.6	100.3	68.1	62.4	4.0		1.78	15.6	8.8
Kherson[g]	58.8	21.1	21.2	97.2	61.4	50.7	8.4		.99	6.0	6.1
Zhitomir[h]	76.7	28.5	10.5	95.1	40.1	24.5	2.5		2.71	9.8	3.6
Vinnitsa[i]	58.0	23.9	8.0	92.9	35.6	24.1	3.8		2.99	6.34	2.1
Kamenets-Podolsk[j]	32.1	14.4	2.3	72.4	12.0	10.6	0.5		6.30	21.2	3.4
Chernigov[k]	35.2	20.1	3.6	67.4	30.0	27.0	3.0		5.58	9.0	1.6
Uman'[l]	44.8	19.3	2.0	....	20.0	18.9	0.5		9.65	38.2	4.0
Pavlograd[m]	18.8	11.5	2.6	....	....	(94.1%)	(5.3%)		4.43	17.8	4.0

a Statistics for 1926 are from Union of Soviet Socialist Republics, Tsentralnoe Statisticheskoe Upravlenie, *Recensement de la Population de l'URSS*, XI, XII, XIII (Moscow, 1929): XI, 76–77 (Zhitomir) and 162–63 (Chernigov); XII, 27 (Kiev), 20–21 (Vinnitsa), 204–5 (Kamenets-Podolsk), 210–11 (Uman'), 299 (Poltava), and 310–11 (Kharkov); XIII, 13–14 (Kirovograd), 36–37 (Kherson), 248–49 (Dniepropetrovsk), and 308–9 (Pavlograd). The 1939 figures are from Frank Lorimer, *The Population of the Soviet Union: History and Prospects* (Geneva: League of Nations, 1946), pp. 250–53.

b *Nova Doba*, September 6, 1942, p. 3; *Nastup*, September 6, 1942, p. 2 (from *Dnipropetrovs'ka Hazeta*); Leontii Forostivs'kyi, *Kyïv pid vorozhymy okupatsiiamy* (Kiev under Enemy Occupations) (Buenos Aires: Mykola Denysiuk, 1952), p. 44. All of these reports are based on the city administration census of April 1, 1942. After that date, the population declined still more, but no later breakdown by nationalities is available.

c *Krakivs'ki Visti*, February 24, 1942, p. 2, based on a census taken by Professor Sosnovyi in December, 1941, evidently at the instance of the city administration. Only the proportion (65%) of the Ukrainians in the total population is given, but it has been assumed that the great majority of the remainder was Russian. The total population declined rapidly in the succeeding years, reaching a low of 200,000 after the German reconquest in March, 1943, of which 80 percent were Ukrainian according to their own declaration (interview with Mayor Semenenko in *L'vivs'ki Visti*, May 23–24, 1943).

d *Nastup*, February 22, 1942, p. 2, based on a city administration census. The figures include the suburb of Amur-Dniepropetrovsk. See also *Krakivs'ki Visti*, February 17, 1942, p. 5. Another report (*Ukraïns'ka Diisnist'*, February 1, 1942, p. 1) gives a total of 350,000, of which 300,000 were Ukrainian.

e *Ukraïns'kyi Visnyk*, November 1, 1942, p. 7. Only the proportion of Ukrainians in the total (93.1%) is given, but, as in the case of Kharkov, it may be assumed that by the date of the count the vast majority of the remainder was Russian.

f *Ukraïns'kyi Visnyk*, June 14, 1946, p. 7; *Ukraïns'ka Diisnist'*, July 10, 1942, p. 1; *Nastup*, July 12, 1942, p. 2, all based on census of the city administration.

g *Deutsche Bug-Zeitung*, July 22, 1942, p. 2; *Ukraïns'kyi Visnyk*, September 6, 1942, p. 6.

h *Nastup*, December 27, 1941, p. 3. About 15.5 percent of the population was Polish; *Krakivs'ki Visti*, October 24, 1941, p. 2, based on a count by the police passport division, lists 2,000 Russians and 7,000 Poles in a total of 42,000.

i *Nastup*, February 1, 1942, p. 2, based on a census of January 1, 1942. About 6 percent of the total was Polish.

j *Krakivs'ki Visti*, January 25, 1942, p. 2, based on a census of the local administration.

k *Krakivs'ki Visti*, May 3, 1942, p. 4; *L'vivs'ki Visti*, April 11, 1942, p. 2, based on the first statistical reports of the city administration.

l *Ukraïns'kyi Visnyk*, November 1, 1942, p. 7.

m *Ukraïns'ka Diisnist'*, February 10, 1943, p. 1.

Note on Sources

Sources for the study of Ukrainian nationalism during the Second World War are extremely varied. Published personal narratives, always important, have increased in number and length during the last thirty years. The footnotes refer heavily to such materials, and a few of the generally significant published memoirs are listed in the selective bibliography which follows this section.*
Ukrainian memoirs, like most others, however, have serious defects as sources for the history of political events. On the nationalist side, memoirs are usually highly colored by the views or prejudices of the authors, since the tempestuous Ukrainian nationalist politics have rarely been conducive to impartial reflection. Moreover, the flight of the nationalists from Eastern Europe as the Soviet armies advanced resulted in the loss of many of the documents which might have enhanced the reliability of their memoirs. In many cases the personal circumstances of the writers have made it impossible for them to check their narratives against documents available since the war. Soviet memoirs of wartime events, on the other hand, suffer from restrictions imposed by the official line.

Fortunately, it is in many cases possible to check postwar narratives against contemporary records. In this respect, documents from the German archives are most valuable. Some of these documents, originally composed by Ukrainian nationalist leaders themselves, provide direct evidence of nationalist thinking and activity. Most of the documents concerning aspects of Ukrainian nationalism are reports by German political, military, or police officials; they are of course subject to error due to misinformation or negligence of the authors. Occasionally, the desire of an official of the Nazi dictatorship to put himself in a better light before his superiors, or to advance a policy he preferred, led to intentional distortion. Since the reports were for official use only, and as a rule were written by officials who were personally not deeply involved in Ukrainian affairs, the element of intentional coloring is comparatively minor.

A second very important body of contemporary sources consists of published material. Some publications were issued clandestinely; while the authors

---

*Since full facts of publication are provided for the first use of each published item *in each chapter*, the reader can locate references on special topics without it being necessary to list all such items again in the selective bibliography.

may have had numerous reasons for distortion, at least they were not subject to German censorship. By far the larger amount of available contemporary printed material, however, was published under German censorship. Consequently, numerous facts had to be omitted and many views colored to make them acceptable to the Germans. German censorship was not iron-clad, however; the numerous ways in which publications in territories occupied by the Germans could express real views and present facts have been touched upon throughout this study. Because of censorship contemporary published sources present comparatively little material of direct political relevance. They do, however, present valuable information on the closely related topics of religious, cultural, and economic activity. Moreover, they describe the overt activities of individuals in specific places at specific times; it is often possible to check such facts in postwar descriptions of covert political activities against the framework obtained from these contemporary published sources. The extent to which facts alleged by the postwar informant conform to the contemporary sources permits one to make a partial evaluation of the reliability of the informant. Contemporary Soviet sources on nationalist activities are much sparser, but for some events they provide valuable information which shifts in Soviet policy have caused to be deleted from postwar publications.

Oral Sources

Important as are the contemporary sources, a rounded picture of the wartime nationalist movements could not have been obtained without the aid of unpublished accounts by participants. Some of these are in the form of manuscripts—a few have since been published—made available during the early 1950s to the author of this study. Most unpublished accounts were obtained, however, through oral interviews. For reasons which should be clear to the reader of this study, it has been necessary to preserve the anonymity of the informants. The code system adopted makes it possible for the author to determine the source of each statement, however, and in many cases it will be possible for him to suggest persons whom an inquirer might approach for further information on a given topic.

The interviews were conducted during 1952-53 in Europe, Canada, and the United States. Before beginning the interviews, the author made a thorough examination of the greater part of the German documents and the published materials, contemporary and memoir. He was also fortunate enough to secure advice and information from a number of scholars who had worked on related studies of the Ukraine and of wartime Eastern Europe. These preliminary investigations enabled him to form an over-all picture of the topic. For many sections of the study, he could establish a reliable account lacking only a limited number of details. This approach was essential for the success of the interviews. Prospective informants were more inclined to furnish information when they learned that the author had acquired the background knowledge of subjects which were of intense personal interest to them. The preliminary investigation also enabled the author to determine some of the key questions, or at least to know which areas of his topic needed probing. An equally useful result of this investigation was that the knowledge acquired enabled the author to assess the validity of many statements while the informant was still available, so that dubious statements could be questioned or further information elicited.

Before the stage of interviewing was reached, however, prospective informants had to be selected and located. If a number of interviewers with ample time had been engaged in the study, it might have been desirable to interview *all* or a considerable portion of émigrés from the East Ukraine and large numbers from the West Ukraine. Such an approach might have yielded valuable information of a statistical nature. The émigrés are in many respects an atypical selection from the entire population, however. It is difficult, if not impossible, to evaluate responses given years after the events by a large number of interviewees on complicated subjects like wartime attitudes. Moreover, such extensive interviewing would have been quite impossible for an individual investigator with a limited number of months at his disposal.

Under the circumstances, the only practical approach was to concentrate on interviewing persons who had had key roles in the events studied. As described above, the preliminary investigation enabled the author to determine the principal areas on which information was needed. It also enabled him in many cases to determine who had held a position which enabled him to acquire such information. The postwar Ukrainian press frequently indicated whether such persons were still alive and gave some hint concerning their present whereabouts. With this information, exact addresses could usually be obtained. Worthwhile informants, whose value the author had not previously recognized, were provided directly by interested organizations and individuals. It is felt, however, that it would have been most unwise to have relied exclusively or predominantly upon such secondhand channels for obtaining a list of informants. Few persons, even among active nationalists, were familiar with all or most of the aspects of the study and were rarely acquainted with a very large proportion of the possible informants. Reliance on interested organizations and individuals for contacts would also, at least to some degree, have resulted in a slanting of the approach, since such channels consciously or unconsciously select informants sympathetic to them.

In addition to a number of Germans, Russians who had lived in the Ukraine and Ukrainians who desired continued union of the Ukraine and Russia (both categories are referred to in subsequent paragraphs as "Russophiles") were interviewed. Both Germans and Russophiles were chosen and located in a manner similar to that employed in the case of Ukrainian nationalists, although of course German and Russian individuals and organizations, rather than Ukrainian nationalist ones, usually served as intermediaries.

Because informants had been selected on the basis of their probable ability to provide information on specific aspects of the study, no generalized questionnaire was employed. Where possible a "non-directive" approach, designed to induce the interviewee to volunteer information he thought important, was used during the first stage of the interview. When specific information desired was not furnished spontaneously, however, detailed questions were put, and if necessary cross-examination employed. If the initial discussion had convinced the informant that the author was engaged in an impartial effort to establish the truth, and that his investigation made it necessary for him to be detailed and persistent in his inquiries, such "detective" methods were not usually resented, although of course some informants avoided revealing desired information.

The informants were frequently busy persons who could not spare an indefinite amount of time. This was especially the case since all rendered their assistance without financial compensation. In some cases an informant could give only a half-hour to answer a few especially important questions, in others several meetings totaling many hours could be arranged.

It would be impossible to give the total number of informants, since frequently at a gathering or in an organizational office a very large number of persons were encountered who furnished a useful hint or an impression of the wartime scene. In the case of seventy-three informants, however, it was felt worth while to conduct more or less systematic interviews and to prepare summary records of the information furnished, classified under the names of the interviewees. A large majority of these records are cited by code number in the footnotes of this study; since one informant frequently furnished more than one interview, the total number of code numbers exceeds seventy-three.

Of the seventy-three informants referred to above, fourteen were former German officials who had been involved in Ukrainian affairs during the war. Of these eleven had been active in the East Ukraine (and in some cases in the West Ukraine as well, and frequently in Berlin in connection with policy toward the Ukraine); three had significant experience in the West Ukraine only. Nine Russophiles were interviewed. Two were pre-1939 émigrés who did not visit the East Ukraine during the war but were active in politics concerning it. The other seven were residents of the Soviet East Ukraine until 1941 or later. Twenty-nine of the interviewees were West Ukrainian nationalists. Of these nineteen were not active in the East Ukraine; their information concerned the background of political activity in the West Ukraine and among the emigration. The remaining ten had extensive experience in the East Ukraine during the war. Seven of the interviewees were East Ukrainian nationalists who had emigrated before 1939. Of these only one was active in the East Ukraine during the war, but the others had important information on nationalist political developments in the emigration or in the West Ukraine, and several were able, through extensive contacts, to gather much information on the wartime East Ukraine. Finally, there were fourteen East Ukrainian interviewees who had remained in the East Ukraine until 1941 or later.

Information obtained from interviews and unpublished manuscripts constitutes an essential, although not a predominant part of the material used in this study. Among the informants were a considerable proportion of the leading personalities mentioned in the text. Moreover, in a very large number of cases information could be obtained from all or several of the conflicting groups concerning events in which they participated. A special effort was made to obtain all sides of a controversial issue, when adequate published sources were not available for one or more groups of participants, and as a rule this effort was successful. It is regrettable that the names of the informants cannot be given in connection with specific items of information which they provided. In many cases, even indication of the point of view represented by the anonymous informant would have provided a clue to his identity because the number of possible witnesses is frequently very limited.

While the use of oral informants for the study of recent political situations involves the disadvantage of inability to cite sources, there are numerous compensating advantages. Subjects, like the present one, which involve widespread clandestine activities, can scarcely be analyzed unless the participants themselves furnish information. Moreover, even when a published memoir exists, it cannot be called to account for discrepancies or asked for additional information as can the living witness. Beyond these advantages, there is the intangible but very real asset of contact with the actors of the drama studied, a contact which gives the author a "feel" for the situation and insights into the psychology of his subjects which would be difficult to achieve in any other fashion.

Above all, in turning to oral informants, timeliness is essential. The most obvious reason is that many available shortly after the events studied, die or disappear soon afterward. Even by the time the second edition of this work appeared (only eight years after its initial publication) at least nine of my informants had passed away, and others would have been unreachable. Now, thirty-seven years after my interviews, nearly all crucial eyewitnesses are forever unavailable, personally, to historians. A more subtle reason is the dimming and distortion of memories as time passes. Throughout the work I have hinted at this problem, and in this note on sources have suggested ways I sought to overcome it. All the same, I am sure my interviews would have been more productive if they had been made very quickly after the close of the Second World War. This was not possible for me, although in fact my interviewing was as timely as that of larger projects relying on information from Soviet defectors. Nor does the overall effort to utilize oral reports from wartime émigrés compare unfavorably, in timing, with later projects for interviewing emigrants from the USSR. Looking back, however, I can only counsel the future analyst of oral information to proceed with all deliberate speed.

Contemporary Documents

Unfortunately, the availability of official archives tends to vary, chronologically, inversely to the availability of oral informants. Often, government documents are designedly withheld until the death of most participants in the events treated. In this respect, the student of wartime Ukrainian nationalism has been exceptionally fortunate. In 1951 I worked briefly for the War Documentation Project, cataloging selections from the immense mass of captured German documents then held by the U.S. Government in Alexandria, Virginia. Even cursory examination of these documents aroused my interest in the Ukrainian nation, and acquainted me with the parameters of its problems, so well known to German specialists but in the early 1950s practically unknown to Americans. My work for the War Documentation Project was subject to security classification. Entirely apart from legal considerations, people of my generation regarded fidelity to their pledge of confidentiality as a matter of personal honor. Consequently, in the first and second editions of this book, I did not use any data derived from documents still classified. After the book had been virtually completed, I returned to work for the War Documentation Project on analytical studies of Soviet partisans (reported in condensed form in *Soviet Partisans in World War II* [1964], after official declassification of the studies and their documentary sources). Although the subject was tangential to Ukrainian nationalism, in my book I was still careful not to use positive information gained in the analyses. Nevertheless, in a purely negative sense some of this information enabled me to avoid incorrect assumptions or formulations which I might otherwise have employed in writing.

More important, my general familiarity with the German documents enabled me to seek out publications and declassified documents which treated the same topics as those still classified. Counseled by various colleagues, notably the War Documentation Project director, the late Fritz T. Epstein, I discovered that a high proportion of the most important German documents referring to Ukrainian nationalism had been declassified shortly after the Second World War in connection with war criminal trials. Portions of those documents dealing with Ukrainian nationalists had frequently been omitted from the massive publication series of the International Military Tribunal and related agencies as not relevant to the judicial proceedings. But, once declassified, the entire documents selected by these agencies were usually placed (often in photographic or mimeographed copies) in various depositories open to scholars, as follows:

National Archives of the United States, Washington:

PS (Paris—Storey, referring to documents collected at Paris for the Nuremberg Trials by Colonel Robert G. Storey, an American officer).

EC Economic (referring to Nuremberg collection on cases arising in connection with economic matters).

USSR Exhibit (referring to documents presented by the Soviet prosecution staff at Nuremberg).

Library of Congress, Washington (reproductions available, often, in other major research libraries):

HH Himmler File (Manuscript Room).

NO Nuremberg, Organizations (referring to documents collected for proceedings against Nazi organizations).

NOKW (Nuremberg, Oberkommando der Wehrmacht, referring to documents collected for trials of German army officers).

Yiddish Scientific Institute, New York:

Occ E (referring to all documents on German occupation in Eastern Europe).

Centre de Documentation Juive Contemporaine, Paris:

CXL (referring to all documents on Eastern Europe).

The vast majority of captured German documents have been returned to the Federal Republic of Germany. Since the 1960s, however, microfilm copies on deposit in the U.S. National Archives have been available to scholars as follows:

T designates the overall series of captured documents, followed by a two- or three-digit numeral indicating the German institutional provenance of large collections of documents. Very approximate guides to these collections are available at the Archives, but, though indispensable, these guides often do not provide adequate clues to specific microfilm reels, among the tens of thousands in the German document series.

Basically, the researcher must be guided by knowledge of the German institutions (SS agencies, military formations, etc.) involved in particular Ukrainian affairs she or he is investigating. The situation is complicated by the fact that pertinent documents often appear in numerous copies, widely scattered in the German institutional files. In these circumstances, a most valuable guide is the series *Litopys UPA*, published by Ukrainian scholars concerned with the nationalist guerrilla organization. Volumes VI and VII of the series contain careful reprints of several hundred German documents, including German translations of many wartime Ukrainian items. The great majority of the *Litopys* German reprint items were assembled in the Federal Republic of Germany archives from the originals now on deposit in Karlsruhe and Freiburg/Breisgau. In a very few instances I was unable to collate these reprinted items with counterparts in the National Archives **T** collections; but in the vast majority of cases I could verify *Litopys* reliability and include a *Litopys* page reference as well as a **T** reel designation. Conversely, I was able to discover a large number of relevant documents (mostly not directly pertinent to the UPA) in the National Archives **T** collection which do not appear in the *Litopys*. Consequently, about half of my sources declassified since 1963 do *not* contain *Litopys* references.

In addition to the official collections discussed above, I was able to use a small number of documents from private collections, as follows:

German documents in the UHVR archive, New York, reprinted in *Litopys*, Vols. VI and VII.

Letter from Bauer to Schenck and Bizantz (all officials in the Generalgouvernement), dated August 18, 1943. In the possession of Liubomyr Makarushka.

Pastoral letter of Metropolitan Andrei Sheptits'kyi, July, 1941. Single printed sheet in the possession of Volodymyr Stakhiv.

Proclamation of leading citizens of Kiev recognizing Ukrainian state proclaimed in L'vov, June 30, 1941, dated July 6, 1941. Typescript in the possession of Volodymyr Stakhiv.

Proclamation of the Ukrainian state in L'vov, June 30, 1941. Typewritten copy in the possession of Volodymyr Stakhiv.

252 / NOTE ON SOURCES

UHVR, document among uncataloged captured materials in the Hoover Library on War, Revolution, and Peace, Palo Alto, California, obtained for me by Alexander Dallin.

Contemporary Newspaper and Periodical Files

Deutsche Bug-Zeitung. Amtsblatt des Generalkommissars für den Generalbezirk Nikolajew. Nikolaev, semiweekly. March, 1942-November, 1943, in Library of Congress.

Der Deutsche in Transnistrien. Odessa, weekly. July, 1942-January, 1944, in Library of Congress.

Deutsche Ukraine Zeitung. Lutsk, daily. January, 1942-January, 1944, in Library of Congress.

Klich (The Call). Berlin, weekly. August-December, 1942, in Institut für Weltwirtschaft, Kiel.

Komunist (The Communist). Kiev, daily.* October, 1939-November, 1941 (numerous gaps), in New York Public Library and Library of Congress.

Krakauer Zeitung. Cracow, daily. November, 1939-February, 1945, in Library of Congress.

Krakivs'ki Visti (Cracow News). Cracow, daily. January-August, 1942, in Library of Congress; January, 1940-October, 1943, and July, 1944-April, 1945, in Institut für Weltwirtschaft, Kiel.

L'vivs'ki Visti (L'vov News). L'vov, daily. January, 1942-March, 1944, and May-June, 1944, in Institut für Weltwirtschaft, Kiel.

Nastup (Attack). Prague, weekly. January, 1940-December, 1943, in Institut für Weltwirtschaft, Kiel.

Natsionalist (The Nationalist). Prague, monthly supplement to *Nastup*. January, 1940-December, 1943, in Institut für Weltwirtschaft, Kiel.

Nova Doba (The New Era). Berlin, weekly. February 15, 1942, Christmas, 1943, and March-December, 1943, in Institut für Weltwirtschaft, Kiel.

---

*After the fall of Kiev to the Germans in September, 1941, *Komunist* was published for a time in Saratov, then in Moscow (see K. Litvin, "Slavnyi shliakh" [Glorious Path], *Radians'ka Ukraïna*, July 15, 1945, p. 3). *Sovetskaia Ukraina* (see below) also continued as a Soviet publication, but I have not been able to determine its place of publication.

Nove Ukraïns'ke Slovo (The New Ukrainian Word). Kiev, daily. August 31, September 3, 11, 14-21, 1943, in Library of Congress.

Pravda Ukrainy (Truth of the Ukraine). Kiev, daily. August, 1944-December, 1946 (numerous gaps), in Library of Congress.

Radians'ka Ukraïna (The Soviet Ukraine). Kiev, daily. August, 1944-December, 1946 (numerous gaps), in Library of Congress.

Sovetskaia Ukraina (The Soviet Ukraine). Kiev, daily. August-November, 1941 (numerous gaps), in New York Public Library.

Ukraïns'ka Diisnist' (Ukrainian Reality). Prague, semimonthly. November, 1940-March, 1944, and June, 1944-April, 1945, in Institut für Weltwirtschaft, Kiel.

Ukraïns'kyi Visnyk (The Ukrainian Messenger). Berlin, irregular (monthly, semimonthly, and weekly at different times). January, 1940-April, 1945, in Institut für Weltwirtschaft, Kiel.

Volyn' (Volhynia). Rovno, semiweekly. January 1, 1943-November 18, 1943, in Library of Congress.

Za Ukraïnu (For the Ukraine). Berlin, semiweekly. January-February, 1945, in Institut für Weltwirtschaft, Kiel.

Selected Bibliography

Abshagen, Karl. *Canaris, Patriot und Weltbürger*. Stuttgart: Union Deutsche Verlagsgesellschaft, 1949.

Armstrong, John A. "Collaborationism in World War II: The Integral Nationalist Variant in Eastern Europe," *Journal of Modern History*, XL (September, 1968), 306-410.

———. *The Soviet Bureaucratic Elite: A Case Study of the Ukrainian Apparatus*. New York: Frederick A. Praeger, 1959.

———. (ed.). *Soviet Partisans in World War II*. Madison: University of Wisconsin Press, 1964.

Bandera, Stepan (Stephen). "V desiatu richnytsiu stvorennia Revoliutsiinoho Provodu OUN" (On the Tenth Anniversary of the Creation of the Revolutionary Directorate of the OUN) *Surma* (The Trumpet) (February-March, 1950), 1-8.

Baran, Stepan (Stephen). *Mytropolyt Andrei Sheptyts'kyi* (Metropolitan Andrew Sheptyts'kyi). Munich: Vernyhora, Ukraïns'ke Vydavnyche Tovarystvo, 1947.

Bilinsky, Yaroslav. *The Second Soviet Republic: The Ukraine after World War II*. New Brunswick: Rutgers University Press, 1964.

Bociurkiw, Bohdan B. "The Uniate Church in the Soviet Ukraine," *Canadian Slavonic Papers*, VII (1965), 89-113.

Borovets', Taras. *Armiia bez derzhavy: Spohady* (An Army without a State: Reminiscences). Winnipeg: Volyn', 1981.

Borys, Jurij. *The Sovietization of Ukraine, 1917-1923. The Communist Doctrine and Practice of National Self-Determination*. Edmonton: Canadian Institute of Ukrainian Studies, 1980.

Boshyk, Yury (ed.). *Ukraine during World War II: History and Its Aftermath, a Symposium*. Edmonton: Canadian Institute of Ukrainian Studies, 1986.

Chartorys'kyi, Mykola C. *Vid Sianu po Krym: Spomyny uchasnyka III podhidnoï grupy-Pivden'* (From the San to the Crimea: Memoirs of a Participant in the Southern Task Force). New York: Howerla, 1951.

Chubai, Mstyslav Z. *Reid organizatoriv OUN vid Popradu po Chorne More* (The Raid of the Organizers of the OUN from Poprad to the Black Sea). Munich: Tsitsero, 1952.

Conquest, Robert. *Harvest of Sorrow: Soviet Collectivization and the Terror Famine*. New York: Oxford University Press, 1986.

Dallin, Alexander. *German Rule in Russia, 1941-1945: A Study of Occupation Policies*. London: Macmillan & Company, Ltd., 1957.

Danilenko, Sergei T. *Dorohoiu Han'by i Zrady* (On the Road of Shame and Treachery). Kiev: "Naukovo Dumka," 1970.

Dmytruk, K. E. *S krestom i trezubtsem* (With Cross and Trident). Moscow: Izdatel'stvo Politicheskoi Literatury, 1979.

Dmytryshyn, Basil. *Moscow and the Ukraine, 1918-1953: A Study of Russian Bolshevik Nationality Policy*. New York: Bookman Associates, 1956.

Doroshenko, Dmytro. *History of the Ukraine*. Translated by Hanna Keller. Edmonton: The Institute Press, Ltd., 1939.

Entsyklopediia Ukraïnoznavstva (Encyclopedia of Things Ukrainian). Edited by Zenon Kuzelia and Volodymyr Kubiiovych. Munich: Naukove Tovarystvo im. Shevchenka, 1949.

Farmer, Kenneth C. *Ukrainian Nationalism in the Post-Stalin Era: Myth, Symbols and Ideology in Soviet Nationalities Policy*. The Hague: Martinus Nijhoff, 1980.

Fedorov, Oleksii. *Podpol'nyi obkom deistvuet* (The Underground Oblast Committee in Action). Literary editor, Evg. Bosniatskii. Moscow: Voennoe Izdatel'stvo Ministerstva Vooruzhennykh Sil Soiuza SSR, 1950.

Forostivs'kyi, Leontii. *Kyïv pid vorozhymy okupatsiiamy* (Kiev under Enemy Occupations). Buenos Aires: Mykola Denysiuk, 1952.

Halushko, E. M. *Narysy istoriï ideolohichnoï ta orhanizatsiinoï diial'nosti KPZU v 1919-1928 rr.* (Outline of the History of the Ideological and Organizational Activity of the Communist Party of the Western Ukraine in 1919-28). L'vov: Vydavnytstvo L'vivs'koho Universytetu, 1965.

Heike, Wolf-Dietrich. *The Ukrainian Division "Galicia," 1943-45: A Memoir.* Ed. Yury Boshyk. Toronto: The Shevchenko Scientific Society, 1988.

Heyer, Friedrich. *Die Orthodoxe Kirche in der Ukraine von 1917 bis 1945.* Köln-Braunsfeld: Verlagsgesellschaft Rudolf Müller, 1953.

Hilberg, Raul. *The Destruction of the European Jews.* Chicago: Quadrangle Books, 1961.

Hrushevs'kyi, Michael. *A History of the Ukraine.* Edited by O. J. Frederiksen. Introduction by Professor George Vernadsky. New Haven: Yale University Press, for the Ukrainian National Association, 1941.

Il'nyts'kyi, Roman. *Deutschland und die Ukraine, 1934-1945: Tatsachen europäischer Ostpolitik, ein Vorbericht.* 2 vols. Munich: Osteuropa Institut, 1955.

Istoriia Mist i Sil Ukraïns'koï RSR (History of Towns and Villages of the Ukrainian SSR). 26 vols. Kiev: Holovna Redaktsiia Ukraïns'koï Radians'koï Entsyklopediï, 1964-74.

Istoriia Ukraïns'koho Viis'ka (History of the Ukrainian Army). 2nd ed. Winnipeg: Vydavets' Ivan Tyktor, 1953.

Kostiuk, Hryhory. *Stalinist Rule in the Ukraine: A Study of the Decade of Mass Terror (1929-39).* New York: Frederick A. Praeger, 1960.

Kovpak, Sidor. *Vid Putivlia do Karpat* (From Putivl' to the Carpathians). Literary editor, Ie. Herasimov. Kiev: Ukraïns'ke Derzhavne Vydavnytstvo, 1946.

Krawchenko, Bohdan. *Social Change and National Consciousness in Twentieth-Century Ukraine.* New York: St. Martin's Press, 1985.

_____ (ed.). *Ukraine after Shelest.* Edmonton: Canadian Institute of Ukrainian Studies, 1983.

Lawrynenko, Jurij. *Ukrainian Communism and Soviet Russian Policy toward the Ukraine: An Annotated Bibliography.* New York: Research Program on the USSR, 1953.

Lebed', Mykola (Nicholas). *UPA: Ukraïns'ka Povstans'ka Armiia* (UPA: The Ukrainian Insurrectionary Army). Presove Biuro UHVR, 1946.

Leibbrandt, Georg (ed.). *Ukraine.* Berlin: Bücherei des Ostraumes, n.d.

Litopys ukraïns'koï povstans'koï armii (Chronicle of the Ukrainian Insurrectionary Army). 9 vols. Toronto: Vydavnytstvo Litopys UPA, 1977-83.

Luckyj, George S. N. *Literary Politics in the Soviet Ukraine, 1917-1934*. New York: Columbia University Press, 1956.

Lysiak, Oleh (ed.). *Brody: Zbirnyk stattei i narysiv* (Brody: A Collection of Articles and Sketches). Munich: Bratstvo kol. Voiakiv Pershoï UD UNA, 1951.

Markus, Vasyl. *L'Incorporation de l'Ukraine Subcarpathique à l'Ukraine Soviétique, 1944-1945*. Louvain: Centre Ukrainien d'Etudes en Belgique, 1956.

Martynets', V. *Ukraïns'ke pidpillia vid UVO do OUN: Spohadi i materiialy do peredistorii ta istoriï ukraïns'koho organizovanoho natsionalizmu* The Ukrainian Underground from the UVO to the OUN: Memoirs and Materials Concerning the Prehistory and the History of Organized Ukrainian Nationalism). Winnipeg, 1949.

Matla, Zynovii. *Pivdenna pokhidna hrupa* (The Southern Task Force). Munich: Tsitsero, 1952.

Mazepa, Izaac. *Ukraïna v ohni i buri revoliutsiï, 1917-1921* (The Ukraine in the Fire and Storm of the Revolution, 1917-1921). 3 vols. Munich: Prometei, 1950-51.

Medvedev, Dmitrii. *Sil'nye dukhom* (The Strong in Spirit). Moscow: Voennoe Izdatel'stvo Ministerstva Soiuza SSR, 1951.

Mirchuk, Petro. *Akt vidnovlennia ukraïns'koï derzhavnosty, 30 chervnia 1941 roku* (The Act of Renewal of Ukrainian Statehood, June 30, 1941). New York: Holovna Uprava Organizatsiï Oborony Chotyr'okh Svobid Ukraïny, 1952.

Motyl, Alexander J. "The Rural Origins of the Communist and Nationalist Movements in Wołyń *Województwo*, 1921-1939." *Slavic Review*, XXXVII (September, 1978), 412-20.

_____. *The Turn to the Right: The Ideological Origins and Development of Ukrainian Nationalism, 1919-1929*. Boulder: East European Monographs, 1980.

_____. "Ukrainian Nationalist Political Violence in Inter-War Poland." *East European Quarterly*, XIX (March, 1985), 45-55.

Nalyvaiko, Nykon. "Legiony v natsional'nykh viinakh" (Legions in National Wars), *Narodna Volia* (The People's Will), October 27, 1949, p. 2; November 3, 1949, p. 3.

Organizatsiia Ukraïns'kykh Natsionalistiv, 1929-1954 (Organization of Ukrainian Nationalists, 1929-1954), 1955.

Ortyns'kyi, Liubomyr. "Druzhyny Ukraïns'kykh Natsionalistiv (DUN)" (The Brotherhoods of Ukrainian Nationalists [DUN]). *Visti Bratstva kol. Voiakiv 1. UD UNA* (News of the Brotherhood of Former Soldiers of the 1st Ukrainian Division of the Ukrainian National Army) (June-July, 1952), 4-5.

OUN u Viini (The OUN in the War). Information Section of the OUN (UNR), April, 1946.

Pan'kivs'kyi, Kost'. *Vid derzhavy do komitetu* (From State to Committee). New York: Zhyttia i Mysli, 1957.

Pidhainy, Oleh S. *The Formation of the Ukrainian Republic*. Toronto: New Review Books, 1966.

Potichnyi, Peter, and Yevhen Shtendera (eds.). *Political Thought of the Ukrainian Underground, 1943-1951*. Edmonton: Canadian Institute of Ukrainian Studies, 1986.

La Renaissance nationale et culturelle en Ukraine de 1917 aux années 1930. Paris: Institut National des Langues et Civilisations Orientales, 1986.

Rudko, Vasyl' ("R. Lisovyi"). "Rozlam v OUN" (The Split in the OUN), *Ukraïns'ki Visti* (Ukrainian News), May 23, 1949, p. 3; October 20, 1949, p. 3; October 23, 1949, p. 3; October 27, 1949, p. 3; November 3, 1949, p. 3; November 6, 1949, p. 3.

Rudnyts'ka, Milena (ed.). *Zakhidnia Ukraïna pid Bol'shevykamy* (The West Ukraine under the Bolsheviks). New York: Naukove Tovarystvo im. Shevchenka v Amerytsi, 1958.

Rudnytsky, Ivan L. (ed.). *Rethinking Ukrainian History*. Edmonton: Canadian Institute of Ukrainian Studies, 1981.

Saunders, David. *The Ukrainian Impact on Russian Culture, 1750-1850*. Edmonton: Canadian Institute of Ukrainian Studies, 1985.

Shankovs'kyi, Lev. *Pokhidni hrupy OUN* (March Groups of the OUN). Munich: Vydavnytstvo "Ukraïns'kyi Samostiinyk," 1958.

Shevelov, George Y. "The Language Question in the Ukraine in the Twentieth Century." *Harvard Ukrainian Studies*, XI (June, 1986), 71-171.

Shtul', Oleh ("O. Shuliak"). *V im'ia pravdy: Do istoriï povstanoho rukhu v Ukraïni* (In the Name of Truth: On the History of the Insurrectionary Movement in the Ukraine). Rotterdam, 1947.

Stakhiv, Ievhen (Eugene) ("E. Pavliuk"). "Borot'ba ukraïns'koho narodu na skhidno-ukraïns'kykh zemliakh, 1941-1944: Spomyny ochevydtsia i uchasnyka" (The Struggle of the Ukrainian People in the Eastern Ukrainian Lands, 1941-44: Memories of an Eyewitness and Participant), in *Kalendar Provydinnia na 1947 rik. Stovaryshennia Ukraïns'kykh Katolikiv v Amerytsi* (Calendar for 1947 of the Providence Society of Ukrainian Catholics in America). Philadelphia: Ameryka, 1947.

———. "Geneza evoliutsii OUN" (Genesis of the Evolution of the OUN), *Ukraïns'kyi Prometei* (Ukrainian Prometheus), Nos. 44, 45, 46 (1955).

Stepovyi, Iurko. *Syn Zakarpattia: Ukraïns'ke revoliutsiine pidpillia v Kyievi 1941-1942 r.* (A Son of Transcarpathia: The Ukrainian Revolutionary Underground in Kiev 1941-1942). Munich, 1947.

Stets'ko, Iaroslav. *30 chervnia 1941: Proholoshennia vydnovlennia derzhavnosty Ukraïny* (June 30, 1941: Proclamation of the Renewal of Statehood of the Ukraine). Toronto: League for the Liberation of Ukraine, 1967.

Subtelny, Orest. *Ukraine: A History*. Toronto: University of Toronto Press and Canadian Institute of Ukrainian Studies, 1988.

Sullivant, Robert S. *Soviet Politics and the Ukraine, 1917-1957*. New York: Columbia University Press, 1962.

Szporluk, Roman. "West Ukraine and West Belorussia," *Soviet Studies*, XXXI (January, 1979), 76-98.

Thorwald, Jürgen. *Wen sie verderben wollen: Bericht des grossen Verrats*. Stuttgart: Steingrüben-Verlag, 1952.

Vynnychenko, Volodymyr. *Vidrodzhennia natsiï: Istoriia ukraïns'koï revoliutsiï, marets' 1917 r.-hruden' 1919 r.* (The Rebirth of a Nation: A History of the Ukrainian Revolution, March, 1917-December, 1919), 3 vols. Vienna, 1920.

Index

Abramovych (Nikanor), see Nikanor, Bishop
Abwehr, contacts with nationalists, 23, 51-52, 81*n*; see also Canaris, Admiral
Action Française, 12
Administrators as nationalists, 185-87
Agrarian question, attitudes of URDP and UNDP on nationalization, 193; nationalism and, 11, 91-93, 123, 189-90, 214
"*Akt*" (OUN-B proclamation in L'vov, June 30, 1941), 56-61, 91
Alexander, Archbishop, 147, 152, 154-55
Alexius, Archbishop, 148-51, 153, 156-58, 196
All-Ukrainian Aid Committee (Vseukraïns'kyi Komitet Dopomohy), 168
All-Ukrainian Congress of Ukrainian Independists, 92
All-Ukrainian Cooperative Bank, see Ukraïnbank
All-Ukrainian Cooperative Society (Vseukraïns'ka Kooperatyvna Spilka), 169
American Committee for Liberation of the Peoples of Russia (later American Committee for Liberation from Bolshevism and American Committee for Liberation), 229-30
Anatole, Archibishop, 148
Andriievs'kyi, Dmytro, 135; background of, 22
Andropov, Iu. V., 237
Anglo-American allies, nationalist attitude toward, 129-30
Anthony (Abashidze), Archbishop, 148
Anthony (Martsenko), Archbishop, 147, 160*n*
Anti-Bolshevik Bloc of Nations (ABN), 229, 236
Arkypenko, Eugene, 140*n*, 193
Arlt, Fritz, 33, 111-12, 138-39
Armija Krajowa (Polish Home Army), 112
Austro-Hungarian Empire, influence of, on Ukrainian nationalism, 11-12
Autocephalous Orthodox Church in Poland, 147
Autocephalous Orthodox Church in Ukraine, see UAPTs
Autonomous Orthodox Church in Ukraine, see Ukrainian Autonomous Orthodox Church

Babak, Theodore, 126*n*
Bahazii, Volodymyr, 74, 83-84, 165-66
Bandera, Stephen, 37-38, 43, 56-57, 59, 60*n*, 68*n*, 129, 133-34, 137-38, 228-29, 236
Bandera faction, see OUN-B
Baran, Stephen, 44
Baranivs'kyi, Anthony, 77, 103
Baranovs'kyi, Iaroslav, 22, 26, 38, 135*n*
Baranovs'kyi, Roman, 22
Basil, Metropolitan, see Lypyns'kyi, Viacheslav
Bazar, OUN-M activity in, 77, 194
Benjamin, Archbishop, 147*n*, 150
Berger, Gottlob (SS Obergruppenführer), 129
Beria, Lavrenti, 230
Bessarabia, nationalism in, 49, 62; Soviet Union in, 49
Beyer, Hans Joachim, 25*n*, 64
Bidar, Roman, 74
Bohatyrchuk, Theodore, 140
Bohatyrchuk, Volodymyr, 157, 168
Boiko, George, 197
Borkenau, Franz, 114
Bormann, Martin, 32*n*, 136*n*
Borovets', Taras, 70-72, 102-4, 108-15, 133-34, 194, 212, 235
Brezhnev, Leonid I., 232, 233, 237
Brotherhoods of Ukrainian Nationalists, 52
Buchko, Bishop John, 41
Bukovina: nationalism in, 62, 212; OUN in, 48, 62, 65; Soviet Union in, 44-45
Bul'ba, Taras, see Borovets', Taras
"Bul'ba" bands, 97-101 (*maps*); Germany and, 135
Buniachenko, General, 142

Canadian Institute of Ukrainian Studies, 236
Canaris, Admiral, 21, 28-29
Carpathian Sich, 16, 22
Carpatho-Ukraine: autonomy of, 15-16; Communist Party in, 134; Hungary and, 134; Kovpak's band in, 101 (*map*); nationalism in, 15-16, 132, 212; OUN-M and, 25, 27-28, 62; Soviet Union in, 134; UPA and, 225-26
Catholic Church, Germany and, 153

261

Chas, 49
Chekaniuk, A. T., 45
Chelm district: denationalization of, 36; Greek Catholic Church in, 31-32; Orthodox Church in, 31-32, 149-50; Polish-Ukrainian massacres in, 112
Chermeryns'kyi, Iaroslav, 67, 80, 135*n*
Chernenko, K. U., 237
Chernigov *oblast*: destruction of OUN-M group in, 78; Kovpak's partisan band in, 105; partisan activity in, 95, 98-101 (*maps*); population of, 243
Chernovtsy, 49
Chetniks, compared to moderate Ukrainian partisans, 114
Chornovil, Viacheslav, 235
Chuchkevych, Ostap, 59, 64
Church: in Kharkov, 199-200; in Mariupol', 208; nationalism and, 145-61, 216; Soviet Union, and, 132; SS Division Galicia and, 130-31; in villages, 191; *see also* under specific church, e.g., Orthodox Church
Cities: intelligentsia of, 183; middle class of, 182-83; populations of, 243-44; starvation in, 87-88; *see also* under specific names, e.g., Kharkov
Coastal area: nationalism in, 205-7; OUN-B in, 206-7; UAC in, 206; UAPTs in, 206-7
Collective farm system: Germany and, 86-87, 189; *see also* Agrarian question; Agricultural policy
Collectivization, *see* Agrarian question
Committee for the Liberation of the Peoples of Russia, *see* KONR
Communism: nationalism and, 2, 6; OUN and, 211-18; students and, 14; in West Ukraine, 12
Communist Party: in Carpatho-Ukraine, 226; partisan activity in Ukraine and, 95-123; partisan direction by, 95-96; tactics of, and OUN, 213-17; Ukrainian cultural life and, 8-10, 171, 192, 232-35; Ukrainian nationalism and, 9-11, 220; in Ukrainian SSR, 180, 186, 230; underground agents, 73-74, 102, 148*n*, 167, 192, 211, 221, 239; UPA and, 104, 220-21
Conference of Oppressed Peoples of East Europe and Asia, 118
Cooperatives: nationalists in, 169; under Soviet Union, 182
"Cossack hundreds," 125
Cracow News, see Krakivs'kyi Visti
Crimea, nationalism in, 209
Culture: Communist Party and, 9-10; under Germany, 170-74; nationalists and, 3-4; *see also* Education; Press

Damaskin, Bishop, 148-49, 153, 196
Daniel, Julius, 233
Danilevskii, N. T., 5

D'Annunzio, Gabriele, 14
Denikin, A. I., General, 7
Diatchenko, Colonel, UNR leader, 63
Dilo, 45
Dimitrius, Bishop, 157
Dionysius, Metropolitan, 147, 149-50, 152
Directory, 7
Displaced persons (DPs), Ukrainians as, 228
Dnieprodzerzhinsk, 205
Dniepropetrovsk: nationalism in, 157, 164; OUN-B in, 61, 157, 166, 183; population of, 243-44; postwar Communist apparatus in, 237; Russophiles in, 157, 164, 166; UAC in, 157; UAPTs in, 157
Dnipropetrovs'ka Hazeta, 164*n*, 179
Dobriansky, Leo, 237
Dolenko, Volodymyr, 185, 197
Donbas: nationalism in, 164, 207-9; OUN in, 208; Russians in, 164, 179, 207; UPA in, 221
Dontsov, Dmytro, 14, 25*n*, 91*n*, 117, 229
Doroshenko, Dmytro, 18
Drohobych oil fields, 110
Druzhyny Ukraïns'kykh Natsionalistiv, *see* DUN
Dubrovs'kyi, V. V., 173, 185, 197
DUN (Brotherhoods of Ukrainian Nationalists) — Druzhyny Ukraïns'kykh Natsionalistiv, 52-53
Dziuba, Ivan, 232-34
Dzvin (The Bell), 175, 180*n*, 204*n*

East Ukraine, 2, 46; geographical variations of nationalism in, 194-210; German occupation and nationalism in, 63-67, 72-84, 86-94; 186; 195; German policy failures in, 85-90; language of, 3-4, 75, 79-80, 117-18, 142, 164, 171, 181, 181*n*, 189, 191, 197, 200, 217, 232; nationalism in, 8-11; nationalist partisan activities in, 226; OUN in, 51, 162; OUN-B in, 61-62, 90-91, 214; OUN-M in, 62, 65-66, 74-80, 91-92; postwar nationalism in, 235-36; postwar political groups, 228-30; regions of, 198 (*map*); repatriation after Second World War, 227-28; URDP and, 229
EDES (non-Communist Greeks), compared to moderate Ukrainian partisans, 114
Education: émigré activities, 170-71; under Germany, 171-72; nationalists and, 170-72; *see also* Students
Émigrés, nationalist activities of, 226-30, 236-37
Emmanuel, Bishop, 158-59, 196

Farmer, Kenneth A., 235
Fascism, OUN and, 213
Fedorov, Oleksii, 95, 105
Fichte, Johann, 14
Filipov (Kharkov writer), 79-80
Finland, UNR and, 22

First Ukrainian Division, 142-44
Forostivs'kyi, Leontii, 140n, 157, 165
France: UNR and, 21
Frank, Hans, 32-34
Franko, John, 4
Free Cossacks, 108, 196
Front of Ukrainian Revolutionists (Front Ukraïns'kykh Revolutsionistiv), 108

Galicia, 53-54; flight of Jews from, 54; Generalgouvernement and, 42, 76n, 109; Greek Catholic Church in, 5, 25, 47, 112, 145, 151, 222-23; influence of, on Ukrainian nationalism, 12-14, 44, 110, 144, 186; integral nationalism in, 14; Kovpak's band in, 100-101 (maps), 109-10; nationalism in, 211; OUN in, 40; OUN-B partisan activity in, 102, 110-11; OUN-M in, 64-65; partisan activity in, 221-23; partisan support in, 115, 224-25; Poland and Poles in, 5, 8, 11, 110-12; Rumania and, 76; Soviet Union and, 31, 44, 46, 144; UPA postwar activities in, 222-25; Wehrmacht in, 124-27, 221
Galician Division, see SS Division Galicia
Gavrushevych, John, 36, 52, 59, 135n
Genadius, Bishop, 157
Generalgouvernement Polen: anti-Polish feelings of Ukrainians in, 36; composition of, 31, 35n, 76n; Galicia in, 36, 75, 76n; German military training and, 127, 130-32; nationalism in, 31-34; Orthodox Church in, 149; OUN-B and, 48; OUN conflict and, 32-36; Poles in, 33-36; Ukrainian Central Committee formation in, 34-35; Ukrainian community organizations in, 33-34; Ukrainian culture and, 35-36
Geographical variations of nationalism, 194-210
George (Korenistov), Bishop, 154n
German army, see Wehrmacht
German Intelligence Service, see Abwehr
German police, see SP
German-Soviet Boundary and Friendship Treaty (1939), 46
Germany: agricultural policy of, 86-88, 178; "Bul'ba" forces and, 134; Carpatho-Ukraine and, 15-16; Catholic Church and, 153; collective farm system and, 86-87; culture under, 172-73, 178; education under, 165, 169-72, 183-84; Het'manites and, 18-19, 75; KONR and, 139-44; labor policy of, 88-90, 136n, 182; limitations on power of, 163-64, 174, 179; national committee formation by, 127; nationalism and, 14, 15, 28-29, 73-93, 140-44, 184, 217-18; nationalism and occupation of East Ukraine by, 73-93, 163-65, 187; nationalism in, and Ukrainian nationalism, 5; nationalism in East Ukraine and, 90-93; nationalists and, 142-44; nationalists in Ukrainian municipal administration established by, 163-71; Orthodox Church and, 148, 153, 157-58, 191; Ostarbeiter program of, 88-89, 96, 106, 135, 136n, 139, 141, 143, 160n, 170, 178-79, 189; OUN and, 32-34, 51, 73-81; OUN-B and, 40, 51-65, 134; OUN-B in East Ukraine and, 61-70; OUN-B in Galicia and, 51-65; OUN-B repression by, 90-91; OUN-M and, 40, 51, 62-63, 67, 73-81; OUN-M repression by, 77-85, 91-92; partisan activity and, 98-101 (maps), 106; policy of, in East Ukraine, 85-90; press under, 174-80; reprisals of, against partisans, 96; Soviet Union and, 13, 17, 19, 21, 32, 46, 49; SS Division Galicia and, 127-32, 144; Ukrainian policy of, 7, 76-77; UNR and, 18-19, 75; UPA and, 220-27; use of former Soviet troops by, 136; see also Generalgouvernement Polen
Gorbachev, M. S., 237-39
Göring, Hermann, 19
Governments, in Ukraine (1917-20), 6-8
Greek (Ukrainian) Catholic Church: in Chelm district, 31-32; in Galicia, 5, 46, 112, 131-32, 145, 151; influence as Ukrainian Catholic Church, 229; nationalism and, 6, 130-31, 145, 238; nationalist parties and, 23-24, 57-58, 130; OUN and, 24-26; Soviet postwar persecution of, 132, 222-23; Soviet Union and, 46, 132, 148; SS Division Galicia and, 130-31; UAC and, 152-53; UAPTs and, 152-53; UPA and, 108n, 222-24

Haievs'kyi (Kiev professor, later UAPTs bishop), 154, 167, 183
Haivaz, Iaroslav, 74
Halan, Iaroslav, 222
Harvard Ukrainian Research Institute, 236
Herder, Johann Gottfried von, 14
Het'manites, 7, 18n, 25, 27, 75, 156; Germany and, 18-19; ideology of, 18-19; importance of, 19; leaders of, 18; location of, 18, 28
Hilarion, Archbishop, 149, 151-52, 159, 199n
Himmler, Heinrich, 76, 126, 130, 136
Hiob, Bishop, 160n
Hitler, Adolf, 32n, 76, 141; attitude of, toward Ukrainians, 32-33, 125
Holos, 141
Horbovyi, Iaroslav, 36
Horbovyi, Dr. V. (OUN-B leader in Cracow), 53, 138
Hrushevs'kyi, Michael, 4, 10
Hryhorenko, General Peter, 235
Hrynenko, George, 180n
Hryn'okh, John, 57, 58, 62, 131n, 229
Hungary: Carpatho-Ukraine and, 15-16; revolution of 1956, 224, 231
Hupalo, Constantine, 173

Iarii, Richard, 42, 52; background of, 23; OUN-B and, 42-43
Iatseniuk, Alexander, 66, 77*n*, 185, 188
Iatseniuk (the younger), 66, 77, 108, 113, 188
Iavors'kyi, Matvii, 10
Ihor, Bishop, 153, 196, 200
Ilnits'kyi, Roman, 59
Institute for the Study of the USSR, 230
Integral nationalism: background of, 212-13; origin of, 12; policies of, 13, 25-26; in West Ukraine, 13-15
Intellectuals as nationalists, 156, 182-87, 216-17
Internatsionalizm chy Russifikatsiia? (Internationalism or Russification?), 232-34
Irliavs'kyi, John, 84
Istoriia mist i Sil Ukraïns'koï RSR (History of the Towns and Villages of the Ukrainian SSR), 233-34
Ivanov, General, 44

Jews: deportation from Zhitomir, 66; Dziuba and, 235; effect of Holocaust of, on handicrafts and professions, 170; flight from Galicia to escape Germans and Ukrainian persecution, 54; intellectuals in service of Communism, 11; as lawyers in Kharkov, 185; nationalist press on, 117-18; NKVD massacre of Zionists, 54; physicians in UPA, 115-16; in Soviet trading system, 182; SP massacres of, 77, 130; in Ukrainian cities before 1917, 6

Kalenda (deputy chief of Kiev police), 67
Kamenets-Podolsk, 8; destruction of OUN-M group in, 78; population of, 243-44
Kaminskii, Bronislav, 142*n*, 224
Kandiïv, George, 126*n*
Kandyba, Dr. (OUN-M leader), 67, 74, 78-79, 92, 135, 167
Kapustians'kyi, General Mykola, 22, 63, 135
Karlovtsi Synod, 160
KGB, *see* NKVD
Kharkov: church in, 199-200; cooperatives in, 168; Germany in, 75; lawyers in, 185-86; nationalism in, 75, 79-80, 173-75, 183, 196, 199; nationalists in administration of, 165; OUN-M in, 75, 199; population of, 243-44; Soviet Union in, 132, 172, 199
Kherson: nationalism in, 206-7; population of, 243-44; UAC in, 170
Khmel'nyts'kyi, Bohdan, 4, 105, 195
Khoroshyi, *see* Michael (Khoroshyi), Bishop
"Khrin," 107-8, 109*n*, 113, 115, 157-58
Khronoviat, Michael, 63, 127
Khrushchev, Nikita, 133, 223, 230-32; quoted, 133
Khvylovyi, Nicholas, 231

Kiev: cooperatives in, 169, 183; deportation of workers from, 89; German capture of, 73-75; German repression of OUN-M in, 76-80, 83-85; nationalism in, 187, 195-96; nationalists in administration of, 73-74, 165-66, 183-84; OUN-M in, 73-80, 162, 183-84, 203; partisan activity in area of, 97-101 (*maps*), 226; population of, 165, 170, 242-43; Russians in, 3, 79-81, 168; Russophiles in, 74, 168; Soviet Union in, 132, 197; students as nationalists in, 84; UAC in, 155-56; UAPTs in, 155
Kinkelin, Dr. (official in Ostministerium), 126, 140*n*
Kirichenko, Aleksei, 230-32
Kirn, Captain (Wehrmacht liaison to UPA), 137
Kirovograd: ethnic composition of, 206; OUN-B in, 70; population of, 243-44; UAPTs in area of, 206
Kliachevs'kyi, Dmytro, 112, 137
Klich, 142*n*
Klymishyn, Nicholas, 60
Klymiv, John, 48, 58, 70
Koch, Erich, 76, 82-84, 87, 104, 154-55, 169, 173*n*
Koch, Hans, 64
Kolkhoz, *see* Agrarian question
Komitet Osvobozhdeniia Narodov Rossii, *see* KONR
"Kommissars," German order to shoot, 77, 86, 95, 186
Kononenko (OUN-M organizer in Kharkov), 197
Konovalets', Eugene, 13, 15, 22, 24, 27-28, 37-38, 42-43, 56, 62, 69, 135
KONR (Committee for the Liberation of the Peoples of Russia) — Komitet Osvobozhdeniia Narodov Rossii: civilians and, 141-42; formation of, 139; Germany and, 139, 160; protests against, 140-41; ROA and, 141; Russians in, 140, 160, 230
Konyk, Bohdan, 67, 74
Korotych, Vitalyi, 238
Koshyk, John, 84
Kostelnyk, Gabriel, 222
Kostomarov, Nicholas, 4
Kostopol' area, as partisan center, 48, 70-72
Kovel', Red partisan band near, 104
Kovpak, Sidor, 105, 105*n*
Kovpak's Red partisan band, 100-101 (*maps*); activity of, 107, 109-10; formation of, 105; in Galicia, 109-10, 126
Kozmyk, John ("Petrenko"), 84*n*
Kozyi, Stephen, 68
Krakivs'ki Visti, 35
Kravtsiv, Bohdan, 141
Krivoi Rog, OUN-B in, 70, 171, 175
"Kruk," 107, 113, 115
Krymins'kyi (OUN leader in Galicia), 48
Kuban', nationalism in, 209; Russians in, 209

Kubiiovych, Volodymyr, 34, 40, 42*n*, 127, 143
Kurmanovych, General, 22, 127, 135
Kursk *oblast*, nationalism in, 209
Kuts, Alexander, 69

Laba, Dr., 131, 131*n*
Labor Policy of Germany in East Ukraine, 135-36, 136*n*
Lawyers as nationalists, 184-86
League for the Liberation of the Ukraine, 10
Lebed', Nicholas, 43, 58-59, 113, 116, 229
"Left Bank" area, nationalism in, 197-201
Leibbrandt, Georg, 32*n*
Lelchitsi, captured by Kovpak's Red partisan band, 105
Lemko area, Poland in, 31, 33*n*, 34, 149
Levits'kyi, Boris, 103
Levits'kyi, Constantine, 44-45, 58, 64
Levits'kyi, Dmytro, 45
Litavry, 78
Liubchenko, Arkadii, 79, 91, 180*n*, 183, 197
Liudvipol' district, as partisan center, 71-72, 109
Livyts'kyi, Andrew, 19-21, 71, 103, 139, 229
Lopatyns'kyi, Volodymyr, 36, 38, 62
Lukin, Alexander, 103-4
Lypkivs'kyi, Metropolitan Basil, 146, 149, 152, 157
Lypyns'kyi, Viacheslav, 18
Lytvynenko, Colonel, 71

Magunia (Generalkommissar in Kiev), 83
"Magyarophiles," 226
Mahonin, Jakob, 129
Maikovskii, Vadym, 126*n*
Makarushka, Liubomyr, 127*n*, 128
Mariiupil's'ka Hazeta, 177, 180, 208*n*
Mariupol': church in, 208; nationalism in, 171, 177, 208-9
Maurras, Charles, 12, 14
Mayors, nationalists as, 165
Mazepa, Professor Isaac, 139
Mel'nyk, Andrew, 24, 29, 62-63, 133, 135, 138-40; background of, 24; Bandera faction and, 37-41; church and, 24-28, 41; power of, 23-29; problems of, 27-28
Michael (Khoroshyi), Bishop, 206
Middle class of cities, 182-83
Mirgorod, 179, 201
Mishchenko (Communist Party official in L'vov), 44
Mitrynga, John, 43, 103, 113, 212
Mitsyk, John, 69
Molotov-Ribbentrop pact: German attitude toward Ukrainian nationalism and, 21; OUN and, 32; UNR and, 21
Monastery of the Caves (Pecherska Lavra), Kiev, 149, 231
Monastyris'ka uprising, 53

Moroz, Valentyn, 235
Mstyslav, Bishop, 154, 156-57, 159; *see also* Skrypnyk, Stephen
Municipal administration: departments under, 163-64; nationalists in, 163-80
Muzichenko, George, 140*n*, 141
Myron, Dmytro, 36, 203*n*

"Nachtigall," 51-54, 55, 56-57, 62, 112
Narodnaia Volia, 14, 91, 213
Nastup, 28*n*, 69
Nationalism, 2, 12-20, 211; in Bessarabia, 49; in Bukovina, 49, 65, 212, 225; in Carpatho-Ukraine, 16, 212, 226; channels of activity for, 162-80; church and, 145-61; in coastal areas, 205-6; Communist Party and, 12; in Crimea, 201; deficiencies of, 216-17; described, 21-22; in Donbas, 207-8; émigré politics after Second World War, 229-30; foreign nationalisms and, 5-6; in *Generalbezirk* Taurien, 206; geographical variations in, 194-210; German control and, 28-29, 73-93, 135-36, 216; Greek Catholic Church and, 5, 57-58, 130, 222, 229; intellectuals and, 165, 216; in Kharkov, 75, 79-80, 173-75, 183, 197, 199; in Kherson, 206-7; KONR and, 139-42; in Kuban', 209-10; in Kursk *oblast*, 209; leaders of, 4, 7; in Mariupol', 171, 177, 208-9; in Odessa, 206; organization and activities after Second World War, 228-29, 236-39; peasants and, 8, 11, 181, 201, 216; in Podolia, 195; Polish-German war and, 29-30; political aspect of, 1-2; political thought of, 212-14; in Poltava, 200; present status of movement, 238-39; relative importance of, 211, 214; in "Right Bank" area, 195-96; in Rostov district, 209; Russian, 80-81; Russian Empire and, 4-6; Russian revolutionary tradition and, 14; social structure and, 6, 181-93; Soviet Union and, 133-34, 235; Stalin and, 9-10; in steppe area, 201-6; stimuli to, 2-4; students and, 8, 10, 182; summary of activities in East Ukraine, 237-39; support for, 209-10, 212; UAPTs and, 148-50, 183, 191, 217; urban-rural differences in, 189-90; in villages, 190-93; in Volhynia, 212
Nationalists: administrators as, 180-87; contacts with Abwehr, 16, 23, 51-52; in cooperatives, 168-69, 196; culture and, 172-74; education and, 165, 169-72, 196; Germany and, 143-44; groups in postwar Ukraine, 235-36; groups outside postwar Ukraine, 228-30; intellectuals as, 165, 181-83, 185, 196; lawyers as, 185-86; as mayors, 165; military ideals of, 124, 128; in municipal administrations, 165-80; in police departments, 164, 192, 195; press and, 174-80, 195; propaganda and, 174-80; in public institutions, 163-67; SS Division Galicia and, 124-30; technical specialists as, 187-92; UAC and, 156-59; UAPTs

Nationalists (*continued*)
and, 157-59; and Wehrmacht, 27-28, 34, 51-62, 73-75, 81*n*, 103, 130, 136-37; in welfare departments, 167-68; women as, 187-88; youth and, 188-89
Natsional'no Trudovoi Soiuz (National Workers' Union), *see* NTS
Nazi Germany, *see* Germany
Nicholas, Exarch of West Ukraine, 147-48
Nikanor, Bishop, 153-55
Nikolaev: deportation of workers from 89*n*; nationalism in, 163, 206; OUN-B in, 69, 206; OUN-M in, 65, 78; UAC in, 206; UAPTs in, 206
NKVD: attacks on OUN émigré leadership, 236; executions in Vinnitsa, 195; German orders to shoot officials of, 77; partisans and, 95, 116, 137, 159, 220-23; plan of UPA to attack, 222; repression of OUN and Zionists in Galicia, 53-54
North Caucasus, rebellion in, 224
Northern Ukraine: partisan activity in, 97-101 (*maps*); *see also* names of cities, e.g., Kiev
Nova Doba, 142*n*, 196
Nova Rada, 49
Nova Ukraïna, 79-80, 175, 177, 197, 199, 208
Nove Ukraïns'ke Slovo, 83, 178*n*, 179, 180*n*, 199
Novyi Chas, 44
NTS (National Workers' Union) – Natsional'no Trudovoi Soiuz, 204
Nymchuk, John, 45

Oberländer, Theodor, 54*n*, 75*n*
Odessa: nationalism in, 206; Russians in, 205
Ohiienko, John, *see* Hilarion, Archbishop
Ohlendorf, SS officer, 126
Ohloblyn, Alexander, 74
"Olevsk Republic," 72, 99 (*map*), 194
Oliinyk, Peter, 67, 80
Omel'chenko, Tymosh, 40, 42*n*
Omelianovych-Pavlenko, Michael, 7, 63, 128
Onats'kyi, Eugene, 135
Organization of Ukrainian Nationalists, *see* OUN
Organizatsiia Ukraïns'kykh Natsionalistiv, *see* OUN
Orlo, 24
Orthodox Church: in Chelm district, 30-31, 149; Germany and, 148, 153-55; nationalists and, 146, 156-57, 208; organization of, 145-46; OUN and, 156; in Poland, 147-48; Russian Revolution and, 146-47; Soviet Union and, 147-48, 150, 231; state and, 145; in Ukraine, 146-47; in Volhynia, 147-50, 157-59; in Zhitomir, 148-49; *see also* UAPTs, Ukrainian Autonomous Orthodox Church
OUN (Organization of Ukrainian Nationalists) – Organizatsiia Ukraïns'kykh Natsionalistiv: Bandera faction split from, 43-44; in Bukovina, 49; Carpatho-Ukraine and, 15-16, 27-28; Church and, 24-26, 119, 156-58; Communist tactics and, 217-18; congress of partisan forces of, 118; courage of, 215; defects of, 213-15; distribution of, 27; in Donbas, 207-8; extremist activities of, 201, 212-13; Fascism and, 213; formation of, 15; in Galicia, 27, 30; Germany and, 28-29, 134, 140-44, 215-17; ideology of, 24-26, 78-79, 181*n*, 187, 215-16; intellectuals in, 186-87, 189, 192, 216-17; internal conflicts in, 36-44; lawyers in, 186-87; leadership of, 22-27; members of, in public institutions, 163-74; military ideals of, 124-25; Molotov-Ribbentrop pact and, 29; nationalism in Generalgouvernement and, 41; in police, 166-67; Polish-German war and, 28-30; press and, 174-79; problems of, 25-27; Provid and members of, 22-24; representation in Rada, 228-29; in Soviet-occupied territories, 48-49; UAC and, 157-59; UAPTs and, 157-59; in Volhynia, 48-49; youth in, 188-89; *see also* OUN-B; OUN-M; OUN-r; OUN-s; Bandera; Mel'nyk; Nationalism
OUN-B (Organization of Ukrainian Nationalists – Bandera faction): arguments of, 42; in Carpatho-Ukraine, 226; in coastal area, 206; demands of, 37-42; in Dniepropetrovsk, 157, 183, 204; in East Ukraine, 5, 60-62, 65-70, 90-91, 161, 171, 173, 177, 179, 199, 203, 209, 214; formation of, 39, 41, 43; in Galicia, 43, 53-60, 91, 106, 110-12, 115, 212; Galician conference of, 119-23; Generalgouvernement and, 41, 53; German repression in East Ukraine and, 69-70, 90-91; Germany and, 51, 62, 134; in Greater Germany, 41; Iarii and, 42-43; ideology of, 91, 104, 117-23; in Kirovograd, 70; Kovpak's partisan band and, 109; in Krivoi Rog, 70; Mel'nyk and, 39; Mel'nyk forces and partisan activity, 48*n*, 107-8; military units of, 51-52, 62, 110; OUN-M and, 62-64; partisan activity of, 97, 100-101 (*maps*), 106-8, 110, 113-16, 214; postwar change of OUN-r, 228; purges of, in UPA, 114-15; Second World War and, 53-54; Senyk-Stsibors'kyi murder and, 68-70; slogan of, 90*n*; SS Division Galicia and, 127-29; in steppe area, 203-5; strength of, 115-16; sub-factions in, 43; in UHVR, 229; Ukrainian Central Committee and, 40; UNO and, 40-41; UPA and, 113-16, 158; youth and, 188-89; *see also* Bandera, Stephen; OUN-r
OUN-M (Organization of Ukrainian Nationalists – Mel'nyk faction): arguments of, 41-43; in Bazar, 77; Bukovina and, 49, 65, 78; in Carpatho-Ukraine, 226; in Chernigov, 78; East Ukraine, 62, 65-66, 74-80, 91-92, 214; in Galicia, 62-63; German repression of, 77, 79-80, 83-85, 92-93; Germany and, 40, 51, 62-63, 67, 127, 135; ideology of, 91-92; in Kamenets-Podolsk, 78; in Kharkov, 73,

79-80, 169, 183, 199; in Kiev, 73-75, 79-80, 83-85, 171, 174, 183-85, 187; League of Ukrainian writers and, 84; OUN-B and, 48*n*, 60-69, 113-14, 188; partisan activity in Volhynia, 107, 109; partisan activity of, 97-100 (*maps*), 107-13, 214; in Podolia, 195; in Polessia, 194; postwar change to OUN-s, 228; press and, 175*n*; prestige of, 84; in Proskurov, 65, 179, 195-96; SS Division Galicia in, 127-30; strength of, 114; in Uman', 65; UNR and, 62-63; UPA and, 71-72; in Vinnitsa, 179; in Zhitomir, 65-70, 174, 195; *see also* OUN-s

OUN-r (Organization of Ukrainian Nationalists — revolutionary), 228-29; activities in Western countries, 228-29; representation in Rada, 228; Soviet attacks on, 236

OUN-s (Organization of Ukrainian Nationalists — solidarist), postwar activities of, 228

Ovcharenko, F. D., 234

Paliïv, Dmytro, 128
Palladius, Bishop, 149, 152
Panchyshyn, M. I., 45
Pan'kivs'kyi, Constantine, 64, 64*n*
Panteleimon (Rudyk), Bishop, 83, 156-57, 160
Pareto, Vilfredo, 14
Partisans: activity of, in Ukraine, 95-116, 133, 193; in Carpatho-Ukraine, 225-26; Communist Party and, 95-116; German reprisals against, 96; local support of, 96, 104-5; myth of Red partisans, 220; OUN-B members as, 97, 100-101 (*maps*), 106-8, 110, 113-16; OUN-M members as, 100-101 (*maps*), 103, 107-9, 113-14; Red army soldiers and, 95; rural support lost, 222; tactics of Wehrmacht against, 96; UNDP members as, 104; UNR and, 103, 107-8, 113-14; UPA and, 102-3
Pavlograd, population of, 188, 243-44
Pavlovs'kyi (chief of Zhitomir city administration), 66
Peasants: nationalism and, 8, 121-22, 155-56, 181, 187-89, 191, 196; in postwar Ukrainian SSR, 221-22, 226, 239; Soviet Union and, 8, 222
Peasant-Workers Association (Selians'ko-Robitnycha Partiia — Sel-Rob), 12
Pelens'kyi, Zenon, 44
Perevertun, Professor (director of All-Ukrainian Cooperative Society, 169
Petliura, Simon, 7-8, 11, 19-20, 20*n*, 69, 79, 192
Petriv, General Vsevolod, 7, 53, 53*n*, 58*n*, 128, 139
Platonius, Bishop, 159
Pochaïvs'ka Lavra (monastery), 147, 149, 150, 157
Podgaitsi uprising, 53
Podgornyi, Nicholas V., 232

Podolia: Jewish population of, 195; nationalism in, 195-96; OUN-M in, 195-96; partisan activity in, 100-101 (*maps*); UAC in, 196; UAPTs in, 196

Pohidny hrupy, *see* Task forces

Poland: Chelm district and, 31-32, 36*n*; Galicia and, 5, 110-11, 133-34; in Lemko area, 31; Orthodox Church in, 147; and Soviet treaty for population exchange, 133; UNDO and, 12, 24; Ukrainian-Polish massacres and, 110-18; UNR and, 7, 11, 20-21; UPA and, 110-11, 221; UVO and, 13, 23; West Ukraine and, 12; *see also* Generalgouvernement Polen

Polans'kyi, George, 56

Polessia: German reprisals against partisans in, 106; nationalism in, 70-72, 194; OUN-B partisans in, 115; partisan activity in, 105-6

Polessian Stronghold, *see* Polis'ka Sich

Police departments, nationalists in, 166-67

Police detachments, in Generalgouvernement, 36, 40, 51

Polish-German war: OUN and, 28-30; Ukraine and, 17-30; UNR and, 19-21

Polis'ka Sich (Polessian Stronghold), 71-72, 102, 106; partisan activity of, 102-4

Poltava: destruction of OUN-M group in, 77; nationalism in, 200; population of, 243-44

Polykarp, Bishop, 147, 150, 152-55, 159

Potapenko, I., 203, 204*n*

Press: in Generalgouvernement, 35; under Germany, 163, 174-80; nationalists and, 174, 175*n*; nationalists on Jews, 178; OUN and, 196; OUN-M and, 196; Russophiles in, 78-79, 179; Soviet Union and, 178-80; Ukrainian newspapers, 176 (*map*); of Ukrainian SSR, 175; in villages, 193; and Wehrmacht 175-79, 209

Prokopovych, Viacheslav, 20-22

Promethean movement, 20; escape of members from Soviet forces, 21; Poland and, 20

Pronchenko, Michael, 180*n*, 183, 203, 204*n*

Propaganda: nationalists and, 174-80; in villages, 192-93

Proskurov, OUN-M in, 65, 179, 195-96

Prosvita societies, 8, 44, 66, 84, 171-74, 183, 196, 199, 209-10, 218; in villages, 189, 191-93

Provisional Government in Petrograd, Rada and, 7

Prykhod'ko, Victor, 8

Public institutions, nationalism in, 163-64

Rada, *see* Ukrainian Central Rada; Ukrainian National Rada
Radio Liberty, 230, 237
Raievs'kyi, Captain (UNR leader), 103, 113
Rebet, Leo, 36, 59-60
Red Army soldiers, partisans and, 95

Rehei, Vasyl', 204
Reichenau, Field Marshal von, 106
Reichskommissariat Ukraine, 81, 154, 159, 169-70, 172; administrative structure of, 82, 163, 166-67; German policy in, 87, 153-55; Kovpak's partisan band in, 105-6; nationalist repression in, 83-84, 166, 177; organization of, 75-77, 82, 166, 177; physiography of, 75-77, 81-82, 94, 152
Reichsministerium für die besetzten Ostgebiete (Reich Ministry for the Occupied Eastern Territories), 75, 125, 153-54, 159-60, 177
Religion, *see* Church *and also* under names of specific churches
Repatriation after Second World War, 227-28
"Right Bank" area, Kovpak's partisan band in, 105; nationalism in, 195-96
ROA (Russian Liberation Army) — Rossiskaia Osvobeditelnaia Armiia, Russians as officers in, 141-42, 142n
Rohach, John, 67, 74, 80
"Roland," 52, 62, 112
Rosenberg, Alfred, 75, 84, 125-26, 139n, 140-41, 153, 154, 170, 173n
Rosokha, Stephen, 28n
Rossiskaia Osvoboditelnaia Armiia, *see* ROA
Rostov district, nationalism in, 209
Rudenko, R. A., 223n
Rudyk, *see* Panteleimon (Rudyk), Bishop, 148
Rumania: Ukraine and, 48-49, 62, 65, 76n, 76, 205-6; UNR and, 21
Russia, Communist, *see* Soviet Union
Russian Empire, Ukrainian nationalism and, 5-6
Russian language, in Ukraine, 3-4, 164-65, 181-82, 205-7, 239
Russian Liberation Army (Rossiskaia Osvoboditelnaia Armiia) — *see* ROA
Russian Orthodox Church: Revolution and, 146-47; UAC and, 146
Russians: in Carpatho-Ukraine, 226; charges of Ukrainian nationalists against, 140, 167n; dominance in KONR, 139; dominant position in pre-Revolutionary Ukraine, 9, 11; in Donbas, 164, 207; in German administration in the Ukraine, 82n; identification as Ukrainian, 204; in Kuban', 209; myth of, 220; in Odessa, 205-6; as officers in ROA, 142; predominance among workers, 6, 8; as Orthodox priests, 150; as prisoners of war, attitude toward Ukrainians, 142n; UPA and, 224, 226; in Zhitomir, 66; *see also* KONR; NTS; ROA; Russian language; UAC; Vlasov
Russophiles: 82n, 184, 202, 247-48; defined, 247; in Dniepropetrovsk, 157, 167-68, 178, 179, 204; in Kiev, 74, 83, 126, 157, 186; in the press, 80-81, 179; and UAC, 157-60; in Vinnitsa, 167, 195; *see also* KONR; NTS; ROA; Russian Language; UAC; Vlasov
Ruzanov, Alexander, 96n
Ryvak, Vasyl', 103

Saburov, Alexander, 95
Sadovs'kyi, Colonel (UNR leader), 71
Sahaidachnyi, Peter, 75, 175
St. Vladimir's Cathedral (Kiev), 154-55
Sal's'kyi, Volodymyr, 20
Samvydav (samizdat) publication, 235
Sambor uprising, 53
SB (Security Service) — Sluzhba Bezpeky, 43, 116, 213
Schenkendorff, General von, 124-25
Second World War: nationalism after, 219-39; OUN and, 29-30; OUN-B and, 51-53; UNR and, 20-21
Security Service, *see* SB
Selians'ko-Robitnycha Partiia — Sel-Rob, *see* Peasant-Workers Association
Semenenko, Alexander, 143, 185, 197
Senishyn, Nicholas, 61
Senyk, Omelian, 24, 25n, 26, 67-70, 68n, 135n; background of, 23; Bandera faction's charges against, 38-39
Sergius, Patriarch, 147
Shandruk, General Paul, 139, 143
Shcherbatiuk, Leonidas, 104, 113
Shcherbitskii, V. V., 237
Shelest, Peter E., 232-35
Sheptyts'kyi, Metropolitan Andrew, 5, 25, 41, 46, 57, 112, 132, 151-52; Galician Division and, 130-31; quoted, 58; and SP massacre of Jews, 130
Sherstiuk, mayor of Krivoi Rog, 203
Shevchenko, Taras, 1-4
Shevchenko Scientific Society, 236
Shreter, *see* Timothy (Shreter), Bishop
Shtepa, Constantine, 80-81, 140n, 157, 180n
Shtul', Oleh, 71, 108, 113, 134, 228
Shubs'kyi, OUN-M leader, 69
Shukhevych, Roman, 43, 51, 52n, 58, 62, 112, 118, 223
Shul'gin, *see* Shul'hyn, Alexander
Shul'ha, OUN-M leader, 69
Shul'hyn, Alexander, 20, 21
Shums'kyi, Alexander, 9, 169, 184
Sicherheitspolizei, *see* SP
Sichovoi Stril'tsi (Sich Sharpshooters), 13, 15, 22, 24
Simon, Bishop, 147, 155
Siniavskii, Andrew, 233
Skaba, A. D., 232, 234, 236
Skoropads'kyi, Paul, 7, 17-19, 139
Skrypnyk, Nicholas, 9, 169
Skrypnyk, Stephen, 150, 154-55, 184; *see also* Mstyslav, Bishop
Slipyi, Bishop Joseph, 58, 131-32
Sluzhba Bezpeky, *see* SB
Smal'-Stots'kyi or Smal'-Stocki, Roman, 20
Sobor of Volhynian Bishops, 149-51
Social Revolutionaries, UNR and, 19
Social structure, nationalism and, 181-93
Society for the Preservation of Historical and Cultural Monuments, 235

Soiuz Ukraïns'koï Natsionalistychnoï Molodi, *see* SUNM
Solzhenitsyn, Alexander, 231, 233
Sotsialistychna Kharkivshchyna, 175
Southeast Asians, compared to Ukrainian nationalists, 129-30
Soviet Ukraine, *see* East Ukraine
Soviet Union: in Bessarabia, 49; in Bukovina, 48-49, 132; in Carpatho-Ukraine, 134, 137; in Galicia, 44-48, 53-54, 132-34, 136-38, 148; Germany and, 13, 17, 19, 21, 32, 46, 49, 53, 58, 140; Greek Catholic Church in Galicia and, 44, 46, 132, 148, 153, 222-23; Greek Catholic Church, postwar persecution of, 222-24, 227; influence of constitution on UHVR, 121; in Kharkov, 132, 172, 186; in Kiev, 91, 132, 195; myth of, 220, 231; Orthodox Church and, 147-50, 159; Orthodox Church in Volhynia and, 148; partisan activity in Ukraine and, 95-96, 105, 116, 220, 232; partisan resistance to, 136-38, 220, 225; peasants and, 12, 86-87, 96, 123, 137-38; press and, 178-80, 231-35; reconquest of Ukraine by, 132-34, 137; repatriation of Ukrainians after Second World War, 227-28; self-determination of Communist parties and, 9; support for, in Ukraine, 12; UPA repression by, 116, 223-25; in Volhynia, 48, 116, 132, 150; in West Ukraine, 44-50, 131-34, 148
SP (Sicherheitspolizei), 77, 83, 130, 166, 172, 200, 206
SS Division Galicia, 142; in battle, 132; church and, 130-31; Germany and, 126-32; organization of, 127-32, 142; support of, 110*n*, 131, 134; and UPA, 132
SS Einsatzgruppen, 54, 59, 64, 69-70, 76-77, 186
Stakhiv, Eugene, 173*n*, 208
Stakhiv, Volodymyr, 59
Stalin, Joseph, 10, 230; and Kovpak, 105; Ukrainian nationalism and, 140
Stariukh, OUN-B leader, 59
Stasiuk, Nicholas, 180, 208
Stefaniv, Colonel, 63
Steppe area: nationalism in, 201-7; OUN-B in, 204-7
Stets'ko, Iaroslav, 43, 54, 56-60, 57*n*, 64, 112, 139*n*, 229; background of, 37; OUN policy and, 37, 54, 56-60
Strokach, Timothy A., 96
Stsibors'kyi, Nicholas, 23-24, 25*n*, 27, 67-70, 68*n*, 92, 135*n*; Bandera faction's charges against, 37-39
Students: Communism and, 14; exchange visits of East and West Ukrainian, 47-49; nationalism and, 8-9; nationalist activities of, in Kiev, 84; SUNM and, 14; *see also* Education
Suliatits'kyi, Captain, OUN-M leader, 74

SUNM (Union of Ukrainian Nationalistic Youth) — Soiuz Ukraïns'koï Natsionalistychnoï Molodi: students and, 14; UVO and, 15
Sushko, Roman, 27-28, 51, 63, 71, 127, 135*n*; background of, 23; Bandera faction and, 40, 51; Generalgouvernement organizations and, 34
Suslov, M. A., 231, 237
Sylvester, Bishop, 154
Symonenko, R. H., 236

Tarkovych, George, 67
Task forces (*Pokhydny hrupy*), 60-61, 69
Taurien, *Generalbezirk*, nationalism in, 207
Technical specialists, as nationalists, 184
Teliha, Olena, 78, 84, 187
Theophilus, Archbishop, 148, 199-200
Third Congress of Soviets, 9
Third Extraordinary Great Congress of the OUN (August 21-25, 1943), 118-19, 129*n*
Timothy (Shreter), Bishop, 147*n*
Tiutiunnyk, George, 9, 22, 77
Transcarpathian *oblast*, *see* Carpatho Ukraine
Transnistria, Ukraine and, 76, 205
Tsuman' area, as center of OUN-B partisans, 109
Turchmanovych, OUN-B leader, 103

UAC, *see* Ukrainian Autonomous Orthodox Church
UAPTs (Ukrainian Autocephalous Greek Orthodox Church) — Ukraïns'ka Avtokefal'na Pravoslavna Tserkva: in coastal area, 206; in Dniepropetrovsk, 157; formation of, 146, 149-52; Germany and, 130, 153-54; influence among émigrés, 229; in Kirovograd area, 205; nationalists and, 149, 153, 157-59, 215; in Nikolaev, 206; organization of, 149-50; OUN and, 156; in Podolia, 196; in Poltava, 200; in steppe area, 205; UAC and, 157-61; UPA and, 158-59; UNR and, 156; in villages, 191; in Zhitomir, 196
Ufa, Soviet evacuation of Ukrainians to, 73
UHVR (Ukraine Supreme Liberation Council) — Ukraïns'ka Holovna Vyzvol'na Rada, 120, 229; administrative structure of, 120-21; and Anglo-Americans, 129; formation of, 119; ideology of, 119-23; political elements in, 119, 236-67; representation in Rada, 229
Ukraïna, 10
Ukraïnbank (All Ukrainian Cooperative Bank), 169

Ukraine: culture of, and Communist Party, 9-10; defined, 1*n*, 202; émigré nationalism after Second World War, 228-30; Germany in, 1, 31-32 (*see also* Generalgouvernement Polen); governments in (1917-20), 7-9; Orthodox Church in, 146-61; partisan activity in, 94-123, 97-101 (*maps*); physiography of, 94-95; Polish-German war and, 17-31; postwar dissidents and nationalism in, 219-39; postwar political leadership in, 230-34, 237-39; repatriation after Second World War, 227-28; Rumania and, 205-6; Russian language in, 3-4, 164-65, 181-82, 205-7, 239; social structure of, 6; *see also* East Ukraine; Northern Ukraine; West Ukraine
Ukrainian Academy of Arts and Sciences, 73
Ukrainian Academy of Arts and Sciences in America (UVAN), 236
Ukrainian Autocephalous Orthodox Church (Ukraïns'ka Avtokefal'na Pravoslavna Tserkva), *see* UAPTs
Ukrainian Autonomous Orthodox Church: in coastal area, 205-7; in Dniepropetrovsk, 157, 204; formation of, 149; Germany and, 154, 159-60; Greek Catholic Church and, 151-52; in Kherson, 206; in Kiev, 157; nationalists and, 154, 196; in Nikolaev, 206; opposition to, 150; in Podolia, 196; reorganization of, 149-50; Russian Orthodox Church and, 159-60; and Russophiles, 155, 157, 158-60; split in, 152-53; UAPTs and, 158-61; UPA and, 158-59; in villages, 191
Ukrainian Central Committee (Chelm), 33
Ukrainian Central Committee (Generalgouvernement), 34-35, 127, 171, 211-12; cultural accomplishments of, 34-35; OUN-B and, 40; support for, 212
Ukrainian Central Rada, 7, 10, 201, 208; *see also* Ukrainian National Rada
Ukrainian Communist Party, *see* Communist Party
Ukrainian Community, 18
Ukrainian Congress Committee (U.S.), 230, 237
Ukrainian Insurrectionary Army, *see* UPA
Ukrainian Liberation Army (Ukraïns'ke Vyzvol'na Voisko), 142
Ukrainian Liberation Movement, 230
Ukrainian Military Organization, 14-15
Ukrainian National Committee, 33, 53, 64, 143
Ukrainian National Council (various provisional bodies), 33, 64, 84
Ukrainian National Democratic Union, *see* UNDO
Ukrainian National Rada (postwar émigrés), 229
Ukrainian National Rebirth, 70
Ukrainian National Union, *see* UNO
Ukrainian Party of Labor (Ukraïns'ka Partiia Pratsi), 12
Ukrainian People's Republic, *see* UNR

Ukrainian People's Revolutionary Army (UNRA), 113
Ukrainian Popular Democratic Party, *see* UNDP
Ukrainian Popular Self-Defense, 110
Ukrainian Red Cross, 168, 183*n*, 187
Ukrainian Republican Army, Polish Army and, 20, 62
Ukrainian Revolutionary Democratic Party, *see* URDP
Ukrainian Social Democratic Party, UNR and, 19
Ukrainian Soviet Socialist Republic, *see* Ukraine
Ukrainian Supreme Liberation Council, *see* UHVR
Ukraïno nasha Radians'ka, 234
Ukraïns'ka Avtokefal'na Tserkva, *see* UAPTs
Ukraïns'ka Holovna Vyzvol'na Rada, *see* UHVR
Ukraïns'ka Hromada, *see* Ukrainian Community
Ukraïns'ka Narodna Demokratychna Partiia, *see* UNDP
Ukraïns'ka Narodna Respublika, *see* UNR
Ukraïns'ka Narodna Revoliutsiina Armii, *see* UNRA
Ukraïns'ka Narodna Samooborona, *see* Ukrainian Popular Self Defense
Ukraïns'ka Natsional'na Vidrozheniia, *see* Ukrainian National Rebirth
Ukraïns'ka Povstans'ka Armiia, *see* UPA
Ukraïns'ka Viis'kove Organizatsiia, *see* UVO
Ukraïns'ke Natsional'ne Demokratychna Ob'iednannia, *see* UNDO
Ukraïns'ke Natsional'ne Ob'iednannia, *see* UNO
Ukraïns'ke Slovo, 67, 74, 78, 164*n*, 175, 178, 196
Ukraïns'ke Vyzvol'ne Voisko, *see* UVV
Ukraïns'kye Dobrovolets', 141
Ukraïns'kyi Holos, 196
Ukraïns'kyi Khliborob, 140*n*, 193
Ukraïns'kyi Kraievyi Komitet (Ukrainian Regional Committee), 64
Ukraïns'kyi Visnyk, 28*n*
Uman', OUN-M in, 65; population of, 243-44
UNDO (Ukrainian National Democratic Union)—Ukraïns'ke Natsional'ne Demokratychne Ob'iednannia: nationalism in Generalgouvernement and, 34; Poland and, 12, 34, 44; postwar revival of, 229; representation in Rada; Soviet control of Galicia and, 44
UNDP (Ukrainian Popular Democratic Party)—Ukraïns'ka Narodna Demokratychna Partiia: formation of, 104; members as partisans, 104; representation in Rada, 229
Union of Russian Officers, 205
Union of Soviet Socialist Republics, *see* Soviet Union

INDEX / 271

Union of Ukrainian Federalist Democrats, 230
Union of Ukrainian Nationalistic Youth, 14-15
Union of Ukrainian Youth, 10*n*
United States, postwar nationalist organizations in, 230, 236
UNO (Ukrainian National Union) — Ukraïns'ke Natsional'ne Ob'iednannia, 40, 63
UNR (Ukrainian People's Republic) — Ukraïns'ka Narodna Respublika, 7-8, 18, 27, 62; distribution of members of, 18; failure of, 8, 20, 212; Finland and, 22; France and, 21; Germany and, 18-19, 75; members as partisans, 103, 108-9; military ideals of, 124; Molotov-Ribbentrop pact and, 21; origin of, 18; Polish-German war and, 20-22; Poland and, 7, 11, 20-21; Rumania and, 21; UPA and, 108; Volhynia, active underground operations in, 48, 70-72; West Ukraine and, 13; Second World War and, 21-22
UNRA (Ukrainian People's Revolutionary Army) — Ukraïns'ka Narodna Revoliutsiina Armiia, 113
UPA (Ukrainian Insurrectionary Army) — Ukraïns'ka Povstans'ka Armiia, 71; Congress of, 118-21; decline in activities of, 138, 222-24; during German occupation, 127-29; Galician Conference of, 118; and Greek Catholic Church, 222-24; Jewish physicians as, 115-16; membership of, 115-16; as myth, 219; OUN-B and, 112-23, 158; OUN-M and, 103-4, 108, 114; partisan activity of, 102-13, 136-38, 220; postwar activities of, 220-27; postwar underground activities, 222-23; Soviet repression of, 116, 222-24; strength of, 115-16, 224; summary of accomplishments of, 224; UAC and, 157-59; UAPTs and, 158; UNR and, 103, 108-9; Wehrmacht and, 137-38, 220
URDP (Ukrainian Revolutionary Democratic Party): formation of, 229; representation in Rada, 229
USSR, *see* Soviet Union
UVO (Ukrainian Military Organization) — Ukraïns'ka Viis'kova Organizatsiia: Poland and, 13, 24, 41
UVV (Ukrainian Liberation Army) — Ukraïns'ke Vyzvol'ne Voisko, 142-44

Valiis'kyi, Colonel, 71
Villages: church in, 191; nationalism in, 189; political activity in, 192-93; press in, 193; propaganda in, 192-93; Prosvita in, 191-92
Vil'na Ukraïna (Dnepropetrovsk), 45
Vil'na Ukraïna (L'vov), 160*n*
Vinnitsa: nationalism in, 62, 166, 195; NKVD executions in, 195; OUN-M in, 65, 179, 195; population of, 243-44; Russophiles in, 166, 195
Vlasov, Andrew, 125-26, 137, 193, 216, 230; KONR and, 139-43; Shandruk and, 143-44

Volhynia: German reprisals against partisans in, 96; nationalism in, 102, 104, 123, 159; Orthodox Church, 147, 149-50; OUN in, 48-49; OUN-B in, 48*n*, 109-10, 112-23; OUN-B partisan activity in, 107-8, 110, 115, 157-58; partisan activity in, 98-101 (*maps*); partisan support in, 102, 104, 225; Soviet Union and, 46, 48, 104, 132, 150; UNR in, 48, 70-72
Voloshyn, Augustin, 16, 25, 41
Voloshyn-Berchank, Free Cossack leader, 108
Volyn', 150
"Volynets'," *see* Iatseniuk (the younger)
Voskobiinyk, Michael, 179, 180*n*, 201
Vseukraïns'ka Kooperatyvna Spilka, 169
Vseukraïns'kyi Komitet Dopomohy, 168

Wallace, Donald Mackenzie, quoted, 3
Wehrmacht: and nationalists, 27-28, 34, 51-62, 73-75, 81*n*, 103, 130, 136-37, 173*n*, 204, 209; tactics used against partisans, 106, 116; and press, 175-77, 208-9; treatment of Soviet prisoners, 85-86; use of Ukrainian troops, 71-72, 124-26, 142, 209, UPA contacts of, 136-37, 221; *see also* Abwehr; Canaris, Admiral
Welfare departments, nationalists in, 168
West Ukraine, 2; Communism in, 14, 44; inhabitants as displaced persons after Second World War, 227-28; integral nationalists in, 14-16; nationalism in, 11-17, 215; peasants in, 223-26; Poland in, 11-12; problems in, 11-12; Soviet control of, 44-48, 50, 132-34, 224; UNR and, 13; UPA partisan activities in, 220-27; *see also* Bukovina; Carpatho-Ukraine; Galicia; Generalgouvernement Polen; Volhynia
Wilhelm, German emperor, 19
Women as nationalists, 187, 221
Wrangel, General P. N., 7
Writers as nationalists, 183-84, 231-36

Yalta agreement, 227
Youth, nationalists and, 156, 188-89

Zakhvalins'kyi (OUN-M police chief in Kiev), 67, 74
Zaporozh'e, OUN-B in, 203
Zaporozhian Cossacks, 7, 22
Zaporozhian Sich, 4, 171, 232
Zatons'kyi, Volodymyr, 8
Za Ukraïna, 141
Zhitomir: deportation of Jews from, 66; deportation of workers from, 89; Kovpak's partisan band in, 106; nationalism in, 77, 164, 172, 174, 185-86, 188; Orthodox Church in, 148-49; OUN-B in, 61-66; OUN-M in, 65-70, 77; partisan activity in, 98-101 (*maps*), 108; population of, 66, 243-44; Russians in, 66, 186; UAPTs in, 196
Zionist, as victims of KNVD, 54